I0868718

Financial Technology and Disruptive Innovation in ASEAN

Muhammad Anshari
Universiti Brunei Darussalam, Brunei

Mohammad Nabil Almunawar
Universiti Brunei Darussalam, Brunei

Masairol Masri
Universiti Brunei Darussalam, Brunei

A volume in the Advances in Finance, Accounting, and Economics (AFAE) Book Series

IGI Global
DISSEMINATOR OF KNOWLEDGE

Published in the United States of America by
IGI Global
Business Science Reference (an imprint of IGI Global)
701 E. Chocolate Avenue
Hershey PA, USA 17033
Tel: 717-533-8845
Fax: 717-533-8661
E-mail: cust@igi-global.com
Web site: http://www.igi-global.com

Copyright © 2020 by IGI Global. All rights reserved. No part of this publication may be reproduced, stored or distributed in any form or by any means, electronic or mechanical, including photocopying, without written permission from the publisher.
Product or company names used in this set are for identification purposes only. Inclusion of the names of the products or companies does not indicate a claim of ownership by IGI Global of the trademark or registered trademark.

Library of Congress Cataloging-in-Publication Data

Names: Anshari, Muhammad, 1977- editor. | Almunawar, Mohammad Nabil, 1960- editor. | Masri, Masairol, 1974- editor.
Title: Financial technology and disruptive innovation in ASEAN / Muhammad Anshari, Mohammad Nabil Almunawar, and Masairol Masri, editors.
Description: Hershey, PA : Business Science Reference, [2019]
Identifiers: LCCN 2018058914| ISBN 9781522591832 (hardcover) | ISBN 9781522591856 (ebook) | ISBN 9781522591849 (softcover)
Subjects: LCSH: Financial services industry--Technological innovations--Southeast Asia. | Financial institutions--Southeast Asia.
Classification: LCC HG3290.8.A6 F56 2019 | DDC 332.10959--dc23 LC record available at https://lccn.loc.gov/2018058914

This book is published in the IGI Global book series Advances in Finance, Accounting, and Economics (AFAE) (ISSN: 2327-5677; eISSN: 2327-5685)

British Cataloguing in Publication Data
A Cataloguing in Publication record for this book is available from the British Library.

All work contributed to this book is new, previously-unpublished material.
The views expressed in this book are those of the authors, but not necessarily of the publisher.

For electronic access to this publication, please contact: eresources@igi-global.com.

Advances in Finance, Accounting, and Economics (AFAE) Book Series

ISSN:2327-5677
EISSN:2327-5685

Editor-in-Chief: Ahmed Driouchi, Al Akhawayn University, Morocco

MISSION

In our changing economic and business environment, it is important to consider the financial changes occurring internationally as well as within individual organizations and business environments. Understanding these changes as well as the factors that influence them is crucial in preparing for our financial future and ensuring economic sustainability and growth.

The **Advances in Finance, Accounting, and Economics (AFAE)** book series aims to publish comprehensive and informative titles in all areas of economics and economic theory, finance, and accounting to assist in advancing the available knowledge and providing for further research development in these dynamic fields.

COVERAGE

- Investments and Derivatives
- Economics of Innovation and Knowledge
- Economic Policy
- Finance and Accounting in SMEs
- Accounting information systems
- Corporate Finance
- Fiscal Policy
- Stock Market
- Bankruptcy
- Theoretical Issues in Economics, Finance, and Accounting

IGI Global is currently accepting manuscripts for publication within this series. To submit a proposal for a volume in this series, please contact our Acquisition Editors at Acquisitions@igi-global.com or visit: http://www.igi-global.com/publish/.

The Advances in Finance, Accounting, and Economics (AFAE) Book Series (ISSN 2327-5677) is published by IGI Global, 701 E. Chocolate Avenue, Hershey, PA 17033-1240, USA, www.igi-global.com. This series is composed of titles available for purchase individually; each title is edited to be contextually exclusive from any other title within the series. For pricing and ordering information please visit http://www.igi-global.com/book-series/advances-finance-accounting-economics/73685. Postmaster: Send all address changes to above address. ©© 2020 IGI Global. All rights, including translation in other languages reserved by the publisher. No part of this series may be reproduced or used in any form or by any means – graphics, electronic, or mechanical, including photocopying, recording, taping, or information and retrieval systems – without written permission from the publisher, except for non commercial, educational use, including classroom teaching purposes. The views expressed in this series are those of the authors, but not necessarily of IGI Global.

Titles in this Series

For a list of additional titles in this series, please visit:
https://www.igi-global.com/book-series/advances-finance-accounting-economics/73685

Foreign Business in China and Opportunities for Technological Innovation...
Anna Visvizi (Deree – The American College of Greece, Greece) Miltiadis Lytras (Deree – The American College of Greece, Greece) Xi Zhang (Tianjin University, China) and Jie Zhao (Anhui University, China)
Business Science Reference • ©2019 • 284pp • H/C (ISBN: 9781522589808) • US $195.00

Handbook of Research on Global Issues in Financial Communication and Investment ...
Hasan Dinçer (Istanbul Medipol University, Turkey) and Serhat Yüksel (Istanbul Medipol University, Turkey)
Business Science Reference • ©2019 • 540pp • H/C (ISBN: 9781522592655) • US $365.00

Behavioral Finance and Decision-Making Models
Tripti Tripathi (Jiwaji University, India) Manoj Kumar Dash (Khallikote University, India) and Gaurav Agrawal (Indian Institute of Information Technology and Management Gwalior, India)
Business Science Reference • ©2019 • 333pp • H/C (ISBN: 9781522573999) • US $215.00

Global Challenges in Public Finance and International Relations
Deniz Şahin Duran (Tokat Gaziosmanpaşa University, Turkey) Yusuf Temür (Tokat Gaziosmanpaşa University, Turkey) and Doğan Bozdoğan (Tokat Gaziosmanpaşa University, Turkey)
Business Science Reference • ©2019 • 304pp • H/C (ISBN: 9781522575641) • US $225.00

International Financial Reporting Standards and New Directions in Earnings Management
Jonas da Silva Oliveira (Instituto Universitário de Lisboa (ISCTE-IUL), Portugal) Graça Maria do Carmo Azevedo (University of Aveiro, Portugal) and Augusta da Conceição Santos Ferreira (University of Aveiro, Portugal)
Business Science Reference • ©2019 • 342pp • H/C (ISBN: 9781522578178) • US $225.00

For an entire list of titles in this series, please visit:
https://www.igi-global.com/book-series/advances-finance-accounting-economics/73685

IGI Global
DISSEMINATOR OF KNOWLEDGE

701 East Chocolate Avenue, Hershey, PA 17033, USA
Tel: 717-533-8845 x100 • Fax: 717-533-8661
E-Mail: cust@igi-global.com • www.igi-global.com

Editorial Advisory Board

Ganjar Alfian, *Dongguk University, South Korea*
Youssef Abu Amuna, *Al-Azhar University, Egypt*
Mohd Hairul Azrin Haji Besar, *Universiti Brunei Darussalam, Brunei*
Eriyatno, *IPB University, Indonesia*
Anas Miftah Fauzi, *IPB University, Indonesia*
Ahmed M. Khalid, *Universiti Brunei Darussalam, Brunei*
Adnan Kisa, *Kristiania University College, Norway*
Andino Maseleno, *Universiti Tenaga Nasional, Malaysia*
Muhammad Shodiq, *Bank CIMB Niaga, Indonesia*
Muhammad Syafrudin, *Dongguk University, South Korea*
Mustafa Z. Younis, *Jackson State University, USA*

Table of Contents

Detailed Table of Contents

implemented by companies and categorized. Financial technology companies are generally start-ups founded with the purpose of disrupting financial systems and corporations that rely less on software. But Fintech is not confined to start-ups only. Fintech comprises a vessel of technical aspects that describes an emerging financial services sector in the 21st century. The chapter aims to provide key insights into the evolution of the FinTech sector in emerging markets like ASEAN and India by and industry experience in this area. Both industry survey reports and peer-reviewed research is used as secondary data. The critical challenges to be addressed at the policy level, regional differences and future implications are being discussed thereby creating bridges the FinTech in ASEAN context to create a coherent framework.

Chapter 3
The Future of FinTech in ASEAN 63
Hazik Mohamed, Stellar Consulting Group, Singapore

FinTech and the digital economy offer opportunities for ASEAN to rebuild trust and confidence in a financial system that had lost them. Some technologists imagine this world without intermediaries, while others just want a faster and more efficient way of transacting. Banks, FinTech companies, and regulators need to collaborate to create an ecosystem to drive greater access to financial services in the integrated ASEAN economy. The authors discuss projected trends in technology and its use in the next few crucial years. They also recommend strategies that involve various market participants and stakeholders coming together and working towards shared goals of a unified ASEAN economic community by increasing financial inclusion for the unbanked and the seamless cross-border flow of goods, services, and payments in a safe and secure manner.

Chapter 4
Paving the Way for the Development of FinTech Initiatives in ASEAN 80
Mahani Hamdan, Universiti Brunei Darussalam, Brunei
Muhammad Anshari, Universiti Brunei Darussalam, Brunei

Financial technology (FinTech) is not one to be ignored under any circumstances. It is not only growing as a concept but a phenomenon that has been manifested in non-financial sectors using innovative technology to bring financial services straight to the customers. The creation and practical applications of FinTech supported by government regulations and financial policies, high mobile adoption, rising rates of internet penetration, and increasingly literate and millennial generation, strongly indicates that the various scopes of FinTech in ASEAN are very promising in supporting economic growth and financial inclusion. This chapter will provide an

overview of FinTech and examine the development of FinTech initiatives to shed light on some challenges and solutions facing the ASEAN's financial landscape today and in the future.

Businesses have been forerunners in providing innovative techniques and technology to the market. These emerging processes, techniques, and technologies have disrupted the existing ones and met the requirements of the existing customers. Today's banking and financial sector is facing an unprecedented change wherein various new players are entering the market and disrupting the traditional modes of operation. These players are a part of the latest disruption in the banking and financial sector, which is popularly known as Fin Tech (which is an amalgamation of finance and technology). They are providing alternative solutions and business models that are overhauling the manner in which this sector and its customers function. This disruption not only opens doors for completely different business opportunities but also poses challenges to the existing set up of business. The chapter aims to study the emerging trends associated emerging opportunities and challenges of FinTech in the banking and financial sector globally.

A portmanteau of financial technology (FinTech) centralizes on the innovative use of smart mobile devices to design and deliver financial services and products, elevating an innovative way of delivering financial services. The chapter mainly focuses on the definition and the importance of FinTech to the financial ecosystem especially in the Southeast Asia region. It focuses on how financial technology (FinTech) came to be, how transactions in the past mostly use cash, and then shifted to credit card and then shifted to a cashless transaction, for example using e-wallet or simply using smartphone for any financial transaction. The research found out how the huge percentage of internet users in the Southeast Asia region were the cause of the development of FinTech companies in the region for FinTech startups. It also showed how FinTech helped to provide solutions for financial inclusion, especially unbanked population.

The main objective of this chapter is to investigate the effects of cybercrime on the banking sector in ASEAN. Global challenges on the evolution of cybercrime are in continuous dynamics in the case of emerging or developing countries, so that sustainable development plays an essential role. Moreover, the propagation effects can generate significant damages in the banking sector. Efficient bank management is essential in the context of providing advanced techniques for cyber security. Traditional cyber security measures are insufficient to ensure data protection and online information privacy. Consequently, investigations of cyber-criminal activity must become a priority especially in the context of globalization.

Financial inclusion is a term that is used to describe easy access of financial products and services for everyone. G20 countries, including Indonesia, show high commitment to accelerate financial inclusion. Financial inclusion also facilitates the achievement of 17 Sustainable Development Goals. Fintech or digital financial technology is one of the most recent innovations in financial industry. It has grown at a rapid speed in the recent years. Fintech provides products and services with low costs, better quality, and stable financial landscape. With its flexibility and simplicity, Fintech may facilitate the offering of financial services to people who are "unbanked," or to small business at low cost and low risk. Hence, this chapter thoroughly discusses FinTech's role in supporting financial inclusion in Indonesia. Indonesia is one of the G20 countries that is committed to conduct financial inclusion. Specifically, this chapter elaborates financial inclusion, Fintech in Indonesia, and role of Fintech in supporting financial inclusion in Indonesia.

While fintech is relatively new in Indonesia, it is visibly emerging and setting for a new path. This chapter is attempting to shed a light on customer adoption and their perceptions toward fintech products and services in Indonesia. This study is descriptive and exploratory by nature. Data gathered from primary surveys as well as secondary sources. This study identifies several factors that significantly affect customer adoption and perception towards fintech products and services, namely relative advantages, trialability, and simplicity. Trust, responsiveness, and empathy are also served as important variables that should be considered as well. It is expected that this study will help researchers and academics who are interested in studying the phenomenon of fintech more broadly.

This chapter aims to address the current FinTech situation in Brunei as well as the possibility of encouraging the growth opportunities and adoption of FinTech into the nation's daily life. Although the development of FinTech has been prevalent across the globe, Brunei has only begun to creep up to its Association of South East Asian Nations (ASEAN) counterparts in the race of FinTech growth. Although existing research on FinTech adoption is prevalent, there is little evidence to indicate a substantive research has been conducted on ASEAN FinTech, particularly in Brunei.

This exploratory research study looked into the younger population of Brunei Darussalam in terms of the feasibility of eWallets. By utilizing the unified theory of acceptance and use of technology (UTAUT) model established by Venkatesh et al., this research hoped to assess the country's technological readiness and the level of acceptance of eWallet adoption in a future of an e-Payment economy for the purpose of to improve the efficiency of financial institutions as well as for the provision of new services for the convenience of the customers. The study found that none of the main four constructs of the UTAUT model to be predictors of behavioral intention but rather, attitude towards using technology and anxiety. This may be as a result of the younger populace being in constant interaction with various types of technology, paired with the rising internet connectivity which led to the minimal impact of a new technology, in this case, eWallets.

Financial technology (FinTech) has been developing at a tremendous rate all around the globe. This chapter will show how banking and financial system has evolved by financial technology which affected the way of how society is living now. There is a rapid change of FinTech for the past few years in Indonesia. These changes have made an impact to the people in Indonesia. As for the exploration to the rise of FinTech in Indonesia, it is important to understand the development and challenges of FinTech in Indonesia by looking changing Indonesian people's behavior in terms of FinTech's adoption include payment channel system, digital banking, peer-to-peer (P2P) lending, and crowdfunding.

The institution of Waqf always played a pivotal role of sustainable economic development in a Muslim society throughout the history of Islam. However, recently, even with the introduction of the modern Islamic finance a few decades ago, the institution has been struggling to rejuvenate its past glory. The key issues are lack of availability of data and historical records, weak transparency and public disclosure, improper audit and compliance practices. The advent of the blockchain has offered a ray of hope for the revival of the Waqf institution. The blockchain has already proved itself as a game changing breakthrough. Similarly, the Waqf institution could be invigorated with the innovative and efficient use of the blockchain. Moreover, the use of smart contracts on blockchain could further enhance the performance and efficacy of the Waqf institution. It is strongly believed that with the firm Islamic jurisprudential foundations of the Waqf, blockchain, and smart contracts will ensure that the Waqf institution could partake in the economic development of the whole Muslim world.

Foreword

FinTech is a global phenomenon which can be characterized as a process to introduce transformative and disruptive innovation to financial services. FinTech firms are generally able to move faster and provide new applications either directly to customers, or in partnership with large financial services institutions. It is, therefore, feared that such innovations or disruptions may take market shares away from Financial Institutions (FIs) and provide a more economical, efficient, competitive and convenient markets and options to customers. Hence fear of disruption is a growing concern for financial services firms. According to a 2018 executive survey, 80% of top executives feared that their firms were at risk of disruption and displacement from highly agile, data-driven competitors. A counter argument is whether these innovations are disruptions or provide healthy competition to market participants. These fears are even more serious in ASEAN region which is fast in adapting new technologies including FinTech. In this perspective, it is imperative to investigate the factors which disrupt the role, structure, and competitive environment for financial institutions and the markets and societies in which they operate.

The book *Financial Technology and Disruptive Innovation in ASEAN* is therefore very timely documenting research findings and expert views from academics, practitioners, business managers and policy makers on a variety of multi-disciplinary issues and challenges financial industry is facing with the current fast pace of innovative technology. Chapters in the book document the FinTech's experts their views and initiate discussion on a range of FinTech's development and achievements in ASEAN member states.

I commend editors from UBD School of Business and Economics (UBDSBE) to take this brave initiative of compiling this important book which provides conceptual understanding and shares practical experience, beneficial to governments, practitioners, as well as general public in the ASEAN region to realize the potential benefits and challenges of disruptive innovations. I am sure, the research compiled in this book will help to develop new business models, applications, processes, products, or services with an associated material effect on financial markets and institutions and the provision of financial services.

Ahmed M. Khalid
Universiti Brunei Darussalam, Brunei

Foreword

Over the past few decades, the Internet and massive adoption of smartphones have affected a major transformation on the industry. Furthermore, a fusion of Big Data, Internet of Things, Cloud Computing, 3D Printing, Artificial Intelligent (AI), RFID technologies is a transformation namely Industry 4.0 focusing on interconnectivity, real-time analytic and processing, machine learning, and automation. Industry 4.0 is the notion of an industrial revolution that will alter the way we live, work and interact with one and another. This impact is clearly evident in the banking and financial industry.

The emergence of FinTech start-up companies supported with advanced technologies has become major disruptions in financial services including in ASEAN that enables financial solutions and innovative business models resulting in the fusion of finance and smart mobile technology.

The book *Financial Technology and Disruptive Innovation in ASEAN* is conceptually and practically beneficial for governments, education institutions, practitioners, and the public to help ASEAN realizes its potential and challenges ahead. It could result in proposing new business models, applications, processes, products, or services with an associated material effect on financial markets and institutions and the provision of financial services.

Finally, I hope this book can inspire readers in the midst of deindustrialization's trends in some ASEAN countries. I thank the editors who have successfully compiled and presented this book of FinTech on a wide range of FinTech's development, and general progress reports of FinTech in ASEAN members that fit the theme of the book are also covered. While the authors comprise a multi-disciplinary approach for the dissemination and discussion of research or best practices on the FinTech in ASEAN resulting on quality of research-based studies which contribute to theory, lesson learned and best practices, critical understanding and policy formulation on FinTech and general progress reports of FinTech in ASEAN are also discussed.

Muhammad Shodiq
Bank CIMB Niaga, Indonesia

Preface

The role of financial services in the financial industry is vitally important. As the technology evolves, the delivery of the services is being shifted from traditional delivery systems to the innovative delivery systems that heavily use information and communication technology (ICT) to serve public in much better ways. Utilizing ICT to deliver financial services as well as creating new financial products and services accessible through the Web/Apps has attracted much attention lately and it has marched to a new area called Financial Technology (FinTech), which can be considered as disruptive innovation in financial sectors. Many innovations have been created in FinTech, and some of them are disruptive innovations that threaten the existing players in the financial industry.

The advancement in ICT, broadband Internet connection, and the extensive use of smartphones are the enabling factors in FinTech evolution (Anshari et al., 2019a). FinTech innovations has led to new business models, applications, processes, or products that affect financial markets and institutions and the provision of financial services. FinTech includes five major areas which are finance and investment, operations and risk management, payments and infrastructure, data security and monetization, and customer interface. It covers many types of financial services such as crowdfunding, money transfer, loan, Peer-to-Peer (P2P) lending, asset management, mobile payment, and fundraising.

FinTech is now widely used around the world. Eventually FinTech will either disrupt or complement existing financial services (Anshari et al., 2019b). Since ASEAN is undergoing a paradigm shift from Government-to-Government (G2G) to Community-to-Community (C2C) relationships with the emphasis on integration and collaboration. The combined economies of ASEAN make it a major of economic power after EU, USA, China and Japan. The combined population of ASEAN creates the world's third largest market with more than 600 millions of people. There are potential readers that is waiting to find the book to discuss about FinTech in ASEAN.

The book *Financial Technology and Disruptive Innovation in ASEAN* is expected to become a major literature and reference for FinTech development, especially in the recent ASEAN's context, featuring conceptual, case studies, recent development, best practices, comparative assessment, business processes, as well as strategies and outputs in studies of FinTech from multiple domains of knowledge. To ensure the quality, each chapter in this book was reviewed in two rounds. Readers are likely to be academicians and students who can use chapters in this book for their references on the latest development of financial technology, researchers academia to gain perspective of disruptive innovation in financial sector, government organizations who interested in the field of FinTech, business owners who need to understand the phenomenon of FinTech, technopreneurs who seek innovative ideas on FinTech, financial & banking practitioners who need to understand recent development of FinTech, policy makers who need to understand the major core of FinTech in ASEAN, and also general public who seek information the emergence of FinTech.

The book covers wide range of topics from disruptive innovation, emerging market, financial inclusion, e-Payment, e-Trading, e-Wallet, Peer to Peer (P2P) Lending, Blockchain Technology, Cryptocurrency, Crowdfunding, Cybercrime, Banking Sector, Cybersecurity Regulations, Sustainable Development, Globalization, Legal Framework, Artificial Intelligence, Cloud Computing, Collaboration, Hackathon, Machine Learning, Internet of Things, both in the ASEAN region and in several specific countries such as Brunei Darussalam, India, Indonesia, Romania, Malaysia, Oman, Saudi Arabia, and Singapore.

The book includes 13 chapters that address the recent FinTech initiative in ASEAN with respect to process, strategies, challenges, lesson learnt, as well as outcomes. The following is the summary of each chapter.

Chapter 1 titled "Financial Technologies: Concept, Application, and Challenges" by Debra Hooi Chern Lee (Universiti Tunku Abdul Rahman, Malaysia), Mobashar Rehman (Universiti Tunku Abdul Rahman, Malaysia), Hui Nee Au Yong (Universiti Tunku Abdul Rahman, Malaysia), and Manzoor Ahmed Hashmani (Universiti Teknologi PETRONAS, Malaysia) explores the concept of Financial Technology (FinTech) and how it has progressed to where it is today. This understanding is further supplemented with the applications of FinTech and the challenges it has to tackle in order to continue to evolve in a favorable manner. This chapter also delves into the concept of blockchain technology (BCT) to comprehend how it holds the power to impact society through revolutionary applications. As the world heralds an era of FinTech, this chapter aims to give insights on the potential of FinTech and how it cross borders to change the lives of many.

Chapter 2 titled "Financial Technology Implications: Emerging Markets Context" by Arjun R (National Institute of Technology Karnataka, India), Nishmitha N (National Institute of Technology Karnataka, India), and Suprabha K R (National Institute of Technology Karnataka, India) examines the particularities of the financial technology industry, how is FinTech defined and how can the financial technology solutions implemented by companies be categorized. Financial technology companies are generally start-ups founded with the purpose of disrupting financial systems and corporations that rely less on software. But FinTech is not confined to start-ups only. FinTech comprises a vessel of technical aspects that describes an emerging financial services sector in the 21st century. The chapter also provides key insights into the evolution of the FinTech sector in emerging markets like ASEAN and India by and industry experience in this area. The critical challenges to be addressed at the policy level, regional differences and future implications are being discussed thereby creating bridges the FinTech in ASEAN context to create a coherent framework.

Chapter 3 titled "The Future of FinTech in ASEAN" by Hazik Bin Mohamed (Stellar Consulting Group, Singapore) affirms that FinTech and the digital economy offer opportunities for ASEAN to rebuild trust and confidence in a financial system that had lost them. Some technologists imagine this world without intermediaries, while others just want a faster and more efficient way of transacting. Banks, FinTech companies and regulators need to collaborate to create an ecosystem to drive greater access to financial services in the integrated ASEAN Economy. We discuss projected trends in technology and its use in the next few crucial years. We also recommend strategies that involve various market participants and stakeholders coming together and working towards shared goals of a unified ASEAN Economic community, by increasing financial inclusion for the unbanked and the seamless cross-border flow of goods, services and payments in a safe and secure manner.

Chapter 4 titled "Paving the Way for the Development of FinTech Initiatives in ASEAN" by Mahani Hamdan (Universiti Brunei Darussalam, Brunei Darussalam) and Muhammad Anshari (Universiti Brunei Darussalam, Brunei Darussalam) states that FinTech is not one to be ignored under any circumstances. It is not only growing as a concept but a phenomenon that has been manifested in non-financial sectors using innovative technology to bring their financial services straight to their customers. The creation and practical applications of FinTech supported by government regulations and financial policies, high mobile adoption, rising rates of Internet penetration and the increasingly literate and millennial generation, strongly indicates that the various scopes of FinTech in ASEAN are a very promising theme in supporting economic growth and financial inclusion. This chapter will provide an overview of FinTech and examine the development of FinTech initiatives to shed light on some challenges and solutions facing the ASEAN's financial landscape today and expected in the future.

Chapter 5 titled "FinTech: a Study of Enablers, Opportunities, and Challenges in the Banking and Financial Services Sector" by Vibha Bhandari (College of Applied Sciences Nizwa, Oman) mentions that businesses have been forerunner in providing innovative techniques and technology to the market. These emerging processes, techniques and technologies have disrupted the existing ones and met the requirements of the existing customers. Today's banking and financial sector is facing an unprecedented change wherein various new players are entering the market and disrupting the traditional modes of operation. These players are a part of the latest disruption in the banking and financial sector, that is popularly known as FinTech. They are providing alternative solutions and business models that are overhauling the manner in which this sector and its customers function. This disruption not only opens doors for completely different business opportunities but also pose challenges to the existing set up of business. The study in its current form and scope aims to study the emerging trends associated emerging opportunities and challenges of FinTech in the banking and financial sector globally.

Chapter 6 titled "Financial Technology and Innovative Financial Inclusion" by Sumarsono (Universitas Islam Negeri Sunan Kalijaga Yogyakarta, Indonesia), Abdullah Al-Mudimigh (Dar Al Uloom University, Saudi Arabia), and Muhammad Anshari (Universiti Brunei Darussalam, Brunei Darussalam) states that a portmanteau of FinTech centralizes on the innovative use of smart mobile devices to design and deliver financial services and products, elevating an innovative way of delivering financial services. The study mainly focuses on the definition and the importance of FinTech to the financial ecosystem, especially in the Southeast Asia region. It focuses on how Financial Technology (FinTech) came to be, how transactions in the past mostly use cash then shifted to a credit card then shifted to a cashless transaction, for example, using an e-wallet or simply using a smartphone for any financial transaction. The research found out how the huge percentage of internet users in the Southeast Asia region was the cause of the development of FinTech companies in the region for FinTech startups. It also showed how FinTech helped to provide solutions for financial inclusion, especially the unbanked population.

Chapter 7 titled "The Effects of Cybercrime on the Banking Sector in ASEAN" by Cristi Spulbar (University of Craiova, Faculty of Economics and Business Administration, Romania) and Birau Ramona (C-tin Brancusi University of Targu Jiu, Faculty of Education Science, Law and Public Administration and University of Craiova, Faculty of Social Science, Romania) investigates the effects of cybercrime on the banking sector in ASEAN. Global challenges on the evolution of cybercrime are in continuous dynamics in the case of emerging or developing countries, so that sustainable development plays an essential role. Moreover, the propagation effects can generate significant damages in the banking sector. Efficient bank management is essential in the context of providing advanced techniques for cyber security. Traditional cyber security measures are insufficient to ensure data protection and online information privacy. Consequently, investigations of cyber-criminal activity must become a priority especially in the context of globalization.

Chapter 8 titled "Financial Inclusion: Does Fintech Help in Indonesia?" by Dian Agustia (Universitas Airlangga, Indonesia) and Nadia Anridho (Universitas Airlangga, Indonesia) explores financial inclusion is a term that is used to describe easy access to financial products and services for everyone. G20 countries, including Indonesia, show high commitment to accelerate financial inclusion. Financial inclusion also facilitates the achievement of 17 Sustainable Development Goals. FinTech or digital financial technology is one of the most recent innovations in the financial industry. It has grown at a rapid speed in recent years. Fintech provides products and services with low costs, better quality, and stable financial landscape. With its flexibility and simplicity, Fintech may facilitate the offering of financial services to people who are "unbanked", or small business at low cost and low risk. Hence, this paper thoroughly discusses FinTech's role in supporting financial inclusion in Indonesia. Indonesia is one of the G20 countries which is committed to conducting financial inclusion. Specifically, this paper elaborates financial inclusion, FinTech in Indonesia, and the role of FinTech in supporting financial inclusion in Indonesia.

Chapter 9 titled "Customer Adoption and Perception Towards Fintech in Indonesia: A Diamond in the Rough or a Dime a Dozen?" by Nofie Iman (Faculty of Economics and Business, Universitas Gadjah Mada, Indonesia) states that FinTech is relatively new in Indonesia, it is visibly emerging and setting for a new path. This article is attempting to shed a light on customer adoption and their perceptions toward FinTech products and services in Indonesia. This study is descriptive and exploratory by nature. Data gathered from primary surveys as well as secondary sources. This study identifies several factors that significantly affect customer adoption and perception towards FinTech products and services, namely relative advantages, and simplicity. Trust, responsiveness, and empathy are also served as important variables that should be considered as well. It is expected that this study will help researchers and academics who are interested in studying the phenomenon of FinTech more broadly.

Chapter 10 titled "The Growing Opportunities of Financial Technology in Brunei" by Fakhriyah Abdullah Thani (Universiti Brunei Darussalam, Brunei Darussalam) explores the current FinTech situation in Brunei as well as the possibility of encouraging the growth opportunities and adoption of FinTech into the nation's daily life. Although the development of FinTech has been prevalent across the globe, Brunei has only began to creep up to its ASEAN counterparts in the race of FinTech growth. Although existing research on FinTech adoption is prevalent, there is little evidence to indicate a substantive research has been conducted on ASEAN FinTech, particularly in Brunei.

Chapter 11 titled "Advancing Towards a Cashless Society: The Acceptance of eWallet in Brunei Darussalam" by Munirah Ajeerah Arine (Universiti Brunei Darussalam, Brunei Darussalam), Hidayatul Aziyah Zain (Universiti Brunei Darussalam, Brunei Darussalam), and Norzaidah Hidayah Rashid (Universiti Brunei Darussalam, Brunei Darussalam) examines the younger population of Brunei Darussalam in terms of the feasibility of eWallets. By utilizing the unified theory of acceptance and use of technology (UTAUT) model established by Venkatesh et al. (2003), this research hoped to assess the country's technological readiness and the level of acceptance of eWallet adoption in a future of an e-Payment economy for the purpose of to improve the efficiency of financial institutions as well as for the provision of new services for the convenience of the customers. The study found that none of the main four construct of the UTAUT model to be predictors of behavioural intention but rather, attitude towards using technology and anxiety. This may be as a result of the younger populace being in constant interaction with various types of technology, paired with the rising internet connectivity which led to the minimal impact of a new technology, in this case, eWallets.

Chapter 12 titled "An Overview of Financial Technology in Indonesia" by Muhammad Anshari (Universiti Brunei Darussalam, Brunei Darussalam), Mohammad Nabil Almunawar (Universiti Brunei Darussalam, Brunei Darussalam), and Masairol Masri (Universiti Brunei Darussalam, Brunei Darussalam) discusses how banking and financial system has evolved by financial technology which affected the way of how society is living now. There is a rapid change of FinTech for the past few years in Indonesia, these changes have made an impact on the people in Indonesia. As for the exploration to the rise of FinTech in Indonesia. Furthermore, the chapter explores the development and challenges of FinTech in Indonesia by looking changing Indonesian people's behavior in terms of FinTech's adoption include payment channel system, digital banking, Peer-to-Peer (P2P) Lending and Crowdfunding.

Finally, Chapter 13 titled "Using Blockchain and Smart Contracts for Waqf Institutions" by Farrukh Habib (International Shari'ah Research Academy for Islamic Finance [ISRA], Malaysia) and Abu Umar Faruq Ahmad (King Abdulaziz University, Saudi Arabia) discusses the institution of Waqf always played a pivotal role of sustainable economic development in a Muslim society throughout the history of Islam. However, recently, even with the introduction of the modern Islamic finance a few decades ago, the institution has been struggling to rejuvenate its past glory. The key issues are lack of availability of data and historical records; weak transparency and public disclosure; improper audit and compliance practices. The advent of the blockchain has offered a ray of hope for the revival of the Waqf institution. The blockchain has already proved itself as a game changing breakthrough. Similarly, the Waqf institution could be invigorated with the innovative and efficient use of the blockchain. Moreover, the use of smart contracts on blockchain could further enhance the performance and efficacy of the Waqf institution. It is strongly believed that with the firm Islamic jurisprudential foundations of the Waqf, blockchain and smart contracts will ensure that the Waqf institution could partake in the economic development of the whole Muslim world.

After the summaries of the chapters included in the book, the book portrays and assesses FinTech's adoption, challenges, and its future directions of the ASEAN members in the Industry 4.0 era. The emphasis of the book is on quality, research-based studies which contribute to theory, lesson learnt and best practices, critical understanding and policy formulation on FinTech. We hope you all find them useful and interesting for research, teaching, and policy studies.

Thank you,

Muhammad Anshari
Universiti Brunei Darussalam, Brunei

Mohammad Nabil Almunawar
Universiti Brunei Darussalam, Brunei

Masairol Masri
Universiti Brunei Darussalam, Brunei

REFERENCES

Anshari, M., Almunawar, M. N., & Masri, M. (2019a). Financial Technology and Disruptive Innovation in Business. *International Journal of Asian Business and Information Management*, *12*(3).

Anshari, M., Almunawar, M. N., Masri, M., & Hamdan, M. (2019b). *Digital Marketplace and FinTech to Support Agriculture Sustainability. Energy Procedia, Elsevier*, *156C*, 234–238.

Venkatesh, V., Morris, M. G., Davis, F. D., & Davis, G. B. (2003). Unified theory of acceptance and use of technology (UTAUT). *Management Information Systems Quarterly*, *27*, 425–478. doi:10.2307/30036540

Acknowledgment

The team would like to express our gratitude and appreciation to the Universiti Brunei Darussalam School of Business & Economics (UBDSBE) for the full support. We also would like to acknowledge the positive supports of our expert advisory panel. Special thanks go to the anonymous referees for their valuables suggestions that greatly improved the manuscripts.

Chapter 1
Financial Technologies:
Concept, Application, and Challenges

Debra Hooi Chern Lee
Universiti Tunku Abdul Rahman, Malaysia

Mobashar Rehman
Universiti Tunku Abdul Rahman, Malaysia

Hui Nee Au Yong
Universiti Tunku Abdul Rahman, Malaysia

Manzoor Ahmed Hashmani
Universiti Teknologi PETRONAS, Malaysia

ABSTRACT

This chapter explores the concept of Financial Technology (FinTech) and how it has progressed to where it is today. This understanding is further supplemented with the applications of FinTech and the challenges it has to tackle in order to continue to evolve in a favourable manner. Being a key player in the FinTech sector, this chapter also delves into the concept of blockchain technology (BCT) to comprehend how it holds the power to impact society through revolutionary applications. As the world heralds an era of FinTech, this chapter aims to give insights on the potential of FinTech and how it cross borders to change the lives of many.

DOI: 10.4018/978-1-5225-9183-2.ch001

Copyright © 2020, IGI Global. Copying or distributing in print or electronic forms without written permission of IGI Global is prohibited.

THE CONCEPT OF FINTECH

Based on Google Trends (2018), the search term 'FinTech' has grown worldwide by more than 5000% over the past five years, gaining it the status of a 'Breakout' query. FinTech, which denotes 'Financial Technology', is the intertwinement between technological innovation and finance in which it improves the delivery of financial and banking services through the application of Information Technology (IT) (Gai, Qiu, & Sun, 2018; Ozili, 2018). In other words, FinTech is an industry consisting of companies that make financial systems and the delivery of financial services more efficient through the use of technology (CB Insights, 2015).

The growing interest in FinTech is not surprising as not only is it shifting paradigms in many areas of the finance industry, but it is also transforming everyday lives as a third of consumers worldwide use FinTech services regularly, with 84% of them aware of their use of FinTech (Ernest & Young FinTech Global Network, 2017). Examples of FinTech application in everyday life include easy payment services such as Paypal, mobile payment services like Apple Pay or simply purchasing items online via credit card.

With this, it is clear that FinTech is no longer a hype but has become a major gamechanger in the field of finance, with 83% of financial firms believing that FinTech start-ups are posing a threat to various aspects of their business (PwC, 2016). This leads to an inevitable need in financial institutions to re-evaluate their existing business models and embrace FinTech in order to remain relevant in this field while gaining a competitive edge (Lee & Shin, 2018) as the emergence of cloud computing, open software, easier access to computing power and data servers mean that even small, innovative technology start-ups can quickly turn their ideas into marketable products.

The global FinTech sector continues to thrive as it raised $41.7 billion in investments during first half of 2018, which surpasses the record total for the whole of 2017 (FinTech Global, 2018). Investments in FinTech are in an all-time high compared to previous years as it was reported that global investment in FinTech companies totaled $19.1 billion in 2015, and it was $13.8 billion in the United States alone (Ancri, 2016).

Much like how the saying goes 'if you can't beat them, join them', much of this growth in investment comes from traditional financial institutions investing in external FinTech start-ups in the form of joint ventures as well as from their own internal FinTech projects (Lee & Shin, 2018). The banks have clients and scale but the new FinTech entrants usually have the innovation edge, especially at the "client experience" interface.

This continuous growth in investment is leapfrogging the development of FinTech to lead breakthroughs in domains such as trust management, big data, cloud computing and data analytic techniques (Gai et al., 2018). More importantly, these ventures contribute to the innovations that lie at the crux of FinTech such as cryptocurrencies and the blockchain, new digital advisory and trading systems, artificial intelligence and equity crowdfunding (Larios-Hernández, 2017). There is a positive feedback cyclic nature to this as this wave of innovations further accelerate the growth of existing financial institutions and attract new affluent investors, which enables more research and development in FinTech (Nakashima, 2018).

The rise of the technology-savvy and connected generation of investors has necessitated innovative investment solutions which offer greater convenience, channel access, transparency and lower cost. The importance of digital technology is in democratising finance. FinTechs are offering technology-enabled solutions that enhance accessibility, convenience and tailored products.

Evidently, FinTech is not just revolutionary to financial institutions and business operators, but it is also causing a big stir in the mundaneness of life. In fact, FinTech has been likened to the Internet of Things (IoT), which is said to be the fourth industrial revolution as FinTech is disrupting existing industry structures and blurring the frontiers of industries (Nakashima, 2018; Philippon, 2016). Some of the notable digital disruptors are the blockchain technology, dark pools and high frequency trading (HFT), robo-advisors (Preetha, 2015).

According to EY's Banking in Emerging Markets GCC FinTech Play 2017 report, the risk of FinTech disruption for both Islamic and traditional financial institutions across emerging markets is real, with the Finance function of banks at the centre of the disruption (Noordin, 2017). Successful digital money solutions should: 1) meet the needs of the market by filling a critical gap; 2) address muscle memory in users, becoming second nature to them and hitting the all-important tipping point for adoption; and 3) confront structural challenges to keep users away from the temptation of paper money (Citigroup, 2016a). Collaboration among FinTechs and traditional financial institutions especially in digital payments, money transfer and lending are now becoming the norm.

In Southeast Asia, the disruption is more pronounced in 'payments', with relatively less FinTechs in capital markets and wealth management. FinTechs are making a push in social payments and remittances in retail, and targeting the payables and receivables flows in SME banking (Financial Planning Standards Board, 2016). FinTech for Financial Inclusion has to be transformative. For an economy to embrace the FinTech, technology enablers needed i.e. very online population, rising internet penetration, modest smartphone penetration and low cash dependence relative to GDP per capita (Citigroup, 2018). FinTechs concentrate efforts on storing relevant experience on technological innovations include the unbanked, close the gender gap of financial inclusion, help us manage climate change risks, mitigate the challenges of de-risking, and bring down the costs of cross-border remittances (Hannig, (2017).

FinTech given its significant potential to disrupt the business model and appeal to a wider audience by promising user-friendly services. FinTech is disrupting the financial services industry, forcing banks to clarify their digital strategies, develop new capabilities and transform their cultures. It helps companies further refine the customer experience and expand their e-banking and online solutions. The FinTech disrupters will force existing banks to accept lower margins, cut costs and improve the quality of financial services. The dramatic changes in financial services can be said to be driven by technology innovation, intensified regulations, changes in consumer behaviour and the need for cost reduction, this global trend is expected to continue in the future. FinTech innovations are transforming financial services in terms of consumer experience, efficiency, credit risks, compliance risks, operational risks and data (Ancri, 2016). Change makes it more difficult for authorities to monitor and respond to risks in the financial system. Hence, there is an imperative need for transformative FinTech (Hannig, 2017).

These digital disruptions can be attributed to the dynamics of the FinTech ecosystem, in which it encompasses five key elements: FinTech start-ups, technology developers, the government, financial customers and traditional financial institutions (Lee & Shin, 2018).

First, FinTech start-ups lie at the very center of the ecosystem as they drive major FinTech phenomena such as the unbundling of financial services, which is a glaring disruption in the finance industry (Lee & Shin, 2018). Due to the unbundling of financial services, there are nine categories of FinTech start-ups: financing, payment, asset management, insurance (insurtech), loyalty programs, risk management, exchanges, regulatory technology (regtech) while the rest will be categorised as others (Haddad & Hornuf, 2016).

Since consumers now have the power to pick and choose individual finance services from a range of different FinTech providers, traditional financial institutions are at a disadvantage as consumers no longer have to rely on a single financial institution to manage their finances (Lee & Shin, 2018). For instance, a consumer may use PayPal for payments while choosing Kabbage for loans and making investments through Betterment.

Technology developers play a role in FinTech's ecosystem as they create a conducive environment that facilitates the growth of FinTech start-ups through platforms such as social media, big data analytics, cloud computing, artificial intelligence, smartphones and mobile services. In return, the FinTech sector helps these technology developers gain revenue (Lee & Shin, 2018).

Governments provide a regulatory environment for FinTech as economic policies, national economic development plans and regulation levels affect FinTech service provisions. Looser regulatory requirements are in favour of FinTech expansion as this enables FinTech start-ups to provide more accessible, customised and cost-effective financial services as compared to traditional institutions (Lee & Shin, 2018). On the other hand, FinTech benefits the government through the generation of a higher tax revenue by encouraging an increase in aggregate expenditure and in the volume of financial transactions (Ozili, 2018). Lastly, traditional financial institutions is a vital component in the FinTech ecosystem as their strength in economies of scale and financial resources enables them to provide funding to FinTech start-ups in exchange for gaining insights of FinTech applications in order to gain resilience in this competitive industry (Yang, 2015).

Financial customers are not only the source of revenue for FinTech companies, but they are also the muse for FinTech development (Lee & Shin, 2018; Nakashima, 2018). Although large organisations play a big role in generating revenue, individual customers and small and medium-sized enterprises (SMEs) are actually the predominant revenue source for FinTech start-ups. Due to the tech-savviness of the younger generation, millennials (individuals of age between 18 and 34) are the primary contributors to FinTech consumption, especially those with higher income (Lee & Shin, 2018). However, there is an undeniable disparity in accessibility to FinTech and this continues to inspire FinTech providers to improve the inclusion of digital financing (Ozili, 2018).

Hence, it can be noted that these five elements symbiotically play a part to ensure that the evolution of FinTech will continue to be one that improves the way people live by offering greater happiness or satisfaction in their lives (Lee & Shin, 2018; Nakashima, 2018).

THE EVOLUTION OF FINTECH

Although FinTech may seem like a relatively new innovation, this marriage between finance and technology actually has a long history that goes all the way back to the late 19th century. Over the span of the past 150 years, FinTech has evolved over three main eras and is currently still under much development (Arner, Barberis & Buckley, 2015).

From a historical perspective, finance and technology have been in a mutualistic relationship since their earliest stage of development. An example that illustrates this the written records of financial transactions during the Mesopotamian civilisation, as written records is one of the earliest form of information (Arner et al., 2015).

However, it was the advances in telegraph technology around the year 1866 that led to the birth of Victorian Internet which kickstarted the first wave of FinTech, also known as FinTech 1.0. The Victorian Internet connected western Europe to North America, thus enabling the instantaneous transmission of financial information between the major financial markets of London and New York. This revolution in business practices in addition to technological improvements such as in railroads and steamships led to the first age of financial and economic globalisation that marked FinTech 1.0 (Arner et al., 2015; Khan, 2018).

Although this era was heavily interlinked with technology, it remained largely an analogue industry that focused on infrastructure through the laying of transatlantic telegraph cables (Arner et al., 2015). After the post-World War I recession, the latter part of FinTech 1.0 began to focus on computerisation as great lengths were taken to develop codes and code breakers in order to secure military communication (Khan, 2018). These efforts proved to be fruitful as they led to FinTech's first major milestone – the opening of the world's first Automated Teller Machine (ATM) by Barclays in 1967 (Raza, 2018). This, along with the establishment of a global telegraph exchange network and the pioneering invention of the first handheld financial calculator, helped propel FinTech into its second era – FinTech 2.0 (Arner et al., 2015).

The commencement of FinTech 2.0 in 1967 marked a shift in financial services as they moved from an analogue industry to a digital one. For instance, the telegraphic system set in place during FinTech 1.0 became electronic in the 1970s while financial firms progressively replaced most forms of paper-based mechanisms with FinTech innovations such as Bloomberg terminals by the 1980s (Arner et al., 2015).

Highlights of the second phase of FinTech include the establishment of the world's first digital stock exchange – NASDAQ, in 1971. This holds much significance as it shaped the electronic trading to the one we know today.

Another milestone of FinTech during this period is the launch of the Society of Worldwide Interbank Financial Telecommunications (SWIFT) in 1973. The SWIFT system is the first and still the most commonly used global payment systems to this very day as it provides the communication protocol between financial institutions, thus enabling large volumes of international payments among them (Khan, 2018).

That being said, the real turning point for FinTech 2.0 was in the 1990s due to the internet revolution. This begun in 1995, where online account checking was first made available via the World Wide Web (WWW). Shortly after that, e-commerce business models started to emerge and were made possible through the founding of Paypal in 1998, which addressed the issue of online payment processing (Arbor Ventures, 2018). The combined impact of these developments made the internet and digitalisation the two key elements of FinTech 2.0, with electronic finance (e-finance) being the star of this age (Arner et al., 2015; Lee & Shin, 2018).

The second era of FinTech was brought to end abrupt end in 2008 due to the global financial earthquake that left the world financial system on the brink of collapse. In actuality, the 2008 global financial crisis was a blessing in disguise for FinTech as it helped elevate this sector to unprecedented levels (Haddad & Hornuf, 2016).

As the public had a growing distrust towards formal financial institution after the crisis, new entrants such as FinTech start-ups were able to successfully penetrate world of finance (Arner et al., 2015). Since FinTech start-ups had a relatively clean track record in that point of time, they could take advantage of the public's lack of confidence in traditional financial institutions to bloom in spite of the fragile state of the finance industry (Lee & Shin, 2018).

Not to mention, FinTech start-ups had a leverage at that time as they were unencumbered by the stricter financial regulatory reformations imposed on traditional banks after the crisis (Santander InnoVentures & Oliver Wyman, 2015). In attempt to prevent the 2008 financial crisis from reoccurring, new stringent regulatory compliances were set in place while existing ones were accelerated. This resulted in the reduced profitability of traditional financial firms, which encouraged them to massively invest in IT in order to address these changes (Khan, 2018).

The third factor leading to the sudden upsurge of FinTech start-ups is the downsizing of IT teams as well as back office employees in companies that were badly affected by the 2008 financial crisis in efforts to reduce operational costs (Arner et al., 2015). This massive job loss ushered a new age of FinTech start-ups as many of these highly skilled but unemployed people began to look for new opportunities and found a demand in the area of crowdlending and crowdfunding, which is one of the prominent FinTech services today (Haddad & Hornuf, 2016). This demand arose as a consequence of the financial crisis as there was an increased cost of debt for many small firms and in some cases, banks stopped lending money to businesses. Hence, these firms were under much pressure due to credit lines or bank loan rejections and had to resort to equity crowdfunding as an alternative source of external finance (Schindele & Szczesny, 2016; Lopez-de-Silanes et al., 2015).

Of course, the skyrocketing popularity of smartphones led by the launch of the Apple iPhone back in 2007 also greatly facilitated the accelerated growth of FinTech as their ubiquity was perfect for FinTech start-ups to provide direct point-of-sales (POS) and stored value systems to individuals (Arner et al., 2015; Khan, 2018; Rooney, 2018).

As a result, FinTech 2.0 was very much driven by FinTech start-ups, with little participation from conventional banks. It is also notable that while these initial innovations brought substantial attention and revenue to the FinTech sector, the financial solutions provided by these start-ups were relatively simple and were largely limited to improving transactions that already existed. Nonetheless, these four factors set the stage for the third phase of FinTech – FinTech 3.0, which is also its current era (Arbor Ventures, 2018).

FinTech 3.0 is very much different from its previous eras as it is not only aimed at improving the efficiency of pre-existing financial services, but it also has ambitions in redefining these services while innovating new solutions. Armed with artificial intelligence, greater computing power and an increased participation from large financial institutions, FinTech 3.0 brings a new horizon to the financial world as it introduces us to revolutionary inventions such as the blockchain technology and cryptocurrencies, which may lead to the obsolescence of traditional fiat currencies (Arbor Ventures, 2018; Khan, 2018).

A major FinTech milestone in this era is the invention of the world's first and largest cryptocurrency – Bitcoin (BTC) by Satoshi Nakamoto in 2009. This digital token took the world by a storm as the value of 1 BTC climbed from a meagre 8 cents in July 2010 to nearly a staggering $20,000 in December 2017, making it a gold rush amongst investors and traders in this digital age (Kharpal, 2018).

More importantly, the creation of Bitcoin also birthed the concept of blockchain technology as Nakamoto invented blockchain as a core component of Bitcoin, where blockchain serves as a public transaction ledger for the digital token. This holds much significance as blockchain represents the first fully functional distributed ledger technology (DLT) in which it utilises a peer-to-peer network that eliminates the need for a trusted party to facilitate digital relationships such as cryptocurrency transactions (Nakamoto, 2008). With this innovation in information registration and distribution, the third stage of FinTech 3.0 has seen changes in traditional banks as 69% of them experimenting with private blockchains (EdgeVerve Systems, 2017).

In fact, many countries are becoming more crypto-friendly. One of such countries is Singapore, where the Monetary Authority of Singapore (MAS) announced "Project Ubin" in 2016 as an attempt to explore blockchain as the country shows interest in launching its own digital currency (Kharpal, 2017). Additionally, the highly regarded Ngee Ann Polytechnic in Singapore is already using blockchain to verify the authenticity of the public institute's diplomas, proving that FinTech is impacting countries in immeasurable ways (Lago, 2018).

FinTech 3.0 also encompasses FinTech 3.5, which emphasises on financial inclusion and economic development in developing countries, especially in Africa and Asia (Arner et al., 2015). A good example would be the meteoric rise of FinTech in China, where their financial system used to be described as nothing short of underdeveloped but has since transitioned into a cutting-edge institutional system due to the expansion of FinTech implementations such as mobile payments via Alipay (Shim & Shin, 2016).

Evidently, FinTech is always evolving as it is driven by weaknesses in the financial landscape, market demands, regulation policies and availability of technological resources (Haddad & Hornuf, 2016). In any case, it is important to realise that every evolution brings opportunities and risks that must be carefully considered in order to support market developments while abiding core mandates such as systemic stability, consumer protection and market competition (Arner et al., 2015).

COMPARISON WITH FIAT MONEY

Before delving into the frills and thrills of currencies such as fiat currency or cryptocurrency, it is important to understand how and why money lies at the core of economics (Paulsen, 2012).

From a technological point of view, money is simply a record-keeping device in which it provides a (possibly limited) form of societal memory of transactions (Kocherlakota, 1998). This gives money three standard roles in an economy:

1. A store of value
2. A medium of exchange
3. A unit of account

Hence, virtually anything can be considered as money as long as it fulfils these three major functions (Quickonomics, 2016).

Currently, fiat money the most dominant form of money in the economic market. It can be defined as any legal tender issued by the government and controlled by a central authority such as the central bank (Goyal, 2018; Quickonomics, 2016). This is precisely what makes it so prevalent – the government order behind its designation regulates it and makes it a requirement for all people and organisations within the country to accept it as a means of payment. Its widespread acceptance is also attributed to the people's trust in the central authority as its value is guaranteed by its issuer (Rotman, 2014). A traditional example of this form of currency is the paper bills of the US Dollar while electronic examples of it include bank credit.

The truth is, fiat money itself is intrinsically useless (Kocherlakota, 1998; Paulsen, 2012). Instead, its value is derived from the relationship of supply and demand as well as the public's confidence in the issuing government. However, this serves as a double-edged sword as it puts this form of money at risk of inflation and deflation (Investopedia, 2015; Quickonomics, 2016).

It is beyond the shadow of doubt that monetary economics is often associated with inflation in which how the quantity of money or its growth rate will affect the prices and quantities of goods. However, this view of money has been challenged with the idea that this focus is misplaced. Since money is essentially a record-keeping device as aforementioned, the true focal point should be on making sure that the record-keeping of financial transactions is done in the most efficient way possible (Kocherlakota, 1998).

This brings us to cryptocurrency, which is a type of unregulated, digital money that is issued and usually controlled by its developers, which means that it is not backed by a central government nor a bank (Rotman, 2014). As of March 2018, there are over 1600 cryptocurrencies in existence, with Bitcoin, Ethereum and Ripple being some of the more prominent examples (Frankel, 2018).

Much like fiat money, cryptocurrency also does not have any intrinsic value (Rahman, 2018; Rotman, 2014). However, cryptocurrency is less prone to inflation because it cannot be infinitely printed to create more supply. Rather, most of them were designed to be capped at a certain number. For example, only 21 million BTC will ever exist based on a predetermined algorithm, where the last BTC will only be mined in the year 2140. This is also the reason why it is possible to determine the number of digital coins circulating at any particular point in time whereas this cannot be done for fiat money (Goyal, 2018).

Unfortunately, many people seem to confuse the price volatility of cryptocurrency with inflation. While political and economic stability have a major impact on fiat money, it is actually technology, adoption rate and demand that heavily influences the value of digital coins (CryptoFarmer, 2018). However, it is undeniable that this high volatility of cryptocurrency is its biggest drawback as it labels cryptocurrency as an abstract concept that is harder to understand and contend with, which drives potential users away due to fear, mistrust and misunderstandings (Goyal, 2018).

Just from their definitions alone, it is clear that there are many other pronounced differences between fiat currency and cryptocurrency. Other than the aspect of legality, these two forms of money also have obvious distinctions when it comes to tangibility as cryptocurrencies do not physically exist, unlike fiat money. As such, cryptocurrencies have the advantage of portability and transferability as there is no physical weight to them (Chizurum, 2018).

The intangible nature of cryptocurrencies gives rise to dissimilarities in terms of storage and exchange, where it can only be stored in digital wallets and exchanged digitally. In contrast, fiat money has the advantage of versatility as it can be stored and exchanged physically as hard cash or digitally through payment providers such as Paypal or even in conventional banks (Goyal, 2018). Another notable gulf is that exchanges done via cryptocurrency is irrevocable as there is no way to cancel transactions made using it – the recipient has to start another transaction to send the digital coins back to the sender. While this may be cumbersome for some, it ensures that cryptocurrencies provide a secure medium (Rotman, 2014).

An important point to note is that cryptocurrency is based on a decentralised system whereas fiat money lies on a centralised system. Unlike how the government and central bank controls fiat currency, cryptocurrency does not have a single entity that controls it. Every device that mines cryptocurrency and makes transactions through it makes up part of the network, which eliminates the need for intermediaries such as banks or payment processors.

As such, cheaper transfer fees and faster confirmation times can be achieved with cryptocurrency (Zainuddin, n.d.).

Another glaring difference between cryptocurrency and fiat money is the issue of privacy. Customers may remain anonymous when making transactions via digital coins as no one can view the amount nor location of the digital wallet (Rotman, 2014). With fiat money, the government and bank has access to an individual's financial information as much of their fiat money is stored in banks. Alas, this makes cryptocurrency the perfect tool for criminals as they can avoid detection and identification since transactions made with digital coins cannot be traced easily (Chizurum, 2018).

However, the key point is that cryptocurrency is a better record-keeper of financial transactions due to its underlying blockchain technology. At its core, cryptocurrency is nothing but a digital file that records every transaction that took place in its network in an open ledger called the "blockchain" (Rotman, 2014). This makes cryptocurrency more transparent as compared to fiat currency. While this may seem contradictory as the users' identities are concealed, transparency and privacy can coexist through the blockchain technology as each user is given a public address where other people may view the holdings and transactions that he or she carried out, which reduces the risk of fraud. This public address is created through a combination of several cryptographic operations that prevents identification of the person behind it (Lisk Academy, n.d.; Yap, 2017).

Ultimately, both fiat money and cryptocurrency have their own strengths and weaknesses. Nevertheless, with the advent of problems pertaining to fiat money such as hyperinflation, kleptocracy and fraudulent crimes, cryptocurrency might be the answer to many of these issues as it creates a trustless system, where trust is not even needed as it is immutable and incorruptible (Lisk Academy, n.d.).

INDUSTRIES AND APPLICATIONS WHERE FINTECH IS AND WILL BE SUITABLE

Finance Industry

As its name implies, FinTech is the perfect catalyst for the revolution across the whole finance industry, no matter if it's a bank, insurance firm, brokerage company or saving and loan associations. This is possible with the rise of

FinTech's ingenious innovation – intelligent automation, which could help the finance sector gain up to $512 billion in new global revenue by the year 2020 (Middleton, 2018).

According to the report "Growth in the Machine" by Capgemini's Digital Transformation Institute (2018), intelligent automation is the right combination of robotic processing automation (RPA), artificial intelligence (AI) and business optimisation processes. This FinTech is a powerful driver of revenue as not only can it cut operating costs while improving customer satisfaction, retention and loyalty but it also enables targeted marketing, extended business hours and a competitive leverage.

The launch of OCBC Bank's specialised mortgage chatbot application "Emma" in 2017 is a solid testimony of how intelligent automation can be a hidden ace in a financial institute (Lee, 2017; Tay, 2018). The chatbot made headlines as it helped the bank generate over $100 million of revenue since its debut, with 90% of the customers satisfied with their interaction and this percentage is expected to rise as Emma continues to undergo further training to ensure the best customer experience (Capgemini, 2018).

As explored previously, FinTech is responsible for numeral disruptions in the finance industry, especially due the unbundling of financial services. One of the financial services that is undergoing much digital reimagination is payment services due to the introduction of cashless payment solutions via cryptocurrency, mobile payment (m-payment) as well as innovative "backend as a service" (BaaS) payment processing models.

For instance, mobile devices such as smartphones can now act as wallets thanks to the development of m-payment services which can be utilised in a plethora of ways from performing electronic transactions such as paying bills to purchasing physical products such as through vending machines, ticketing machines or any manned point-of-sale (POS) systems (Iman, 2018).

Referring to Table 1, digital-banking penetration for transactions and services is on the rise across both developed and emerging countries (Härle et al., 2015). Among emerging Asian countries, China ranked the top, followed by Vietnam and Malaysia.

As payments represent the platform for the entire banking relationship, even nonbank players such as telcos, local payment specialists and global players are keen to capture payment revenue. Players such Alibaba in China, Globe in Philippines and PayPal across Asia Pacific are already gaining traction. The biggest payment company in Asia today is not a bank; it's Alipay (DBS Group Research, 2015). The payments technology has also created opportunities. Innovative solutions such as payments with a single

Table 1. Percentage of respondents using online banking 2014

Developed Asia	Percentage	Emerging Asia	Percentage
Australia	96	China	57
Hong Kong	93	India	18
Japan	83	Indonesia	36
Korea	96	Malaysia	41
Singapore	94	Philippines	13
Taiwan	92	Thailand	19
		Vietnam	44

Source: McKinsey survey on personal financial services in Asia, 2007-14 as quoted by Härle et al. (2015)

tap or near-field communications, face/voice recognition and fingerprint verification are designed to support more secure and convenient payments. According to Viknesh and Abdulwahab (2017), customer experience is affected by perceived ease of use, security and privacy, attitude, knowledge to use, digital efficacy, government support and perceived behavioural control (Viknesh & Abdulwahab, 2017).

It is worth noting that the year 2015 is a key milestone of electronic payment as the number of Interbank GIRO transactions (149 million transactions) surpassed the number of cheques cleared (148 million cheques) for the first time (Ibrahim, 2016). The Sun Daily reported that Bank Negara Malaysia (BNM) established a Financial Technology Enabler Group (FTEG) to formulate and enhance regulatory policies to facilitate the adoption of technological innovations, and would serve as the dedicated contact point for FinTech related queries. ("Banks willing to work with FinTech companies", 6 June 2016). The financial services industry is capital intensive, involves larger amounts of money, control of credits and other risks, and highly regulated. Legal frameworks and business processes designed to protect consumers have to fully keep up to the changes in the digital landscapes.

Even though FinTech companies pose a threat to the financial institutions, it also presents an opportunity to collaborate with the startups. Malaysian banks that are not ready will experience negative consequences on their bottom line and profitability (Nazri & Hoolash, 2017). Among the local financial institutions, the speed of FinTech adoption defers from one with another. The four local banks that are leading the charge in digital finance are Maybank, CIMB, RHB Bank and Hong Leong Bank. Maybank launched MaybankFintech, the first by a bank in Southeast Asia in 2015, and digital services including Malaysia's first mobile wallet, MaybankPay and Samsung

Pay in 2016 (Maybank, 2017). CIMB Bank launched the CIMB FinTech to drive innovation as well as to incubate new ideas; digitise operations; and transform the Group (CIMB, 2017). RHB expects that significant innovation to come in areas such as lending, payments, wealth management and customer engagement. Secondly, RHB has also started its FinTech accelerator program. Thirdly, RHB have established a dedicated 'Digital Center of Excellence', as reported in The Sun Daily ("Banks willing to work with FinTech companies", 6 June 2016.). RHB Bank collaborated with Startup bootcamp FinTech, and launched RHB Pay Anyone and RHB TradeSmart Global Trading System in 2016 (RHB, 2016). Hong Leong Bank launched HLB LaunchPad, a mentorship and developmental program targeted at nurturing technology start-ups, piloted in-branch mobile servicing solution and introduced eFD via FPX in 2017 (HLBB, 2017), and its FinTech development plans are in areas such as Peer-to-Peer ("P2P") lending, e-wallet and e-payment providers, supply chain financing and providers of new credit scoring technologies (HLBB, 2018). These banks adopt the FinTech towards better mobile banking, cash management and understanding customer behaviour for higher productivity.

Referring to Table 2, Malaysia was ranked 22nd, which was a drop of 2 ranks from year 2014; Malaysia still need to improve on especially on digital money solutions, propensity to adopt and technology and financial infrastructure.

Table 2. Digital Money Index 2016 (selected countries)

Rank	Country	Change in rank from 2014	Government and market support	Technology and Financial Infrastructure	Digital Money Solutions	Propensity to adopt
2	Singapore	0	1	3	7	8
3	United States	0	4	12	6	1
5	Hong Kong	0	3	1	20	12
9	Japan	0	5	18	8	4
21	Korea, Republic of	0	25	50	5	14
22	Malaysia	-2	10	20	27	23
37	Indonesia	0	41	45	51	34
38	China	1	27	63	41	46
40	Thailand	3	43	35	60	37
45	Philippines	-3	61	32	62	35
63	India	-9	57	37	49	74

Source: Citigroup (2016a)

Transportation Industry

With the ubiquity of mobile devices and the convenience that comes with it, it's not surprising that m-payment services are penetrating many daily activities, be it dining or shopping. In 2016, approximately 68 percent of China's population were users of m-payment, leading up to an astronomical total of $760 billion in m-payment transactions (Wang et al., 2017). Technological advances have also encouraged the proliferation of m-payment systems as consumers can now perform transactions through short message service (SMS), near-field communication (NFC) and quick response (QR) codes (de Luna, Liébana-Cabanillas, Sánchez-Fernández, & Muñoz-Leiva, 2018).

These m-payment systems are shaking up the transportation industry, more specifically the public transportation sector as its adoption in this sector is useful for ticket purchasing and validation (Fontes et al., 2017). In China, Alipay is already a popular payment option for bus and subway passengers in over 50 cities, including Beijing, Shanghai and Hangzhou. Since this m-payment service uses an offline QR code-based payments that only require 0.3 seconds to complete, it is no wonder that this FinTech is ideally suited for hustle and bustle of public transport stations as it helps shorten queues and eliminates the need for small change (Finextra, 2018). This method of payment proves to be successful as Alipay has aggressive and ambitious plans to expand to around 50 new cities by 2019 in order to top competitors such as Tencent who are also players aiming to dominate this competitive field (Chen, 2018).

Gaming Industry

Cryptocurrency is changing the gaming industry radically as a blockchain-driven game economy is beginning to take shape, especially with the development of Ethereum games. Released in November 2017 by Axiom Zen, CryptoKitties is one of the first blockchain-based games where players collect and breed unique virtual cats and then auction their virtual cats for cryptocurrency. The game is definitely one to look out for as in September 2018, a CryptoKitty was sold for 600 ETH (Ethereum), which is equivalent to a shocking $172,000 (Serrels, 2018). This proves that a cryptocurrency marketplace for gamers is feasible as it is every gamer's dream to be able to earn "real" money from playing games (Egovora, 2018).

There are also games where the cryptocurrency is used as their in-game payment currency. With the newfound partnership between AppCoins, a digital coin that is spearheading the use of cryptocurrency in the applications economy and Unity, a major game engine, game developers can now explore a new stream of revenue as gamers can now make in-game purchases using digital currency. There are high hopes that this venture will be successful as the quantity of payments using AppCoins has risen by 590 percent between September and October 2018 as its service is compatible with popular gaming platforms such as the Nintendo Switch and the PlayStation 4 in addition to iOS and Android mobile devices (Blenkinsop, 2018).

Eco-Industrial Development

FinTech proves itself to be multifaceted as it can also be implemented in the benefit distribution in payments for ecosystem services (PES) as well as REDD+, which is a global initiative that gives land users some financial incentives to reduce carbon and methane emissions from their land. Traditionally, payments from the scheme implementors (typically a government agency or a non-governmental organisation) would have to bypass lower-tiers of governments before accruing at the community level. Only then can the community representatives disburse the payment participating households or individuals.

FinTech brings a new approach to the PES/REDD+ benefit distribution as the participants in the PES/REDD+ schemes only need to register a mobile money account with the scheme implementors, thus skipping many links in the chain and reducing the associated risk of corruption and elite capture while enabling payments to be made in a more secure, instantaneous and effortless manner (Thompson, 2017).

This type of payment is also known as the government-to-peer (G2P) payment service offered through FinTech, which is salient in expanding financial inclusion especially in developing countries. This is why there are at least 19 G2P programmes operating in developing countries such as Pakistan (Arner, Buckley, & Zetzsche, 2018).

Hence, FinTech continues to astound us as it penetrates other industries and blooms steadfastly through the digital disruptions it creates. Unbeknownst to many, FinTech has truly begun to affect even the most inconspicuous parts of our daily lives due to its ubiquity, adaptability and versatility.

CHALLENGES WHICH FINTECH IS FACING AT THE MOMENT AND IN THE FUTURE

It is unavoidable that FinTech has to face formidable hurdles as it is crucial to ensure that the sector continues to improve as it evolves. Currently, the challenges FinTech face can be categorised into six major dimensions – financial inclusion, regulation, security and privacy, technology integration, shortage of skilled human resources and lastly, customer management (Lee & Shin, 2018; Ozili, 2018).

Financial Inclusion

To date, FinTech still struggles in expanding financial inclusion due to a variety of reasons. One of such reasons is the religious beliefs of certain communities towards technological developments (Ozili, 2018). For instance, Bitcoin was embroiled in a controversy amongst Islamic scholars as some regarded Bitcoin as halal while the others thought of it as something forbidden as it is an enabler for crimes such as tax evasion (The New Arab, 2018). Understandably, its questionable permissibility led to Bitcoin's weak foothold in the Muslim community and financial firms, which highlights a weakness in the financial inclusion of FinTech innovations such as cryptocurrency. When Muhammad Abu-Baker of Indonesia's Blossom Firm declared Bitcoin as compliant under Syariah Law in his research paper published in April 2018, the digital coin's value skyrocketed by over $1,000 in just less than one hour as it was now potentially open to a new market of 1.6 billion Muslims (Cuthbertson, 2018). This may be an indication of just how much influence financial inclusion has on FinTech products.

Another challenge FinTech has to deal with as it strives for greater financial inclusion is financial illiteracy especially in rural and poor communities due to difficulties in attaining a holistic education. This is an onerous problem as individuals from such communities often do not trust in efforts taken to persuade them to adopt digital finance services in addition to the fact that they see little incentives to use digital channels which they do not or cannot understand. There is hope to rise above this obstacle as people in aboriginal or impoverished communities have a higher likelihood of trusting friends or family members who are already FinTech users, which provides some insight on the approaches FinTech can take to connect with them (Ozili, 2018).

Regulation

Regulation of FinTech remains to be a heavy pressure on FinTech start-ups as intuitions are required to produce escalating amounts of financial, risk and compliance data while being simultaneously regulated in multiple jurisdictions with multiple framework (Treleaven, 2015). Not to mention, FinTech start-ups have to also consider the balance between low cost business models and the compliance costs they come with (Arner, n.d.).

While this increased intrusion of regulation enables the systemic risk analysis of the FinTech and finance industry, it comes at a price as now FinTech firms are burdened with stringent regulatory compliances. This is a major barrier that discourages the innovation of new FinTech products, which highlights the need for regulatory support for innovation in this sector (Treleaven, 2015).

This situation is made worse when many emergent FinTech firms have difficulty in identifying their regulatory obligations due to its complexity, which can result in licensing delays and hefty fines (Arner, n.d.; Rampton, 2017). An incident demonstrating this occurred when the Financial Crimes Enforcement Network (FinCEN) levied its first fine on virtual currency exchange back in the year 2015, in which Ripple Labs was fined $700,000 due to the firm's failure to register under FinCEN as well as failing to implement and maintain an adequate anti-money laundering (AML) program (Ferro, 2015).

FinTech start-ups can also be seen to operate in a legislative grey areas when regulations fail to keep pace with the technological advances (Global Banking & Finance Review, 2018). This is because both regulators and industry officials lack up-to-date analytical and data skills to cope with the rapid changes in technology, especially with the inter-connectedness of financial markets due to the global nature of FinTech (Iwamoto et al., 2018).

Thankfully, FinTech has started to respond to these challenges through the development of regulatory technology (RegTech), which presents an opportunity to apply innovative FinTech paradigms and big data analytics to regulation and compliance through algorithmic and automatic regulation. Other efforts have also begun to take shape in order to help FinTech firms overcome the regulatory difficulties faced, such as regulatory sandboxes where new FinTech products, models and services can be safely tested with customers (Treleaven, 2015).

Security and Privacy

The issue of regulation is important as its implementation is essential in protecting consumers from the misuse and mishandling of their private data in FinTech companies. As the use of FinTech proliferates, its cyber vulnerabilities become more alarming as the increased sophistication and scale of cyber-attacks pose a significant threat to the security and privacy of customers' data on digital channels (Ozili, 2018).

While FinTech start-ups do not have the same budgets as conventional banks when it comes to data security, the customer information these start-ups hold is just as sensitive. This means that FinTech firms need to do more with less resources in ensuring overall security excellence by building a heavily fortified network as well as maintaining a firewall configuration (O'Dwyer, 2017).

FinTech firms that fail to pay careful attention on the potential security threats truly operate at their own peril as they will be the next targets of hackers and other cybercriminals. Take Wonga for example, where this FinTech firm known for its payday lending was hit with a massive data breach in 2017 that ended up affecting almost 250,000 of its users in which sensitive data such as their names, addresses and bank account numbers were stolen (Jamieson, 2017).

These cybercriminals find their way into the systems of these companies primarily through social engineering techniques such as phishing as well as the technical hacking technique such as penetration testing. However, they vary their attack methodologies depending on the target or even after a specific period, which means FinTech firms have to always be on their toes in order to abate this disaster (O'Dwyer, 2017). One way to do this is by employing dynamic security solutions such as a moving target defence (MTD), which leaves hacker in frustration as it enables systems to recognize attack point patterns and identify potentially malicious behaviour without additional programming (Global Banking & Finance Review, 2018).

Concerns regarding data collection and data privacy is another issue the FinTech sector has to grapple with. It is an open secret that many FinTech companies collect large amounts of their customers' data for analytical purposes in sales and marketing, where the data harvested includes sensitive personal data and financial records. In fact, some of them have begun to gather alternative data, where they track and trace the digital footprints of their customers such as on social media (Ng, 2018).

This practice poses legal questions regarding consumer awareness and consent on the collection of their data as well as raises the issue of data ownership. Moreover, it also means that more third-parties can have authorised access to consumers' sensitive data through these FinTech firms, thus making further compromises on consumer data privacy as the third-party may have different approaches to data security (Ng, 2018).

Hence, it is no wonder that FinTech companies are attractive in the eyes of cybercriminals as they hold valuable data that can used for lucrative exploitation. Unfortunately, many FinTech start-ups find it challenging to upkeep a set of comprehensive and transparent privacy terms that is in compliance with current regulations as the harsh truth is that most of them are profit-driven and consequently allocate fewer resource for data security and privacy (Ng, 2018).

Technology Integration

To prevent the stagnation of FinTech development, partnerships and joint ventures between traditional financial institutions and FinTech start-ups is necessary as this plays a part of the FinTech ecosystem. However, traditional banking processes may be incompatible with new FinTech models, especially if there is no solid integration plan to bridge them together (Lee & Shin, 2018).

From a FinTech perspective, the onboarding process of technology products in financial companies appears to be complex and under-resourced. Based on a report published by Accenture (2018), this process involves four phases – prospecting, proof of concept, procurement and implementation. The report noted that tactical miscoordination between FinTech start-ups and conventional financial institutions is a challenge that slows down the adoption of FinTech in financial services. The proof of concept phase clearly illustrates this point as the majority of conventional financial institutions judged product feasibility with compliance and security as the top concerns while FinTech firms generally emphasised on funding sources and alignment between use cases and product roadmaps.

The lack of mutual understanding and clear communication between these two entities are apparent to be inhibitors in the efforts to accelerate FinTech mainstream adoption, which further amplifies the need for improvements in technology integration with financial services. One way is to prioritise regular and timely two-way communication between them in order to break free from the confinements of their own mental models in which they perceive that they have different working worlds due to the differences in size, regulation, bureaucracy, cash flows and other factors. For instance, financial institutions can improve productivity by streamlining the decision-making process and give prompt rejections on FinTech ideas instead of baiting developers with a series of "maybe's" that lead to a dead end (Accenture, 2018).

In regard to issues with FinTech integration, the lack of readiness in financial institutions to embrace FinTech is also another formidable challenge. According to the British Bankers Association (BBA), the footfall for branches has reduced by 30% in the last three years and the number of banking-related mobile applications has doubled in 2013. In other words, the development of alternative channels and lower footfall has led banks to trim their branch networks (DBS Group Research, 2015). The spending has been shifting from physical outlets to IT that it will be banking without branches, investing without brokers and paying without paper.

According to Citigroup (2016b), FinTech companies have both scale and innovation in China. Emerging markets with a high percentage of unbanked population, relatively weak consumer banks, and a high penetration of mobile phones have big opportunities as they are ripe for FinTech disruptions. Nevertheless, based on the survey titled "Catching the FinTech Wave" produced by PricewaterhouseCoopers (PwC) Malaysia and the Asian Institute of Chartered Bankers (AICB), 82% of Malaysian financial institutions saw FinTech as a threat to their businesses, however, there was still lack of readiness among the financial institutions in embracing FinTech because merely 47% of the Malaysian financial institutions have placed FinTech at the heart of their strategy (Ganeshwaran, 2016).

Customer Management

A key area that FinTech has to deal with is the loss of human touch in its customer service. Due to the rise of artificial intelligence and machine learning, some FinTech business models leave clients feeling like they are dealing with a faceless entity as they interact with robo-advisors like OCBC Bank's chatbot "Emma". While the younger generations such as Generations X and Y can somewhat adapt to this due to their tech-savviness, older clients may find it uncomfortable or even unsettling. While intelligent automation is highly productive and can offer personalised service around the clock, it presents another challenge as it is also highly costly for FinTech start-ups to employ (Lee & Shin, 2018).

FinTech is not just about the technology, it is also about the people. So how can these FinTech firms avoid becoming soulless revenue generators? For one, having customer's needs and interests as a driver of FinTech adoption and innovation is key. In the end, the aim of any FinTech is to improve the lives of people by making things more convenient and making them feel satisfied. As the world move towards automation, FinTech companies should also consider offering some level of direct human interaction in their customer service by having a dedicated team to support customers whenever they need help as they continue on their journey with the company (Global Banking & Finance Review, 2018).

MANAGERIAL CONTEXT AND IMPLEMENTATION IN A BUSINESS ORGANIZATION

FinTech is a great tool for all businesses, no matter how small or big they may be. However, there is an entry barrier for its implementation in business organisations due to the regulatory challenge as delved on in the previous section.

Nonetheless, FinTech also shines bright when embraced by businesses due to its usefulness in managing a business' cash flow. In this context, other than the aforementioned innovations such as global payment systems, some of FinTech's notable contributions include artificial intelligence, automation, cloud accounting and open banking (Plumb, 2018). These offer business greater access to data and more powerful tools that could lead to better insight and decision-making in budgeting, forecasting, analysis and resource management.

With the rapid development of technology, artificial intelligence and machine learning in software and apps could just give businesses a glimpse far greater insights than manual analysis can currently offer. With this new breed of business intelligence, business organizations can grasp the opportunity to adjust their marketing in time to take advantage of the situation at hand (Plumb, 2018; Totka, 2018).

One of such tools is Fluidly, an artificial intelligence-powered cashflow management software that enables forecasting in real time and automated credit control. Applications such as these are a huge help for small or medium enterprises (SMEs) as the prospect of having real-time and month-end reports without the cost of employing management accountants will help ease the financial burden of the business organization. After all, he biggest killer of any business is running out of money as 82 percent of them fail due to poor cash flow management skills (Flint, 2018). In addition, overall organizational productivity can be boosted since these FinTech innovations also streamline business processes such as data entry, which in turn helps save much time. This means that more resources can be freed up and used for more value-adding projects.

REFERENCES

Ancri, C. (2016, October 19). *FinTech Innovation: An Overview*. Washington, DC: Board of Governors of the Federal Reserve System.

Arbor Ventures. (2018). *FinTech—Past, present and future*. Retrieved from https://medium.com/@ArborVentures1/fintech-past-present-and-future-eac0f8df2722

Arner, D. W. (2016). *FinTech: Evolution and regulation*. Retrieved from https://law.unimelb.edu.au/__data/assets/pdf_file/0011/1978256/D-Arner-FinTech-Evolution-Melbourne-June-2016.pdf

Arner, D. W., Barberis, J., & Buckley, R. P. (2015). The evolution of FinTech: A new post-crisis paradigm. *Geo. J. Int'l L.*, *47*, 1271.

Arner, D. W., Buckley, R. P., & Zetzsche, D. A. (2018). *Fintech for financial inclusion: A framework for digital financial transformation*. Alliance for Financial Inclusion.

Banks willing to work with fintech companies. (2016, June 6). *The Sun Daily*.

Blenkinsop, C. (2018). Why making in-app game purchases using crypto is about to get easier. *Coin Telegraph*. Retrieved from https://cointelegraph.com/news/why-making-in-app-game-purchases-using-crypto-is-about-to-get-easier

BlockchainHub. (n.d.). *Smart contracts*. Retrieved from https://blockchainhub.net/smart-contracts/

Chen, M. (2018). Mobile payment firms eye city transport. *China Daily*. Retrieved from http://www.chinadaily.com.cn/a/201805/21/WS5b022003a3103f6866ee98d7.html

Chizurum, C. (2018). Cryptocurrency versus fiat money: Pros and cons. *Cryptoblockwire*. Retrieved from https://cryptoblockwire.com/cryptocurrency-vs-fiat-money/

CIMB Group Holdings Berhad. (2017). *CIMB Annual Report 2017*. Retrieved from www.cimb.com

Citigroup. (2016a). *Digital Money: Releasing The Flow Of Digital Money Hitting The Tipping Point Of Adoption*. January.

Citigroup. (2016b). *Citi GPS: Global Perspectives & Solutions*. March.

Citigroup. (2018, March). *Citi GPS: Global Perspectives & Solutions*

Cryptoboer. (2018). *Cryptocurrencies vs. fiat money: major differences and similarities*. Retrieved from https://www.cryptoboer.nl/2018/01/27/cryptocurrencies-vs-fiat-money-major-differences-and-similarities/

Cuthbertson, A. (2018). Bitcoin market opens to 1.6 billion Muslims as cryptocurrency declared halal under Islamic law. *The Independent*. Retrieved from https://www.independent.co.uk/life-style/gadgets-and-tech/news/bitcoin-islamic-law-muslims-cryptocurrency-market-permissible-sharia-news-price-surge-a8302761.html'

DBS Group Research. (2015, April 14). ASEAN Banks, Regional Industry Focus.

de Luna, I. R., Liébana-Cabanillas, F., Sánchez-Fernández, J., & Muñoz-Leiva, F. (2018). Mobile payment is not all the same: The adoption of mobile payment systems depending on the technology applied. *Technological Forecasting and Social Change*. doi:10.1016/j.techfore.2018.09.018

Detwiler, D. (2018). One nation's move to increase food safety with blockchain. *IBM*. Retrieved from https://www.ibm.com/blogs/blockchain/2018/02/one-nations-move-to-increase-food-safety-with-blockchain/

EdgeVerve Systems. (2017). Blockchain technology: from hype to reality.

Egorova, K. (2018). Gaming company allows players to win cryptocurrency in its new first-person shooter. *Coin Telegraph*. Retrieved from https://cointelegraph.com/news/gaming-company-allows-players-to-win-cryptocurrency-in-its-new-first-person-shooter

EY FinTech Global Network. (2017). EY FinTech Adoption Index 2017. *The Rapid Emergence of FinTech.* Retrieved from http://www.ey.com/GL/en/Industries/Financial-Services/ey-fintech-adoption-index

Ferro, S. (2017). Regulators just demonstrated they are serious about making digital currency companies follow the rules. *Business Insider*. Retrieved from https://www.businessinsider.com/ripple-just-got-slapped-with-a-700000-fine-2015-5/?IR=T

Financial Planning Standards Board. (2016). FinTech and the Future of Financial Planning.

Finextra. (2018). *Alipay targets China's public transportation networks.* Retrieved from https://www.finextra.com/newsarticle/31977/alipay-targets-chinas-public-transportation-networks

FinTech Global. (2018). *2018 is already a record year for global FinTech investment.* Retrieved from http://fintech.global/2018-is-already-a-record-year-for-global-fintech-investment

Flint, M. (2018). Cash flow % of small businesses fail. *Reason, 82.*

Fontes, T., Costa, V., Ferreira, M. C., Shengxiao, L., Zhao, P., & Dias, T. G. (2017). Mobile payments adoption in public transport. *Transportation Research Procedia, 24*, 410–417. doi:10.1016/j.trpro.2017.05.093

Frankel, M. (2018). How many crytocurrencies are there? *Fool*. Retrieved from https://www.fool.com/investing/2018/03/16/how-many-cryptocurrencies-are-there.aspx

Gai, K., Qiu, M., & Sun, X. (2018). A survey on FinTech. *Journal of Network and Computer Applications, 103*(January), 262–273. doi:10.1016/j.jnca.2017.10.011

Ganeshwaran, K. (2016, November 26). FinTech seen as threat to business of institutions. *The Star Online*.

Gem. (n.d.). *Healthcare solutions.* Retrieved from https://enterprise.gem.co/health/

Global Banking & Finance Review. (2018). *The three biggest FinTech challenges facing the industry right now.* Retrieved from https://www.globalbankingandfinance.com/the-three-biggest-fintech-challenges-facing-the-industry-right-now/

Google Trends. (2018). *fintech*. Retrieved from https://trends.google.com/trends/explore?date=all&q=fintech

Goyal, S. (2018). The difference between fiat money and cryptocurrencies. *Yahoo*. Retrieved from https://finance.yahoo.com/news/difference-between-fiat-money-cryptocurrencies-132027811.html

Haddad, C., & Hornuf, L. (2016). The emergence of the global fintech market: Economic and technological determinants. *Small Business Economics*, 1–25.

Hannig, A. (2017, December 20). FinTech: What's in it for financial inclusion? Alliance for Financial Inclusion.

Härle, P, Havas, A, Kremer, A, Rona, D, Samandari, H (2015). The future of bank risk management.

Hong Leong Bank Berhad. (2017). *Sustainability Report 2017*.

Hong Leong Bank Berhad. (2018). *Annual Report 2018*.

Ibrahim, M. (2016, April 4). Accelerating the migration to electronic payments in Malaysia [Speech of the Deputy Governor of the Central Bank of Malaysia]. In Inaugural Malaysian E-Payments Excellence Awards, Kuala Lumpur.

Iman, N. (2018). Is mobile payment still relevant in the fintech era? *Electronic Commerce Research and Applications*, *30*, 72–82.

CB Insights. (2015, November 19). *Disrupting Banking: The FinTech Startups That Are Unbundling Wells Fargo, Citi and Bank of America*. Retrieved from https://www.cbinsights.com/blog/disrupting-banking-fintech-startups/

International Monetary Fund. (2018). The Core Principles for Islamic Finance Regulations and Assessment Methodology. *Staff Report*, *18/193*(May), 35.

Investopedia. (2015). *Is fiat money more prone to inflation than commodity money?* Retrieved from https://www.investopedia.com/ask/answers/041515/fiat-money-more-prone-inflation-commodity-money.asp

Iwamoto, K., & Lee, J. (2018). *Banks, regulators lack skills to cope with pace of fintech innovation*. Retrieved from https://asia.nikkei.com/Spotlight/Asia300-Summit-2018/Banks-regulators-lack-skills-to-cope-with-pace-of-fintech-innovation

Jamieson, S. (2017). *Wonga data breach could affect nearly 250,000 customers' bank details.* Retrieved from https://www.fintech.finance/01-news/wonga-data-breach-could-affect-nearly-250000-customers-bank-details

Khan, F. (2018). Evolution of fintech—A timeline. *Datadriveninvestor.* Retrieved from https://www.datadriveninvestor.com/2018/06/15/evolution-of-fintech%E2%80%8A-%E2%80%8Aa-timeline/

Kharpal, A. (2017). Singapore aims to finish its own cryptocurrency trial next year. *CNBC.* Retrieved from https://www.cnbc.com/2017/10/26/singapore-cryptocurrency-blockchain-trial.html

Kharpal, A. (2018). Bitcoin market share is at the level it was just after it hit its near-$20,000 record high. *CNBC.* Retrieved from https://www.cnbc.com/2018/08/07/bitcoin-market-share-near-level-when-price-hit-record-high.html

Kocherlakota, N. (1998). The technological role of fiat money. *Federal Reserve Bank of Minnianapolis Quarterly Review, 22*(3), 2–10.

Kumar, S. (2018). Financial inclusion can leapfrog with blockchain technology. *Yourstory.* Retrieved from https://yourstory.com/2018/01/financial-inclusion-leapfrog-blockchain-technology/

Lago, C. (2018). How Singapore is using blockchain outside of cryptocurrencies. *CIO-Asia.* Retrieved from https://www.cio-asia.com/article/3291758/blockchain/how-singapore-is-using-blockchain-outside-of-crypto-currencies.html

Larios-Hernández, G. J. (2017). Blockchain entrepreneurship opportunity in the practices of the unbanked. *Business Horizons, 60*(6), 865–874. doi:10.1016/j.bushor.2017.07.012

Lee, I., & Shin, Y. J. (2018). FinTech: Ecosystem, business models, investment decisions, and challenges. *Business Horizons, 61*(1), 35–46. doi:10.1016/j.bushor.2017.09.003

Lee, J. (2017). OCBC chatbot 'Emma' helps customers sign $70m in home loans. *StraitsTimes.* Retrieved from https://www.straitstimes.com/business/banking/ocbc-chatbot-emma-helps-customers-sign-70m-in-home-loans

Lisk Academy. (n.d.). *Blockchain transparency explained.* Retrieved from https://lisk.io/academy/blockchain-basics/benefits-of-blockchain/blockchain-transparency-explained

Lopez-de-Silanes, F., Phalippou, L., & Gottschalg, O. (2015). Giants at the gate: Investment returns and diseconomies of scale in private equity. *Journal of Financial and Quantitative Analysis, 50*(3), 377–411. doi:10.1017/S0022109015000113

Mansfield-Devine, S. (2017). Beyond Bitcoin: Using blockchain technology to provide assurance in the commercial world. *Computer Fraud & Security, 2017*(5), 14–18. doi:10.1016/S1361-3723(17)30042-8

Maybank. (2017). Annual Report 2017.

Middleton, C. (2018). FinTech: Intelligent automation could add $512 billion to finance sector. *Internet of Business*. Retrieved from https://internetofbusiness.com/fintech-intelligent-automation-could-add-512-billion-to-finance-sector/

Nakamoto, S. (2008). Bitcoin: a peer-to-peer electronic cash system.

Nakashima, T. (2018). Creating credit by making use of mobility with FinTech and IoT. *IATSS Research, 42*(2), 61–66. doi:10.1016/j.iatssr.2018.06.001

Nasdaq. (2018). Nasdaq blockchain strategy. Retrieved from https://business.nasdaq.com/media/Blockchain Mutual Fund Strategy SEB and Nasdaq 2018_tcm5044-61791.pdf

Nazri, M and Hoolash, R. (2017). Are Malaysian banks doing okay with the FinTech wave? *Malaysian Business*.

Noordin, KA. (2017, July 5). Disrupting Islamic finance. The Edge Malaysia.

O'Dwyer, M. (2017). Reducing security breaches in FinTech is a business priority. *IPSwitch*. Retrieved from https://blog.ipswitch.com/reducing-security-breaches-in-fintech-is-a-business-priority

Ozili, P. K. (2018). *Impact of digital finance on financial inclusion and stability. Borsa Istanbul Review*. doi:10.1016/j.bir.2017.12.003

Paulsen, D. (2012). Why fiat money is a safe asset. *Economics Letters, 116*(2), 193–198. doi:10.1016/j.econlet.2012.02.016

Philippon, T. (2016). *The fintech opportunity (No. w22476). National Bureau of Economic Research*. doi:10.3386/w22476

Preetha, N. (2015) Digital Disruption: Game Changer for the Capital Market Industry. engage@SIDC, 1(2), 4-6.

PwC. (2016). *Customers in the spotlight: How FinTech is reshaping banking*. Retrieved from https://www.pwc.com/gx/en/industries/financial-services/publications/fintech-is-reshaping-banking.html

Quickonomics. (2016). *The four different types of money.* Retrieved from https://quickonomics.com/different-types-of-money/

Rahman, A. J. (2018). Deflationary policy under digital and fiat currency competition. *Research in Economics*, *72*(2), 171–180. doi:10.1016/j.rie.2018.04.004

Rahman, A. R. (2017). We need responsible disruption. Accountants Today, (Mar/Apr), 18–20.

Rampton, J. (2017). Move fast, but be careful: The challenges of FinTech. *Due*. Retrieved from https://due.com/blog/move-fast-careful-challenges-fintech/

Raza, S. (2018). FinTech – the evolution of modern financial technology in the 21st century. *Value Walk*. Retrieved from https://www.valuewalk.com/2018/03/fintech-evolution-financial-technology/

Rooney, K. (2018). After the crisis, a new generation puts its trust in tech over traditional banks. *CNBC*. Retrieved from https://www.cnbc.com/2018/09/14/a-new-generation-puts-its-trust-in-tech-over-traditional-banks.html

Rotman, S. (2014). Bitcoin Versus Electronic Money. *Cgap*, (January), 4. Retrieved from https://openknowledge.worldbank.org/bitstream/handle/10986/18418/881640BRI0Box30WLEDGENOTES0Jan02014.pdf?sequence=1&isAllowed=y

Santander InnoVentures & Oliver Wyman. (2015). Rebooting Financial Services.

Schindele, A., & Szczesny, A. (2016). The impact of Basel II on the debt costs of German SMEs. *Journal of Business Economics*, *86*(3), 197–227. doi:10.100711573-015-0775-3

Serrels, M. (2018). Someone just bought a cryptocurrency cat for $172,000. *CNET*. Retrieved from https://www.cnet.com/news/cryptokitties-bought-a-digital-cat-for-172000/

Shim, Y., & Shin, D.-H. (2016). Analyzing China's FinTech Industry from the Perspective of Actor – Network Theory, *40*, 2015–2017.

Tay, V. (2018). OCBC Bank's Emma: How a chatbot aided in generating leads and conversions. *Marketing Interactive*. Retrieved from https://www.marketing-interactive.com/ocbc-banks-emma-how-a-chatbot-aided-in-generating-leads-and-conversions/

The New Arab. (2018). *Is Bitcoin halal? Islamic scholars wade into cryptocurrency debate.* Retrieved from https://www.alaraby.co.uk/english/news/2018/4/9/is-bitcoin-halal-islamic-scholars-wade-into-cryptocurrency-debate

Thompson, B. S. (2017). Can Financial Technology Innovate Benefit Distribution in Payments for Ecosystem Services and REDD+? *Ecological Economics*, *139*, 150–157. doi:10.1016/j.ecolecon.2017.04.008

Totka, M. (2018). 7 Secrets for using fintech to manage small business cash flow revealed. *SmallBiztrends*. Retrieved from https://smallbiztrends.com/2018/11/managing-cash-flow-with-fintech.html

Treleaven, P. (2015). Financial regulation of FinTech Financial regulation. EY Global Financial Services Institute, 3(3).

Viknesh, V., & Abdulwahab, A. S. (2017). The Impact of Digitalization of Retail Banks in Malaysia on Customer Experience. *International Journal of Accounting & Business Management*, *5*(2), 197–213.

Woetzel, J., Seong, J., Wang, K. W., Manyika, J., Chui, M., & Wong, W. (2017). Digital China: Powering the Economy to Global Competitiveness.

World Bank. (2018). *Financial inclusion on the rise, but gaps remain, global findex database shows.* Retrieved from https://www.worldbank.org/en/news/press-release/2018/04/19/financial-inclusion-on-the-rise-but-gaps-remain-global-findex-database-shows

Yang, S. (2015). Why Wall Street is pouring money into companies that want to eat its lunch. *Business Insider*. Retrieved from https://www.businessinsider.com.au/wall-street-invests-in-fintech-startups-2015-3

Zainuddin, A. (n.d.). Guide to centralized cryptocurrencies: what makes a coin centralized? *Master the Crypto*. Retrieved from https://masterthecrypto.com/centralized-cryptocurrencies-coin-centralized/

ADDITIONAL READING

Buchak, G., Matvos, G., Piskorski, T., & Seru, A. (2018). FinTech, regulatory arbitrage, and the rise of shadow banks. *Journal of Financial Economics, 130*(3), 453–483. doi:10.1016/j.jfineco.2018.03.011

Chishti, S., & Barberis, J. (2016). *The FinTech book: the financial technology handbook for investors, entrepreneurs and visionaries*. John Wiley & Sons. doi:10.1002/9781119218906

Dapp, T., & Slomka, L. (2015). FinTech reloaded–Traditional banks as digital ecosystems.

Demirguc-Kunt, A., Klapper, L., Singer, D., Ansar, S., & Hess, J. (2018). *The Global Findex Database 2017: Measuring Financial Inclusion and the FinTech Revolution. The World Bank*. doi:10.1596/978-1-4648-1259-0

Gabor, D., & Brooks, S. (2017). The digital revolution in financial inclusion: International development in the fintech era. *New Political Economy, 22*(4), 423–436. doi:10.1080/13563467.2017.1259298

Gomber, P., Koch, J. A., & Siering, M. (2017). Digital Finance and FinTech: Current research and future research directions. *Journal of Business Economics, 87*(5), 537–580. doi:10.100711573-017-0852-x

Leong, C., Tan, B., Xiao, X., Tan, F. T. C., & Sun, Y. (2017). Nurturing a FinTech ecosystem: The case of a youth microloan startup in China. *International Journal of Information Management, 37*(2), 92–97. doi:10.1016/j.ijinfomgt.2016.11.006

Nicoletti, B. (2017). *The future of FinTech: Integrating finance and technology in financial services*. Springer. doi:10.1007/978-3-319-51415-4

KEY TERMS AND DEFINITIONS

Artificial Intelligence: The application of computer science such that a system can learn, reason and store information.

Blockchain: Blocks of data where each block is chained to the next through the use of hashes.

Cryptocurrency: A digital form of currency.

Distributed Ledger Technology: The storage of data as a digital list of transactions where each participant in the network as the exact same copy of it.

Fiat Money: A medium of exchange in which its value is derived from supply and demand as well as human belief.

Financial Technology: The combination of finance and information technology.

Chapter 2
Financial Technology Implications:
Emerging Markets Context

Arjun R.
National Institute of Technology Karnataka, India

Nishmitha N.
National Institute of Technology Karnataka, India

Suprabha K. R.
National Institute of Technology Karnataka, India

ABSTRACT

The chapter examines the particularities of the financial technology industry and explores how FinTech is defined and how the financial technology solutions can be implemented by companies and categorized. Financial technology companies are generally start-ups founded with the purpose of disrupting financial systems and corporations that rely less on software. But Fintech is not confined to start-ups only. Fintech comprises a vessel of technical aspects that describes an emerging financial services sector in the 21st century. The chapter aims to provide key insights into the evolution of the FinTech sector in emerging markets like ASEAN and India by and industry experience in this area. Both industry survey reports and peer-reviewed research is used as secondary data. The critical challenges to be addressed at the policy level, regional differences and future implications are being discussed thereby creating bridges the FinTech in ASEAN context to create a coherent framework.

DOI: 10.4018/978-1-5225-9183-2.ch002

Copyright © 2020, IGI Global. Copying or distributing in print or electronic forms without written permission of IGI Global is prohibited.

INTRODUCTION

Financial technology (or FinTech) is the new technology and innovation that aims to compete with traditional financial methods in the delivery of financial services. The use of smartphones for mobile banking and investing services are examples of technologies aiming to make financial services more accessible to the general public. FinTech is blurring lines between technology and financial services. It is a rapidly evolving segment of the financial services sector where tech-focused start-ups and other new market participants are disrupting how the financial services industry traditionally operates (Gabor and Brooks, 2017). New FinTech companies and market activity are reconstituting the competitive landscape, changing the definition of a player in the financial services sector. Financial technology (FinTech) has appeared as a relatively new industry in India. It has companies that use technology to offer financial services. These companies operate in insurance, asset management and payment etc. India has experienced the emergency of numerous FinTech start-ups, accelerators and incubators over the last few years. India is doing everything to establish itself as a global FinTech hub. With a large market of unserved customers, increasing mobile/internet banking, favorable demographics, an active start-up ecosystem and a large talent pool, ASEAN & India has strong opportunity (Hoontrakul, 2018).

One of definition of FinTech is "*the new applications, processes, products, or business models in the financial services industry, composed of one or more and provided as an end-to-end process through the Internet and used to computerize insurance, trading, and risk management*". Also, Bitcoins' and blockchain are the new internet technology with the potential to transform the financial industry and disrupt markets around the world. The online banking system that is internet banking will typically be part of the system operated by a bank and is in contrast to

The objectives of this chapter are summarized as:

Objective 1: What major factors that favor the financial technology in emerging markets?

Objective 2: How does trend for FinTech usage vary across different sectors and verticals?

Objective 3: What is scenario about conditions of FinTech sector in India?

Objective 4: Why does FinTech hold challenges as well as potential for ASEAN?

To answer these questions the study adopts mixed methods of research. Specifically, secondary data from research publications in peer-reviewed and indexed journals, industry white reports and other recent sources are being used. The unique contribution of study is it bridges the current research challenges in FinTech in ASEAN as well as Indian context to create a coherent framework to be empirical tested. Survey reports includes EY FinTech that uses EY Consumer Banking survey results (55,000 consumers surveyed worldwide which showed decreased dependence on their traditional bank and increased excitement about alternatives). Second industry report by Economist derives data from September and October 2018 survey of 25 executives to assess corporate attitudes towards FinTech in ASEAN, all of whom had an interest in operating in the region. Nearly half (44%) of survey respondents are already doing business in ASEAN, while other half (52%) are watching to enter in the next three years.

Background of ASEAN

With more than 600m people, ASEAN is regarded as a development opportunity for businesses, given the large prospective customer base. This is particularly pertinent for companies generally, and technologically enabled ones specifically, looking at a comparative advantage in terms of digital skills vis-à-vis most countries in the region. Regardless of their home of operations, FinTech companies across the world are interested in tapping into the growing ASEAN market. Average incomes are growing and societies are gradually getting online, comprising via smartphones, which enable the distribution of new products or services to a growing population across the region.

This chapter shows important changes between the seven key markets within ASEAN, across areas such as technological readiness, business culture and regulation. Successful FinTech entrepreneurs approach the several markets within ASEAN with an appreciation of their distinct characteristics, opportunities and challenges. Among the seven ASEAN countries, Singapore leads across most areas of measurement undertaken (Gnirck and Visser, 2016). Its smartphone diffusion is more than twice that of Thailand, and the average income is also much greater than its other ASEAN neighbors. It is therefore not unexpected that the city state is also home to four in ten of the region's FinTech's, more than any other country.

Nimtrakoon (2015) found that investors attracted in the firms operating in ASEAN countries, must to develop their vision and concern about the priority of using Intellectual Capital (IC) to choose their portfolio by looking at the value creation ability and IC of various firms. Additionally, firms in each country tend to place a different degree of emphasis on components of value added intellectual coefficient to generate corporate value. The results showed that a positive relationship amongst IC and market value, endorsing that firms with greater IC tend to have greater market value. Similarly, a positive association existed between IC and financial performance measures.

ASEAN embodies the aspiration of 10 uniquely different countries in Asia to bring about greater economic prosperity, and social and cultural progress for the people of ASEAN (Figure1). To achieve the 2025 ASEAN Economic Community (AEC) plan for regional economic integration, three strategic measures stand out as critical for the continued development of FinTech in the region:

1. Expand broadband access to more people and businesses to help bridge the digital divide between rural and urban areas.
2. Create a unified payment infrastructure to support mobile financial services, reducing the costs and complexities of cross-border payments and promoting financial inclusion.
3. Harmonise government policies and coordinate legal and regulatory frameworks in the areas of digital identity, privacy, trade and e-commerce.

Figure 1. ASEAN citizens who have a smartphone (% of population)

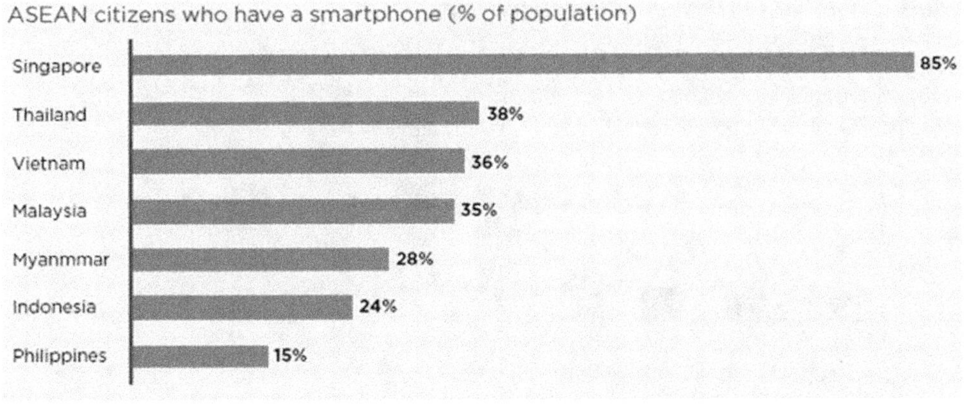

Funding is powering the rise of FinTech in ASEAN as an engine of economic growth and prosperity has caught the eye of global investors and there is an abundant supply of early-stage funding in the area. Investment in Southeast Asia FinTechs soared 33 per cent year-on-year to US$252 million in 2016, according to Tracxn. Total investment in the region is poised to exceed US$338 million. Outside the traditional forms of backing from angel investors and venture capitalists (VCs), crowdfunding, venture debt and bank venture funds have also donated to the rise of fund available for capitalizing in ASEAN FinTechs.

While FinTechs are still in their initial stage in ASEAN, digital platforms such as e-commerce have thrived, backed by internet giants who have the financial power to make large, billion dollar investments in the next unicorns of ASEAN. The battle for the consumer wallet and mindshare continue to drive investment as internet giants seek to create a foothold in ASEAN, starting in Singapore, Indonesia and Thailand. The global FinTech industry attracted more than US$24 billion in investment in 2016, ten times the level received in 2010 (Figure 2). FinTech investment in Asia exceeded North America for the first time in 2016, led by blockbuster deals in China, including Alipay and Lu.com raising US$4.5 billion and US$1.2 billion respectively(Figure 3).

Indonesia, Malaysia and Thailand are fast catching up with Singapore as a favored FinTech home, supported by high levels of mobile adoption, rising rates of internet penetration and an progressively urban, literate and young population. This has attracted large numbers of investors and FinTechs to focus their attention on the region.

ASEAN also is observing evident progress in FinTech. In 2016, investments in the Southeast Asian FinTech market increased to US$252 million, compared

Figure 2. Global FinTech investment activity

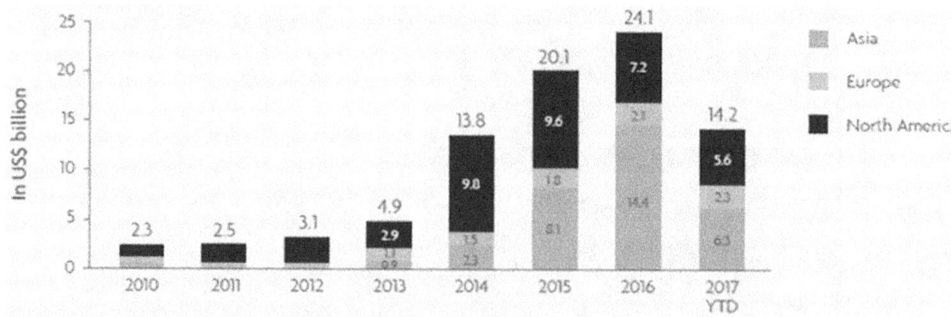

Figure 3. FinTech distribution in ASEAN

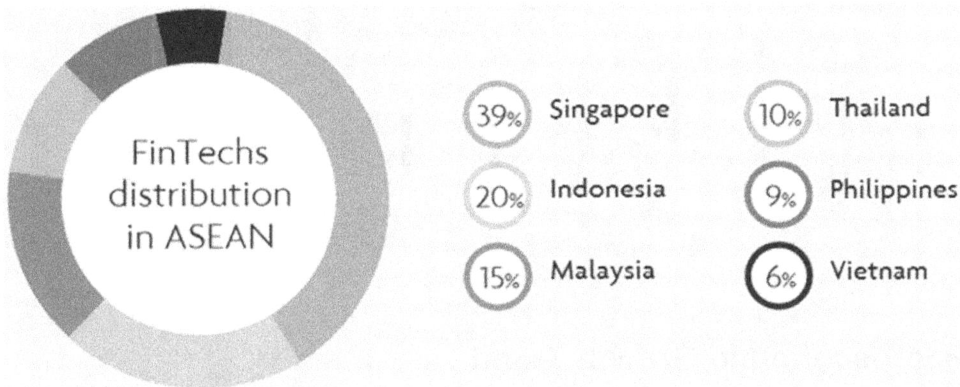

Figure 4. FinTech funding in ASEAN

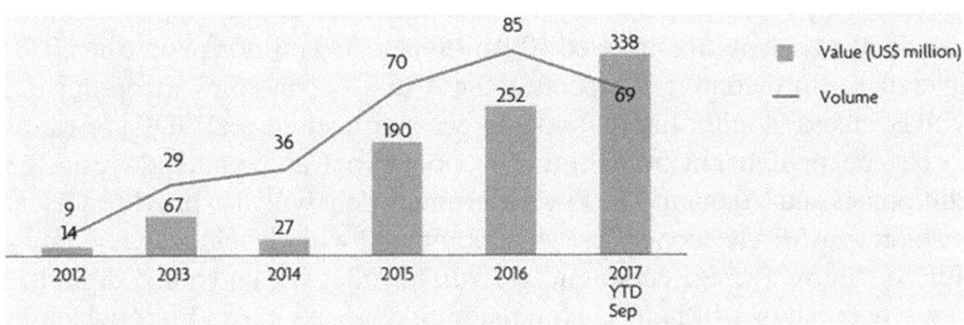

with US$190 million in 2015, a rise of about 33 per cent. Total investment up to September 2017 has already exceeded that of 2016 to reach US$338 million (Fig. 4). Most of the funding in the region is from seed and angel investors.

DRIVERS OF FINTECH

Robust Macroeconomic Growth

Robust GDP growth, favorable demographics, digital readiness and regulatory initiatives offer a plethora of prospects for FinTechs across the ASEAN region. Better cross-border interoperability and policy regulation will also help ASEAN to exploit the full benefits of digital technology (Figure 5).

Figure 5. Real GDP average growth (%)

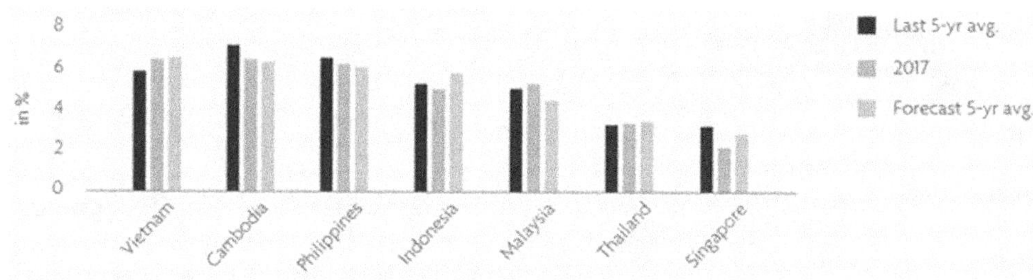

Macroeconomic Growth Trend

Around 50 per cent of ASEAN's population is below 30 years of age. By 2030, this huge young population will enjoy bigger levels of literacy and contain many first-time career seekers. Southeast Asia's urban population is also likely to rise by an estimated 100 million, to 373 million people by 2030. Overall, the forthcoming prospects of the ASEAN economies are optimistic, with Business Monitor International forecasting average real GDP growth of six per cent or higher in the emerging economies of Cambodia, Indonesia, the Philippines and Vietnam. The low government debt will also provide a fiscal cushion to ASEAN economies when compared with developed economies (Fig.5). Above average economic growth, together with a young, digitally-savvy population will help to stimulate middle-class expenditure which in turn will drive demand for financial services.

Low Banking Penetration

The ASEAN Economic Community's Vision for 2025 is focused on closing the digital gap, improving financial access and literacy, escalating the scope of intermediary facilities (such as digital payments) and developing financial services for smaller firms and lower income groups. It supports information and communication innovation and technological developments such as big data and data analytics.

As at 2014, more than half of the adult population of ASEAN does not have access to banking services, which means more than 264 million adults in Southeast Asia are unbanked. The gap widens in rural areas, where 74 per cent of the population does not have access to a bank account (Figure 6). Key barriers to financial inclusion include the lack of personal documents and

Figure 6. Adults with an account (2014) (%)

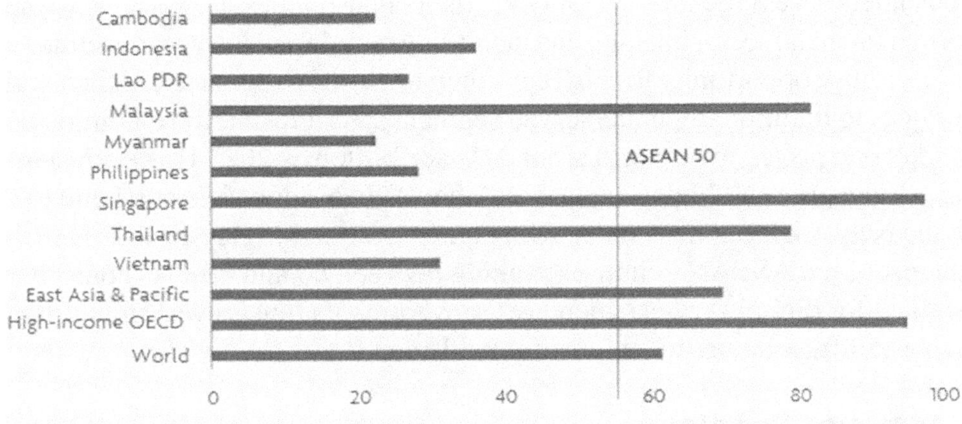

credit history, poor financial infrastructure, logistical and delivery challenges, restrictive regulations and financial products offered by banks in major cities that are more suited for an urban population. The large unbanked/underbanked population of ASEAN makes it an attractive region for FinTech companies to develop solutions and to go to market.

Digital Adoption

With the exception of Singapore, ASEAN countries are in the early stages of their digital journey. The fraction of internet users varies, with Singapore, Malaysia and Philippines having penetration levels of above 50 per cent, but in Indonesia the number is only 25.4 per cent (Kartawijaya, R., & Hamsal, 2018). Nevertheless, the region ranks third globally in terms of the number of mobile users, behind only China and India.

ASEAN ranks fourth globally in terms of the number of internet users, behind China, India and the US. Estimates show that combined, Indonesia, Malaysia, Philippines, Singapore, Thailand and Vietnam represent the world's fastest growing internet market (~14 per cent five-year compound annual growth rate (CAGR)) with an current internet user base of 315 million prediction to grow to around 480 million by 2020.

Mobile access in these countries is high, even in comparison with the developed markets of the United Kingdom and the United States. Digital research firm GfK estimates that in 2016, around 90 per cent of online consumers access the internet daily via their smartphones. Low access to the formal financial sector but high and increasing mobile and internet penetration offers a huge opportunity for FinTech companies in the region to bid financial services to traditionally underserved segments. As a result, the e-commerce market is expected to be worth around US$88 billion by 2025.However, apart from Singapore and Malaysia, many of the ASEAN countries rank quite low in the Network Readiness Index (Singapore at #1 and Malaysia at #31, with the rest of the ASEAN countries ranking between 60 and 80). As consumer demand for digital services increases, governments must invest in building a robust infrastructure to support future demand

Consumer Readiness

Consumers worldwide are becoming more receptive to substitute lending channels. In the past, the main drivers of competition in the financial services industry were price, product and scale of the branch network. Today, consumer experience is the main driver of channel choice. The emphasis now is on simplicity, speed, convenience, round-the-clock connectivity and responsiveness to consumer needs.

FinTechs appear to have an upper hand in conceptualizing extremely simple and intuitive customer experiences. According to EY's Consumer Banking Survey 2016, 42 per cent of consumers globally have used an online/mobile-only non-bank financial service in the past year, signaling their willingness to try out FinTech solutions. Furthermore, 21 per cent of

Figure 7. Trust in primary financial service providers

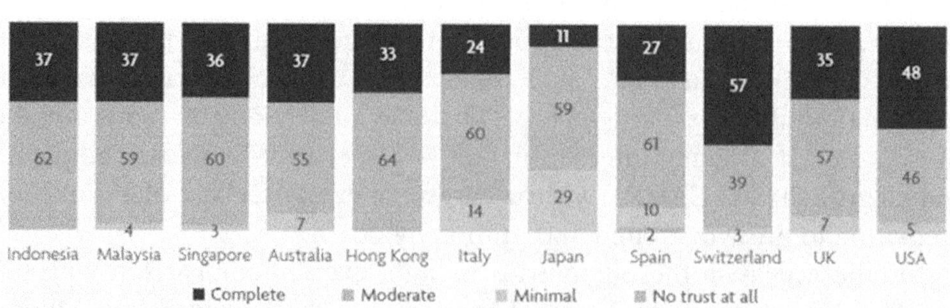

consumers indicated that they would consider trying out a FinTech solution in the future. In ASEAN, more consumers have used non-bank financial services in the past 12 months; 64 per cent in Indonesia, 49 per cent in Malaysia and 45 per cent in Singapore. The remainder have not used them yet, are averse to using them, do not plan to use them in the future or do not know/are unsure of how to use them.

One reason for this could be the absence of trust in online-only FinTechs, which have only been around for a few years and the consumers' desire to put their savings in safe and regulated financial institutions. For example, 54 per cent of Malaysian banking consumers said that they would not trust a financial service provider without physical branches.

Unlike the relationship consumers have with their bank, the relationship between FinTechs and consumers has not been time-tested. Ninety-four per cent of global consumers have not moved their primary relationship to new companies offering simpler services than traditional banks (Figure 7). Consumers in ASEAN still believe that banks are relevant, despite their willingness to try out FinTech services – 75 per cent in Malaysia, 70 per cent in Singapore and 68 per cent in Indonesia still believe that banks have an important role to play in helping them achieve their life's goals because of their expertise across all types of financial products (Riyanto *et al.*, 2018).

Regulators Adopting to Changes

Most ASEAN countries have already identified FinTech as a major growth area and have taken steps to cultivate a supportive environment for FinTechs. Singapore is the market leader in ASEAN with the Monetary Authority of Singapore (MAS) taking a number of steps to endorse FinTech. Backed by a supportive regulatory regime and progressive policy initiatives, Singapore stands competitively among global FinTech hubs (Figure 8).

The launch of the AEC in 2015 has the potential to unlock opportunities in ASEAN. Currently, the region has differing levels of digital penetration, internet speeds, infrastructure and standards. In an effort to push innovation across the ASEAN block, the International Finance Corporation together with MAS and the ASEAN Bankers Association have established the ASEAN Financial Innovation Network (AFIN) to enable real-time collaboration and

Figure 8. Benchmarked ranking of FinTech ecosystems globally

2015 rank by ecosystem attribute					
Region	Talent • Talent availability • Talent pipeline	Capital • Seed • Growth • Listed	Policy • Regulatory regimes • Government programmes • Taxation policy	Demand • Consumers • Corporates • Financial Institutions	Total points
United Kingdom	2	3	1	3	9
California	1	1	6	2	10
New York	3	2	7	1	13
Singapore	4	7	2	6	19
Germany	6	4	5	5	20
Australia	5	5	3	7	20
Hong Kong	7	6	4	4	21

Relative rank: 1 = highest, 7 = lowest

cross-border policy harmonization for better interoperability. The industry sandbox approach under AFIN will help FinTechs, banks and regulators to test new innovations and to work towards financial inclusion. It gives banks in the region access to FinTech firms with whom they can collaborate to offer banking connectivity in a cost-efficient manner. The objective of the network is three-fold:

1. Address issues of connectivity, local compliance and cross-border compatibility
2. Create an industry sandbox to provide a cloud-based testing environment through which banks and FinTech players can develop, test and refine digital finance and inclusion solutions. The cloud-based approach will help in distribution of FinTech solutions to financial institutions located in multiple jurisdictions; and
3. Facilitate discussions among participating regulators on cross-border policy harmonization

Figure 9. Opportunities specific to ASEAN

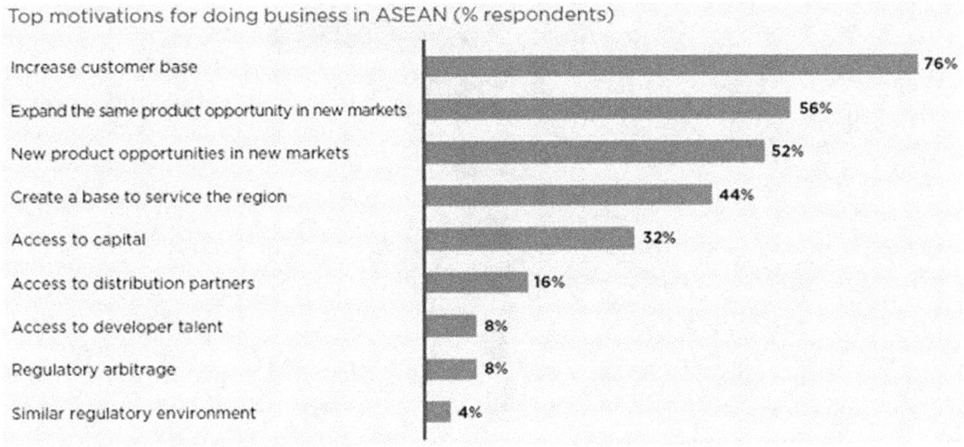

Opportunities in ASEAN

About three-quarters (76%) of FinTech executives say their top motivation for doing business in ASEAN is increasing their customer base. This is followed by expanding the same product opportunity in new markets (56%) and new product opportunities in new markets (52%) (Figure 9).

TRENDS OF FINTECH

Payments

Online payments and mobile wallets (digital payments) dominate the ASEAN FinTech industry. The main driver of the payments innovation boom has been an expansion of internet access, combined with rising smartphone ownership – enabling real-time access and a sharp increase in the number of young, tech-savvy consumers. According to a Visa survey, 36 per cent of the population in Southeast Asia are active internet users and 70 per cent shop online at least once a month. (Figure 10).

Figure 10. Density of ASEAN FinTech industry by category

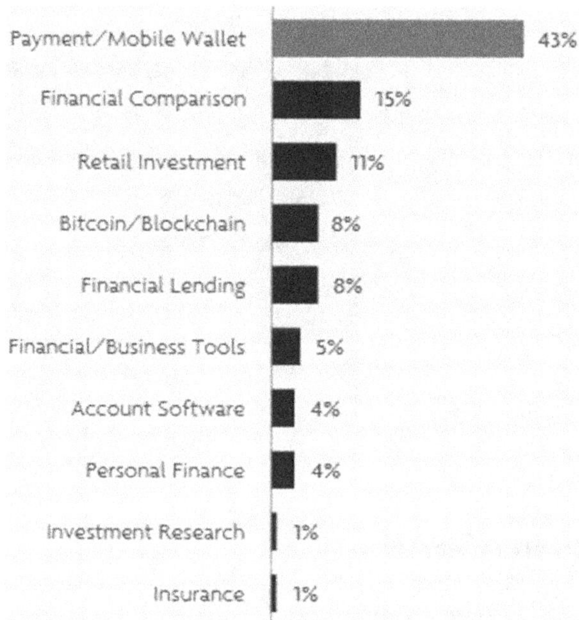

Figure 11. Digital wallets penetration survey results (2015)

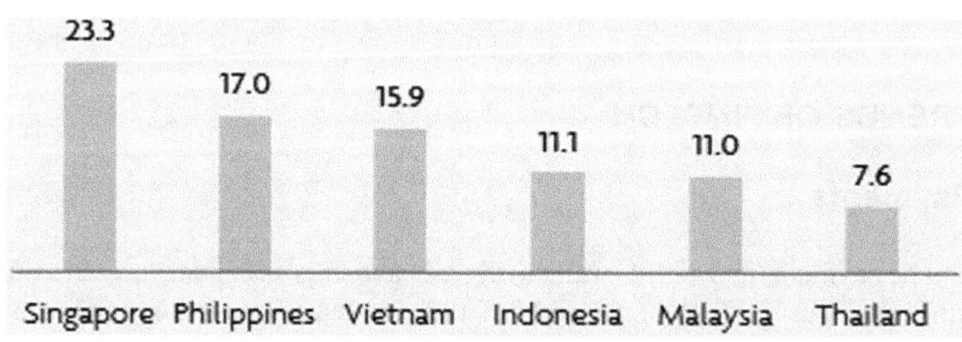

Digital Wallets

Singapore is the most mature cashless payments market with the highest digital wallet penetration at 23.3 per cent, followed by Philippines, Vietnam, Indonesia, Malaysia and Thailand. The increase in smartphone penetration in these countries is expected to provide a strong push to digital wallet adoption in the future(Figure 11). There is also strong potential for penetration of

Figure 12. Digital payments transaction value and growth rate

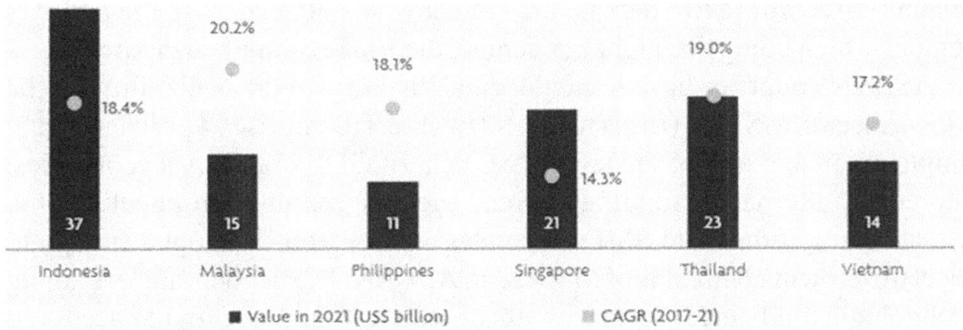

digital payments into areas such as wage payments (71 per cent received in cash), government transfers (69 per cent received in cash) and utility bills (89 per cent paid in cash). In the next five years, digital payments are expected to record double-digit five-year CAGRs across countries, with Malaysia expected to grow by 20.2 per cent CAGR from 2017 to 2021(Huei *et al.* 2018). Indonesia is also not far behind with 18.4 per cent growth and is expected to have the highest digital payments transaction value of US$37 billion in 2021 (Figure 12).

Peer-to-Peer (P2P) Lending

The P2P lending segment has matured quickly in Europe, America, and across China since 2005. Allied Market Research predicts that the P2P market will grow at a CAGR of 51.5 per cent (2016-2022) to reach US$460.3 billion by 2022.The next growth frontiers are ASEAN, where P2P lending is still at a

Figure 13. No. of P2P lending platforms in ASEAN by country (YTD 2017)

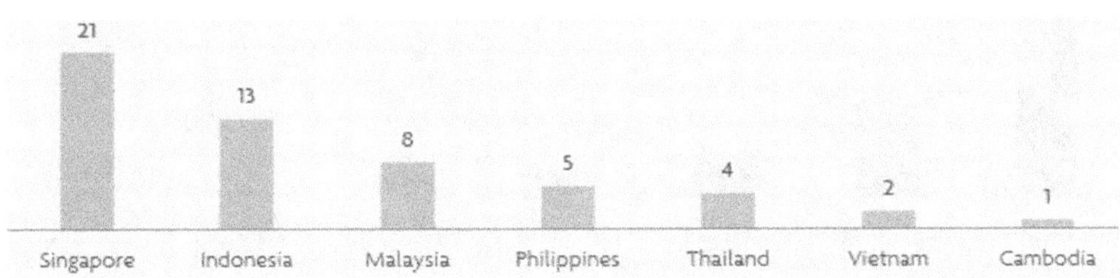

nascent stage (less than 0.1 per cent of all loans are originated through P2P lenders). According to Tracxn data, there are 54 P2P lenders in the ASEAN region, which comprise eight per cent of the FinTech market(Figure 13).

ASEAN countries have limited formal banking credit availability for the MSME sector. MSMEs (firms with<100 workers) comprise 74 per cent of total employment and approximately 41 per cent of GDP in ASEAN economies. Moreover, alternative funding sources such as venture and angel capital, private equity funds and SME exchanges are not well-developed enough to meet the growing demands of MSMEs in ASEAN. P2P lenders are leveraging technological advances to narrow this credit gap and to provide access to capital for this underserved segment.

Case Study: Cryptocurrency start-ups gain popularity in Philippines remittance industry24In recent years, several crypto currency start-ups have emerged in the Philippines, providing low-cost remittance services for overseas workers. Blockchain-based remittance service providers such as Coin.ph and Toast are helping expand financial access. Coins.ph has attracted more than a million users and established a network of more than 22,000 disbursement and collection locations throughout the Philippines. In the case of Toast, the target audience is overseas workers in Singapore and Hong Kong. Moreover, mainstream Bitcoin adoption is also surging as Filipinos are turning to it for remittance payments mainly due to the inefficiency of the local banking system. According to a 2016 report, 20 per cent of remittances from the Philippines to South Korea are processed in Bitcoin. Notably, in early 2017, Bankgko Sentral ng Pilipinas (BSP), the central bank, legalized Bitcoin as a payment method and is also regulating the local Bitcoin exchanges.

Figure 14. Number of savings & investment FinTechs by ASEAN country (YTD 2017)

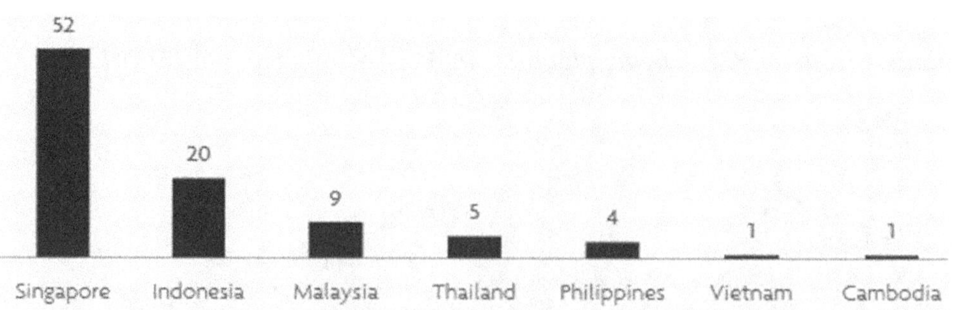

Savings and Investments

The consumer savings and investment management industry is witnessing a phase of significant demographic shift as assets are transferred to the millennial generation. FinTech start-ups offering digital investment services are gaining popularity with millennials, who are tech-savvy, believe in a do-it-yourself approach and generally prefer to avoid face-to-face business interactions(Figure 14).

Rise of Robo-advisors in ASEAN: The emergence of the millenial generation, combined with the rise of middle-income consumer groups (traditionally unserved by wealth managers), has led to robo-advisors gaining

Figure 15. Robo-advisors AUM by country (US$ million)

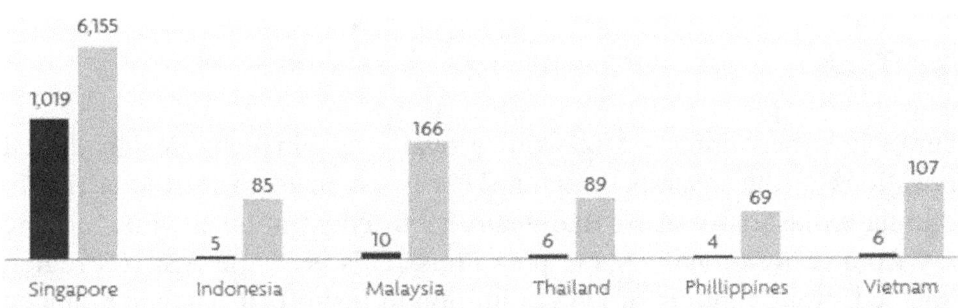

Figure 16. Snapshot of various opportunities

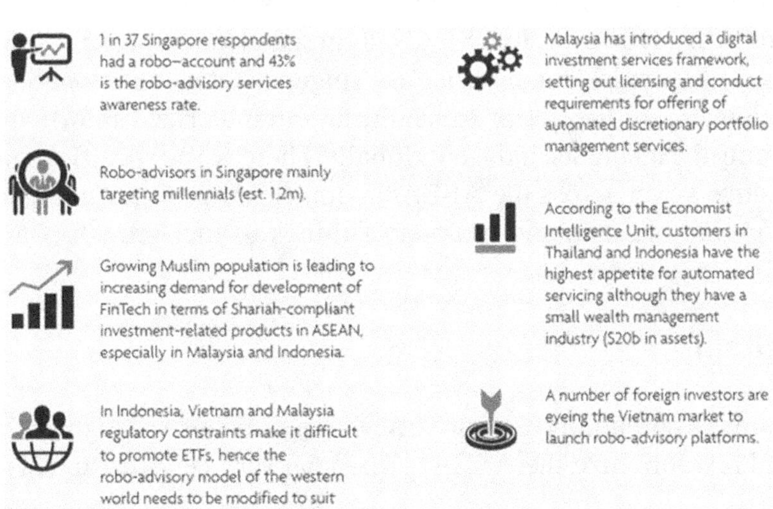

traction. The rise of robo-advisors seeks to complement, not replace existing financial advisors who serve the wealthy in ASEAN. EY's 2016 Consumer Banking Survey found that though 65 per cent of global consumers think having a digital presence is highly important, an equal percentage also think physical presence is highly important. Nearly 60 per cent indicate that they want to visit a branch or speak to a real person to purchase a new product or get advice, and say it is important that they can speak to a person at their bank 24/7 (55 per cent of consumers) (Figure 15)(Figure 16).

Emerging Technology Areas

While payments, P2P lending and savings and investment remain the primary areas wherein FinTechs in ASEAN have focused their initiatives, some of the other emerging technology areas also hold strong promise

InsurTech

InsurTech is becoming a buzzword globally as FinTechs design digital innovations in the insurance sector. This is expected to lead to a rise in usage-based insurance and dynamically-adjusted premiums, while moving away from conventionally static premiums. This year, the ASEAN region witnessed strong funding of US$75 million in InsurTech. The most funded company in this category is Singapore Life (US$50 million).

And online aggregators, which enable better-informed insurance choices, are the most popular FinTech model across Western countries, as well as in India and China. However, in ASEAN, aggregators are not as prevalent, and even where they exist, for instance in Singapore, the functionality is still basic. Telematics – the act of transmitting computerized information – is transforming the insurance industry globally.There are no specific regulations on telematics as yet across the ASEAN countries. InsurTech companies are also leveraging big data and internet of things to fuel growth (Raikwar *et al.*, 2018).

Blockchain

Blockchain is a potentially disruptive new-age distributive ledger technology that could revolutionize the ASEAN financial services industry, with wide applications in payments and trade transactions. Currently in the ASEAN region, beyond the payments and remittances market, blockchain exists largely in the pilot stage. Blockchain awareness is on the rise and ASEAN governments are keen on utilizing the benefits of blockchain to facilitate financial and economic development, as well as good governance. In March 2017, the MAS concluded its proof-of-concept project to test the use of blockchain in domestic interbank payments, working with the R3 consortium of financial institutions. The Malaysian Industry-Government Group for High Technology, an industry-government think tank, is collaborating with Bloke, a domestic cryptocurrency and blockchain advocacy body to develop the country's blockchain industry and encourage foreign players to enter the market.

Artificial Intelligence

Experts in the financial services domain believe that Artificial intelligence (AI) has the potential to become the primary channel through which financial service providers and customers will interact with in the next three years. In the ASEAN region, AI is still in its infancy. The banking sector has been a first mover in adapting AI but has faced difficulty in scaling up, mainly due to the lack of a skilled workforce and sufficient data. Among ASEAN countries, Singapore is planning to set up the world's largest AI hub by 2018 with the aim to establish itself as a global leader in AI technologies. It plans to incubate 100 start-ups and build intellectual property in the area of AI. The Bangko Sentral ng Pilipinas, the central bank of Philippines, is looking to utilize artificial intelligence in regulatory and consumer protection functions.

AN OUTLOOK FROM INDIAN PERSPECTIVE

Market Size and Growth in India

According to the report of The National Association of Software and Services Companies (NASSCOM), India has an existence of around 400 companies in the FinTech space, with an investment of about $420 million in 2015. The NASSCOM report also estimated the FinTech software and services market to grow 1.7 times by 2020, making it worth $8 billion.

The India FinTech Awards (IFTA) is a platform to celebrate and recognize the best innovations from FinTech companies. The Indian FinTech background is as follows – 34% in payment processing, followed by 32% in banking and 12% in the trading, public and private markets. Accelerators and incubators i.e., it is a company that helps new and startup companies to develop by providing services such as management training or office space, tapping the start-up ecosystem is being developed as FinTech hub and the local government of Andhra Pradesh, had opened FinTech Valley Tower to promote the investments in this area. India FinTech Forum represents the Indian FinTech firms as part of the Global FinTech Hubs Federation (GFHF).

In 2017, Adopting FinTech is another challenge which usually slows down the innovation, and in order to change their behavior more effort on marketing and consumer education is required. Government efforts towards promoting digitization of financial systems and reducing cash transactions in the economy have been very effective in shifting consumer focus towards digital changes for financial transactions, where the payment sector have benefited more.

Further, the FinTech sector is finding its way into the budget speech for 2017. India has the highest expected return on investment on FinTech projects at 29% versus a global average of 20%. Support from the government has increased the users' adoption plans such as Jan Dhan Yojana, Aadhaar and the emergence of UPI provided good base for FinTech companies and has also increased financial position in the country. The 'Payments' segment is the most funded in Indian FinTech landscape, because of demonetization. However, banking technology solutions are also facing strong growth and allowing financial institutions to create continuous solution delivery for end users. In spite of significant reductions in incoming global investments in the FinTech space, the India opportunity remains promising and favorable. India offers the largest unbanked population, along with a strong technology and business ecosystem.

The Indian Governmental Initiatives

The Government of India has recently pushed for financial inclusion, digitization and start-up activity has led to the introduction of policies recently which provide a strong foundation to the FinTech sector in India (Gupta and Xia, 2018).

1. **India Stack**: Through the introduction of India Stack, the government has provided a world-wide technological framework to entrepreneurs, innovators and corporations, allowing for the fastest growth of FinTech ventures. This situation somewhat resembles the policy that was offered by the government to the telecom industry in the 90's, with FinTech taking centre stage in many reform initiatives.
2. **Start-up India Program**: It was launched by the central government, includes the simplification of regulatory processes, tax exemptions, patent reforms, mentorship opportunities and increased government funding.
3. **Jan Dhan Yojana (PMJDY)**: Due to this policy the Financial inclusion in the country has grown significantly, it is one of the world's biggest financial inclusion program, with an aim to facilitate the creation of bank accounts for large unserved sections of India's billion plus population.
4. **Aadhaar Adoption**: The RBI approved Aadhaar based biometric authentication, which will allow for bank accounts to be opened through e-KYC at any Banking Correspondent (BC) location. This will allow financial services companies to do e-KYC checks more economically, thereby reducing transaction costs for customers.
5. **National Payments Council of India Initiatives:** The National Payments Council of India (NPCI), has introduced the Unified Payments Interface (UPI), which has influenced the growth of mobile phones as acquiring devices, significantly reducing the cost of infrastructure for FinTech ventures and also the digital banking is expected to grow faster than ever before. These initiatives are very helpful for a digitally enabled financial sector in India, also encourages technologies and banking experience in India.
6. **Public Relations**: The Indian government has also played a strong role in encouraging and educating consumers in the economy towards digitized monetary systems. The industry is still suffering from regulatory uncertainties and doubts, particularly with respect to new business models enabled by FinTech applications such as P2P transactions, crowdfunding and data security.

FinTech Ecosystem

FinTech is a dynamic segment of the financial services sector that is gaining much importance and disrupting the traditional financial services value chain.

New Fin Tech companies and market activity are reconstituting the competitive landscape, blurring the identity of a player in the financial services sector. Below are a few sectors in FinTech that track actively and are the key areas to look at for the next wave of innovations.

1. **Integrated Digital Banking**: Financial Services companies face intense pressure to increase efficiencies and reduce costs while delivering next-generation digital services. Companies with financial technology start-ups and other non-traditional market entrants can give them the agility they need to support digital transformation and create a digital ecosystem that will retain existing customers and attract new ones (Thompson, 2017). New start-ups are emerging to meet both customer and bank needs can implement this technology.
2. **Alternate Lending***:* Alternative finance refers to financial channels and instruments that have emerged outside of the traditional finance system such as regulated banks and capital markets. Examples like online marketplaces are crowd funding, peer-to-peer consumer and business lending, invoice trading third party payment platforms, etc. (Wonglimpiyarat, 2018).
3. **Robo- Advisory***:* It is the use of algorithms to support the entire investing process from setting financial goals to portfolio re-balancing and monitoring whilst bringing more transparent, traceable, and efficient and customer centric standards along the overall value chain. Robo advisors destroy traditional techniques with Direct-to-Consumer (D2C) platforms. These platforms provide an easier, faster, and more user-friendly investment based solutions to both end investors and asset and wealth managers (Kamruzzaman, J., & Sarker, 2006).
4. **Cyber and Financial Crime***:* Is an increasing concern for all financial institutions, from the largest global organizations to the smallest companies and partnerships. Preventing and detecting Financial Crime.
5. **Digital Payments**: FinTech is altering the way consumer and helpful in making wholesale payments. FinTech start-ups are taking payments to the next level in terms of speed, convenience, efficiency and multichannel accessibility.
6. **Augmented (AR) and Virtual Reality (VR)**: AR involves a real-time view of the physical world around us, which is then improved by digital information. VR, on the other hand, involves creating a simulated world, instead of reflecting the real world around us.

Bitcoins

Bitcoin is an experimental, decentralized digital currency that enables instant payments to anyone, anywhere in the world. It uses peer-to-peer technology to operate with no central authority managing transactions and issuing money are carried out collectively by the network. Bitcoin is designed around the idea of using cryptography to control the creation and transfer of money, rather than relying on central authorities.

Blockchain

The blockchain is a new technology that combines a number of mathematical, cryptographic and economic principles to maintain a database involving multiple participants without the need for any third-party validator or reconciliation. It is a single, shared, immutable write only ledger of transactions that is updated when multiple, decentralized actors achieve a consensus on the validity of a participant's new entries. The blockchain has the potential to disrupt the banking industry to its core through its adoption for storing, lending, moving, trading, accounting, reconciling and guaranteeing money through its consensus ledger, cryptographic security and digital signature.

Online Banking

Online banking, also known as internet banking, e-banking or virtual banking, is an electronic payment system that enables customers of a bank or other financial institution to conduct a range of financial transactions through the financial institution's website. The online banking system will typically connect to or be part of the core banking system operated by a bank and is in contrast to branch banking which was the traditional way customers accessed banking services. Online banking has many features and facilitates in common:

1. A bank customer can perform non-transactional tasks through online banking such as, Viewing account balances, Downloading bank statements and applications for M-banking, E-banking, Viewing images of paid cheques.
2. Bank customers can transact banking tasks through online banking, including – Funds transfers, bill payments, Investment purchase or sale, Loan applications and transactions, Credit card applications and so on.

3. Some financial institutions offer special internet banking services, for example: Personal financial management support, such as importing data into personal accounting software. Some online banking platforms support account aggregation to allow the customers to monitor all of their accounts in one place whether they are with their main bank or with other institutions.

SECTOR CHALLENGES AND ISSUES IN FUTURE

Issues, Controversies, Problems

The digital delivery of financial services has been a focal point for investors over the past several years. While the macro-economic and political dynamics are changing, the FinTech industry remains ripe for continued innovations (Hoontrakul, 2018).

1. **Investment shake-Ups:** Everyone is used with FinTech now and even many investors are interested too. Many new investors, even within established venture capital firms, lack an understanding of how the industry works. Their actions are creating noise and interference in the marketplace. However, capital across the board has apparently slowdown. Hope many successful companies will continue to find funding despite the broader slowdown.
2. **Regulation:** Governments at all levels have taken an increasing interest in the financial services industry, post the global financial crisis. Old and new policies will have a significant effect on the success and failure of new companies. Following the U.S. presidential election, there is a widespread belief that FinTech entrepreneurs' burdens will be reduced in launching their business.
3. **Technology:** The financial services industry is largely automated on old technologies. New technologies present the opportunity to have superior products and services, but it can be challenging to get industry participants.

ASEAN Context

Government policy (licensing requirements and regulations) are said to be the biggest barrier to introducing new products or services in ASEAN, according to four in ten survey takers (40%). "Many people assume it can be done relatively easily but the culture is different and you have to make sure you have local staff," says Julian Fenwick, managing director at Governance Risk & Compliance Solutions, a "regtech" company that helps FinTechs and traditional financial services institutions comply with local regulations. Established in 2012 the company uses technology solutions to meet local compliance rules and has 250 clients across the world.

ASEAN markets differ significantly in terms of consumer preferences, technology infrastructure, regulations and policies. There are three areas that could be developed further to encourage greater levels of FinTech innovation and digital adoption.

1. Expanding broadband access: In ASEAN, internet connectivity is increasing but large gaps still exist. Internet connectivity remains relatively poor in rural areas, especially in Indonesia, Thailand, the Philippines and Vietnam. Universal broadband access and widespread digital literacy will help to level the playing field between urban and rural populations and promote e-commerce and digital wallets.
2. Creating a unified payment infrastructure: Creating a unified payments network will help ASEAN to reduce the costs and complexities of cross-border payments within the region. This includes implementing Real Time Gross Settlement (RTGS) systems, ACH systems domestically and common infrastructure standards.
3. Policy harmonization: Consumer protection laws vary significantly across ASEAN. At present, only Singapore, Malaysia and the Philippines have dedicated data protection laws. Indonesia, Myanmar and Vietnam have data privacy requirements as part of their respective electronic transaction laws. To create a common, unified and safe environment for customers, legal and regulatory frameworks around privacy, customs, digital trade, dispute resolution, cross-border data flow, e-commerce, and intellectual property can be harmonized.

Steps taken to create digital identities for delivery of financial and social services will lead to interoperability across ASEAN countries, boosting

Figure 17. Challenges in FinTech

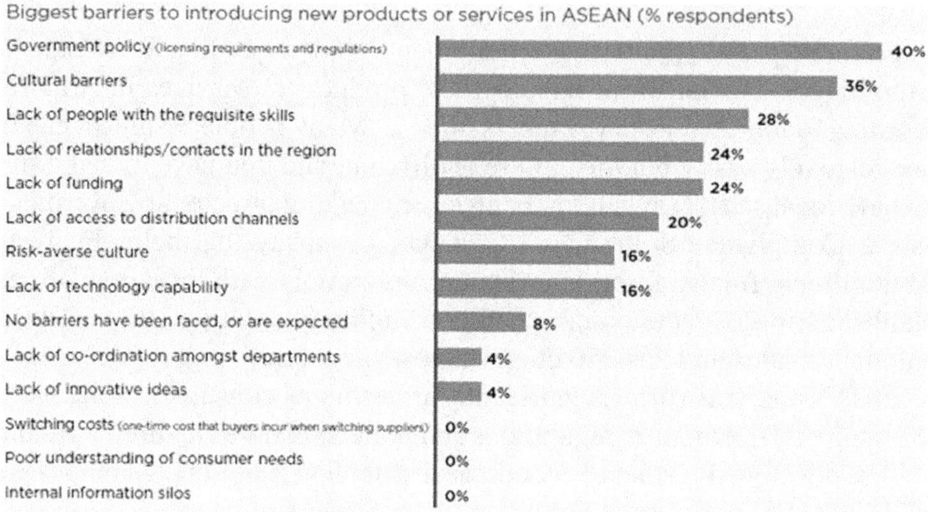

FinTech adoption in the region. Though it is important to achieve harmonization of regulations and practices across ASEAN, it might be challenging to achieve this in the short term. In the meantime, it is important that a regulatory framework be developed to help a FinTech operating in one country understand and navigate the markets in other ASEAN countries efficiently(Figure 17).

SOLUTIONS AND RECOMMENDATIONS

To build a sustainable financial services ecosystem, which includes a vibrant FinTech sector, it is imperative that ASEAN countries take steps to create an environment where technical, entrepreneurial and financial services talent can flourish. Currently, the FinTech workforce is relatively small in ASEAN, though the numbers are increasing. To nurture talent, countries can encourage STEM (science, technology, engineering and mathematics) education in schools and undertake a review of infocomm curriculum to replace/revise old curriculum with relevant material and skill development. Academic pathways and education initiatives are the first steps to build a healthy pipeline of talent. Universities can play a key role in providing graduate pathways to FinTechs, promoting the sector and, in the longer term, adapting curriculums (e.g. towards entrepreneurship) and spearheading research (e.g. into artificial intelligence). Having an intra-ASEAN support system that accommodates foreign talent through simple and flexible immigration policies and programmes would also be helpful in alleviating the FinTech talent supply crunch.

In order to grasp the opportunities and overcome the barriers in ASEAN, FinTech companies can consider a number of recommendations:

1. Tap into the potential: Every ASEAN market is growing in terms of size, online access and smartphone penetration—identify which country is the best match for the business.
2. Develop an understanding of local regulations: Each ASEAN market is unique and requires in-depth knowledge of how to do business. Regtech firms are of value.
3. Consider local partnerships: Local actors understand the local environment and can ease the transition of doing business in another country.
4. Collaborate with big banks and others: Traditional financial institutions are looking for innovative ideas whereas FinTech companies can gain customer access and knowledge. There are also opportunities to collaborate with organizations in other sectors.
5. Stay the course: Many markets require time, patience and investment in order to succeed, and local business culture can reward those who stay the course without leaving too soon.

LIMITATIONS AND FUTURE RESEARCH DIRECTIONS

As opined by Gomber *et al.* (2017), the future of FinTech solutions will be driven both by innovations on the technology level and by the reaction of politicians and regulators to the new developments. Customers will appreciate technological solutions that ease usage and reduce transaction costs. Limitations of current study is that findings of earlier studies need to be validated through primary data using survey instrument. The generalizability or theory building entirely relies on inferences from probability sampling based data-sets captured from stakeholders covering ASEAN and/or Indian markets and is costly and time consuming process. Future research can utilize by addressing local concerns to proliferate FinTech (Gupta and Xia, 2018)

CONCLUSION

A booming global industry, FinTech brings new innovations to traditional financial services and in the process can help reach new population segments and enable the provision of new products and services to existing customers. Regulations, however, have largely lagged behind in this fast-developing movement, and cultural barriers are limiting expansion opportunities. Shim and Shin (2016) found that there are telecom policy implications that affect FinTech in China. This needs to be empirically validated. In ASEAN, the opportunities and challenges may be greater than any other region, given the diverse socio-economic and demographic composition of its members, ranging from the small, advanced city state of Singapore to the Indonesian consumer market of more than 260m people, the world's fourth-largest population. Although the financial industry has traditionally been an early adopter and intensive user of new developments in information and communication technology, the emergence of innovative business models and the new competitors have a tremendous influence on industry dynamics (Chuen *et al.* 2015).

In a rapidly changing economic environment and in the light of challenging and cost-intensive regulatory requirements, incumbent providers of banking business and financial services are facing a substantial transformation: Digital Finance. A more technology-savvy clientele across generations, new technologies, and the digitalization of the industry challenges business models of traditional service providers. Both novel forms of disintermediation and new competitors can be observed in all relevant business functions in financial services. Against this background, most players in the industry try to design customized, intelligent, and flexible, however cost-efficient, financial products and services and strive to achieve new levels of customer centricity.

Global peer-to-peer money transfer systems, improved smartphone usage in financial transactions and the ability to use wearables also for financial transactions are interesting research topics and provide the basis for future FinTech business models. Beyond this, given the high dynamics in this field and the need for fast, nevertheless efficient regulatory answers, any academic insights on the impact of regulatory measures.

ACKNOWLEDGMENT

Due acknowledgement for extended to all faculty, scholars of the School of Management, NIT Karnataka, India. Additional thanks to the editorial team.

REFERENCES

Andreasson, K. (2018). FinTech in ASEAN: Unlock the opportunity. *The Economist.*

Chuen, K., Lee, D., & Teo, E. G. (2015). Emergence of FinTech and the LASIC principles. *Journal of Financial Perspectives*, *3*(3).

Gabor, D., & Brooks, S. (2017). The digital revolution in financial inclusion: International development in the fintech era. *New Political Economy*, *22*(4), 423–436. doi:10.1080/13563467.2017.1259298

Gnirck, M., & Visser, G. (2016). Singapore, the FinTech Hub for Southeast Asia. *The FinTech Book: The financial technology handbook for investors, entrepreneurs and visionaries*, 58-60.

Gomber, P., Koch, J. A., & Siering, M. (2017). Digital Finance and FinTech: Current research and future research directions. *Journal of Business Economics*, *87*(5), 537–580. doi:10.100711573-017-0852-x

Gupta, A., & Xia, C. (2018). A Paradigm Shift in Banking: Unfolding Asia's FinTech Adventures. In Banking and Finance Issues in Emerging Markets (pp. 215-254). Emerald Publishing Limited.

Hoontrakul, P. (2018). Asia's Digital Economy. In *Economic Transformation and Business Opportunities in Asia* (pp. 269–312). Cham: Palgrave Macmillan. doi:10.1007/978-3-319-58928-2_8

Huei, C. T., Cheng, L. S., Seong, L. C., Khin, A. A., & Bin, R. L. L. (2018). Preliminary Study on consumer attitude towards FinTech products and services in Malaysia. *International Journal of Engineering & Technology*, *7*(2.29), 166-169.

Kamruzzaman, J., & Sarker, R. A. (2006). Artificial neural networks: Applications in finance and manufacturing. In *Artificial Neural Networks in Finance and Manufacturing* (pp. 1–27). IGI Global. doi:10.4018/978-1-59140-670-9.ch001

Kartawijaya, R., & Hamsal, I. (2018). FINTECH: FinTech Entrepreneurs versus Banks in Indonesia. *Advanced Science Letters*, *24*(1), 264–266. doi:10.1166/asl.2018.11978

Nimtrakoon, S. (2015). The relationship between intellectual capital, firms' market value and financial performance: Empirical evidence from the ASEAN. *Journal of Intellectual Capital*, *16*(3), 587–618. doi:10.1108/JIC-09-2014-0104

Raikwar, M., Mazumdar, S., Ruj, S., Gupta, S. S., Chattopadhyay, A., & Lam, K. Y. (2018, February). A blockchain framework for insurance processes. In *2018 9th IFIP International Conference on New Technologies, Mobility and Security (NTMS)* (pp. 1-4). IEEE. 10.1109/NTMS.2018.8328731

Riyanto, A., Primiana, I., & Azis, Y. (2018, August). Disruptive Technology: The Phenomenon of FinTech towards Conventional Banking in Indonesia. *IOP Conference Series. Materials Science and Engineering*, *407*(1), 012104. doi:10.1088/1757-899X/407/1/012104

Sharf, S. (2016, November 7). The FinTech 50: The Complete List 2016. *Forbes*.

Shim, Y., & Shin, D. H. (2016). Analyzing China's FinTech industry from the perspective of actor–network theory. *Telecommunications Policy*, *40*(2-3), 168–181. doi:10.1016/j.telpol.2015.11.005

State of FinTech in ASEAN. (2017). *EY report*. Retrieved on 04-02-2019 from https://www.ey.com/Publication/vwLUAssets/ey-state-of-FinTech-in-asean/%24File/ey-state-of-FinTech-in-asean.pdf

Thompson, B. S. (2017). Can financial technology innovate benefit distribution in payments for ecosystem services and REDD+? *Ecological Economics*, *139*, 150–157. doi:10.1016/j.ecolecon.2017.04.008

Wonglimpiyarat, J. (2018). Challenges and dynamics of FinTech crowd funding: An innovation system approach. *The Journal of High Technology Management Research*, *29*(1), 98–108. doi:10.1016/j.hitech.2018.04.009

Chapter 3
The Future of FinTech in ASEAN

Hazik Mohamed
Stellar Consulting Group, Singapore

ABSTRACT

FinTech and the digital economy offer opportunities for ASEAN to rebuild trust and confidence in a financial system that had lost them. Some technologists imagine this world without intermediaries, while others just want a faster and more efficient way of transacting. Banks, FinTech companies, and regulators need to collaborate to create an ecosystem to drive greater access to financial services in the integrated ASEAN economy. The authors discuss projected trends in technology and its use in the next few crucial years. They also recommend strategies that involve various market participants and stakeholders coming together and working towards shared goals of a unified ASEAN economic community by increasing financial inclusion for the unbanked and the seamless cross-border flow of goods, services, and payments in a safe and secure manner.

DOI: 10.4018/978-1-5225-9183-2.ch003

Copyright © 2020, IGI Global. Copying or distributing in print or electronic forms without written permission of IGI Global is prohibited.

INTRODUCTION

The demand for FinTech solutions in ASEAN is underscored by the rapid adoption of technology, high-levels of mobile usage and rising rates of internet penetration, an increasingly urban, literate and young population, as well as a segment of consumers and micro, small and medium-sized enterprises (MSMEs) underserved by traditional banking solutions. These factors and the economic potential of ASEAN have also attracted large numbers of investors to the region.

To realise the potential benefits FinTech innovation can bring to the region will require commitment and collaboration. Banks, FinTech companies and regulators should continue to collaborate to create an ecosystem to drive greater access to financial services in ASEAN. Building the ASEAN FinTech ecosystem is complicated and it involves various market participants and stakeholders coming together and working towards shared goals of a unified ASEAN Economic Community, increased financial inclusion for the unbanked and the seamless cross-border flow of goods, services and payments.

This dynamic region is ripe for technology transformation across sectors such as e-commerce, travel and hospitality, and, of course, financial services. Technology unicorns Lazada, Go-Jek, SEA (formerly Garena) and Grab are just the beginning of a bigger push of ASEAN tech companies enabling connectivity, consumption and economic growth. Where 2010 saw the rise of Chinese tech giants and 2015 the re-awakening of the Indian subcontinent, the next five years will be marked by the tremendous opportunities in ASEAN. With roughly US$2.2 trillion in annual trade flows and over 50,000 financial institutions providing banking services to consumers and businesses, financial technology is at the core of the ASEAN growth story.

Furthermore, only 27% of the region's 635 million people have a bank account (as of April 2016) according to KPMG. This implies that 438 million people do not have access to traditional financial services in this region and in poorer countries like Cambodia, only 5% have bank accounts, which is one of the major reasons for sustained poverty in the region. In addition, only 3% are protected by insurance. So, it is not hard to imagine the opportunity for FinTech in ASEAN. According KPMG, reaching the unbanked population in ASEAN could increase the economic contribution of the region from US$17 billion (2016) to US$52 billion by 2030. FinTech startups have the potential to usher in serious change (both sense of the word) in the region.

Notably also, Southeast Asia has a higher than global average mobile phone penetration rate. While Singapore reached a smart phone penetration rate of approximately 80% in recent years, mobile phone connectivity in Myanmar (93%), Cambodia (173%), Vietnam (131%) and Thailand (133%) grew rapidly over the years (2012-2017). Every month the population of Bosnia-Herzegovina (approximately 3.7 million people) is being added to the internet in ASEAN as users. A Thai consumer spends on average 4.4 hours per day on social media, and data connection in the countryside of Myanmar may be better than in certain modern Western cities. Financial services provided by FinTech companies over the mobile phone, such as money transfers at low cost and short-terms loans, could help bring people out of poverty in the region.

In an EY survey conducted in October 2017 of 125+ institutional investors deeply interested and active in the FinTech sector in ASEAN, it was noted that there was greater than US$2 billion in capital commitments available. On the opposite end, a survey of 230+ FinTech companies, conducted in the same timeframe for the same jurisdiction, capital requirements were established at just greater than US$1 billion. Numerically, there is about two dollars of capital for every dollar worth in a FinTech opportunity.

This chapter discusses the multi-faceted nature of the FinTech future for the ASEAN market. These include its technological trends moving into and beyond 2020, and how consumer behavior has shifted with the digital transformation of services along with its regulations (or lack thereof). It also presents the possible models of collaboration between FinTech startups and financial institutions like banks and regulatory authorities. We also highlight challenges that face organisations that want to adopt frontier technologies like AI, blockchain and machine learning including challenges in technical expertise and capacity-building, and in dealing with change resistance within their own organisations.

Technological Trends of the Digital Economy and the Internet of Things (IoT) Era

Digital transformation and new technology adoption have changed the way of doing businesses (not only in ASEAN but all around the globe too) and these new ways have resulted in reshaping the existing models of businesses and the creation of new innovative ones. In general, digital financial services in most developing countries has developed independently of the efforts of financial regulators, and usually led by mobile telecommunications companies. In many jurisdictions, market regulators only started to address potential risks to consumers and financial stability once mobile payments had already become of mainstream in the domestic financial system.

The digital transformation shift has also changed the expectations and wants of the customers. Today, customers want banking (and other financial services) from anywhere they are and at any time, regardless if they are in the office, or at home in the evenings, or out running errands. This digital behavior of customers has set a new bar for the services industries, and the industry is trying to cope with the needs of these digital mindsets by using omni channels and advanced technologies. Having better insights into how customers behave in their preferred buying channels also allows businesses to identify the right moment to intervene and develop a comprehensive strategy that works holistically across channels such as search, video, social, and display (Mohamed & Ali, 2019). The modes in which fintech has become relevant to every customer without the need for an array of disparate customized solutions are with chatbots and robo-advisory solutions. Built into messaging apps, chatbots come as close to the customer as possible by being a personal assistant in any enterprise. They provide a pertinent answer and allow the clients to complete a purchase immediately with the help that is provided.

Looking in the future, what will the financial services sector will look like in 2020 for ASEAN? Will artificial intelligence replace operations? Will performing financial functions occur in an instantaneous manner from the palm of our hands? Will there be enough disruption so that large banks will no longer exist? We discuss areas where the forecast for the future of digital technology will expand.

Open Platforms

It appears that there is a trend towards open platforms. Even an internet giant like Google, which had covetously protected its search algorithms, has opened up its AI algorithms to the coding community as an open-source resource. We can project the open system materializing in two aspects: first, new platforms can be built with as much proven open sourced software. Examples include databases a company uses, such as Hadoop, PostgreSQL and MongoDB. Second, open API system or Application Programming

Interface. This open API provides future flexibility as well as the ability to have other non-influenced voices providing continuous feedback to suggest new ways in approaching a problem.

An open system fits perfectly into the overarching need for transparency in the financial markets system, and more transparency will lead to better product and cost control. However, the main problem with an open system is information leakage. To have a fully open system to increase transparency and at the same time make sure the amount of information leakage is minimal will be the fine art that would need to be mastered by tomorrow's industry leaders.

Web and Mobile (IoT Devices)

Another area is the integration of multiple devices connected together to make up the Internet of Things (IoT). The advent of financial markets-specific containers such as Openfin, which creates an ease of integration amongst platforms and institutions by making an application native to any screen, allows the transformation to mobile to be extremely easy. The more institutions standardize the usage of these infrastructures, the easier application deployment and integration will be.

Cloud-Based (IoT Infrastructure)

Increasingly, the IT infrastructure for most organisations are becoming cloud-based. Public clouds, private clouds, cloud as a disaster recovery (DR), and cloud communications are here to stay and will increase exponentially as the adoption of cloud-based computing accelerates. We predict that all companies, regardless of size, will build on a cloud-based infrastructure, and consider a server-less environment with adequate cyber-security measures. Cloud computing will also serve as an opportunity to consolidate platforms and connectivity.

Widespread Use of Artificial Intelligence (AI)

The short-term prediction is that AI and cognitive platforms will all be a major part of every solution going forward. With the explosion of big data, AI technologies are key to understanding and improving the use of this big data. AI is advancing at the fastest pace and will integrate into our daily lives by 2020 (Juniper Research, 2016) in almost every aspect. However, effective use of AI is data quality, and reconciliation. If the quality of the data coming in is poor, then there will be poor output — quality of output is highly dependent on the quality of input. This example shows that the holy grail in terms of our platform's goals is to improve data quality, improve data matching of non-structured data, and help AI algorithms sieve data impurities on their own.

INDUSTRY AND STARTUP COLLABORATION

It is paramount that both ASEAN financial institutions and FinTech companies meet the needs of digital transformation and keep on the track of innovation to remain relevant and sustainable. Traditional financial institutions are considered slow in reaction to changes due to may limitations, including additional regulatory controls and risk averse culture. However, ASEAN financial institutions do have some key advantages. They have, over a relatively short period of time, built customers' trust, able to adapt quickly, large network of interested individuals, ethical businesses and financing resources. To remain competitive, ASEAN banks have to overcome old business models which cannot be modified by implementing new technologies. Furthermore, the most efficient way to evolve is for the traditional financial institutions to embrace new partnerships and collaborations with younger and forward-looking start-ups and FinTech developers who provide the technological skill-sets to reinvent the future of banking and financial services.

Industry Models for FinTech Adopters

Interoperability, coordination and collaboration are the important elements of any developed and successful ecosystem around the globe. This involves different governments, public and private sectors indigenously and outside the region. Public and private sectors can establish safe, secure, reliable and affordable open and shared platform for digital payments, banking services and other financial alternatives by converging themselves via digital channels, including decentralized shared ledgers. This will work as the catalyst of financial inclusion and will also enhance the adoption of basic and primary financial services at a larger scale.

This trend of interoperability, coordination and collaboration is pervasive and is prevailing around the world. For example, the Postal Savings Bank of China (PSBC), China's largest lender having branch network of 40,000 branches, has deepen cooperation with Ant Financial and Tencent in internet and mobile finance. The online banks also align with Chinese Government's policy by providing access to financial services to the unbanked Chinese (Duflos, 2015). P2P lenders Jimubox, RenRenDai and Minshengyidai and China Minsheng Bank are helping each other to manage and safeguard funds of investors (Ernst and Young, 2016). The Dianrong.com and the regional Bank of Suzhou set up collaboration agreement in 2014 to target small enterprises (Finextra, 2014). More examples exist around the globe.

Interoperability, coordination and collaboration involve different branches of the government, public and private sectors, indigenously as well as outside the region. Public and private sectors can establish safe, secure, reliable and affordable shared platforms for digital payments, banking services and other financial alternatives by converging themselves via digital omni channels. This will work as the catalyst of financial inclusion and will also enhance the adoption of basic and primary financial services at a larger scale to those who may not have access previously.

A comprehensive analysis of different models of collaborations between FinTech companies and banks have been done in two reports provided by (Ernst and Young, 2017; TheCityUK, 2017). There are different collaboration models explained and discussed in these reports. Some of the prominent models are detailed in the following sub-sections.

Hackathons

This model is not very formal, usually is a fun way to invite startups and FinTech companies to provide a solution on a particular use case or business challenge. Hackathons typically take place in teams and groups of coder-entrepreneurs and programmers. In these events, the organizers set off to test early-stage protypes and ideas in an attempt to solve specific problems and offer solutions. Financial institutions (FIs) can get quick and innovative solutions through this kind of events while FinTech companies get to pitch their ideas and a shot at getting funded or recruited. An example of this model is the LGB innovation lab set by the Lloyds Banking group to test prototypes and find solutions to their operational issues.

Start-Up Corporate Accelerator Model

In this model, FinTech companies submit their applications to FIs to propose solutions or innovation to existing problems in the form of products or services. FIs then short-list a number of FinTech applicants to further develop the proposed innovative services and products. They work together in 12-week programs where every aspect of the solution is refined and perfected through industry experts' mentorship and internal sources that FIs are willing to provide. Beyond merely a collaborative arrangement, this model eventually involves equity agreements where FIs take equity stake in the FinTech companies that successfully graduate from their intensive accelerator programs.

Enterprise Solutions

In this model, FIs select products or services developed a FinTech vendor and test them in focused groups or pre-selected group of customers. Upon successful trials, the FI then scales up the product to its wider market segment. This is a straight-up commercial type of collaboration in which both parties work towards an enterprise solution that can be disseminated to the business organization.

Model of Corporate Venture Capital (CVC)

Corporate Venture Capital (CVC) is the investment of corporate funds directly in external startup companies. This is a simple arrangement in which the IFI takes a minor stake in one or many up-and-coming FinTech companies, to secure access to innovative products and services once these FinTech come into the market and start operations.

Hybrid Model

Hybrid model combines two or more than two models in a manner that both financial institutions and FinTech platforms will get benefits and share the rewards of collaboration and cooperation. This may include a collaborative agreement based on support and cooperation, and also a commercial agreement which may be based on any other model like CVC, Start-up Corporate Accelerator model. Hackathons also can help ASEAN financial institutions to attract innovative and creative minds who can create much-needed solutions.

In a hybrid model all involved parties can reap more benefits and also reduce risks and uncertainty regarding intellectual rights, ownership, costs and profits.

Regardless of any models chosen, the main entities within the innovation ecosystem are the regulators, FinTech companies, FIs, venture capitalists, government agencies, strategy and technology consultants, media and academia. They need to be fully cooperative and supportive of each model. Every crucial component gives support to each other and strengthens each other for the attainment of common and collective objectives. Each of the party plays its role and use their resource and capability to provide solutions. Regulators may provide innovation-friendly policies and environment that gives incentives to FinTech platforms to test and refine their innovative ideas, and FIs may provide financing or access to their internal sources and financial expertise. Incubators and regulatory sand-boxes allow for the trial of prototypes in a controlled environment, while the media and academia may provide insights into trends and conduct proof-of-concept research to determine viable solutions for the gap in the industry.

CHALLENGES FOR FINTECH ADOPTERS

Regulatory Issues

According to International Data Group (IDC), it is estimated that the banks, investment banks and insurance companies globally are investing around US$85bn only in regulatory oversight, legislative initiatives and risk control (Broby and Karkkainen, 2016).

Due to technological advancements and innovative models, the scenario of financial industry is also changing especially when it comes to ASEAN FinTech industry. Each passing day, new ideas are developing, new initiatives in the FinTech world are launched and a new platform is getting financing and starting providing services. And these shifts are completely transforming and shifting the world economy (Hayen, 2016). This demands a dynamic and a new set of regulations to foster and propagate the growth of FinTech industry and also to keep consistency and alignment with the continuum of regulations. However, it is also important to note that risk and failure are an integral part of innovation in FinTech solutions. Therefore, it is critical for regulators to ensure safeguards are in place to manage the risks (such as institution-specific micro-financial risks and system-wide macro-financial risks). Providing parameters and regulatory clarity through a framework (for FinTech business models) is essential for FinTech's mass adoption in order to ensure the financial stability of the system. Regulatory sandboxes are only one of the approaches to manage FinTech and may not fit circumstances in different situations and jurisdictions. Market supervisors will have to ensure that financial institutions or firms have robust governance frameworks and such surveillance could be complemented by data-driven supervision.

The rule-making process also needs some changes due to its present unidirectional and inflexible nature. Rigorous and hard regulations which are placed upon traditional financial institutions cannot be applicable on a nascent industry of FinTech (Tsai and Peng, 2017). An agile and results driven process of rule-making is important to set rules and boundaries for the ever-changing environment of finance, in particularly for the FinTech industry (Brummer and Gorfine, 2014). Moving forward, the industry could come to consensus on a set of prudential regulations for FinTech which can be applicable in all regions. The formation of consortiums and alliances among financial institutions, conglomerates, FinTech platforms, academia and regulatory authorities can be a good step forward.

Cybersecurity

While most organisations acknowledge that security is an important consideration in developing computer systems, costs and business performance often take precedence over security. Even though awareness has been elevated on security issues, most organisations focus on applying security only at the commissioning stage of the system development and try to force-fit security into the final design, resulting in ineffective application of security.

Another significant risk management concern is the operational risk that reflects cyber-security, fraud and theft, data privacy and legal issues. While regulatory instruments such as Basel Committee on Banking Supervision (BCBS) capital requirements can create incentives to address certain operational risks, such as business continuity, capital is not sufficient to restore operations if a financial institution suffers a cyber-attack. Cyber-security and critical Information Technology infrastructure resilience has to be given considerable attention by market supervisors of all sectors, especially the banking/financial sector.

Inertia and Stagnation

The hard regulations and legacy culture in an organization are infused with each other. This impedes the path of an organization to move forward especially when it comes to the path of innovation. This culture of layering and folding of management in decision-making traps an organization in the ropes of stagnation. Risk averse behavior of management which becomes more complex when diffused from lower to top management. FinTech provides for quicker, more informed decision making and calculated risk-taking behaviors.

FinTech focuses on access and control of the customers' financial transactions, and ASEAN FinTech will provide the personalization of finance to the customers by using digital channels and innovative business models within the deployment of big data, AI and blockchain. The process from inception and opening of an account or executing an investment to the final rewards and other financial transactions can be directly controlled by the end users in FinTech solutions.

In a financial organization which is encumbered by layers of management, it is not easily possible to do experimentation for new innovative products and business models. Getting approvals alone will take ages. In addition, experimentation involves failure and the fear of failure results in the lack of support of innovation. It is a fact that without experimentation in this era of digitalization, financial institutions will fail to compete and will not be able to provide the services and products which the consumers expect.

For example, a leading financial services company turned to Agile to support its goal of organizing around customer experiences rather than products (Olsen et al, 2017). In doing so, it sharpened the focus on raising speed to market and ensuring consistently high customer loyalty scores for sales and service delivery, especially in predominantly digital channels. The company uses Agile, cross-functional teams of 8 to 10 people, aligned to specific customer episodes. Each team brings together the requisite capabilities in business, design, processes and technology. The company now is taking its experience-led Agile approach to scale across the enterprise, through waves of applied learning sessions, and is well on its way to improving productivity by three to four times.

Lack of Expertise and Talent

The FinTech industry is bringing together IT professionals, data scientists, entrepreneurs, programmers, etc. to the financial services industry. This entry of new and diverse skilled people in the circle of financial services industry make the FinTech industry more diversified and innovative but also somewhat complex.

One way to overcome the dire need of skilled and talented human capital, could be to increase the production of skilled human capital through effective education of intellectual capital in academia and research. The need to bridge academic curricula to the needs of industry is also critical to bring much needed solutions to real problems. Although there are number of institutions which have already began running courses as part of degree programs in conventional FinTech, there are none in ASEAN finance programs. There is not a single course on FinTech with regards to ASEAN Finance (ICD and Thomas Reuters, 2017). This is indeed very alarming and requires immediate resolution. When FinTech and innovation programs are in place, there should be industrial attachment programs for tertiary students in the form of internships, project collaborations, and exchange programs. For the public or older folks who seek alternative career paths, coding academies need to be developed to skill those interested in coding and programming. It is fairly obvious that as the finance industry gets disrupted, the redundant professionals lose their jobs but as the disrupters continue to employ coders, programmers, various IT specialists and data scientists.

At the university and think tank levels, there should be more collaboration across disciplines, and collaborative cross-training and interdisciplinary research programs to complete the FinTech ecosystem to supply quality and knowledgeable talents.

At the bank level, as automation pervades more activities, their workforce must evolve. Thousands of roles are becoming obsolete, including tellers, backoffice processors — even routine call-center agents, as chatbots and robo-advisors take on simple inquiries. Conventional technologies have helped banks to double labor productivity every few years through digitalizing processes and applying more sophisticated industrial methods like capacity planning and Lean Six Sigma. Opimas, a research firm, estimates that by 2025, the rollout of artificial intelligence (AI) technology by financial institutions will reduce employment in the capital markets by 230,000 people, with the largest impact in the asset management industry, where machines will replace around 90,000 people (Olsen et al, 2017). Taiger, for instance, combines machine learning with natural-language processing to automatically identify, extract, cleanse and validate pieces of information from many types of documents. The banking applications include client onboarding, due diligence and combating money laundering. After a large European bank shifted to Taiger's technology for client onboarding, its cost fell 85% and turnaround time shrank from several weeks to seven minutes, with no loss in quality. As AI spreads throughout the industry, bank professionals who previously performed those activities will have to upgrade their expertise to remain relevant.

The greatest talent challenge for FinTech adopters is attracting technical specialists. There is a worldwide shortage of talent in advanced analytics, new technologies such as blockchain and customer experience design. The shortage is worsened by competition from more attractive FinTech startups and companies that are building interesting solutions. Banks will have to get creative in attracting and nurturing top talent, through incentives such as elevating top performers into key roles with more latitude and flexibility for further innovation, whilst adapting their respective organizational cultures to manifest this new reality.

CONCLUSION

Digital disruptions in our way of life are pushing all FinTech adopters to take more defined strategy decisions. Many banks have recognized that they need a truly differentiated strategy as the industry's economics have come under pressure from new technology and non-traditional entrants with disruptive business models. Large non-finance technology firms have also been moving into markets such as payments, raising customers' expectations for better digital tools and simple, convenient service. Ever-stricter capital and liquidity requirements by regulators have reduced banks' own balance sheet leverage. Low interest rates and low economic growth intensify this pressure that weighs on them.

Difficult as strategic choices may be, FinTech adopters may find it even more challenging to adapt their operating models quickly to a new strategy.

At present, much effort and money go into operating legacy processes and dealing with regulatory requirements to keep the bank running. Gartner estimates that banks on average spend roughly 60% of their IT budgets to maintain legacy IT systems as compared to just 24% to grow the business and 16% to transform it (Olsen et al, 2017). The global financial crisis, moreover, prompted a greater scrutiny to fiduciary duties, and mistrust in the banks' legacy talent, systems and processes which is being overhauled by the current disruptive revolution.

Regulatory support provides an ecology that helps to foster and promote the new or young entrepreneurs and also other ASEAN financial institutions to test their innovative business models. Likewise, it is advisable that other organizations like think tanks and research institutions start sharing and discussing new ideas and collaborate with entrepreneurs to enhance regulations which can support further growth of FinTech eco-systems in ASEAN. Such initiatives provide avenues for regulators and governing authorities to discuss the complex multi-dimensional issues faced by FinTech industry and begin engagements with the industry on viable and practical regulations for the community. Regulators do not want industry players just adhering to rules, or checking boxes but rather, embrace regulatory intent, and create sound, secure, unbiased businesses, where regulatory compliance and sound conduct is embedded in the processes and values of everyday operations.

Promising FinTech companies in ASEAN could witness an increase in investment and acquisitions by investors who are looking to ride the next decade of ASEAN growth, as well as ASEAN banks seeking new and innovative digital capabilities. While this is a good position for FinTechs to be in, those who can work effectively with banks to leverage their ASEAN banking network and knowledge of the local customer base will stand a better chance of success.

ASEAN is a huge market for FinTech roll-out, fortified by unrequited demand for financial services from the unbanked and underbanked. Regional banks, regulators, policymakers and academia have acknowledged the need for innovation and are taking steps to create an inclusive ecosystem. If the technology talent puzzle is also solved, ASEAN will be able to leap forward with FinTech and capitalize the new economy as a major player in the global arena.

REFERENCES

Accenture. (2016). *FinTech and the Evolving Landscape: Landing Points for the Industry*. Retrieved from https://www.finextra.com/finextra-downloads/newsdocs/accentureFinTech2016.pdf

Botsman, R., & Rogers, R. (2011). *What's Mine is Yours: How Collaborative Consumption is Changing the Way We Live*. Collins.

Broby, D., & Karkkainen, T. (2016). *FINTECH in Scotland: building a digital future for the financial sector*. Academic Press.

Brummer, C., & Gorfine, D. (2014). FinTech: building a 21st century regulator's toolkit. Milken Institute.

Chishti, S., Barberis, J., & Telfer, J. (2017). *The FINTECH Book: The Financial Technology Handbook for Investors, Entrepreneurs and Visionaries (Unabridged edition)*. Audible Studios on Brilliance Audio.

daCosta, F. (2013). *Rethinking the Internet of Things: A Scalable Approach to Connecting Everything*. New York: Apress. doi:10.1007/978-1-4302-5741-7

Dawson, R. (2014). The New Layer of the Economy Enabled by M2M Payments in the Internet of Things. *Trends in the Living Networks*. Retrieved from http://rossdawsonblog.com/weblog/archives/2014/09/new-layer-economy-enabled-m2mpayments-internet-things.html

Dharmesh, M. (2016). *Racing from Digital Engagement to Customer Intimacy*. Retrieved from https://www.temenos.com/en/market-insight/2016/racing-from-digital-engagement-to-customer-intimacy/

Duflos, E. (2015). *New Accounts in China Drive Global Financial Inclusion Figures*. Retrieved October 2, 2017, from http://blogs.worldbank.org/eastasiapacific/new-accounts-china-drive-global-financial-inclusion-figures

Ernst and Young. (2017). *Unleashing the Potential of FinTechs*. Retrieved from http://www.ey.com/Publication/vwLUAssets/ey-unleashing-the-potential-of-fin-tech-in-banking/$File/ey-unleashing-the-potential-of-fin-tech-in-banking.pdf

Ernst and Young. (2018). *ASEAN FinTech Census 2018.* Retrieved from https://www.ey.com/Publication/vwLUAssets/EY-asean-fintech-census-2018/$FILE/EY-asean-fintech-census-2018.pdf

Gansky, L. (2010). *The Mesh: Why the Future of Business Is Sharing.* Portfolio Penguin.

Hayen, R. (2016). *FinTech: The Impact and Influence of Financial Technology on Banking and the Finance Industry.* Createspace Independent Publishing Platform.

Hitcher, W. (2006). *The Innovation Paradigm.* Retrieved from https://www.icd-ps.org/en/common/viewfile?FilePath=~/Uploads/publication/doc/20171205113348810IFDIReport2017.pdf

CB Insights. (2018). *FinTech Trends to Watch in 2018.* Retrieved from / research/report/FinTech-trends-2018/

Jagtiani, J., & Lemieux, C. (2017). *FinTech Lending: Financial Inclusion, Risk Pricing, and Alternative Information (SSRN Scholarly Paper No. ID 3005260).* Rochester, NY: Social Science Research Network. Retrieved from https://papers.ssrn.com/abstract=3005260

Juniper Research. (2016). *FinTech AI Revenue to Grow 960% by 2021, Driven by Big Data, Distributed Computing & Connectivity.* Retrieved from https://www.juniperresearch.com/press/press-releases/FinTech-ai-revenue-to-grow-960-by-2021-driven-by

King, B. (2014). *Breaking Banks: The Innovators, Rogues, and Strategists Rebooting Banking* (1st ed.). Wiley. doi:10.1002/9781118958247

Mohamed, H., & Ali, H. (2019). Blockchain, Fintech and Islamic Finance — Building the Future of the New Islamic Digital Economy. De|G Press.

Nicoletti, B. (2017). The Future of FinTech: Integrating Finance and Technology in Financial Services. Cham: Palgrave Macmillan.

Olsen, T., Judah, M., Fielding, J., Nielsen, N. P., & Phillips, S. (2017). *New Bank Strategies Require New Operating Models.* Singapore: Bain & Company's Financial Services.

Sironi, P. (2016). *FinTech Innovation: From Robo-Advisors to Goal Based Investing and Gamification* (1st ed.). Wiley. doi:10.1002/9781119227205

Skinner, C. (2016). *ValueWeb: How FinTech firms are using bitcoin blockchain and mobile technologies to create the Internet of value*. Marshall Cavendish International Asia Pte Ltd.

Stefik, M., & Stefik, B. (2006). *Breakthrough: Stories and Strategies of Radical Innovation* (illustrated edition). The MIT Press. Retrieved from http://gen.lib.rus.ec/book/index.php?md5=B1A5F9B3FFE65BF5C53490B52C7B78D6

Tapscott, D., & Tapscott, A. (2016). *Blockchain Revolution: How the Technology Behind Bitcoin Is Changing Money, Business, and the World.* Penguin.

TheCityUK. (2017). *Transformation and innovation: a guide to partnerships between financial services institutions and FinTechs*. Retrieved from https://www.thecityuk.com/assets/research-report/Transformation-and-innovation-A-guide-to-partnerships-between-financial-services-institutions-and-FinTechs.pdf

Tsai, C., & Peng, K.-J. (2017). *The FinTech Revolution and Financial Regulation: The Case of Online Supply Chain Financing (SSRN Scholarly Paper No. ID 3035386)*. Rochester, NY: Social Science Research Network. Retrieved from https://papers.ssrn.com/abstract=3035386

Villasenor, J. (2016). *Ensuring Cybersecurity in FinTech: Key Trends and Solutions*. Retrieved May 11, 2018, from https://www.forbes.com/sites/johnvillasenor/2016/08/25/ensuring-cybersecurity-in-FinTech-key-trends-and-solutions/

Chapter 4
Paving the Way for the Development of FinTech Initiatives in ASEAN

Mahani Hamdan
Universiti Brunei Darussalam, Brunei

Muhammad Anshari
https://orcid.org/0000-0002-8160-6682
Universiti Brunei Darussalam, Brunei

ABSTRACT

Financial technology (FinTech) is not one to be ignored under any circumstances. It is not only growing as a concept but a phenomenon that has been manifested in non-financial sectors using innovative technology to bring financial services straight to the customers. The creation and practical applications of FinTech supported by government regulations and financial policies, high mobile adoption, rising rates of internet penetration, and increasingly literate and millennial generation, strongly indicates that the various scopes of FinTech in ASEAN are very promising in supporting economic growth and financial inclusion. This chapter will provide an overview of FinTech and examine the development of FinTech initiatives to shed light on some challenges and solutions facing the ASEAN's financial landscape today and in the future.

DOI: 10.4018/978-1-5225-9183-2.ch004

Copyright © 2020, IGI Global. Copying or distributing in print or electronic forms without written permission of IGI Global is prohibited.

INTRODUCTION

The use of Information and Communication Technology (ICT) has a long history in the financial services and business industries. Financial services industry, being regarded as the early adaptors of ICT (Puschmann, 2017), has brought about the fastest digital revolution of Financial Technology (FinTech). From simply providing and supporting back end technological support for financial service providers to a more user centric services and automation of decision-making (Dorfleitner et.al, 2017).The significance of FinTech is very much relevant today because it offers simplified and cost-effective services to customers, gives them access to a variety of value-added services, and enables organisations to meet their needs and preferences. More importantly, FinTech has brought the need to communicate everywhere and at all times without being confined to one space or location. Internet and mobile banking has gradually reduced the physical interaction between customers and financial institutions and replacing money with digital currency. This has considerably reduced customers' need to visit bank branches, which is however viewed as 'disruption' in the financial services ecosystems by the financial service providers.

The issue with FinTech Innovation and its applications are growing too fast that even regulators are struggling to keep up with it, and the financial industry is a high profile industry that demands the paramount security. Although FinTech can be seen as disruptive innovations to traditional banking transactions or conventional services, the growth of FinTech companies has increased rapidly over the years and the new trends in the services industry will also likely continue to expand globally. Figure 1 shows that North America received the largest amount of funding in general, increasing from US$2,583M (in 2013) to US$8,281M (2015). The amount decreased by US$2,390 in 2016, but later increased by US$1,946M in 2017. Asia is the next largest FinTech funded continent – increasing dramatically from 2013 to 2016 by more than 1600%, and decreased for the first time in 2017 by only 10%. Europe FinTech funding grew over 120% in 2017 from US$1,210M to US$2,676M (Gromex, 2018).

Figure 1. Trend of Fintech funding
Source: FinTech trends to watch in 2018

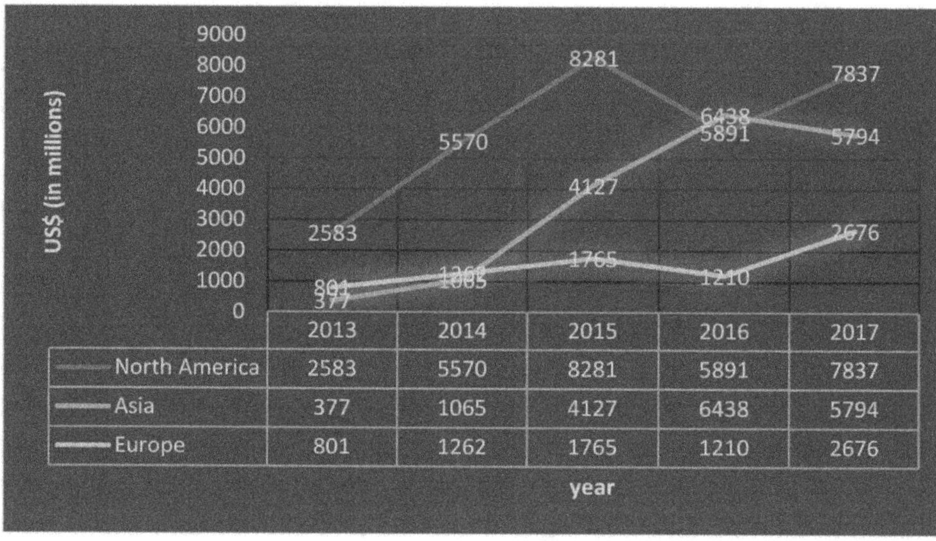

After the global financial crisis in 2008, not only the financial services industry in the ASEAN region has begun to evolve at a rapid pace, the popularity of FinTech is also on the rise in Southeast Asia. ASEAN comprised of ten Southeast Asian countries, already showed their intentions to accommodate FinTech and its investment has surged, jumping 45 percent year-over-year to US$366 million in 2017 (EY, 2018). Iwasaki (2018) indicated the development of FinTech in ASEAN has huge potential to fundamentally change the way countries solve many issues affecting the financial environments such as low bank account holdings and limited access to bank loans and credit cards (Iwasaki, 2018). Given that there have not been many studies on FinTech in ASEAN setting, this chapter aims to provide an overview of ASEAN's FinTech landscape, focusing on the dynamic growth and advancement in FinTech product and application.

AN OVERVIEW OF FINTECH

FinTech can be described as any technological innovation used to deliver financial services such as investment, payment and cryptocurrencies (Wigglesworth, 2016), to customers not confining to any specific sectors or business models (example, peer-to-peer lending). In particular, FinTech has changed the financial services industry, affecting the entire scope of services and products that are traditionally provided by the industry (Arner et al., 2015). In the past, FinTech was used to support back end processing technologies in banking and financial institutions. However today, FinTech has expanded in scope, offering services for the betterment of end customers or users. It started with Automatic Teller Machine (ATM) in 1967 by Barclays Bank to cater for end users (Arner et al., 2015). Table 1 presents the evolution of FinTech, starting from 1993 when the term 'FinTech' was first coined until 2014. FinTech enables the delivery of financial innovation that resulted to new business models, applications, processes, products, or services with an associated material effect on financial markets and institutions, and the provision of financial services (Schindler, 2017). FinTech products include cryptocurrencies such as Bitcoin and Ripple, and mobile-based payment and online payment solutions like Apple Pay, AliPay and many more (Milne, 2015).

The advent of FinTech utilizes ICT to provide financial services to people; develop solutions to payment problems, issue digital currencies and process data analytics; and to make financial operations more efficient (Micu & Micu, 2016). But the paradigm has gradually shifted. FinTech brings with it huge benefits on one hand, and various risks on the other. FinTech has been viewed as a disruptive new market force – a financial technology solution that disrupts the current practices of banking, finance and insurance sectors in doing business (Kursh & Gold, 2016). Generally, FinTech has eased the burden of carrying cash as well as lowering transaction costs for businesses.

Table 1. Evolution of FinTech

1993	FinTech was the original name of the Financial Services Technology Consortium, a project initiated by Citicorp, an effort to overcome a reputation for resisting technological collaboration with outsiders.
1995	Wells Fargo became the first bank to offer an online checking account.
1997	The first virtual banks, without physical branches emerged.
2008	ING Direct launched in Canada, as a subsidiary of the ING group. The financial crisis of 2008, which left the global financial system on the brink of systemic collapse, can be viewed as the turning point for FinTech.
2009	Version 0.1 of Bitcoin SW is released. It includes a Bitcoin generation system that would create a total of 21 million Bitcoins through the year 2040.
2013	Google introduced Google Wallet, which allowed users to make purchases from their mobile phones using NFC technology.
2014	Apple similarly launched Apple Pay in 2014.

Source: Arner, Barberis and Buckley, 2017

In 1990s, FinTech introduced an online banking system in order to reduce reliance on service staff and traditional teller line, the ATM usage and services. Bank branches have also shrunk in size as more customers are pushed onto digital products. The rise of electronic payment (e-payment) has decreased cash transactions, and payment processing devices such as mobile wallet and payment apps can provide ever more secure online payment transactions. For example, Amazon used one click payment system and created "Login and Pay with Amazon" service in 2013 for making payments. Remittance between individuals using email address was also supported (Arner, et.al, 2015).

ApplePay, Google Wallet and AliPay are among the global FinTech players that have a big part in enabling e-payment (Schindler, 2017). ApplePay, an e-wallet that provides customers an alternative of making payments digitally, has been practically used in America since October 2014 (Lee & Lee, 2016). Alibaba and Tencent are two largest internet companies that provide branchless banking services such as Ant Financial and WeBank. Not only they had upgraded their FinTech to keep up, both companies also offer a wider choice of services and better access to banking and financial services (Lee & Teo, 2015). Blockchain is a type of FinTech, aimed at creating a decentralised digital public record of transactions that is secure, anonymous, tamper-proof and unchangeable. Instead of maintaining a private database of records, blockchain technology makes all records public (Gavril, 2017). This implies that people may no longer need a bank to transfer money or keep their account records. Specifically through blockchain technology, crypto-currencies such as Bitcoin and Ripple have become the most widely adopted FinTech product in the world (Milne, 2015). Bitcoin that was developed by Nakamoto, is today's leading crypto-currency that has not only changed the currency markets (Broby & Karkkainen, 2016), but enabled the digital currency transfers to be priced at a wholesale rate that would not be available to most customers and offered full disclosure of how much they are paying (Laven & Bruggink, 2016).

STATE OF FINTECH IN ASEAN

The rapid digitalisation of our economy and financial sectors, gave rise to FinTech in ASEAN as an important part of cooperation to seek out new and innovate solutions to solve problems of financial inclusion. Much of the attention on financial inclusion has been on lifting people out of poverty by introducing them to financial services. The rise of FinTech also provides a great alternative for Small and Medium-Sized Enterprises (SMEs) financing and filled the gaps in ASEAN's sustainable financial system. Digital finance in Southeast Asia brings the benefits of financial services to those who have no access, and allows them to take steps toward a better financial life. FinTech has significantly lowered transaction costs, in which the mass adoption of smart mobile devices with affordable internet access undoubtedly influenced the customers' behaviours on how they want to get access toward financial or banking services. Moreover, there is a shift in the balance of power between financial services regulators and FinTech companies that disrupts the traditional distribution of services to financial institutions and customers in multiple jurisdictions. Some of these FinTech developments in ASEAN member countries which may have been driven generally by the difficult post-crisis environment for banks are presented in the next section.

Brunei Darussalam

The development of FinTech in Brunei Darussalam (Brunei) has been slow and generally insufficient to address financial inclusion in a sustainable manner. FinTech Unit at the Authority Monetary Brunei Darussalam (AMBD) was only established in Brunei in 2017. Although FinTech adoption remains early stage technology development in boosting customer experience, for the most part there has been some progress (ASEAN Today, 2018). To encourage a thriving financial environment for innovative ideas, AMBD launched a regulatory sandbox to facilitate the development of FinTech and developed regulatory guidelines for the sandbox. The regulatory sandbox in Brunei's context is to enable local start-ups to develop and test their FinTech services and applications, and execute programmes for monitoring and evaluation (Biz Brunei, 2017). As AMBD has been actively directing most of its efforts to further facilitate the development of Islamic Banking and Finance, there is a growing market potential of Islamic FinTech in Brunei by promoting mutual consent, timeliness, honesty and goodwill – *Syariah* principles governing Islamic finance products and transactions.

Bank Islam Brunei Darussalam (BIBD), the largest Islamic Bank in the country, currently provides digital banking system called BIBD NEXTGEN to respond to the increasing use of online and mobile banking platforms such as BIBD Mobile, to manage their day-to-day banking requirements. BIBD Mobile is an App that can be downloaded in smartphones and tablets which allows customers to transfer money or pay bills, and BIBD QuickPay, a feature in BIBD Mobile, is a quick cashless payment option whereby customers simply scan QR codes to pay for goods or services (BIBD, 2018). BruPay, a Brunei based FinTech Company that specializes in providing e-payment solutions approved by the AMBD, provides a platform for e-Wallet application that allows customers to make cashless payments as easy as taking pictures, such as for purchasing prepaid top-ups, bills and even transfer money to anyone instantly using a QR Code or a smartphone (Biz Brunei, 2018). While other card-based digital transactions charge 3 percent per transaction, BruPay does not charge commission (transaction) fee and offers the merchants to post their item list to the public (Wong, 2018). One important observation that perhaps explains Brunei's weak level of competitiveness in FinTech sector within the region is that the market is small and the country is also not strong when it comes to innovation. Hence, the alternative way is to replicate models that have proved successful in other countries.

Cambodia

Financial inclusion through FinTech application plays a critical role in Cambodia. Retka (2018) reported that financial inclusion in Cambodia has resulted in an increase in Gross Domestic Product per capita from $1024.9 in 2015 to $1135.2 in 2017. In 2016, the National Bank of Cambodia (NBC) estimated that 71 percent of the country's population had access to financial services, while 59 percent still use formal banking services. Investment of money into FinTech has certainly grown, and is becoming an urgent necessity for helping the unbanked and under-banked population to access financial services, as well as to enable Microfinance Institutions to deliver the services to customers in remote areas at low cost and of a high level of security. The NBC felt there is an obvious need to build supportive environment through the licensing of payment services providers (Serey, 2017), which had just been given such strong political support. Improving financial outcomes with FinTech has been a game changer for promoting development and regional partnership for financial inclusion between China and Cambodia (Ng, 2017).

As FinTech gains more traction and attention in Cambodia, one of the biggest challenges remains educating people to embolden them to switch from cash payments to cashless wallets. They fail to see the need to move beyond operating in cash because traditional cash-based services are common and still highly prevalent in the country. Due to lack of education and awareness, they have also failed to take advantage of all the benefits of online services. Many do not adopt new technologies due to the unavailability of information and instructions in Khmer language in smartphones. English as a language barrier is an issue that needs to be addressed in adopting FinTech (Phong et al., 2016). AlienDev, an IT Company, offers a powerful solution to support learners' needs in Cambodia. The Company developed Khmer Smart Keyboard so locals can understand as they embark on using FinTech app for their everyday financial needs. Wing Company, a successful FinTech startup which performs like mobile money agent network, is targeting the unbanked population to provide them with financial services such remittances, top-ups and mobile payment. Banhji, Cambodia's first FinTech company, has also interestingly used free online accounting software to reach out to thousands of SMEs across the country and help them with inventory management, improved cash flow, accounting and tax compliances and invoice payments (Pesin, 2017).

Indonesia

The World Bank recognizes Indonesian FinTech as the fastest growing industry across Southeast Asia. The industry has brought together citizens into the formal financial system with interventions by the regulators and increased number of FinTech startups, (Hoesin, 2018). The emergence of FinTech has become the best alternative to working for unbanked population, startup companies, and SMEs to grow their businesses. According to *Otoritas Jasa Keuangan* (OJK) – the Financial Services Authority of Indonesia, payment of credit through FinTech in Indonesia has reached IDR 7.8 trillion (approx. USD $534 million) as of July 2018. This revenue comes from 66 local peer-to-peer lending sectors alone (Indonesia Investment, 2018). The estimated US$22.338 billion worth of transactions in the FinTech market for 2018 could experience even greater growth moving into the coming year (FinTech News Indonesia, 2018). The government's support towards the development of FinTech and low transaction fees are vital for effective collaborations with FinTech companies to create synergies and encourage innovation without hampering evolution. In essence, supporting FinTech is a means toward increasing financial inclusion and access for the people of Indonesia while backing positive social and economic outcomes, as well as ensuring stability of the financial services systems.

Nonetheless, there are some real issues in many parts of the Indonesian communities where the issue is much more than just unbanked and underbanked population. The vast majority of the population remains atomised and unorganised, and have not been able to afford good smartphones or access financial services due to lack of sustainable financing and banks' lengthy procedures and administrative barriers. Cheaper smartphones and internet connection will pave a way for financial inclusion and accelerating FinTech innovation, leading to substantial cost savings as well as increasing competitiveness of e-commerce activities in Indonesia. The extent FinTech may pose systemic risks to financial systems is still a matter of concern, despite the government's ambition to make Indonesia the largest digital economy in Southeast Asia by 2o20 and major banks' investment in local startups. The recent ban for using cryptocurrencies to make payments among unbanked population has a major impact on businesses, affecting the way they transact with constituents (Maulia, 2018). This situation has forced the government to restrict market access by capping foreign ownership in e-money providers at 49%, continue doing research on the impacts of FinTech and enact effective policies. These actions are very much needed for risk mitigation to shape the future of financial services that benefits all stakeholders.

Laos

FinTech in Laos is in the very early stages of development, and the government is continuously working on numerous initiatives with industry participants and FinTech companies to allow experimentation while maintaining sector stability. Yet, the underlying issue of many problems faced by the government is the lack of resources and capabilities to build FinTech ecosystems for the startups. This is critical to nurturing the kind of technological innovation necessary to make financial markets and systems more efficient. The Laos government recognizes the potential benefits of FinTech in helping their millennials with finance and how FinTech ecosystem can stimulate the broader local economy and enable growth opportunities for many sectors. But there are also some challenges associated with it. While corporate interest is growing, Laos's FinTech startup sector is still lack of infrastructure it requires for future growth. The lack of dedicated incubators and accelerators, angel investors and venture capitalists also holds back booming of FinTech startup sector (Kong, 2016), because funding remains a major issue for startups. Funding is an existential part of running a startup, and unfortunately not many startups in Laos are investment ready which suggests it is not only money but the startups are also looking for strategic help and advice from their investors.

The millennials in Laos may have grown up with a new respect for FinTech entrepreneurship and their enthusiasm for starting their own business or going out on their own should be nourished to embrace the FinTech economy. Although startups' lack of experience is rarely brought up as an issue, this is a sticking point in FinTech industry and has certainly been a point of discussion. Laos faces challenges in developing FinTech startups because the market is small and at its infancy with consumerism being very new to Laos's citizens. Tung (2015) shared that only less than 10 percent of its seven million populations expressed their confidence and willingness to purchase products and services from local startups, and majority of the population still do not have access to either smartphone or Internet service. Although only 20 percent of the population have access to Internet services, the focus of Laos government is to encourage growth across all industry sectors including low, medium and high-tech firms, not simply fostering more startups. Similar to Indonesia, cheaper and faster Internet will help the FinTech startup ecosystem to thrive in Laos (Kong, 2016). To work towards developing digital solutions that can reach the broadest portion of the population, local startups have been required to refine their business models (Kong, 2016), have a dialogue and build sturdy and beneficial partnerships with multinational organisations, banks and third-party partners or providers (Danchainam, 2018).

Malaysia

FinTech is a fast-moving industry, and its benefits are widely visible and accepted in Malaysia. The proliferation of FinTech apps has been shown to affect the society, and the government policies 'fit for purpose', plays an important role in creating conditions in which businesses flourish. In 2016, the Central Bank of Malaysia launched the Financial Technology Regulatory Sandbox Framework (FTSF), which sets out the criteria for participating in the regulatory sandbox. All the digital products and financial services offered in the country must comply with applicable laws and regulations, and the FinTech companies and financial institutions are given the flexibility to experiment their innovative FinTech solutions in a live controlled environment with the appropriate safeguards. FinTech in Malaysia is seen as an opportunity, rather than a threat or 'disruptive force' to banking industry. FinTech complements banking institutions, and supplements or diversifies the existing financial system. Maybank, one of the most used banks in Malaysia, is among the first few banks to embrace FinTech adoption (Fong, 2016). In 2004, Maybank introduced an online banking for specific transactions to minimise the risk associated with such transactions and safeguard all parties concerned.

The rapid pace of FinTech businesses like MyCash Online, Neuroware and Touch 'N Go is very much dictated by people, and fuelled by global market demands for digital products and services, the constant use of the internet and the intensifying use in mobile applications, which are now part of the everyday routine for many people. With strong community and government support for startup businesses, top 5 of listed tech companies in Southeast Asia are based in Malaysia. In 2015, Malaysia was the first country in Asia Pacific to manage fair treatment in crowdfunding in developing FinTech agenda (Cham et al. 2018). The country has an advantage to get talent and mobility of resources and adequate funding from Singapore's networks to leverage on foreign funds they might bring, as well as its information technology market is expected to continue on its strong growth trajectory. Bernama (2017) further highlighted that Malaysia's conducive infrastructure with strong internet connectivity combined with the government policies serves as a sound foundation for the further strengthening of FinTech startup ecosystem in the region.

Myanmar

Myanmar's financial system is largely controlled by banks, and about 90 percent of the population still lack easy access to formal financial services. This signifies that the country must continue to build sustainable financial services as well as create an ecosystem for financial inclusion. The arrival of mobile financial services and FinTech in the remote Southeast Asian market like Myanmar has not only called out the problems, but offered solutions to address financial inclusion. It opens new opportunities for Myanmar's government to encourage FinTech growth through FinTech ventures' increased capital investment in smartphones and internet penetration to offer a user-friendly digital interface, faster and better service to the unbanked, and a low-cost platform for financial service providers. Wave Money, the first company to receive a license under the new regulation released by the Central Bank of Myanmar, is a joint venture between Telenor, First Myanmar Investments (FMI) and Yoma Bank that offers mobile financial services. Such services provide a safe, convenient and flexible way of receiving, sending and spending money worldwide all on one online account via mobile phones or in person at any of the 4,000 Wave Shop agents.

Myanmar has been late in appreciating the sheer demand for digital information, but today FinTech innovative solutions have begun to reshape the country's business models in response to offering simplified banking services at lower costs or with less hassle or paperwork (FinTechNews, 2017). The government has also taken steps towards achieving its goal to reaching out to 40 percent of the population to have access to financial services by 2020, while encouraging 15 percent of the population to use more than one digital financial product within the same timeframe (Jones, 2016). Mywallet Plus, a FinTech company specialising in online payment and is also a joint venture between LEO TECH Services Pte Ltd in Singapore and MCC Group in Myanmar, has provided consumers and businesses in Myanmar with an online payment platform for utility bill payments, e-commerce processing and consumer bill payments. Although the mobile phone penetration rate in the country barely touched double digits in 2013, and reached only around 50 percent of the population in 2015 (FinTechnews, 2017), with so many people are now increasingly using smartphones, tablets and laptops to conduct their business, mobile virtualisation has become a legitimate and necessary option in Myanmar.

Philippines

With FinTech adoption on the rise, 86 percent of the households in the Philippines are seeking ways to benefit from deploying FinTech and access to services that were previously preserved for the wealthy. Based on the recent data collected by the Bangko Sentral Pilipinas (BSP) in 2015, these households had no savings account because they did not have sufficient money to open an account. They also failed to see the importance to manage one and the need to deposit money in a bank when the service charge alongside the minimum balance was set too high. It was also inconvenient for them to travel long distance when they can even run their business and banking transactions from their home based computer and smartphones supported by internet network speed. The Unisys APAC Banking Insights Survey indicated that majority of the citizens prefer paying their bills over counters. According to Akamai's State of The Internet Connectivity Report in the first quarter of 2017, Philippines was ranked the lowest among Asia-Pacific countries with an average of 5.5 Mbps and placing at 100th in the Global Ranking (Barreiro, 2017). In an effort to improve internet connectivity, an estimated $1.5 - $4 billion worth of investment was approved to deploy national broadband network as well as accelerating the use of wireless fiber optic technology and cables (Philstar, 2017).

A recent study conducted by Voyager Innovations and FINTQnologies Corporation (2017) showed that access to financial services for most provinces in the Philippines have been stagnant for three years (2015-2017), leading to 40 percent remain at the bottom of the country's access to financial and banking services. Low-income provinces only received 0.9 percent of total loan transactions and 2.5 percent of total domestic deposits, in comparison to the high-income provinces where the percentages ranged above 90 percent. Banks and ATMs were also generally located in the high-income provinces, leaving people who live in low-income provinces with no or limited access to financial services. The rising number of local FinTech startups to empower consumers and businesses, and give them direct access to world class financial services (FinTechnews, 2018), has made the country the fastest growing smartphone market in ASEAN. Tagcash is a digital wallet that allows consumers to top up their money through local 7-Eleven convenience stores in the Philippines, bank transfers, local agent networks and the use of bitcoins. Coins.ph is a mobile money transfer platform that is powered by blockchain technology. E-Peso, a product of Genuisys International Systems Corp (GISC), is a virtual Peso currency to support cashless products, high security, AMLA compliance, mobile money and E-Payment. PesoPay, a product of AsiaPay, is an online payment gateway system that aims to provide secure and seamless electronic payment solutions for enterprises. Overall, the FinTech ecosystem in the Philippines is fueled by the startups' commitment to build a cashless economy which will integrate financial inclusion and increase the adoption rate for FinTech solutions (Chin & Collao 2018).

Singapore

Singapore can be considered as one of the most wired countries in ASEAN. With a total population of 5.7 million, the impact of FinTech advancement can be felt from the mobile phone penetration rate which stood at 148 percent and household broadband subscription rate at 104 percent (Tan, Cheah, Chen & Choy, 2017). Singapore as the top leading financial center with 117 foreign banks and five global banks, holds the largest share and distribution of FinTech in the region (Trade, 2016). Currently, there are more than 400 FinTech companies and 30 FinTech innovation lab research centers established in the country (Straits Times, 2016), and this growth has reaped massive economic rewards. In 2017, Singapore achieved the highest record of FinTech funding in ASEAN at US$229.1 million (S$312 million) (KPMG's Pulse of FinTech Report, 2017). The government through its Monetary Authority of Singapore (MAS) has made great strides in FinTech and financial inclusion, and more importantly, user trust gaps have been traversed to get FinTech to where it is today (Fintechnews, 2017). With 76 percent of consumers using card than cash and 69 percent using electronic modes when purchasing, Singapore has been ranked among the top cashless countries globally.

Singapore is also far ahead of other ASEAN cities, and scored consistently high across all sectors including insurance (3rd), banking (5th), investment management (5th), professional services (4th), and government & regulatory (4th) on the Global Financial Centres Index in 2018 (Singapore Business Review, 2018). The country was ranked fourth on GFCI, which gives rise to a prime opportunity for digital wallets to thrive. The rapid growth of smartphones and a strong push for digital wallet or e-wallet has resulted in Singapore having the highest digital wallet penetration rate. Technological change alone does not lead to more demands for digital demand, but factors such as price pressures, income growth and environmental changes all have a part to play. Yu (2017) reported that 87 percent of the country's population have shown a widespread demand for digital wallet, and 80 percent have already adopted smartphones for making e- payments (Google Asia Pacific, n.d.). This achievement is attributable to Singapore's best and strongest payment ecosystem that has significantly enhanced FinTech adoption, and increased MAS's collaborative efforts and partnerships with private players and telecommunications companies.

Thailand

Thailand's economy is expected to grow between 3.8 and 4.0 percent (Bangkok Post, 2018), and a part of the boost may have been from the emergence of FinTech. The country has gradually shifted its focus from increasing labour intensive industries to expanding their human capital for the rising skills demand for technology. Thailand faces challenges in several areas, but there are four that stands out including skilled labour shortage; not making enough return on investment, changes in consumer expectations and the increasing competition from financial technology companies. The World Bank Survey showed 83.5 percent of the workforce in Thailand is unskilled (The Nation, 2016), and such result suggested investment in building well-trained fields' expertise in in science, technology, engineering and mathematics will be crucial to fulfilling the country's digital economy vision. To keep pace with the digitisation of the economy, the government regulated a law to accommodate an inflow of foreign workers to work in sectors suffering labour shortages and develop local talent through skills transfer (Jomo, 1997, p. 82).

Thailand has the potential of being one of Southeast Asia's FinTech Hubs due to its distribution of digital convergence across the country. The country shows remarkable progress on access to finance for the poor where 97 percent of the population was already either banked or given access to formal financial services which has been offered by financial providers (Christopher, 2018). The growth of mobile and internet penetration has also rapidly risen whereby its internet access has increased from 67 percent in 2017 to 84 percent of the population in 2018, and total funds raised by Thailand Tech startups increased from $88m to $271m (Thailand Tech Startup Ecosystem Report, 2018). In 2017, Thailand contributed about 10 percent of FinTech distribution, ranking the country as the fourth rising country in in ASEAN (UOB Group, 2017). The country's startup ecosystem continues to flourish with the increasing number of investments and investors, making it more attractive to be a part of FinTech landscape. The number rose significantly, from one venture capitalist, one accelerator and three funded Tech startups in 2012 to more than 96 venture capitalists, eight accelerators and more than 90 funded Tech startups in 2017.

While digital payment is the largest market segment in the country, contributing a total transaction value of USD 6,440.9m in 2016, the country has yet to offer substantial startups in other segmentation of FinTech services other than digital financial services such as crowd funding, peer-to-peer lending and insurance (Kong, 2016). The National Innovation System which is key to Thailand 4.0's innovative process at the national level, plays a crucial role in building a crowd funding platform that provides financing for entrepreneurial start-ups (Wonglimpiyarat, 2017). Thailand 4.0 places greater emphasis on a value-based, innovation-driven capabilities, with human intellectual capacity replacing physical capital. Despite a stagnant market, FinTech development in Thailand has been ranked seventh among ASEAN countries in FinTech Competitiveness Index, and recognised as the country with stable political environment, secure funding opportunities, strong financial attractiveness and talent, supportive business regulatory advancement, better customer and market constructs like smartphone penetration, innovation ecosystem and business environment (Suchit 2017).

Vietnam

Although FinTech is quite new in Vietnam, the transaction volumes are extremely high with many potential service providers to come. FinTech transaction amount is estimated to reach US$ 7,259m with an annual growth rate of 17.5 percent in period 2017 to 2021. While FinTech is one of the fastest growing sectors and the newest investment trends for startups, the country's domestic economy which heavily dependent on manufacturing industry remains positive. The manufacturing industry continues to drive robust revenue growth due to higher foreign direct investment (FDI) inflows and stronger foreign demand for Vietnamese goods. Digital payment contributed a total transaction value of USD7, 252m, representing the largest market segment in FinTech sector (about 99.9 percent). It is also one that has the largest number of FinTech startups (Tam & Hanh, 2018), in which 58 percent of the startups operate in mobile payment services (about 58 percent). The beginning of digital financial services in Vietnam including savings, credits and insurance and payment facilities through electronic devices, is still at a very nascent stage and proved to be challenging. At present, mobile 'top ups' and utility bill payments conducted through formal bank accounts, internet or cell phones are the most prevalent digital financial activities in Vietnam (Kong, 2016).

In 2017, the Governor of the State Bank of Vietnam established a Steering Committee on Financial Technology with the purpose of advising the

Governor on solutions to improve the FinTech ecosystem, including legal framework to facilitate the development of FinTech businesses in Vietnam and aligns them with the government's guidelines and legislations (Sy.ngo, 2018). Smartphones and services boost internet use in Vietnam, and thereby penetrating the FinTech market even further. E-commerce and M-commerce that have expanded their reach to assist people who were previously underserved by financial services, are growing faster than the capacity of the economy to support them. For example, offering opportunities for private sector companies to partner with Vietnamese government to support infrastructure, meeting the rising demand for digital solutions and softwares, and enhanced use of space technology-based tools and payment for end-users and merchants. The current FinTech industry in Vietnam is dominated by payment solutions. Its remittance solutions, mainly the remittances sent worldwide from United States, accounted for almost USD 14 billion will create the biggest opportunity for businesses and banks to stay relevant in Vietnam.

DISCUSSION

The ASEAN Economic Community's Vision for 2025 is focusing on closing the digital gap, increasing financial access and literacy, expanding the scope of intermediary facilities (such as digital payments) and developing financial services for smaller firms and lower income groups (Businesstimes, 2018). Population growth, invention of the new high-speed technology which increases investment demand for FinTech, development of urbanisation, and widespread of smartphone adoption are seen as part of the economic growth indicators in ASEAN as these supports digital information and communication innovation as well as technological advancements such as big data, data analytics, Industry 4.0 and Internet of Things.

Globally, FinTech has been seen as a disruptive innovation to banking & financial institutions. However FinTech in ASEAN has a rather bigger role to play. History proves that ASEAN has always been the centre of economic integration. Be it social or economic, the innovation and the technological developments taking place in ASEAN's 10 member countries have found its reverberations reaching those of other regions. The geographical expansion of international trade allows for the discovery of new and innovative ways to solve problems of financial inclusion. FinTech offers a sufficiently low cost alternative to persuade people to adopt FinTech solutions and invest in FinTech companies. While non-financial businesses and professions use FinTech to offer products or services without (or less) transacting through banking and financial insitutions (Anshari et al., 2019), FinTech has succeeded as both standalone businesses and vital links in the financial services value chain (examples e-commerce and m-commerce). Market demand for innovative products and services has been pushing FinTech innovation in ASEAN.

In response to the rapid development of FinTech, convenience and security are the main reasons why consumers are adopting FinTech solutions. Singapore-based FinTech companies continue to dominate the ASEAN FinTech market, followed by Thailand and Indonesia (BBVA, 2017). Data from Tracxn showed that Singapore contributes the largest share about with 39 percent of FinTech market in ASEAN. Its strong internet and well-developed infrastructure supported by relevant and timely policies and regulatory practice framework have better positioned Singapore's FinTech companies than most Asian companies in Hong Kong and London, to succeed in global markets. The profitability and scalability of FinTech has caught the attention of investors and FinTech incubators ("State of FinTech"). Thus, countries like Indonesia, Malaysia and Thailand need to catch up with FinTech hubs and FinTech in terms of technology because investment in new technology and in adapting to the changing financial landscape are not deemed a priority before. Conventional banks have so far been unable to engage customers online whereas FinTech has, as their strength lies in online interaction.

The Rise and Development of FinTech

The rapid growth of FinTech development steers ASEAN member countries towards a cashless society. Although e-payment and e-wallet are the preferred cashless payment methods that have been effected in ASEAN member countries, followed by P2P lending, crowdfunding, and retail investments, there are still practical problems to address including internet connectivity, mobile and banking penetration. Singapore has been regarded as the most mature cashless society because it has the highest digital wallet penetration followed by Philippines, Vietnam, Indonesia, Malaysia and Thailand (Tech Collective, 2018). FinTech is easily accepted in ASEAN for the following reasons. Firstly, ASEAN's growth has been powered by its people. The combined ASEAN nation has a huge population of about 630 million across

10 countries, and about half of them are under the age of 30. The number is expected to expand by 373 million by 2030 (Funding Societies, 2018). Considering the growth of emerging ASEAN is largely underpinned by demographic structure and rapid urbanisation, with a young, digitally adept population and rising personal incomes driving demand in the mobile voice and data segments, this makes ASEAN as an attractive zone for FinTech industry to advance and embrace the fourth industrial revolution.

Secondly, the rapid growth of smartphone adoption and cheaper internet connectivity are the other drivers behind the emergence of FinTech, with Cambodia (173 percent), Thailand (133 percent), Vietnam (131 percent) and Myanmar (93 percent) (Viray, 2018). Today, about 3.8 million people in Southeast Asia have been connected to internet, and on average, a person spends 4.4 hours per day on social media in Thailand (Thaivisa, 2018). The high smartphone adoption, cheaper Internet access and many options of digital platform attract the attention of digital-savvy resulting in the increase of the consumption rate. The increase in smartphone penetration has made strong push to adopt e-wallet in ASEAN countries. This massive innovation created for mobile base transfer, e-wallet, and other alternative financing and App-based finance tools with a lot of options, has made things easier to access domestic and international financial services and today, people prefer easier alternatives to compare prices or find online stores for shopping. Mobile services, logistics and infrastructure improvements have made all this possible. By 2025, it is predicted that the middle class of Southeast Asia will increase to over 440 million people (Funding Societies, 2018).

Thirdly, while setting up national FinTech regulatory sandbox in an attempt to stay competitive and keep innovation, it limits ASEAN FinTech companies to scale up and expand their businesses outside their home countries. Regulators monitor and foster the development of FinTech industry in their respective countries, and are mandated to work within national jurisdictions. In response to this, ASEAN FinTech Network (AFN) brings together the FinTech ecosystems of Singapore, Malaysia, Indonesia, the Philippines, Thailand and Vietnam (BBVA, 2017), to create an open platform for collaboration, commitment to build engagement, cooperation and knowledge sharing across the fragmented ASEAN region, all with a focus on driving performance in the industry. It centres its success on training the potential FinTech workforce, improving accessibility of investment capital, global market access and deepening the availability of cutting edge (or core) technology. FinTechs like Blockchain,

Artificial Intelligence and Biometric, which have the potential to create the highest impact on return on investment, have increasingly attracted many investors to invest in FinTech startups in the ASEAN region.

CHALLENGES AND FUTURE DIRECTION

The sustainability of some business models has yet to be tested. FinTech startups in particular, require business models that not only fit and relevant but also sustainable to address financial exclusion (Jones, 2016). The acceptance and adoption of FinTech in ASEAN has affected the entire global financial system by continuously engaging in financial innovations and inclusive finance for inclusive growth and development (Chen, 2016). FinTech businesses are relatively viable when they are small but will struggle to maintain their viability when the activity scale expands. It is also difficult to predict whether potential users of new financial services will become active users. Despite the significant benefits FinTech could offer to consumers, the environment remains challenging to move away from traditional banking systems and practices. Some people remain sceptical about FinTech's fulfilment and customer service support to customers across countries, because there is a deep-rooted anxiety about security of online payments (Iwasaki, 2018).

Since FinTech in some ASEAN countries is still underdeveloped, substantial improvements are necessary because FinTech will drive business models of the future. Countries must address financial inclusion to build a shared future and to reach poor, low and middle-income consumers with useful financial solutions and having access to financial services. To support financial inclusion, FinTech system such as the effectiveness of credit screening system for investment like P2P lending requires continuous review and improvement, while regulators have the task to regulate FinTech innovations in a way that reduces systemic risks and at the same time also allowing for their further development. Despite the various situational contexts, problems affecting each member of ASEAN countries are relatively similar and they all agree on overcoming and improving practical issues in adopting and developing FinTech innovation. There is no doubt that banks and other financial service providers with large network coverage are key FinTech enablers. They can reduce gaps in FinTech initiatives, and take part in FinTech activities. Yet, financial service providers also need more differentiation to convince consumers about their digital products, and provide incentives to change.

Lagarde (2018) reported that there are about 1.7 billion adults who still live without access to financial services, and EY's FinTech Adoption Index indicated one third of the world uses two or more FinTech services, and 20 percent of them are unaware they are using FinTech (EY, 2017). This opening provides an opportunity for FinTech companies to provide new applications or in partnership with financial institutions to reach out the unbanked and under-banked population, SMEs, and agricultural development in ASEAN. Unleasing the potential of FinTech in financial industry, the impact is greater when cooperation can be fostered among countries to make the FinTech initiative workable into single ASEAN market. Syariah compliant FinTech will also enrich the variants of FinTech products and services to target ASEAN's growing Islamic community and broadening their footprint in Southeast Asia such as Brunei, Malaysia and Indonesia. Overall, FinTech has proved to create impacts on financial inclusion, define and shape the future of the global financial industry which looks stronger than ever.

CONCLUSION

Financial inclusion and skills transfer must be integrated in the development of FinTech in ASEAN. FinTech is still in its early stage, but the landscape has become more crowded. Many of the new players including FinTech startups are competing each other effectively in the realm of soft power. There has been a tremendous surge of interest in FinTech innovative solutions from investors particularly in mobile payments like e-payment and e-wallet. This method of mobile payment is prevalent among millennials and young folks in ASEAN FinTech industry, followed by P2P, crowdfunding and retail investments. There are many practical issues for the proliferation of FinTech in ASEAN such as internet connectivity and mobile penetration rate, most noticeably a change in the way we do things today. Moving away from the traditional banks has begun, and may have been the preferred choice of the SMEs, underbanked and unbanked population. Majority of the population among young and tech-savvy consumers have access to smartphones that effortlessly encourage them to actively participate in FinTech activities. Governments remain the most powerful actors on improving ASEAN FinTech's ecosystem. Finally, FinTech with a digital based platform enables multi-channel financial transactions to an extended pool of market and broadens the delivery of financial services efficiently and effectively from a far distance and yet within reach.

REFERENCES

Anshari, M., Almunawar, M. N., Masri, M., & Hamdan, M. (2019)... *Digital Marketplace and FinTech to Support Agriculture Sustainability, Energy Procedia, Elsevier, 156C*, 234–238.

Arner, D. W., Barberis, J. N., & Buckle, R. P. (2015). *The Evolution of FinTech: A New Post-Crisis Paradigm?* Retrieved from https://papers.ssrn.com/sol3/papers.cfm?abstract_id=2676553

ASEANtoday. (2018). *Better late than never? Brunei and its role in the Fintech revolution*. Retrieved 30 October 2018 from https://www.aseantoday.com/2018/06/better-late-than-never-brunei-and-its-role-in-the-fintech-revolution/

Barreiro, V. (2017). *PH has slowest average internet speed in Asia Pacific – report*. Retrieved 20 October 2018 from https://www.rappler.com/technology/news/171680-philippines-akamai-broadband-adoption-internet-speed-rankings

BBVA. (2017). *FinTech in emerging ASEAN: Trends and prospects*. Madrid, Spain: BBVA Research.

Bernama. (2017, December). Malaysia's fintech industry poised for growth. *New Strait Times*. Retrieved from https://www.nst.com.my/business/2017/12/311888/malaysias-fintech-industry-poised-growth

Bernama. (2017, December). Malaysia's fintech industry poised for growth. *New Strait Times*. Retrieved from https://www.nst.com.my/business/2017/12/311888/malaysias-fintech-industry-poised-growth

BIBD. (2018). *BIBD QuickPay*. Retrieved 30 October 2018 from http://www.bibd.com.bn/personal/digital-banking/bibd-quickpay/

BizBrunei. (2017, March 1). AMBD launches sandbox under new FinTech unit: Local start-ups can now test financial technology products and services through the regulatory sandbox. *Biz Brunei*. Retrieved from https://www.bizbrunei.com/2017/03/amdb-launches-sandbox-new-FinTech-unit/

BizBrunei. (2018). *BruPay receives AMBD approval for trial phase*. Retrieved 30 October 2018 from https://www.bizbrunei.com/2018/08/brupay-receives-ambd-approval-for-trial-phase-sandbox/

Broby, D., & Karkkainen, T. (2016). *FINTECH in Scotland: building a digital future for the financial sector*. Academic Press.

BSP. (2015). *National Baseline Survey on Financial Inclusion*. Retrieved 20 October 2018 from http://www.bsp.gov.ph/downloads/publications/2015/NBSFIFullReport.pdf

Businesstimes. (2018). *What is the ASEAN Economic Community?* Retrieved 30 October 2018 from https://www.businesstimes.com.sg/hub-projects/deepening-asean-economic-integration/what-is-the-asean-economic-community

Cham, T. H., Low, S. C., Lim, C. S, Aye, A.K., & Ling, R. L. B. (2018). Preliminary study on consumer attitude toward fintech products and services in Malaysia. *International Journal of Engineering & Technology, 7*(2.29), 166-169.

Chen, L. (2016). From FinTech to Finlife: The case of FinTech Development in China. *China Economic Journal, 9*(3), 225–239. doi:10.1080/17538963.2016.1215057

Chin, C. S., & Collao, J. B. (2018, April 1). *It's time for more FinTech in the Philippines*. Retrieved from https://www.rappler.com/thought-leaders/199315-time-more-FinTech-philippines

Christopher, M. (2018). *FinTech Industry in Thailand holds Unlimited Prospects*. Retrieved from https://www.opengovasia.com/FinTech-industry-in-thailand-holds-unlimited-prospects/

Collective, T. (2018). *Why is Asia leading the Fintech race?* Retrieved 30 October 2018 from https://techcollectivesea.com/2018/01/19/why-is-asia-leading-the-fintech-race/

Danchainam, N. (2018). *10th Digital Finance Working Group in Lao PDR is a clarion call for Digital Finance*. Retrieved 28 October 2018 from http://www.uncdf.org/article/3302/10th-digital-finance-working-group-in-lao-pdr-is-a-clarion-call-for-digital-finance

Dorfleitner, G., Hornuf, L., Schmitt, M., & Weber, M. (2017). *FinTech in Germany*. Springer International Publishing. doi:10.1007/978-3-319-54666-7

EY. (2018). *ASEAN FinTech Census 2018*. Retrieved 30 October 2018 from https://www.ey.com/Publication/vwLUAssets/EY-asean-fintech-census-2018/$FILE/EY-asean-fintech-census-2018.pdf

EY FinTech adoption index. (2017). Retrieved from http://www.ey.com/gl/en/industries/financial-services/ey-FinTech-adoption-index#market_link

FinTech trends to watch in 2018. (2018). Retrieved from https://www.cbinsights.com/reports/CB-Insights_FinTech-Trends-2018.pdf

FinTechnews. (2017). *FinTech in Myanmar, an Overview*. Retrieved 28 October 2018 from http://FinTechnews.sg/8637/myanmar/FinTech-myanmar-overview/

FinTechnews. (2018). *FinTech startups in Philippines*. Retrieved 28 October 2018 from http://FinTechnews.sg/FinTech-startups-philippines/

Fintechnews. (2017a). *Fintech Singapore 2017 in Review*. Retrieved 30 October 2017 from http://fintechnews.sg/15601/fintech/fintech-singapore-2017-review/

Fong, V. (2016). *The emergence of FinTech: Where does Malaysia stand?* Retrieved from http://www.banktechasia.com/FinTech-in-malaysia-2016/

Fundingsocieties. (2018). *Here are the reasons for Fintech's rapid growth in Southeast Asia*. Retrieved 30 October from http://brands.dollarsandsense.sg/fundingsocieties/tag/asean/

Gavril, M. (2017). *The Financial Revolution And The Many Benefits It Brings: Cryptocurrency & Blockchain Technology*. Academic Press.

Gnrick, M. (2017, Aug 22). *The 5 driving factors behind ASEAN's imminent FinTech boom*. Retrieved from https://www.forbes.com/sites/outofasia/2017/08/22/the-5-driving-factors-behind-aseans-imminent-FinTech-boom/#cff91055cf3b

Gromex, M. (2018). *What Can FinTech Expect In The Next 24 Months In The Central And Eastern Europe*. Retrieved 30 October 2018 from https://www.forbes.com/sites/michalgromek/2018/07/27/what-can-fintech-expect-in-the-next-24-months-in-the-central-and-eastern-europe/#5694db9548e2

Gudowicz, Z. (2018). *ASEAN Thailand ICO market*. Retrieved from https://www.cyberius.com/wp-content/uploads/2018/03/ASEAN-Insights-Thailand.pdf

Hoesin, S. (2018). *Unrealized Potential in Indonesia's Growing FinTech industry*. Retrieved 30 October 2018 from https://ifcextapps.ifc.org/IFCExt/Pressroom/IFCPressRoom.nsf/0/E26207B6540F40A9852582DB001098C9

Investment, I. (2018). *Rapid Development of Fintech Industry in Indonesia*. Retrieved 30 October 2018 from https://www.indonesia-investments.com/id/finance/financial-columns/rapid-development-of-fintech-industry-in-indonesia/item8949

ITA. (2016). *FinTech Top Markets Report*. Retrieved from https://www.trade.gov/topmarkets/pdf/Financial_Technology_Executive_Summary.pdf

Iwasaki, K. (2018). Emergence of FinTech companies in Southeast Asia: rising hopes of a solution to financial issues. *Journal of Pacific Business and Industries, 18*. Retrieved from https://www.jri.co.jp/MediaLibrary/file/english/periodical/rim/2018/68.pdf

Jomo, K. S. (1997). *Southeast Asia's misunderstood miracle: Industrial policy and economic development in Thailand, Malaysia and Indonesia*. Boulder, CO: Westview Press.

Jones, B. (2016). *Mobile Money at The Report*. Myanmar: Oxford Business Group.

Kong, A. (2016). *The state of FinTech in Thailand*. Retrieved from https://yostartups.com/the-state-of-FinTech-in-thailand/

Kong, A. (2016). *The State of FinTech In Laos*. Retrieved 28 October 2018 from https://yostartups.com/the-state-of-FinTech-in-laos/

Kursh, S. R., & Gold, N. A. (2016). Adding FinTech and blockchain to your curriculum. *Business Education Innovation Journal, 8*.

Lagarde, C. (2018). *IMF and World Bank unveil Fintech Agenda*. Retrieved 30 October 2018 from https://www.finextra.com/pressarticle/75832/imf-and-world-bank-unveil-fintech-agenda

Laven, M., & Bruggink, D. (2016). How FinTech is transforming the way money moves around the world: An interview with Mike Laven. *Journal of Payments Strategy & Systems*, *10*(1), 6–12.

Lee, D. K., & Teo, E. G. (2015). Emergence of FinTech and the LASIC principles. *The Journal of Financial Perspective*, *3*(3), 24–37.

Lee, S. H., & Lee, D. W. (2016). *Review on FinTech Industry in Oversea*. Academic Press.

Lee, T., & Kim, H. (2015). An exploratory study on FinTech industry in Korea: Crowdfunding case. *International conference on Innovative Engineering Technologies*, 58-64.

Micu, I., & Micu, A. (2016). Financial Technology (FinTech) And Its Implementation on The Romanian Non-Banking Capital Market. *SEA-Practical Application of Science*, *11*, 379–384.

Milne, A. (2015, November 16). *Achieving European policy objectives through Financial Technology*. Brussels, Belgium: ECRI.

Pesin, I. (2017, May 10). *FinTech in Cambodia 2017*. Retrieved 28 October 2018 from https://medium.com/@igorpesin/FinTech-in-cambodia-2017-d74f82f46b7d

Philstar. (2017). *Phl leads in internet speed increase*. Retrieved 20 October 2018 from https://www.philstar.com/business/2017/06/04/1706696/phl-leads-internet-speed-increase

Phong, K., Srou, L., & Solá, J. (2016). *Mobile Phones and Internet Use in Cambodia 2016*. Academic Press.

Puschmann, T. (2017). FinTech. *Business & Information Systems Engineering*, *59*(1), 69–76. doi:10.100712599-017-0464-6

Schindler, J. (2017). *FinTech and Financial Innovation: Drivers and Depth*. Finance and Economics Discussion Series 2017-081. Washington, DC: Board of Governors of the Federal Reserve System.

Serey, C. (2017). *FinTech could be 'game changer'.* Retrieved 28 October 2018 from https://m.phnompenhpost.com/business/FinTech-could-be-game-changer

Straitstimes. (2016). *New fintech innovation hub to take shape in the heart of Singapore's CBD.* Retrieved 30 October 2018 from https://www.straitstimes.com/business/banking/new-fintech-innovation-hub-to-take-shape-in-the-heart-of-singapores-cbd

Suchit, L. N. (2017). *Thailand lags in FinTech development in Asia.* Retrieved from https://www.bangkokpost.com/tech/local-news/1373711/thailand-lags-in-FinTech-development-in-asia

Sy.ngo. (2018). *How Financial Technologies (FinTech) Market Evolves in Vietnam?* Retrieved 28 October, 208 from http://www.antconsult.vn/news/how-financial-technologies-FinTech-market-evolves-in-vietnam.html#ixzz5OuiQSLzE

Thaivisa. (2018). *Thai people spend NINE hours per day online, new study finds.* Retrieved 30 October 2018 from https://tech.thaivisa.com/thai-people-spend-nine-hours-per-day-online-new-study-finds/27033/

Trade. (2016). *2016 Top Markets Report Financial Technology Country Case Study.* Retrieved 30 October 2018 from https://www.trade.gov/topmarkets/pdf/Financial_Technology_Singapore.pdf

TradingEconomics. (2018). *Thailand GDP Growth Rate.* Retrieved 27 October 2018 from https://tradingeconomics.com/thailand/gdp-growth)

Tung, C. (2015). *Cambodia and Laos: the challenge of altering attitudes towards startups.* Retrieved from https://e27.co/cambodia-laos-challenge-altering-attitudes-towards-startups-20151118/

UOBgroup. (2017). *State of FinTech in ASEAN.* Retrieved 27 October 2018 from https://www.uobgroup.com/techecosystem/pdf/UOB-State-of-FinTech-in-ASEAN.pdf

Viray, G. (2018). *4 things fintech startups can learn from the mobile payments boom in Cambodia.* Retrieved 12 November 2018 from https://e27.co/4-things-fintech-startups-can-learn-mobile-payments-boom-cambodia-20180326/

Wigglesworth, R. (2016, January 20). *FinTech: Search for super-logo*, Retrieved from http://mypages.iit.edu/~mdixon7/FinancialTimesArticle_SearchForASuperAlgo_Jan_20_2016.pdf

Wong, A. (2018). BruPay receives AMBD approval for trial phase. *Biz Brunei*. Retrieved from https://www.bizbrunei.com

Wonglimpiyarat, J. (2017). FinTech Crowdfunding of Thailand 4.0 Policy. *Journal of Private Equity*, *21*(1), 55–63. doi:10.3905/jpe.2017.21.1.055

Yu, E. (2017). *More Singapore consumers choose e-payments over cash.* Retrieved 30 October 2017 from https://www.zdnet.com/article/more-singapore-consumers-choose-e-payments-over-cash/

Chapter 5
FinTech:
A Study of Enablers, Opportunities, and Challenges in the Banking and Financial Services Sector

Vibha Bhandari
College of Applied Sciences Nizwa, Oman

ABSTRACT

Businesses have been forerunners in providing innovative techniques and technology to the market. These emerging processes, techniques, and technologies have disrupted the existing ones and met the requirements of the existing customers. Today's banking and financial sector is facing an unprecedented change wherein various new players are entering the market and disrupting the traditional modes of operation. These players are a part of the latest disruption in the banking and financial sector, which is popularly known as Fin Tech (which is an amalgamation of finance and technology). They are providing alternative solutions and business models that are overhauling the manner in which this sector and its customers function. This disruption not only opens doors for completely different business opportunities but also poses challenges to the existing set up of business. The chapter aims to study the emerging trends associated emerging opportunities and challenges of FinTech in the banking and financial sector globally.

DOI: 10.4018/978-1-5225-9183-2.ch005

Copyright © 2020, IGI Global. Copying or distributing in print or electronic forms without written permission of IGI Global is prohibited.

INTRODUCTION

Business has existed since the early times of human race. Though started with simple barter system involving exchange of goods for goods and services, business has undergone multiple changes to meet the varied requirements of human beings. Businesses have reformed and renovated the ways of dealing with the ever-changing requirements of the market. In this reformation and renovation of business models, technology has played a very important role. In fact, it can also be said that change in the business models have been possible due to the new techniques and technologies provided by the businesses themselves. The changes ushered by the technological innovations have made it possible for the businesses to meet the requirements of the existing base and extension or creation of new market bases. Today, technology in business is an inevitable requirement. As time progresses, the business world is leaning more and more towards it, making it almost impossible to separate the two from each other. The primary objective of business is to generate and maximize returns for its stakeholders. To achieve this objective, businesses need to be innovative. Technology facilitates in providing innovative solutions to businesses which in turn makes them profitable and sustainable in the long run. In order to be sustainable, technology needs to be sold and accepted – which is made possible only by business. Thus it can be said that business and technology are complementary to each other and the existence of one without the other is not possible.

While constructing new playing fields for the existing businesses, technology has also posed some challenges for the existing businesses in the related and other fields. For example, the introduction of smart phones have not only created new markets for apps, online transactions, easier communication – thus creating a full package for information sharing, communication and entertainment through the usage of internet .But at the same time seriously damaging the photo reel business, markets for audio and video entertainment, postal services, to name a few. Thus, a new technology not only opens doors for new opportunities but also slims down the existing ones and creates windows of challenges. The same holds true for the banking and financial services sector.

The banking and financial sector today is amidst an insurrection of unprecedented opportunities and challenges which have been ushered by the fourth industrial revolution. This fourth industrial revolution is driven by Financial Technology popularly known as FinTech, which symbolizes innovative products from new startups or the adoption of new approaches by existing players in the financial space, with technology as the key enabler. Industrial Revolutions have overhauled the production processes of goods and services for commercial purposes. While the first industrial revolution resulted into mechanized production, the second led to mass production and the third resulted in automate production. The first industrial revolution employed steam and power, the second one utilized power, and the third one functioned on electronic and information technology for revolutionizing commercial production. The current fourth industrial revolution is building upon the third and is characterized by a fusion of technologies that is blurring the lines between the physical, digital and biological spheres (Schwab, 2016).

FinTech as ushered by the fourth industrial revolution is a broad phenomenon that is evolving daily as more technology entrepreneurs enter the industry and transform it according to social needs. On one hand, FinTech could be considered a financial service, which is intervened by innovative technologies to satisfy the requirements of tomorrow: high efficiency, cost reduction, business process improvement, rapidity, flexibility, and innovation (Dapp, 2014). On the other hand, FinTech also refers to companies – and, even more typically, to start-ups, which serve as enablers of these services (Zavolokina, Dolata, & Schwabe, 2016).

The global FinTech industry has witnessed phenomenal rise in the volume of investments. The total global investment in FinTech remained close to $31 billion, with venture capital investing of $2.1 billion in insurtech across 247 deals and blockchain accounting for $512 million of investment across 92 deals (Pollari & Raisbeck, 2018). The number of FinTech deals globally rose from 1,800 deals in 2016 to 2,700 deals in 2017 (Accenture, 2018). This increase in FinTech investments and deals is spread across continents and indicates the rising demand for new digital innovations in the financial services area, as these technologies prove their value, acceptance and applicability.

This chapter in its current form aims to study the enablers, opportunities and emerging challenges of FinTech in the banking and financial sector.

Enablers of FinTech

For long, the large and established players of the banking and financial sector had advantages of being sole players due to their financial strength, size and area networks. With the advent of the FinTech revolution, this sector is at the brink of major overhaul today. The enablers for this fourth industrial or FinTech revolution can be classified as under:

Global Financial Crisis: The year 2008 witnessed one of the worst financial crisis since the great depression of 30's.This crisis hit the global banking and financial services sector very badly. The banking and financial services sector became busy to save their remaining assets from getting affected by the crisis and recovery of the dues. The regulatory authorities enforced laws and rules to salvage the damage, bring stability to the markets, and restore the residual customer and investor trust. These changed rules and laws demanded immediate and strict compliance from banks and financial services sector. As the banks and financial services sector took time to understand and incorporate these regulatory enforcements in their day-to-day functioning, innovation of products and services took a back stage.

Rising Customer Requirements: During the time of crisis, there was a whole new generation of millennials (also known as Generation Y) who were tech friendly and wanted solutions, which were not being offered by the traditional players in this sphere. This segment of population was globally mobile and wanted products and services that were fast, efficient, effective and pocket friendly. The kinds of services being offered by the traditional players in the market were unable to meet these challenging requirements. This created a gap between what these new age customers wanted and what the market offered.

Emergence of Non-Traditional Financial Players: Due to the financial crisis, the traditional banking and financial sector, got busy with legal compliance and salvaging their assets and reputation and so devising and offering new products and services took a back seat. The non-traditional financial players were quick to realize this gap between increased customer expectations and complacency on part of traditional players .They began filling this gap with compelling offers, taking advantage of the latest technology to deliver better value propositions to customers in a number of areas and even creating new customer segments. These players disrupted the existing structures and paved way for new solutions that were enabled by the advances in Information Technology (IT).

Advances in IT: The advances in IT has led to revolutionary changes in communication, transportation and has been one of the leading facilitators of global business. While the banking sector was stagnant, customer preferences were changing, the world of IT was experiencing tremendous growth and innovation. These innovations were partly propelled by the non-traditional players who incorporated them to provide innovative banking and financial services. Some of notable advances in IT which have brought about the FinTech revolution are as stated below:

- Machine Learning (ML)
- Artificial Intelligence (AI)
- Internet of Things (IoT)
- Chatbots
- Cloud
- Big data
- Application Programming Interface(API)
- Near Field Communication
- Bio metrics
- Robot advisory (Robo-advisory)
- Block chains

These enablers have paved the way for FinTech revolution, which is reforming, restructuring and reinventing the entire way in which today's banks and financial services sector function. Today FinTech is defining the direction, shape and pace of innovation across almost every subsector of financial services. The traditional and non-traditional financial players in this arena have transformed the structure, provision and consumption of banking and financial services . The opportunities created by this revolution are enormous and are vividly changing the banking and financial sector today.

EMERGING OPPORTUNITIES IN THE BANKING AND FINANCIAL SERVICES SECTOR

The demographic and technological enablers of the FinTech revolution have created opportunities for both the traditional and non-traditional players of this sector. Lending, receipts, payments and remittances were traditionally considered forte for the banks and other traditional players like credit unions, insurance companies, asset management companies to name a few. The FinTech revolution has brought a total overhaul to these services and other similar products. Today, not only traditional but also non-traditional companies are coming forward in this arena to provide solutions by bringing in models which are tech as well as customer friendly. The opportunities created in this sector are enormous. The paper in its current form will try to explore a few of these opportunities emerging for the traditional as well as non-traditional players.

Payments, Receipts and Remittances: These areas of financial services were traditionally the forte of banks and other specialized organizations. The adoptions of IT tools have revolutionized these areas. Emergence and rapid use of mobile phones and applications have made it possible to carry out transactions at the touch of a finger. Digital and mobile wallets are giving users alternatives for on-line payments and in-person transactions. The most popular mobile wallets include Apple Pay, Android Pay, Samsung Pay and a large collection of others, including countless retailer and financial institution-branded apps. The most familiar digital wallets are Master Card's Master Pass, Visa Checkout and PayPal (Thienes, 2016). Also, these wallets are collaborating with merchants and crossing over to the brick and mortar space to provide better and enhanced services to their customers. These wallets are also playing an important role in providing financial services to the unbanked and under banked sections of the economies.

The remittance market is worth $582 billion US Dollars and is another area, that is undergoing enormous change. This sector today, is witnessing the involvement of well-capitalized upstart companies with innovative FinTech solutions that are challenging the established players like Moneygram, and Western Union (Shiva, 2016).This development is not restricted to only western part of the world but has made its inroads across the globe. For instance, most adults in Kenya have M-Pesa accounts, which allows people to send money to each other via a text message (African Business Magazine, 2017). Remitting money to African countries costs more than 10% of the value of money sent and is one among the highest transfer fees paid. Applications like these have made these transfers affordable and quick while providing multiple payment options which are safe and secure (Scott-Briggs, 2017).The use of block chain technology in this area is going to further improve this.

Lending: Providing loans for commercial and personal purposes have been one of the leading activities for banks and credit associations, which require the fulfilment of certain regulatory norms. Despite the increase in the number of banks and their expansive network, there are certain sections of the economy that remain unbanked or under banked. Digital lending is the technology that kick started the FinTech movement and is still one of the most prominent user of IT in the financial services area. Online lenders that include peer-to-peer lending platforms as well as underwriter and lending platforms are using data collected from online activities of consumers and businesses. These online lenders are leveraging this data with the help of machine learning technologies and algorithms to assess credit worthiness of the applicants *(Empirica.com, 2018),* to make underwriting decisions, creating computer programs that can automate loan originations without the need for a customer to ever visit the branch *(Rob, 2017).*

Another area experiencing significant innovation is mortgage lending where technology can significantly simplify the process by digitizing forms, prepopulating known information and ensuring that all documents are in order before a customer proceeds for the mortgage process (Morgan, 2017).

Customer Service: The use of chatbots for supporting the customer service interactions in banks is growing. Currently, these chatbots are said to possess the intelligence of a 2-3-year old. However, as machines do not suffer from physical or learning fatigue, the evolution of a chatbot could be best described as more exponential than linear. So, in future more chatbots are anticipated with improved quality of interactions, speed of responses, and accuracy in decision-making. Banks are planning to adopt models based on regression aided by machine learning to offer better products to its customers. With the support of data scientists, banks plan to gain insights into customer behavior, expectations and responses. The insights gained will help to identify the needs of the customer, and thus aid the banks to design and offer customized products for their customers (Sundarajan, 2017).

Asset and Wealth Management: According to Pricewaterhouse Cooper's Global Fintech Survey of 2016, approximately 60% of asset and wealth managers fear of losing their business to the FinTech companies (Barry & Maya, 2016).This fear of loss comes from various sources like online brokerages, wire houses, and robo-advisors to name a few-which are extensively using accurate predictive analysis supported by innovative data and opinion mining, imagery analytics, machine learning and artificial intelligence techniques. This usage has facilitated in managing risks, ensuring compliance, improving trading efficiency and providing better solutions. For instance, innovations under the umbrella of "robo-advisors" are becoming more sophisticated and, thus, enable advisors to service not only the higher net worth accounts but also the affluent masses who are looking for economical alternatives to receive advice on how to manage their assets (Barry & Maya, 2016).

Another IT development that will change the asset and wealth management sector is "blockchain technology" also known as distributed ledgers. Distributed ledgers are highly flexible and can be used to remove friction from the client on-boarding process, streamline management of model portfolios, speed the clearing and settlement of trades, and ease compliance burdens associated with anti-money laundering (AML) and know your customer (KYC). This will result in elimination of redundant functions like reconciliation of proprietary database, reduced operational expenses and increased opportunities to enhance the customer experience. Besides, the traditional asset and wealth managers, this technology will have broader applications for rollovers, trusts, estates, insurance and other transactions where assets are moved between parties or contracts are executed (Nanayakkara, Smith, Nassir, Hatch, Crespigny, & Hinkis, 2017).

It is true that FinTech has created opportunities for traditional and non-traditional service providers in the banking and financial sector. It is changing the manner in which this sector is performing today. But this of technology in the financial sector has its own set of challenges, as discussed in the forthcoming section.

CHALLENGES FOR THE BANKING AND FINANCIAL SERVICES SECTOR

The banking and financial ecosystem today is witnessing disruptions unknown hitherto, like cost commodization, profit redistribution, product customization-to name a few. This has resulted into emergence of players and offerings that are low margin, asset light, scalable, innovative, and compliance easy (LASIC) (Chuen & Teo, 2015).Though the rules and players of the game are changing fast, this sector faces unprecedented challenges today. Some of them area as discussed below.

Talent Acquisition: The financial services sector is facing unprecedented change, where non-traditional financial players are jostling for their place in the market, backed by new technologies. These changes will result into unemployment in the traditional areasand have serious consequences on the jobs of bankers, auditors, lawmakers and accountants. There will be a need to provide alternative employment to these experienced and qualified professionals. Not only this, the future professionals needed in this area shall have to be multi-talented in the fields of design, IT, business, law and marketing. The professionals of tomorrow in this field will be very different from professionals of today-with very different personalities. Acquiring these professionals will be a challenge.

Survival: Banks and other traditional players of this sector are facing fresh challenges from non-traditional players and their offerings that were unknown before. These non-traditional players have read the pulse of the market and created tech savvy and customer friendly products, but are fund and brand scarce. On the other hand the traditional players are fund, time and brand opulent but are scarce on innovative product offerings. Both these players have different strengths and weaknesses and there will be a tough scuffle individually for them to survive. One thing is for sure that the players delivering products which meet and exceed the customer expectations will survive.

Security and Privacy: Each FinTech innovation entering in the market comes with issues of trust and privacy. Every additional device connected to the net is a new attack vector for the hackers. Data is the new gold oil and cybercriminals are waiting to acquire it. The Cambridge Analytica case raises serious issues regarding the use of personal data collected without knowledge or permission to establish sophisticated models of user's personality raises ethical and privacy issue (Davies, 2015).The innovations entering the markets will have to ensure the safety and privacy of the users data. Appropriate mechanisms and procedures need to be designed to ensure that there is no data and security breach.

Regulatory Compliance: As the new models to meet customers' expectations evolve, they pose serious challenges to the law makers. The traditional players were falling under the legal compliance umbrella and were forced to follow the prescribed norms and procedures. But the non-traditional players and their offerings lie outside the legal net. Many times the service providers are not even known to the users and legal system. In such a scenario seeking compliance and adherence to norms and procedures is unimaginable. The regulators will have to adopt a proactive approach and strict adherence to its framework in order to maintain the trust of the customers and at the same time promote the use of better solutions to provide enhanced customer experience and needs.

CONCLUSION

Despite the above challenges, one thing is certain is that FinTech is here to continuously disrupt, innovate, reform, restructure, reinvent and stay in the banking and financial services sector. The future of this sector looks very promising with the emerging dynamics of increased participation of traditional and non-traditional players, customer expectations, regulatory and compliance systems. The road ahead for banking and financial services sector is challenging and tough, but is certainly interesting and worth a watch.

REFERENCES

Accenture. (2018, February 28). *Newsroom Main.* Retrieved from Accenture: https://newsroom.accenture.com/news/global-venture-capital-investment-in-fintech-industry-set-record-in-2017-driven-by-surge-in-india-us-and-uk-accenture-analysis-finds.htm

African Business Magazine. (2017, August 30). Fintech can cut remittance costs to a fraction. *African Business.*

Barry, B., & Maya, B. (2016). *PwC Global FinTech Survey:Beyond automated advice: How FinTech is shaping asset & wealth management.* Pricewaterhouse Coopers.

Chuen, D. L., & Teo, E. G. (2015, September 30). *Emergence of Fintech and the Lasic Principles.* Retrieved from https://papers.ssrn.com/sol3/papers.cfm?abstract_id=2668049

Dapp, T. F. (2014). *Fintech-The digital (r)evolution in the financial sector:Algorithm-based banking with the human touch.* Frankfurt: Deutsche Bank.

Davies, H. (2015, December 11). *The US News.* Retrieved from The Guardian: https://www.theguardian.com/us-news/2015/dec/11/senator-ted-cruz-president-campaign-facebook-user-data

Empirica.com. (2018, March 12). *Top Fintech companies in lending space.* Retrieved March 12, 2018, from http://empirica-software.com/fintech-companies-lending/

Morgan, R. (2017, September 5). The top fintech trends driving the next decade. *ABA Banking Journal.*

Nanayakkara, N., Smith, C., Nassir, Z., Hatch, M., Crespigny, A. C., & Hinkis, R. (2017). *Blockchain innovation in wealth and asset management: Benefits and key challenges to adopting this technology.* Ernst & Young LLP.

Pollari, I., & Raisbeck, M. (2018). *The pulse of fintech.* KPMG.

Rob, M. (2017, September 5). The top fintech trends during the next decade. *ABA Banking Journal.*

Schwab, K. (2016, January 14). *The Fourth Industrial Revolution: What it means and how to respond.* Retrieved from World Economic Forum: https://www.weforum.org/agenda/2016/01/the-fourth-industrial-revolution-what-it-means-and-how-to-respond/

Scott-Briggs, A. (2017, May 30). *Fintech News: Tech Bullion.* Retrieved March 15, 2018, from https://www.techbullion.com/fintech-money-transfer-sector-improving-remittance-industry/

Shiva. (2016). *Fintech Outlook for 2017: Report discussing trends, opportunities and challenges.* Schaumburg: Opus Consulting.

Sundarajan, S. (2017, November 28). *Top 10 fintech trends that could infuence the banking industry in 2018.* Retrieved March 10, 2018, from https://yourstory.com/2017/11/top-10-fintech-trends-influence-banking-industry-2018/

Thienes, C. (2016, June 16). *What's the difference between mobile and digital wallets?* Retrieved March 20, 2018, from http://www.tmgfinancialservices.com/the-future-of-credit/future-of-credit-blog/whats-the-difference-between-mobile-and-digital-wallets

Zavolokina, L., Dolata, M., & Schwabe, G. (2016). *The FinTech phenomenon: antecedents of financial innovation perceived by the popular press.* Financial Innovation.

Chapter 6
Financial Technology and Innovative Financial Inclusion

Sumarsono
Universitas Islam Negeri Sunan Kalijaga Yogyakarta, Indonesia

Abdullah Al-Mudimigh
Dar Al Uloom University, Saudi Arabia

Muhammad Anshari
https://orcid.org/0000-0002-8160-6682
Universiti Brunei Darussalam, Brunei

ABSTRACT

A portmanteau of financial technology (FinTech) centralizes on the innovative use of smart mobile devices to design and deliver financial services and products, elevating an innovative way of delivering financial services. The chapter mainly focuses on the definition and the importance of FinTech to the financial ecosystem especially in the Southeast Asia region. It focuses on how financial technology (FinTech) came to be, how transactions in the past mostly use cash, and then shifted to credit card and then shifted to a cashless transaction, for example using e-wallet or simply using smartphone for any financial transaction. The research found out how the huge percentage of internet users in the Southeast Asia region were the cause of the development of FinTech companies in the region for FinTech startups. It also showed how FinTech helped to provide solutions for financial inclusion, especially unbanked population.

DOI: 10.4018/978-1-5225-9183-2.ch006

Copyright © 2020, IGI Global. Copying or distributing in print or electronic forms without written permission of IGI Global is prohibited.

INTRODUCTION

Financial Technology or better known under the term 'FinTech' is widely used in the financial industry. It is in the center of attention as it has many benefits and more convenient to be used. Financial technology develops technological system in the finance industry. The emergence of FinTech companies make an innovation in the industry where the systems become beneficial for general public and even government around the world. FinTech keeps improving and attracting investors from all over the world. In 2014, $12 billion of private capital was invested into FinTech (Gulamhuseinwala, et al, 2015). It offers more user-friendly and convenient ways of managing finance for people in juxtaposition with traditional methods. FinTech industries provide variation of financial services such as Peer to Peer lending, e-payment, holding assets, investments, crowdfunding, insurance services and many more.

FinTech not only focus on the companies but also common people which are the majority of consumers as they use the services for their daily lives. Some of FinTech examples are "cryptocurrencies such as Bitcoin and Ripple, the use of big data for risk analytics, new peer to-peer and other platforms and distributed ledgers for supporting transaction efficiency" (Milne, 2015). Both start-ups and traditional finance companies are active in FinTech where it changes the way traditional institution works such as the interaction with their customers. "Today, FinTech companies directly compete with banks in most areas of the financial sector to sell financial services and solutions to customers which most of us use now" (FinTech Weekly, para. 2).

For the traditional method, we have to go to the bank itself to make a transaction but with FinTech, we can just do it with our mobile phones through mobile online banking. Although we are more used to human interaction, the risk of using machines during the process is lower. Thus, the probability of making mistakes are rarely made (Dhar, 2016). This is also proved by FinTech Weekly (2017) that "especially millennials (people born between approximately the early 80s and late 90s) and the following generations prefer quick and easy banking services over walking to a branch".

Since FinTech is the product of innovation, technology, business, and economy. The significance of FinTech lies on the movement of technology driven and it will continue to grow bigger especially when technology giants such as Alibaba, Apple, and Google starts to massively introducing FinTech system. It is highly efficient that helps both the individuals and the large corporations FinTech will likely grow larger than what it can be imagined at this stage of time as technology are also improving and growing for the future.

Due to this probability, FinTech is likely to become prominent in the financial sector today and in the future. FinTech provides many privileges compared to traditional financial system. It is important to have background knowledge about FinTech through assessing its meaning and its history.

DEFINITIONS AND SCOPE

There is no concurrence in defining what FinTech exactly is. But many different authors have made attempts to define FinTech according to their own understandings drawn from their conveyed studies and surveys.

Dorfleitner (2017) stated that FinTech represents companies that offer financial services which incorporate advance technologies. Besides providing digital products and services explicitly designed for the banking and financing sector, there are also FinTech that in charge of distributing insurance. These types of FinTech are often called InsurTechs. In addition, it may also offer several of third-party services for instance, providing technical solutions for financial services providers.

According to Schindler (2017), FinTech refers to financial innovation made possible using technology comprising a broad range of services for instance, online marketplace lending, equity crowdfunding and financial applications of machine learning. It is also similar with Arner (2015) who expressed FinTech as the whole stretch of services offered by finance industry which is greatly supported using advance technology.

There are many forms of FinTech. One example is that FinTech can be found in trading and investing. Nowadays, making an investment are helped or advised by automated financial advisors. According to Anthony Back, Robo-advisors and other startups are utilizing sophisticated algorithms to make trading and investing a fully automated online experience. These automated platforms provides investors big savings and offers financial planning services that are usually given or kept hidden for wealthy investors. Some companies that specialize in this kind of work are such as the Wealthfront and the Betterment. FinTech such as the Robo-advisor in the investment game are potentially replacing traditional non technological advisors with a cheaper and more productive alternative.

Another example is in terms of funding is Crowdfunding. Crowdfunding acts as an alternate source of investments for startups or new businesses who does not have a high capital budget. Anthony Back believes that these startups tend to be not in the interest of big firms or companies. However, with online crowdfunding that raises money in a large amount from different individuals worldwide can fund projects of a new business. Kickstarter and Indiegogo are examples of companies that specialize in online crowdfunding and have manage to be successful. This type of financial technology helps promising ideas to reach an end product. Thailand government has set the direction in moving the nation towards a value-based and innovation-driven economy, wherein crowdfunding is one of the policy mechanisms to support SMEs. It explores the dynamics of financial technology crowdfunding under the policy direction of the so-called Thailand 4.0 (Wonglimpiyarat, 2017).

Another example of FinTech can be found in terms of payments. The most mainstream type of cryptocurrency is known as Bitcoin. Cryptocurrency was designed as a peer-to-peer (P2P) payment network without any intervention from any governing state authorities. The founder of Bitcoin, Nakamoto defined his invention as "A purely peer-to-peer version of electronic cash which would allow online payments to be sent directly from one party to another without going through a financial institution". In summary, it can be seen at the table 1 below.

Table 1. Types of FinTech

Types	Descriptions
Online banking	Banking activities are done online, for example making payments, transferring money between accounts, monitor accounts, download transactions, handling loan activity, including applications and repayments.
Payments and transactions	Internet-based method of processing economic transactions. Allows accepting payments over the internet. Typically run by third-party corporations, such as PayPal, Google or Click2Pay.
Market trading	The act of buying and selling products on the web. Traders buy and sell using the trading platform. Investors need to provide capital in the hope of financial gain.
Raw materials management	The management ensures that the raw materials are in the range of productivity and the value is on an affordable scale.
Collective financing	It comprises organisational forms which are owned and governed by citizens – sometimes together with municipalities and other institutions.
Development of financial security systems	To manage and secure the systems from any future imbalances.
Digital wallets	An electronic device that allows individuals to make transactions include purchasing items online using the apps available on their mobile phones.
Peer-to-peer investing	Enables individuals to lend money without using an official financial institution as an intermediary.

History of FinTech

The advancement of ICT and the extensive use of smart mobile devices are the enabling factors to financial technology evolution. Technology has always played a key role in the financial sector in ways that most people take for granted and might not ever see. Despite all that, people are still unaware of what FinTech is and where it originated from. Even though FinTech is relatively new, it has existed long before the term has even been created.

Britannica stated that in 1920s, individual firms, such as oil companies and hotel chains, starts to distribute credit card to customers to make a purchase at their each of their business branch. However, the first official universal credit card to be used was introduced by the Diners' Club in 1950s. This makes carrying cash a lot easier in a sense that all the consumers could just bring their cards.

Zerucha (as cited in Truong, 2016, p. 5) believes that with the success of the credit cards, it has led to the creation of other new technology project. One of which is the Automatic Machine Teller (ATM). ATMs was first introduced by Barclays in 1960s. This allowed people to withdraw their money directly from the ATM instead of going to the bank. Even though ATM is quite useful to avoid long queues in banks, it is only sufficient enough to support the financial industry and this does not mean it replaces the banking industry. In the end, banks still held an important role in performing most of the financial transaction.

According to Pisani, the first electronic stock market was put into operation by NASDAQ in 1970s (Pisani, 2010). This allowed brokers to buy and sell stocks even after market hours. Moreover, to support the storage of a large amount of data in a safe and optimal way, mainframe computers were installed in most of the financial institutions in the 1980s, further enhanced the agility of financial transaction and supports the implementation of e-commerce.

The booming evolution of FinTech was facilitated by the evolving Internet technology. This exceptional progress of the internet has made a necessary thing for the introduction of a lot of FinTech start-ups in many years later especially Singapore as they are the leading regional FinTech Hub.

Figure 1 below shows brief history of FinTech. Despite the rapid growth of financial technology as we see now, FinTech is nothing new. In fact, the origin could be traced back all the way in 1865, where the invention of pantelegraphy started making a breakthrough in the world of banking. Followed by in the 1800s where consumers started using charge plates and

Figure 1. The evolution of FinTech

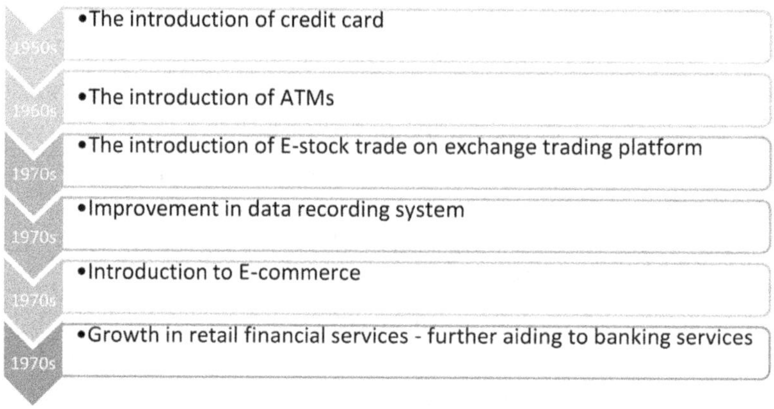

credit coins to exchange goods with merchants. Throughout 1950s and 1960s, modern-day credit card and Automated Teller Machines (ATMs) were introduced – slowly developing the progress of financial services from analogue to digital. Then came along the establishment of the Society of Worldwide Interbank Financial Telecommunications (SWIFT) in the 1973 that has helped to resolve problem relating to international transaction with the means of telecommunication. Furthermore, there has been improvements in record management and financial operation in 1980s. It was noted too this time around there was an increase in online banking as well as E-commerce all through 1990s (Arner, Barberis, & Bukley, 2016).

However, when the global financial crisis fallen on 2007 to 2008, years after came along new innovation in FinTech. This includes the introduction of cryptocurrency like Bitcoin in 2009. Moreover, now in the present serves booming increase in retail financial sectors where online banking could be easily done on mobile phones (Desai, 2015).

Trends in FinTech

Figure 2 shows the trend of FinTech funding according to the regions whereas North America received the most funding in general, increasing from 2013 to 2015, from US$2583M to US$8281M and decreased in 2016 by US$2390. Funding for North America increased again in 2017, by US$1946M from the previous year. Asia is the next most FinTech funded continent – Increasing dramatically from 2013 to 2016 by more 1600%, and decreased for the first time the following year (2017) by 10%. Europe FinTech funding grew over

Figure 2. Trend of FinTech funding
Source: FinTech trends to watch in 2018, 2018

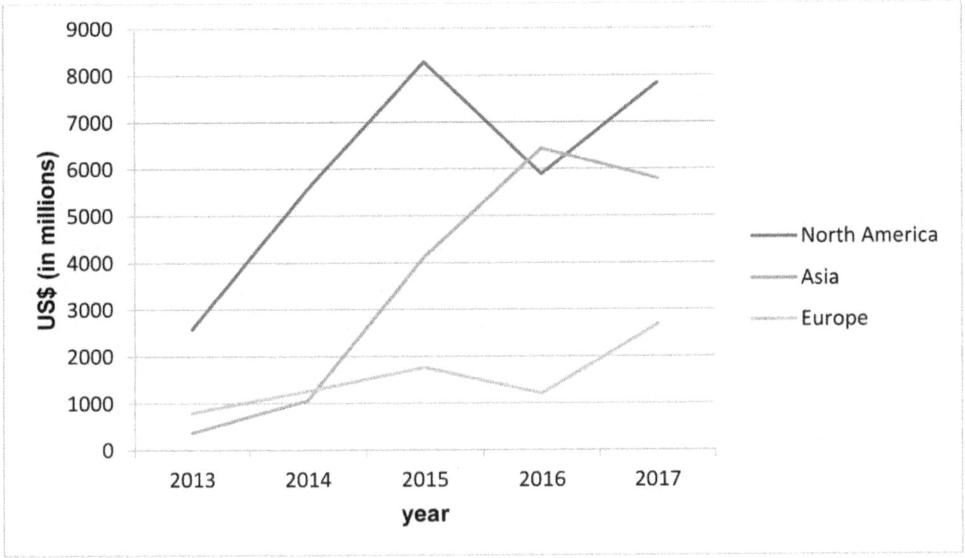

**For a more accurate representation see the electronic version.*

120% in 2017 from US$1210M to US$2676M. Africa, Australia and South America are the least funded continents, with very minimal increase and data throughout.

FinTech in South East Asia

FinTech has become a trend in Southeast Asia in the recent year. This is because FinTech has a potential to solve any problems that affecting the financial environment in these countries. With the situation in Southeast Asia, FinTech has a major impact in the financial area. In Southeast Asia, the financier's region is considered underdeveloped and many countries wanted an improvement through using FinTech system. Before FinTech many things that are difficult can now be achieved by using FinTech. FinTech adoption is fairly a new and recent introduction in ASEAN countries with Thailand and Singapore being its main players in the industry. As stated by Iwasaki (2018), according to a survey done in 2017 by Thai technology media firm Techsauce and market research and consultancy company RUAMKID, Singapore is home to main offices to 43% of FinTech companies in Southeast

Asia, followed by Thailand (19%) and Indonesia housing 12% of FinTech companies. Also in the same survey, electronic payment business such as mobile payment service is the leading business for FinTech companies in Southeast Asia with a huge 43%. Compared to the global trend, less than 20% of companies are involved with the electronic payment business according to lists compiled by CB Insights in 2017. This shows that Southeast Asia FinTech business still have a long way to go to compete with the FinTech in Europe/USA. FinTech startups in Southeast Asia is increasing in the past few years. Vietnam-based company, Service, Coins.ph from the Philippines and Funding Society from Singapore are few examples of FinTech startups based in Southeast Asia. The Southeast Asia region have the potential to become the main hub for FinTech startups across the world. As researched by Iwasaki (2018), according to statistics compiled by CB Insights showed that Venture capital investments in FinTech startups in Southeast Asia snowballed from $11 million in 2012 to $177 million in 2015 (see Figure 3). The Vietnamese government is developing a national financial inclusion strategy which it plans to issue in 2020. The State Bank of Vietnam (SBV) established its FinTech steering committee and a regulatory sandbox framework that the new framework will allow FinTech companies and financial institutions to test new products and services under SBV's close supervision prior to being introduced to the market (Fintechnews, 2018).

The main technologies and business models used by FinTech companies in Southeast Asia are commonly copied from developed countries and China (Iwasaki, 2018). There is little importance on the originality of the technologies and business models in FinTech and that is why there is many FinTech companies in Southeast Asia that are involved in the same businesses. This is evident in the lists by CB Insights where all countries in Southeast Asia is home to at least one FinTech company specializing in electronic payment business. FinTech business in Southeast Asia adopt a business models which combines both high-tech and low-tech models. For example, in situations where mobile payments are available, those services cannot be fully accessed from mobile devices and must be complemented by ancillary services provided by small retailers.

FinTech is known for its financial services by using technology. There are four characteristics of FinTech that can be seen in Southeast Asia. Firstly, a mobile payment service. This is because it can be used even by people that do not have bank accounts. In addition by using smartphone customer can load money into the accounts for paying cash to connect retailers or other

Figure 3. FinTech investment in Asia
Source: E27, 2017

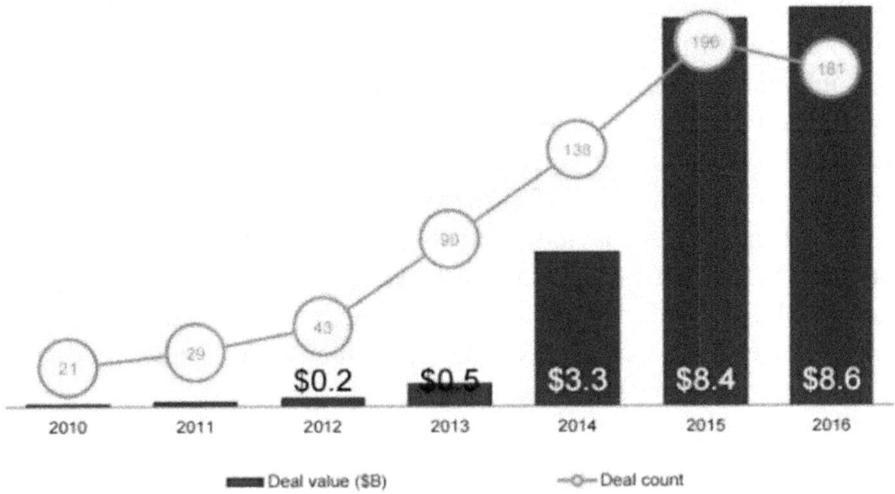

outlets in the local community. Secondly, mobile services allow cash to be transfer using only a mobile phone. Using electronic payments are used as part of their effort to create a domestic infrastructure such as in Thailand and Singapore. Thirdly, transferring cash services to overseas. This is because the services have evolved to meet the demand of a region in which a huge amount of people travel overseas for work. It is easier, cheaper and faster than the traditional way. Last but not least, lending services based on the use of alternative data. They collect and analyze digital footprints and use this information to compensate for or provide alternative data.

Singapore is the home to the most significant share of FinT`ech ventures in ASEAN with 39%. The development of financial infrastructure and supportive regulatory policies have position Singapore well to compete with other global FinTech hubs such a Hong Kong and London. Indonesia, Malaysia as well as Thailand are fast catching up as preferred FinTech home, supported by high mobile adoption, rising rates of internet penetration and increasingly urban, literate and young population. Singapore has the highest online populations where 74.5% of the population has access to the internet. Followed by Malaysia in second place with 70.9% of the population are fond of the internet. While Thailand is in the last place having 33.9% of the population.

CONCLUSION

In conclusion, FinTech industry provides the opportunity in transforming the financial sector to be more advanced by providing a variety of business models and market resolutions which will greatly improve financial services in comparison with traditional ways. Furthermore, in consideration with the affluently trends of FinTech in many countries may find it helpful in ruminating to fully embrace FinTech as the primary sector of future financing. FinTech may replace cash payment and ultimately moving towards e-payment, although many may still prefer using cash, with the involvement in e-payment, publics may have a wide variety of payment methods. Eventually, becoming a cashless society. As current topics suggests, the FinTech industry does not seem to be deserted anytime soon.

REFERENCES

Anshari, M., Almunawar, M.N., & Masri, M. (2019b). Financial Technology and Disruptive Innovation in Business. *International Journal of Asian Business and Information Management.*

Anshari, M., Almunawar, M. N., Masri, M., & Hamdan, M. (2019a). *Digital Marketplace and FinTech to Support Agriculture Sustainability. In Energy Procedia.* Elsevier.

Arner, D. W., Barberis, J. N., & Buckle, R. P. (2015). *The Evolution of FinTech: A New Post-Crisis Paradigm?* Retrieved December 10, 2018 from https://papers.ssrn.com/sol3/papers.cfm?abstract_id=2676553

Desai, F. (2015). *The Evolution of Fintech.* Retrieved from https://www.forbes.com/sites/falgunidesai/2015/12/13/the-evolution-of-fintech/2/#454f8b0e3dd0

Dhar, V. (2016). When to trust robots with decisions and when not to. *Harvard Business Review.*

Dorfleitner, G., Hornuf, L., Schmitt, M., & Weber, M. (2017). *FinTech in Germany.* Springer International Publishing. Retrieved from https://www.fintechweekly.com/fintech-definition

Fintechnews. (2018). *Fintech for financial inclusion in Vietnam*. Retrieved from http://fintechnews.sg/21608/vietnam/fintech-for-financial-inclusion-in-vietnam/

Gulamhuseinwala, I., Bull, T., & Lewis, S. (2015). *FinTech is gaining traction and young, high-income users are the early adopters*. Academic Press.

Iwasaki, K. (2018). Emergence of FinTech companies in Southeast Asia: Rising hopes of a solution to financial issues. *Pacific Business and Industries*, *18*(68), 1–32.

Milne, A. (2015). *Achieving European Policy Objectives through Financial Technology*. European Credit Research Institute.

Pisani, B. (2010). *Man vs machine: how stock trading got so complex*. Retrieved December 10, 2018 from https://www.cnbc.com/id/38978686

Schindler, J. (2017). *FinTech and Financial Innovation: Drivers and Depth*. Finance and Economics Discussion Series 2017-081. Washington, DC: Board of Governors of the Federal Reserve System.

Truong, O. (2016). *How FinTech industry is changing the world*. Retrieved December 10, 2018 from https://www.theseus.fi/bitstream/handle/10024/123633/TRUONG_OANH.pdf?sequence=1

Wonglimpiyarat, J. (2017). FinTech Crowdfunding of Thailand 4.0 Policy. *Journal of Private Equity*, *21*(1), 55–64. doi:10.3905/jpe.2017.21.1.055

Chapter 7
The Effects of Cybercrime on the Banking Sector in ASEAN

Cristi Spulbar
University of Craiova, Romania

Ramona Birau
Constantin Brâncuşi University of Targu Jiu, Romania

ABSTRACT

The main objective of this chapter is to investigate the effects of cybercrime on the banking sector in ASEAN. Global challenges on the evolution of cybercrime are in continuous dynamics in the case of emerging or developing countries, so that sustainable development plays an essential role. Moreover, the propagation effects can generate significant damages in the banking sector. Efficient bank management is essential in the context of providing advanced techniques for cyber security. Traditional cyber security measures are insufficient to ensure data protection and online information privacy. Consequently, investigations of cyber-criminal activity must become a priority especially in the context of globalization.

DOI: 10.4018/978-1-5225-9183-2.ch007

Copyright © 2020, IGI Global. Copying or distributing in print or electronic forms without written permission of IGI Global is prohibited.

INTRODUCTION

The digital age offers infinite opportunities for proliferation of cyber attacks based on highly sophisticated damaging tools. Nevertheless, in the case of cybercrime, developing countries such as ASEAN are characterized by incoherent and insufficient legal regulations issued by government authorities. The Association of Southeast Asian Nations also known as ASEAN was founded on 8 August 1967 in Bangkok, Thailand based on the ASEAN Declaration or Bangkok Declaration by the founding parent member countries, i.e Indonesia, Malaysia, Philippines, Singapore and Thailand. Afterwards, Brunei Darussalam joined the Association of Southeast Asian Nations (ASEAN) on 7 January 1984, and Viet Nam joined the ASEAN on 28 July 1995. Moreover, Lao PDR and Myanmar joined the ASEAN on 23 July 1997, and Cambodia joined the ASEAN on 30 April 1999.

The effects of cybercrime on the banking sector are extremely damaging, but also being propagated through innovative web-based technology and internet communications. In addition, cybercrime is distinguished by various dimensions such as: cyber terrorism, malware attacks, identity theft, cyber stalking, cyber espionage, spam attacks, copyright infringement, computer viruses. Cybercrime activity has reached a very high level in recent years mostly in developing countries. Official statistics provide alarming data on cyber attacks based on different patterns.

The action of effectively combating the negative phenomenon of cybercrime is based mainly on clear and predictable legal framework. Implementing rigorous cybersecurity standards are essential in reducing the effects of cybercrime. Malicious virtual applications represent one of the most prolific forms of cybercrime. Moreover, an action of great financial importance for bank customers is combating bank frauds as essential component of cybercrime that affects the banking system. A cybernetic hacking attack represents an illegal activity focused on obtaining financial benefits due to the deception, cheating and trust extortion of individuals, public institutions, business firms or financial institutions such as banks.

LITERATURE REVIEW

In the literature there are various research studies on investigating the effects of cybercrime on the banking sector. Hamin, Othman and Selamat (2016) have provided an elaborate perspective on financial investigation of cyber terrorist financing and have highlighted the difficulties faced by law enforcement considering the technical, operational and legal challenges with regard to these very sensitive issues. Shekokar, Shah, Mahajan and Rachh (2015) have conducted a research study on detection and prevention of phishing attacks and provided an alternative prevention solution focused on examining the hyperlinks in the source code of the email webpage and the overall appearance of the website.

Bregant and Bregant (2014) have conducted a detailed research study on computer and cyber crimes and have identified several main categories of these criminal activities such as: unauthorized access or hacking, fraud and identity theft, industrial espionage, and general abuse of resources. Moreover, Arumuga Perumal (2008) has investigated the impact of cyber crime on virtual banking and have concluded that cybercriminals have a prolific activity, especially in terms of phishing techniques used to steal personal finances and to manage identity theft with global consequences.

Mongid (2015) has analyzed important issues regarding cost efficiency of the ASEAN banking market and has concluded that the cost efficiency score for Brunei is 58%, for Indonesia is 70%, for Cambodia is 60%, for Laos is 62%, for Myanmar is 48%, for Malaysia is 63%, for Singapore is 80%, for Thailand is 79%, for Phillippines is 67%, and for Vietnam is 69%. Furthermore, Syadullah (2018) has provided an interesting approach on ASEAN Banking Integration Framework (ABIF) and has also discussed concluding issues regarding the level of bank efficiency in ASEAN countries.

Noman, Gee and Isa (2017) have investigated relevant aspects regarding the impact of the competition on financial stability of the banking sector in ASEAN countries and have revealed the existence of a non-linear relationship between competition and financial stability of the banking sector. Moreover, Pradhan, Arvin, Hall and Norman (2017) have examined the linkages between banking sector depth, trade openness, and economic growth based on a panel data set which includes the ASEAN regional forum countries for the period 1961–2012 by using panel cointegration and causality tests and have concluded that there was a general long-run equilibrium relationship among trade openness, banking sector depth and economic growth.

Kim DO, Chu and Nguyen (2017) have conducted a detailed research study on ASEAN financial integration and Vietnamese banking system and have concluded that Vietnamese banks are characterized by a relatively low level of development which makes them vulnerable compared to foreign banks. In addition, Kim Do, Nguyen and Le (2017) have investigated the effects of the credit boom on the soundness of Vietnamese commercial banks and have suggested that credit risk management requires improvements and rapid credit growth generates risks that should not be ignored.

Nguyen (2018) has conducted an interesting empirical study on implications of diversification on cost and profit efficiency of commercial banks in selected ASEAN countries and has revealed that more income - diversified banks had lower overall cost efficiency, while more asset - diversified banks had only lower persistent cost efficiency. On the other hand, Wong and Deng (2016) have conducted an empirical research study on banking efficiency based on a sample data pannel of 39 banks collected for certain member countries in Association of Southeast Asian Nations (ASEAN) and have suggested that large - sized banks in ASEAN are less cost efficient.

Antonescu and Birau (2014) have investigated relevant issues on financial and non - financial implications of cybercrimes in emerging countries and have concluded that the phenomenon of cybercrime is an inevitability of modern era due to recent advances in information technology. In addition, Lagazio, Sherif and Cushman (2014) have conducted a research study on the impact of cyber crimes on financial sector and highlighted potential vulnerabilities on the strategic behavior of financial companies such as: increasingly exaggerated expenses on defence and persistent under - reporting of cybercrime incidents.

Powell and McMillan (2017) have analyzed essential issues regarding bank risk in Malaysia and have revealed that Malaysian banks are characterized by significantly lower risks than the ASEAN region. Moreover, Tahir and Mongid (2013) have investigated the inter - relationship between bank cost efficiency, capital and risk-taking in ASEAN banking and have concluded that bank cost efficiency is the foundation for banks' capital position and risk-taking.

Baker (1999) have provided a detailed analysis of fraud on the Internet and have identified certain sensitive areas such as securities sales and trading, electronic commerce, and the rapid growth of Internet companies. In a complementary manner, Sanusi, Rameli and Isa (2015) have conducted a relevant empirical research study on identification and prevention of fraud schemes in the banking institutions considering that potential victims can be among others, shareholders, depositors, borrowers, the staff and even the banking institution itself.

Chowbe (2011) has provided an exhaustive approach to identifying the characteristic features of cyber criminality and the author has concluded that there are two main categories of cybercrimes, ie the first where the computer is instrument and the second where computer is incidental. On the other hand, Uche (2001) has investigated relevant aspects on the phenomenon of fraud in the Nigerian banking industry the author has suggested that corruption and drug trafficking activities have contributed to the growth of fraudulent activities.

Lokman, Ilyas and Tsuchiyac (2017) have conducted a research study on the impact of phishing attack on online banking and have concluded that the use of online banking platforms to perform these cybercrime activities affects the user's loyalty and interest in online banking. In addition, More, Jadhav and Nalawade (2015) have conducted a research study on the relationship between online banking or e-banking and cyber crimes attacks or computer network attack and have identified several categories of such criminal activities such as: stealing an organization's intellectual property, confiscating online bank accounts, creating and distributing viruses on other computers, posting confidential business information on the Internet and disrupting a country's critical national infrastructure.

Ali, Ali, Surendran and Thomas (2017) have investigated the effects of cyber threats on customer's behaviour in e-banking services and have suggested that it is necessary to increase customer's awareness about available cybercrimes in the very vulnerable context regarding online banking and sensitive financial data. Moreover, Karim (2016) has investigated relevant issues regarding cyber and other technology related crime in the banking sector of Bangladesh and has identified some of the most common such criminal activities, namely: Automated Teller Machine (ATM) frauds, and E-Money Laundering.

Broadhurst (2006) has provided an exhaustive framework on developments in the global law enforcement of cybercrime and has suggested that cybercrime most often happens to be traditional crimes, such as: fraud, identify theft, child pornography. In a much more specialized manner, Akinyomi (2012) has discussed issues of great interest on the dynamic phenomenon of fraud and certain ways of prevention in the Nigerian banking sector and has also revealed the main negative consequences, namely loss of revenue and loss of customers' confidence.

Gaumer, Mortier and Moutaib (2016) have investigated the relationship between financial institutions and cyber crime considering the importance of information systems for cyber criminals which implements a series of criminal activities such as social engineering or advanced persistent threats. Moreover, Choudhury, Basak and Guha (2013) have conducted a detailed analysis on the various implications of the cybercrimes and have identified several categories of this growing phenomenon, such as: child pornography, fraud, e-mail abuse (traditional forms) but also more sophisticated forms like cyber – terrorism.

Leukfeldt, Lavorgna and Kleemans (2017) have conducted a highly documented empirical research study on the activity of cybercriminals operating in phishing and malware attacks and have also provided an innovative insight into the importance of using complementary methods of preventing cybercrime such as virtual ethnography and interviews with cybercrime offenders. In addition, Al – Alawi (2014) has investigated in an interesting manner relevant aspects regarding computer crimes and computer forensics and has also suggested that customer awareness' is essential in order to combat cybercrimes.

AN EMERGING APPROACH TO UNDERSTANDING ASEAN COUNTRIES

The Association of Southeast Asian Nations (ASEAN) has a relatively recent but very interesting history. Moreover, the aims and purposes of the Association of Southeast Asian Nations (ASEAN) highlight the opportunity for efficient functioning as well as for the sustainable development of this group of states. The founding parent countries of the ASEAN are the following: Indonesia, Malaysia, the Philippines, Singapore, and Thailand, also known as the ASEAN - 5. Currently, the Association of Southeast Asian Nations (ASEAN) includes 10 member states, ie: Brunei Darussalam, Cambodia, Indonesia, Laos (Lao PDR), Malaysia, Myanmar, Philippines, Singapore, Thailand, and Vietnam.

The Association of Southeast Asian Nations (ASEAN) was founded in the base of the Bangkok Declaration also known as the ASEAN Declaration which was adopted by the Foreign Ministers at the 1st ASEAN Ministerial Meeting in Bangkok, Thailand on 8 August 1967. In addition, the aims and purposes of the Association of Southeast Asian Nations (ASEAN) have been very clearly stated in the Bangkok Declaration as follows:

1. *To accelerate the economic growth, social progress and cultural development in the region through joint endeavours in the spirit of equality and partnership in order to strengthen the foundation for a prosperous and peaceful community of South-East Asian Nations;*
2. *To promote regional peace and stability through abiding respect for justice and the rule of law in the relationship among countries of the region and adherence to the principles of the United Nations Charter;*
3. *To promote active collaboration and mutual assistance on matters of common interest in the economic, social, cultural, technical, scientific and administrative fields;*
4. *To provide assistance to each other in the form of training and research facilities in the educational, professional, technical and administrative spheres;*
5. *To collaborate more effectively for the greater utilization of their agriculture and industries, the expansion of their trade, including the study of the problems of international commodity trade, the improvement of their transportation and communications facilities and the raising of the living standards of their peoples;*
6. *To promote South-East Asian studies;*
7. *To maintain close and beneficial cooperation with existing international and regional organizations with similar aims and purposes, and explore all avenues for even closer cooperation among themselves.*

The Association of Southeast Asian Nations (ASEAN) member countries focus on achieving a higher level of economic and financial performance in the coming years. The ASEAN Banking Integration Framework (ABIF) is a major project with complex implications that will contribute significantly to the sustainable development of financial services. However, the Qualified ASEAN Banks (QABs) plays an essential role in achieving the proposed objectives regarding the banking sector integration. The ASEAN member countries have optimistic expectations about the financial integration process. The ASEAN Banking Integration Framework (ABIF) has the maturity of the implementation limit in 2020, ie a relatively tight deadline.

A General Approach to the Concept of Cybercrime

In the literature there is no universally accepted definition of cybercrime. Online criminal activity has multiple negative implications in terms of banking system activity. Understanding cybercrime is a major challenge, especially in the context of the global economy. The concept of cyber crime has diversified consequences by reaching global dimensions. Moreover, cybercrime is also known as computer-oriented crime or computer crime. Cybercrime is a very lucrative activity considering the high amounts of money obtained through bank fraud or money laundering. Moreover, a phishing scam represents an illegal activity that follows the user's deception in order to obtain quick and easy financial gains. However, these cybercrime activities are very hard to follow by law enforcement.

The Internet World Stats classify the main regions of the world based on Internet Usage and World Population Statistics updated as of June 30, 2018, and revealed that the number of Internet users is the following: Africa – 464.923.169, Asia – 2.062.197.366, Europe – 705.064.923, Latin America / Caribbean – 438.248.446, Middle East – 164.037.259, North America – 345.660.847, Oceania / Australia – 28.439.277. In addition, the penetration rate (% Pop.) is the following: Africa - 36.1%, Asia - 49.0%, Europe - 85.2%, Latin America / Caribbean - 67.2%, Middle East - 64.5%, North America - 95.0%, and Oceania / Australia - 68.9%. The penetration rate (% Pop.) measured globally is 55.1% at June 30, 2018 (Internet World Stats, n.d).

The legal perspective is still fragile in terms of providing appropriate punishments for cybercrime. In other words, according to the international classification criteria, the founding countries of the ASEAN are the following: Indonesia, Malaysia, the Philippines, Singapore, and Thailand, i.e ASEAN - 5. Moreover, it is important to note that all the founding members of the ASEAN are developing countries.The generating causes of cybercrime in the banking sector generally have a purely financial explanation based on an attempt to achieve easy winnings. Generally, the fight against cybercrime is chaotic in the absence of solid cyber security strategy. Unfortunately, developing countries are very vulnerable due to the lack of an appropriate legal framework.

As a comparative analysis, the Internet World Stats classify the main regions of the world based on Internet Usage and World Population Statistics updated as of March 30, 2017, and revealed that the number of Internet users is the following: Africa - 345.676.501, Asia - 1.873.856.654, Europe - 636.971.824, Latin America / Caribbean - 385.919.382, Middle East- 141.931.765, North America - 320.068.243, Oceania / Australia - 27.549.054. Moreover, the penetration rate (% Pop.) is the following: Africa - 27.7%, Asia – 45.2%, Europe – 77.4%, Latin America / Caribbean – 59.6%, Middle East- 56.7%, North America - 88.1%, Oceania / Australia - 68.1% (Internet World Stats, n.d).

Broadly speaking, Antonescu and Birau (2014) suggested that cybercrime activity includes a wide range of illegal activities such as: cyber bullying, cyber terrorism, identity theft, cyber stalking, virtual pornography (via the Internet), cyber espionage (illegally obtaining confidential data), computer hacking, computer fraud, online harassment, phishing, online piracy, blackmailing proceeding, cyber extortion, spam attacks, copyright infringement, computer virus programs (installing malicious software programs such as Trojan horse viruses). Social platforms are one of the most common and frequent manifestation of cyberspace impact on modern human lives but the effects of cybercrime on the banking sector imply severe consequences, especially in the context of globalization.

The extremely rapid technological evolution leads to the intensification of cyber attacks. It is very important to emphasize that the transmission channels of cyber crimes include certain components of the Internet, ie: e-mails, websites (in particular e-commerce sites), chat rooms, discussion groups, instant messaging (IM), open forums, social networks, messenger or other online services. On the other hand, Antonescu and Birau (2014) have also highlighted the non-financial implications of cybercrimes which include a number of extremely important issues such as: loss of customer confidence, negative publicity (image scandals, reputational damage), diminishing productivity, business discontinuity, loss of confidential customer or company data (informations), unauthorized access to certain product innovations, loss of intellectual property and many others.

The internet banking or e-banking is a significant advance in the implementation of innovative technologies in order to provide more efficient banking services. However, a socio-psychological approach can provide an intrinsic, very interesting insight into the personality of these cybercriminals. Birau (2016 a) has conducted a research study on the influence of sociopathic behavior in the case of corporate management and has suggested that a sociopath is manipulative, devious, arrogant, defiant, offensive, unpredictable, impulsive, insincerity, and unreliable, but can also conceal his real intentions in order to obtain an advantage. It is rather a common activity for cyber criminals to carry out illegal activities on hacking bank systems.

The web banking application can not always provide maximum security against cyber attacks. Birau (2016 b) has investigated the influence of psychiatric disorders and internet addiction on human behavior and has revealed that the reality can be very deformed in cyberspace but the frequently accessed informations have significantly increase the users vulnerability regarding potential virtual dangers. Moreover, Birau (2017) has also analyzed the implications of free internet access on the sociopathic and psychopathic personality based on childhood trauma and suggested that Internet has a very dark side in terms of criminality considering the fact that free internet access provides significant opportunities in committing serious offenses such as child pornography, trafficking in human beings, sexual exploitation of children and women, enforced prostitution, the exploitation of children in begging, organ trafficking and many others.

Analyzing the Vulnerabilities of the Banking System

The banking system is an essential component of economic growth and macroeconomic stability, especially in the context of globalization. The evolution of the banking sector in each country is affected by various changes in the international banking and financial environment. A well - functioning financial system allows an economy to fully exploit its growth potential by providing the necessary financing sources for investment opportunities at minimal cost. Thus, a robust and dynamic economy needs a financial system capable of channeling financial sources to business entrepreneurs who have the capacity to make productive investments. Online banking is a relatively new component of the banking system, very attractive but very vulnerable to cyber attacks.

The World Bank provides a classification of world's countries or economies based on four main groups according to the income criterion, ie low, lower-middle, upper-middle, and high based on gross national income (GNI) per capita, value calculated in the the currency of United States (dollars) by using the World Bank Atlas method. By considering this selection criterion, can be highlighted the following classification of countries for the current 2019 fiscal year by using as a criterion the GNI per capita level for 2017 fiscal year: low-income economies ($ 995 or less), lower middle-income economies (greater than or equal to $ 996 but but less than or equal to $ 3,895), upper middle-income economies (greater than or equal to $ 3,896 but less than or equal to $ 12,055) and high-income economies ($ 12,056 or more). However, Romania is included in the category of upper-middle-income economies ($ 3,896 to $ 12,055).

The official classification of the world economies for 2017 fiscal year provides a relevant perspective for understanding the level of development of the knowledge-based society concept in terms of income levels. The category of low - income economies ($ 995 or less) includes the following countries: Afghanistan, Guinea – Bissau, Sierra Leone, Benin, Haiti, Somalia, Burkina Faso, Korea Dem. People's Republic, South Sudan, Burundi, Liberia, Syrian Arab Republic, Central African Republic, Madagascar, Tajikistan, Chad, Malawi, Tanzania, Comoros, Mali, Togo, Congo, Dem. Republic, Mozambique, Uganda, Eritrea, Nepal, Yemen Republic, Ethiopia, Niger, Zimbabwe, Gambia, The Rwanda, Guinea, and Senegal.

The category of lower – middle - income economies ($ 996 to $ 3,895) includes the following countries: Angola, Indonesia, Papua New Guinea, Bangladesh, Kenya, Philippines, Bhutan, Kiribati, São Tomé and Principe, Bolivia, Kosovo, Solomon Islands, Cabo Verde, Kyrgyz Republic, Sri Lanka, Cambodia, Lao PDR, Sudan, Cameroon, Lesotho, Swaziland, Congo, Republic, Mauritania, Timor – Leste, Côte d'Ivoire, Micronesia, Fed. Sts., Tunisia, Djibouti, Moldova, Ukraine, Egypt, Arab Republic, Mongolia, Uzbekistan, El Salvador, Morocco, Vanuatu, Georgia, Myanmar, Vietnam, Ghana, Nicaragua, West Bank and Gaza, Honduras, Nigeria, Zambia, India, and Pakistan.

The category of upper – middle – income economies ($ 3,896 to $ 12,055) includes the following countries: Albania, Fiji, Namibia, Algeria, Gabon, Nauru, American Samoa, Grenada, Paraguay, Armenia, Guatemala, Peru, Azerbaijan, Guyana, Romania, Belarus, Iran, Islamic Republic, Russian Federation, Belize, Iraq, Samoa, Bosnia and Herzegovina, Jamaica, Serbia, Botswana, Jordan, South Africa, Brazil, Kazakhstan, St. Lucia, Bulgaria, Lebanon, St. Vincent and the Grenadines, China, Libya, Suriname, Colombia, Macedonia, FYR, Thailand, Costa Rica, Malaysia, Tonga, Cuba, Maldives, Turkey, Dominica, Marshall Islands, Turkmenistan, Dominican Republic, Mauritius, Tuvalu, Equatorial Guinea, Mexico, Venezuela, RB, Ecuador, and Montenegro.

The category of high - income economies ($ 12,056 or more) includes the following countries: Andorra, Germany, Oman, Antigua and Barbuda, Gibraltar, Palau, Argentina, Greece, Panama, Aruba, Greenland, Poland, Australia, Guam, Portugal, Austria, Hong Kong SAR China, Puerto Rico, Bahamas, Hungary, Qatar, Bahrain, Iceland, San Marino, Barbados, Ireland, Saudi Arabia, Belgium, Isle of Man, Seychelles, Bermuda, Israel, Singapore, British Virgin Islands, Italy, Sint Maarten (Dutch part), Brunei Darussalam, Japan, Slovak Republic, Canada, Korea, Republic, Slovenia, Cayman Islands, Kuwait, Spain, Channel Islands, Latvia, St. Kitts and Nevis, Chile, Liechtenstein, St. Martin (French part), Croatia, Lithuania, Sweden, Curaçao, Luxembourg, Switzerland, Cyprus, Macao SAR, China, Taiwan, China Czech Republic, Malta, Trinidad and Tobago, Denmark, Monaco, Turks and Caicos Islands, Estonia, Netherlands, United Arab Emirates, Faroe Islands, New Caledonia, United Kingdom, Finland, New Zealand, United States, France, Northern Mariana Islands, Uruguay, French Polynesia, Norway, and Virgin Islands (U.S.).

The most recent FTSE Annual Country Classification Review which was released on September 2018, provides the following classification categories, ie: developed, advanced emerging, secondary emerging and frontier. The developed countries category includes the following: Australia, Austria, Belgium/Luxembourg, Canada, Denmark, Finland, France, Germany, Hong Kong, Ireland, Israel, Italy, Japan, Netherlands, New Zealand, Norway, Poland, Portugal, Singapore, South Korea, Spain, Sweden, Switzerland, UK and USA. The advanced emerging countries category includes the following: Brazil, Czech Republic, Greece, Hungary, Malaysia, Mexico, South Africa, Taiwan, Thailand and Turkey. Moreover, the secondary emerging countries category includes the following: Chile, China (to be reclassified as Secondary Emerging, commencing from June 2019), Colombia, Egypt, India, Indonesia, Kuwait (reclassified as Secondary Emerging, effective in two tranches: 50% on 24 September 2018 and 50% on 24 December 2018), Pakistan, Peru, Philippines, Qatar, Russia, Saudi Arabia (to be reclassified as Secondary Emerging, commencing from March 2019) and UAE. The last category, namely the frontier countries category includes the following: Argentina, Bahrain, Bangladesh, Botswana, Bulgaria, Côte d'Ivoire, Croatia, Cyprus, Estonia, Ghana, Iceland (to be reclassified as Frontier, effective with the annual review of the FTSE Frontier Index in September 2019), Jordan, Kazakhstan, Kenya, Latvia, Lithuania, Macedonia, Malta, Mauritius, Morocco, Nigeria,

Oman, Palestine, Romania, Serbia, Slovakia, Slovenia, Sri Lanka, Tunisia and Vietnam.

Numerous research studies have been conducted in the literature regarding the banking system and its various implications on the economy. Spulbar and Nițoi (2012) have provided a very interesting comparative analysis of banking systems. The analysis of each banking system is divided in a balanced and uniform manner, around three main criteria, i.e: the historical criterion, the descriptive criterion, and the performance criterion. Although the activity of banking institutions with regard to banking products and services is universal, in the organization and functioning activity of various institutions of the banking system, such as commercial banks, savings banks, credit co-operatives, mortgage banks, credit unions banks, there are numerous differences.

Understanding the way in which financial structures work is essential when it comes to reforming them. Restricting access to the financial market is one of the reasons why financial systems differ, and removing them will implicitly lead to accelerating financial convergence. Spulbar and Nitoi (2015) have conducted an empirical research study on cost efficiency of commercial banks in Central and Eastern Europe and have concluded that a high level of macroeconomic stability has a direct impact on the efficiency of commercial banks. In addition, Spulbar and Nitoi (2016) have investigated the relationship between bank efficiency and risk and productivity patterns in Romanian banking system and suggested the fact that there is a direct interdependence between a reduced risk of failure, a higher level of liquidity, a higher rate of financial intermediation, a higher ROE, and efficiency.

The financial structure is traditionally measured by the relative size of the different components of the financial market. A larger financial market is actually a channel for financial assets. In other words, the basic function of the banking system is based on collecting savings and after that channeling financial assets to profitable investments considering bank loans or other banking services. It is not yet known which systems are performing better, financial systems based on banks or financial systems based on financial markets. The structures and functions of financial systems are very complex and in a continuous change, especially in terms of globalization. These banking systems are made up of very heterogeneous financial institutions, ie: commercial banks, insurance companies, investment funds, capital markets and many others.

The vulnerability of the banking systems to cyber attacks is mostly generated by structural and functional fragility. Financial stability is the context in which the financial system works effectively and is able to withstand relatively large economic and financial shocks. Consequently, financial stability is a prerequisite for sustainable economic growth on a non-inflationary basis. Therefore, maintaining financial stability is an important concern of central banks and financial sector supervisors worldwide. Financial stability is also a permanent challenge, largely due to the rapid pace of innovations and the continuous structural evolution of financial systems. Relatively recent changes have included the development of a whole range of financial instruments and an increase in the number of new cross -sectoral participants in the financial markets. These developments have generated an increased number of possible channels through which economic and financial shocks can be generated and propagated with significant consequences.

The globalization process involves certain challenges and risks. Global integration and increased mobility of capital have conducted to a high degree of exposure of the financial system regarding the dynamic changes in financial investor perceptions. In addition, international trade and financial linkages have intensified the cross-border transmission of financial shocks. Globalization also influences the activity of central banks in the case of their main two functions, ie: establishing monetary policy and ensuring financial stability.

CONCLUSION

The concept of cybercrime is characterized by various meanings, given the explosive evolution of this criminal activity worldwide. The rapid expansion of Internet banking services in ASEAN represents significant progress in achieving effective management. ASEAN cyber security is an area of great interest taking into account both its financial and non-financial implications. However, the accelerated growth of the cybercrime phenomenon influences the normal functioning of the banking system in ASEAN.

Banking network communication are characterized by certain vulnerabilities that can be exploited by cyber criminals. Online banking fraud and money laundering are very profitable cybercrime activities that can provide very high and easy financial profits. Consequently, cyber criminals may engage in illegal activities from a very long distance in order to perform online banking frauds. Cyber risk management is very important in combating online criminal attacks. Generally, detection and prevention are a sustainable alternative for improving bank risk management. Anti - phishing measures aim to protect the client of the bank system from the unauthorized access of cyber criminals.

Communication technologies are a very useful advancement in the context of the globalized economy, but are also a major vulnerability in terms of banking system security. The cyberspace is a very attractive domain for busy business people or simple citizens who are conducting their online banking transactions. The topic of cybercrime also includes the so called phishing which is a certain category of cybercrime related with the bank fraud phenomenon. The activity of phishing includes criminal activity that affects sensitive personally identifying information, passwords logins, online banking details and credit card information.

REFERENCES

Akinyomi, O. J. (2012) Examination of fraud in the Nigerian banking sector and its prevention. *Asian Journal Of Management Research*, *3*(1), 184 – 192.

Al-Alawi, A. I. (2014). Cybercrimes, Computer Forensics and their Impact in Business Climate: Bahrain Status, *Research. Journal of Business and Management*, *8*, 139–156. doi:10.3923/rjbm.2014.139.156

Ali, L., Ali, F., Surendran, P., & Thomas, B. (2017). The Effects of Cyber Threats on Customer's Behaviour in e-Banking Services. *International Journal of e-Education, e-Business, e-Management and e-Learning,* *7*(1), 70 – 78. doi:10.17706/ijeeee.2017.7.1.7

Antonescu, M., & Birau, R. (2014). Financial and non-financial implications of cybercrimes in emerging countries. *Procedia - Economics and Finance*, *32*, 618 – 621. doi:10.1016/S2212-5671(15)01440-9

Arumuga Perumal, S. (2008). *Impact of Cyber Crime on Virtual Banking*. Available at SSRN: https://ssrn.com/abstract=1289190

Baker, R. C. (1999). An analysis of fraud on the Internet. *Internet Research, Emerald Publishing Limited*, *9*(5), 348–360. doi:10.1108/10662249910297750

Bhasin, M. L. (2015). Menace of Frauds in the Indian Banking Industry: An Empirical Study. *Australian Journal of Business and Management Research, 4*(12). Available at SSRN: https://ssrn.com/abstract=2676466

Birau, R. (2016a). A framework for investigating the influence of sociopathic behavior in the case of corporate management. *International Journal of Core Engineering and Management, 3*(8), 9 – 11.

Birau, R. (2016b). Investigating the influence of psychiatric disorders and internet addiction on human behavior. *International Journal of Business Quantitative Economics and Applied Management Research, 3*(6), 48 – 52.

Birau, R. (2017). The implications of free internet access on the sociopathic and psychopathic personality based on childhood trauma. *International Journal of Core Engineering and Management, 4*(1), 16 - 20.

Bregant, J., & Bregant, R. (2014). Cybercrime and Computer Crime. In The Encyclopedia of Criminology and Criminal Justice. John Wiley & Sons, Inc. Doi:10.1002/9781118517383.wbeccj244

Broadhurst, R. (2006). Developments in the Global Law Enforcement of Cyber-Crime. *Policing: an International Journal of Police Strategies and Management, 29*(3), 408 – 433. Available at SSRN: https://ssrn.com/abstract=2089650

Choudhury, R. R., Basak, S., & Guha, D. (2013). Cyber Crimes - Challenges & Solutions. *International Journal of Computer Science and Information Technologies, 4*(5), 729 - 732.

Chowbe, V. S. (2011). *An Introduction to Cyber Crime: General Considerations*. Available at SSRN: https://ssrn.com/abstract=1766234

FTSE Country Classification. (n.d.). Retrieved from http://www.ftse.com/products/indices/country-classificatio.

Gaumer, Q., Mortier, S., & Moutaib, A. (2016). Financial institutions and cyber crime – Between vulnerability and security. *Financial Stability Review, 20*, 45 - 52.

Hamin, Z., Othman, R., & Selamat, H. S. (2016). Funding terror in cyberspace: Challenges in the financial investigation of cyber terrorist financing. *Information Journal Elsevier B., 19*(10), 4725–4730.

Internet World Stats. (n.d.). Retrieved from https://www.internetworldstats.com/stats.htm

Karim, S. S. (2016). Cyber-crime Scenario in Banking Sector of Bangladesh: An Overview. *The Cost and Management, 44*(2), 13 – 19.

Kim, H. T., Chu, L. K., & Nguyen, P. M. (2017). Vietnamese Banking System in the Context of ASEAN Financial Integration. *International Journal of Financial Research, 8*(1). doi:10.5430/ijfr.v8n1p155

Kim Do, H. T., Nguyen, N. T. M., & Le, T. H. (2017). Effects of the Credit Boom on the Soundness of Vietnamese Commercial Banks. *International Journal of Financial Research, 8*(3). Doi:10.5430/ijfr.v8n3p57

Lagazio, M., Sherif, N., & Cushman, M. (2014). A multi-level approach to understanding the impact of cyber crime on the financial sector. *Computers & Security, Elsevier, 45*, 58–74. doi:10.1016/j.cose.2014.05.006

Leukfeldt, E. R., Lavorgna, A. & Kleemans, E. R. (2017). Organised Cybercrime or Cybercrime that is Organised? An Assessment of the Conceptualisation of Financial Cybercrime as Organised Crime. *European Journal on Criminal Policy and Research, 23*(3), 287 – 300. doi:10.100710610-016-9332-z

Lokman, A. M., Ilyas, S. S. M., & Tsuchiyac, T. (2017). A Qualitative Exploration of Phishing and its Affect to Trust in Online Banking. *International Journal of Control Theory and Applications, 10*(30), 63-70.

Mongid, A. (2015). Cost Efficiency of the ASEAN Banking Market. *International Business Management, 9*(7), 1580–1586. doi:10.3923/ibm.2015.1580.1586

More, M. M., Jadhav, M. P., & Nalawade, K. M. (2015). Online Banking and Cyber Attacks: The Current Scenario. *International Journal of Advanced Research in Computer Science and Software Engineering, 5*(12), 743 - 749.

Nguyen, T. L. A. (2018). Diversification and bank efficiency in six ASEAN countries. *Global Finance Journal*, *37*, 57 - 78.. doi:10.1016/j.gfj.2018.04.004

Noman, A. H. M., Gee, C. S., & Isa, C. R. (2017). Does competition improve financial stability of the banking sector in ASEAN countries? An empirical analysis. *PLoS ONE. Europe PMC*, *12*(5), e0176546. doi:10.1371/journal.pone.0176546 PMID:28486548

Powell, R. J., & McMillan, D. (2017). New perspectives on bank risk in Malaysia. *Cogent Economics & Finance, Taylor & Francis*, *5*(1). doi:10.1080/23322039.2017.1326217

Pradhan, R. P., Arvin, M. B., Hall, J. H., & Norman, N. R. (2017). ASEAN economic growth, trade openness and banking-sector depth: The nexus. *EconomiA. Elsevier B.*, *18*, 359–379. doi:10.1016/j.econ.2017.05.002

Sanusi, Z. M., Rameli, M. N. F., & Isa, Y. M. (2015). Fraud Schemes in the Banking Institutions: Prevention Measures to Avoid Severe Financial Loss, 7th International Conference on Financial Criminology 2015, 13-14 April 2015, Wadham College, Oxford, United Kingdom. *Procedia Economics and Finance*, *28*, 107–113. doi:10.1016/S2212-5671(15)01088-6

Secretariat A. S. E. A. N. World Bank. (2013). *ASEAN Integration Monitoring Report*. Jakarta: ASEAN Secretariat and the World Bank. Retrieved from https://openknowledge. worldbank.org/handle/10986/16695

Shekokar, N. M., Shah, C., Mahajan, M., & Rachh, S. (2015). An Ideal Approach for Detection and Prevention of Phishing Attacks, ICAC3′15. *Procedia Computer Science*, *49*, 82–91. doi:10.1016/j.procs.2015.04.230

Spulbar, C., & Nițoi, M. (2012). *Comparative analysis of banking systems*. SITECH Publishing House Craiova.

Spulbar, C., & Nitoi, M. (2015). An Examination of Banks' Cost Efficiency in Central and Eastern Europe. *Procedia Economics and Finance*, *22*, 544–551. doi:10.1016/S2212-5671(15)00256-7

Spulbar, C., & Nitoi, M. (2016). The relationship between bank efficiency and risk and productivity patterns in Romanian banking system. *Romanian Journal of Economic Forecasting*, *19*(1), 39–53.

Sustainable Development knowledge Platform, Division For Sustainable Development, UN-DESA, the United Nations, Department of Economic and Social Affairs. (n.d.). Retrieved from https://sustainabledevelopment.un.org/

Syadullah, M. (2018) ASEAN Banking Efficiency Review Facing Financial Services Liberalization: The Indonesian Perspective. *Asian Development Policy Review*, *6*(2), 88-99. Doi:10.18488/journal.107.2018.62.88.99

Tahir, I. M., & Mongid, A. (2013). The Interrelationship between Bank Cost Efficiency, Capital and Risk-Taking in ASEAN Banking. *International Journal of Economics and Management Sciences*, *2*(12), 1 - 15. Available at SSRN: https://ssrn.com/abstract=2766904

The official website of the Association of Southeast Asian Nations. (n.d.). Retrieved from https://asean.org/

The official website of the European Commission – Eurostat. (n.d.). Retrieved from http://ec.europa.eu/eurostat/

The official website of the UNESCO. (n.d.). Retrieved from www.unesco.org

The official website of the United Nations. (n.d.). Retrieved from http://www.un.org/

The official website of the World Bank. (n.d.). Retrieved from http://data.worldbank.org/-

Uche, C. U. (2001). Nigeria: Bank Fraud. *Journal of Financial Crime, Emerald Publishing Limited*, *8*(3), 265–275. doi:10.1108/eb025992

Wong, W. P., & Deng, Q. (2016). Efficiency analysis of banks in ASEAN countries, *Benchmarking. An International Journal, Emerald Publishing Limited*, *23*(7), 1798–1817. doi:10.1108/BIJ-11-2013-0102

Chapter 8
Financial Inclusion:
Does Fintech Help in Indonesia?

Dian Agustia
Universitas Airlangga, Indonesia

Nadia Anridho
Universitas Airlangga, Indonesia

ABSTRACT

Financial inclusion is a term that is used to describe easy access of financial products and services for everyone. G20 countries, including Indonesia, show high commitment to accelerate financial inclusion. Financial inclusion also facilitates the achievement of 17 Sustainable Development Goals. Fintech or digital financial technology is one of the most recent innovations in financial industry. It has grown at a rapid speed in the recent years. Fintech provides products and services with low costs, better quality, and stable financial landscape. With its flexibility and simplicity, Fintech may facilitate the offering of financial services to people who are "unbanked," or to small business at low cost and low risk. Hence, this chapter thoroughly discusses FinTech's role in supporting financial inclusion in Indonesia. Indonesia is one of the G20 countries that is committed to conduct financial inclusion. Specifically, this chapter elaborates financial inclusion, Fintech in Indonesia, and role of Fintech in supporting financial inclusion in Indonesia.

DOI: 10.4018/978-1-5225-9183-2.ch008

Copyright © 2020, IGI Global. Copying or distributing in print or electronic forms without written permission of IGI Global is prohibited.

INTRODUCTION

Financial inclusion is a term that used to describe easy access of financial products and services for everyone. It means that both individual and business have access to financial products and services, such as saving, payment, credit, and insurance. Everyone may choose financial products and services based on their needs.

Financial inclusion seeks to minimize the number of people who do not have financial access, especially banking. Therefore, it is expected that everyone has access to financial services in the future. Those financial services should be good quality, safe, and affordable to everyone in order to increase the community welfare. Financial services must be suitable with people's needs and have some easy requirements for them. Moreover, safe financial services are intended to protect people's rights and obligations from the possible risks posed by the services.

Financial inclusion is one of the most important parts of social and economy inclusion processes to drive economic growth. An inclusive financial system can be achieved through public access to financial services to improve economy capacity, which in turn can reduce economic inequality. Broader access to financial services is important to increase public participation in economics. With the ease in financial access, people can accept help in in preparing their daily lives, planning their long-term goals, and preventing any emergency situations.

Financial inclusion is one of the programs of G-20 countries. This program is a joint program of economic growth among G-20 countries. Therefore, G-20 countries, including Indonesia, are highly committed to accelerate financial inclusion to achieve economic growth. Financial inclusion also facilitates the achievement of 17 Sustainable Development Goals. The goals were formulated on July 19th 2014 and agreed on August 2015. It was also published in United Nations's (UN) resolution on October 21st 2015 and agreed by 193-member countries to use financial inclusion as a tool to achieve sustainable development. Meanwhile, those 17 Sustainable Development Goals include: 1) No Poverty; 2) Zero Hunger; 3) Good Health and Well-Being; 4) Quality Education; 5) Gender Equality; 6) Clean Water and Sanitation; 7) Affordable and Clean Energy; 8) Decent Work and Economic Growth; 9) Industry, Innovation, and Infrastructure; 10) Reduced Inequalities; 11) Sustainable Cities and

Communities; 12) Responsible Production and Consumption; 13) Climate Action; 14) Life Below Water; 15) Life On Land; 16) Peace, Justice, and Strong Institutions; and 17) Partnerships for the Goals.

FINTECH AS AN INNOVATION IN FINANCIAL INDUSTRY

Fintech or *digital financial technology* is one of innovations in financial industry. Fintech is a combination between financial service and technology that changes business model from conventional model to technology-based model. In conventional model, customer needs to go to the bank and deposit their money directly, while in technology-based model, long distance and real-time transactions can be done.

Fintech emphasizes the ease and economics of costs in capturing, sending, storing and analyzing data in digital form. Fintech utilizes technological innovations such as the internet, mobile phone, and data processing. Fintech has changed the availability of information and has reduced physical transactions and costs in producing and distributing financial products and services.

Fintech emerged when people need information technology in every aspect of their life. Fintech has grown rapidly in recent years because it provides low cost products and services, better quality, and a stable financial landscape. Fintech helps selling transactions and payment systems become more effective, efficient, and economical. Fintech also has better infrastructure, big data, data analytics, and mobile devices.

Fintech benefits its players in simplifying transaction chain, reducing operational cost and capital cost, as well as forming transaction information flows. Fintech startup companies offer more attractive services with more choices than traditional financial companies. With its flexibility and simplicity, fintech facilitates the offering of financial services to people who are not reachable and to small businesses at small costs and risks. In this case, Fintech is able to change the financial system while being able to replace and support the role of formal financial institutions.

During the Annual Meetings of International Monetary Fund (IMF) and the World Bank Group (WBG) on October 8-14, 2018, The Bali Fintech Agenda was launched. It is a framework to support the Sustainable Development Goals, especially for low-income country in which access to financial services is still low. It consists of 12 policy elements, such as: 1) Embrace the Promise of Fintech; 2) Enable New Technologies to Enhance Financial Service Provision; 3) Reinforce Competition and Commitment to Open, Free, and Contestable Markets; 4) Foster Fintech to Promote Financial Inclusion and Develop Financial Markets; 5) Monitor Developments Closely to Deepen Understanding of Evolving Financial Systems; 6) Adapt Regulatory Framework and Supervisory Practices for Orderly Development and Stability of the Financial System; 7) Safeguard the Integrity of Financial Systems; 8) Modernize Legal Frameworks to Provide an Enabling Legal Landscape; 9) Ensure the Stability of Domestic Monetary and Financial Systems; 10) Develop Robust Financial and Data Infrastructure to Sustain Fintech Benefits; 11) Encourage International Cooperation and Information-Sharing; and 12) Enhance Collective Surveillance of the International Monetary and Financial System. These elements are launched to help member countries to utilize the benefits and opportunities of financial technology that transforms the provision of banking services as well as to manage the inherent risks. It also helps member countries in developing their own domestic policy related to financial technology.

THE DEVELOPMENT OF FINTECH IN INDONESIA

Similar to other countries in the world, Fintech is also one of the fastest growing sectors in Indonesia. Arner, Barberis, and Buckley (2015) divided Fintech evolution into three different stages. The first stage is Fintech 1.0 in the year of 1866-1987. It was characterized by interconnected analogue activities and pioneered by telecommunications firms. The second stage is Fintech 2.0 in the year of 1987-2008. It was characterized by the digitalization of existing analogue Fintech development such as internet banking and spearheaded by financial institutions. The third stage is Fintech 3.0 in advanced countries and Fintech 3.5 in developing countries in the year of 2008-present. It is dominated by start-ups firms. In Indonesia, Fintech development started with Fintech 2.0 which was pioneered by the financial services industry then it followed by Fintech 3.5 which has been spearheaded by start-ups.

The number of Fintech companies in Indonesia have multiplied since 2015 and forced regulators to formulate a legal framework in order to permit Fintech to operate in formal financial sector and provide protection for the consumers and the state. The Indonesia Fintech Association was established in Jakarta on September 17th, 2015 during Invest Day 2015. It further strengthens the existence of Fintech in Indonesia, particularly with the formulation of regulations which govern Fintech. In 2016, The Indonesia Fintech Association recorded that there were 135 Fintech firms. It was a three-fold increase from 51 Fintech firms in 2015.

Considering that financial sector holds an important role in Indonesia's economic growth, Indonesian government takes some necessary steps to regulate Fintech industry. Such intention was stated by Indonesian president, Joko Widodo, during Indonesia e-Commerce Summit & Expo 2016. Government affirmed that it would pay more attention and support to develop Fintech in Indonesia. Furthermore, it was also predicted that Fintech in Indonesia would grow significantly in 2016 (Febriana, 2016).

Year of 2016 was the starting point when Fintech obtained an official attention from the government. Several legal regulations which were published in 2016 affirmed Fintech's legal position in Indonesia, namely Regulation of Financial Service Authority No.77/POJK.01/2016 on Information Technology-based Services of Lending and Borrowing; Regulation of Bank of Indonesia No. 18/40/PBI/2016 on Implementation of Payment Transaction Process; Bank of Indonesia's Circular Letter No. 18/22/DKSP on digital financial service; and Regulation of Bank of Indonesia No. 18/17/PBI/2016 on electronic money.

On June 16th, 2017, Otoritas Jasa Keuangan (OJK) or Financial Service Authority officially formed the Fintech Advisory Forum. It is a forum to orient Fintech industry development. It also facilitates and ensures smooth, consistent, and constructive coordination between institutions, government ministries and other relevant parties with Fintech start-ups. The Fintech Advisory Forum is expected to create a fair, healthy, competitive and sustainable business climate in the financial services industry in Indonesia. Based on OJK Annual Report (2017), there were 29 Fintech listed in Financial Service Authority in 2017 and it increased to 64 per June 2018. The list will keep growing as there are a lot of unlisted Fintech institutions.

Business Insider (2016) categorized 6 (six) areas of Fintech activities, which are then classified again to at least 20 categories. From all categories, the most important sectors are related to payment and loan (Citi Report, 2016). In Indonesia, the main Fintech activities related to payment are under the regulations of Bank of Indonesia; while those related to loan are under the regulations of Financial Service Authority.

In addition, according to EY ASEAN Fintech Census (2018), in South East Asia region, Indonesia is the second country with the highest number of Fintech after Singapore. Totally, Indonesia has 262 Fintechs while Singapore has 490 Fintechs. Indonesia can be called "booming digital payments market" while Singapore is "Asia's Fintech hotspot". For the incubators, accelerators and innovation labs, Indonesia is in the third rank with estimated number of 20 labs while the first rank is Singapore with the number of 54 labs and the second rank is Vietnam with the number of 24 labs. In terms of hiring the right talent for Fintech, Indonesia is facing more difficulties than Singapore, especially in hiring foreign talent.

INDONESIA'S FINANCIAL INCLUSION HAS WORLDWIDE RECOGNITION

Financial inclusion strategy in Indonesia is outlined under Strategi Nasional Keuangan Inklusif (SNKI) or Financial Inclusion National Strategy. The national strategy includes vision, mission, target, and inclusion policy. The strategy is directed to support three objectives, namely economic development, acceleration of poverty alleviation, and reduction of individual and regions inequality. Those objectives aim to achieve Indonesian communities' welfare.

Strategi Nasional Literasi Keuangan Indonesia or SNLKI (Indonesian National Financial Literacy Strategy) was launched in 2013. This policy was issued by government under Otoritas Jasa Keuangan (OJK) or Financial Service Authority as a guidance to increase knowledge, understanding, and utilization of financial products and services. The launch of this program was supported under OJK Regulation No. 1/POJK.07/2013 on Consumer Protection in Financial Services Sector. Three years later, government issued Presidential Regulation No. 82/2016 on the National Strategy of Financial Inclusion (SNKI) as a law foundation on national financial inclusion. The regulation is supported under OJK Regulation No. 76/POJK.07/2016 on Raising Financial Literacy and Inclusion in the Financial Services Sector among Consumers and/or the Public.

The efforts to achieve financial inclusion in Indonesia has been recognized worldwide. Indonesia, represented by OJK, received Global Inclusion Awards 2017, which was organized by Child and Youth Finance International (CYFI) for the Asia-Pacific Region in Berlin on May 3rd 2017. Indonesia was deemed successful in developing strategies of literacy and financial inclusion using various approaches. Indonesia is also committed to raise financial inclusion target to 75% by 2019 and financial literacy by 2% per year. Positive synergy is the key success which was assessed in the award. The implementation of SNKI and SNLKI with relevant ministries, institutions, and parties, namely Coordinating Ministry of Economic Affairs; Ministry of Finance; Ministry of Education; Ministry of Research, Technology, and Higher Education; Ministry of Religious Affairs; Ministry of Manpower; Ministry of Communication and Information; Bank of Indonesia; OJK; academicians; and non-governmental organizations.

Several products and services have been developed by OJK to improve financial inclusion in Indonesia, such as savings accounts for school student, savings accounts for university students and young people, microfinance services, branchless banking, and financial inclusion month.

Savings Accounts for School Student (SimPel/SimPel iB)

SimPel/SimPel iB is a part of the national financial inclusion programs which intends to create saving culture from early age. The target of this program is primary and secondary school students. In 2017, 279 banks participated in this program, with the number of accounts of 8,045,225 and a volume of IDR 1.63 trillion. There are also cooperation agreements between banks and schools, which reached 199,819 signed agreements.

Savings Accounts for University Students and Young People (SiMuda)

SiMuda is a financial inclusion program which targets university students and young people, ranging from 18 to 30 years old. This age group is a potential group since it is accounted for 24.8% of the total population in Indonesia. In 2017, OJK developed a model for this program together with representatives from banking industry and other industries.

Microfinance Services (Laku Mikro)

This program is set to broaden public financial access to microfinance products and services. It is a joint marketing program from banking industry, non-bank financial industry, and capital market. The products and services of this program are deposit, finance, investment funds, gold, and insurance. It is also accompanied by education and consultation services.

Branchless Banking (Laku Pandai)

In 2017, total 27 banks, which encompass 25 conventional commercial banks and two Sharia banks, offer branchless banking services. The number of branchless banking agents is 740,121 (722,239 individuals and 17,792 outlets) in 34 provinces and 512 cities/regencies in Indonesia. By far, about 13 million customers have opened a basic savings account (BSA) through the branchless banking with a total value of IDR1.03 trillion. Most branchless banking agents are located in Java Island (66.68%), followed by Sumatra (18.96%), Sulawesi (5.17%), Bali-East Nusa Tenggara-West Nusa Tenggara (3.90%), Kalimantan (3.93%), and the remaining 1.35% in Maluku and Papua.

Figure 1. Distribution of branchless banking agents in 2017
Source: OJK Annual Report 2017

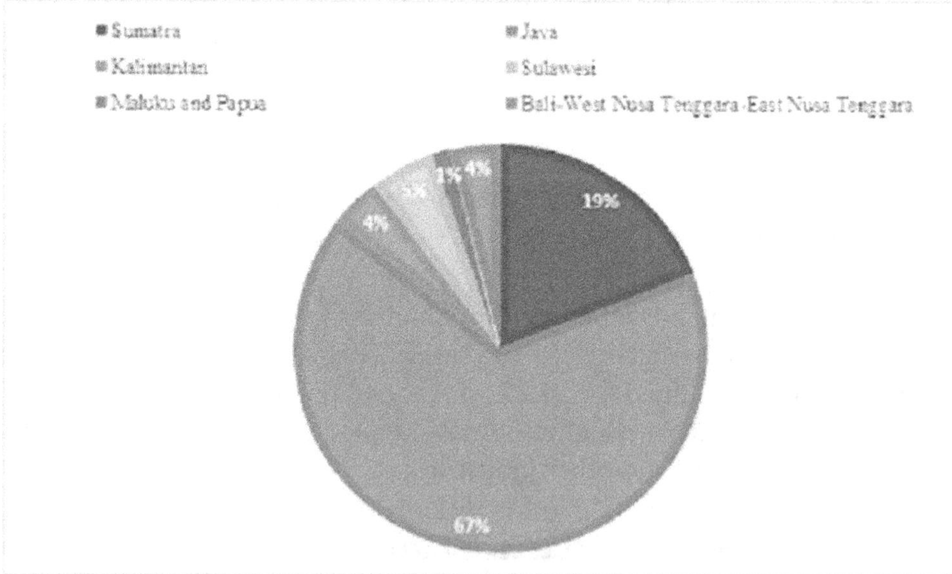

**For a more accurate representation see the electronic version.*

The Financial Inclusion Month

October 2017 was declared as as financial inclusion month, under a theme called "Accelerating Financial Inclusion through Digital Financial Inclusion (DFI)". The activities within the month consisted of: 1) selling financial products and services with various discounts, bonuses, and rewards; 2) educational activities and financial inclusion campaign which were hosted at regional OJK offices and head office together and attended by financial services industry in the form of an exhibition, financial education, socialization, and national seminar. The statistics of financial inclusion month are shown in Table 1.

Based on evaluation and monitoring, those programs show effective results. Based on the survey results of National Financial Literacy in 2013 when this program was launched, literacy index was recorded at 21.8% and inclusion index was at 59.7%. The survey results in 2016 showed that the literacy index was 29.7% and inclusion index was 67.8%. Based on those results, it can be concluded that financial inclusion program has broad, measurable, and continuous positive impacts on Indonesian people. In 2019, OJK sets a target of literacy index to reach 35% and inclusion index to reach 75%.

FINTECH ROLE IN SUPPORTING FINANCIAL INCLUSION IN INDONESIA

Finance is undoubtedly the main component in each business activity of a corporate. A study from World Economic Forum (2015) revealed that limited access to finance is the most frequent occurrence in business world, particularly

Table 1. Financial inclusion month 2017

No.	Description	Achievement		Increase
		2016	2017	
1.	Participating Financial Services Institutions	83	340	309.6%
2.	Programs	196	399	103.6%
3.	Activities	633	1,113	75.8%
4.	Participating Cites	111	171	54%
5.	Number of New Accounts Opened	3,545,812	5,489,145	54.8%

Source: OJK Annual Report 2017

in developing country like Indonesia. As we have known, Indonesian market is dominated by micro, small, and medium enterprises (hereafter, UMKM). It is also recorded that at least 90% UMKM in Indonesia have limited access to finance. Shinozaki (2012) found that collateral requirement and high interest rate for loans are the main obstacles for UMKM to obtain financial access. This requires innovation both in formal and informal safe financial channels in order to provide financial assistance to UMKM.

Growth of financial sector in Indonesia today has not been followed by adequate access to financial services for the society members. Based on Global Findex 2014, it turned out that only 36% of adult population in Indonesia has access to formal financial institution. Widening financial access and deepening financial dimensions, as well as stabilizing domestic financial system are essentially needed to achieve target of economic growth. In National Mid-Term Development Plan (RPJMN) 2015-2019, Indonesian government set the target of economic growth to be 8% in 2019. An attempt of widening public access to financial service in RPJMN 2015-2019 is a part of description in *Nawa Cita*, which aimed to achieve economic independence by driving some strategic sectors in domestic economy. The target of the program is by increasing public's and UMKM's access to financial services.

Citizens of Indonesia have a great need in financial service, particularly the basic service. Such service encompasses non-cash payment, saving, credit or funding, remittance, and insurance. Current financial service in Indonesia is mostly dominated by banking sector as the provider of banking and payment services. An attempt to improve financial inclusion is challenged not only from low financial literacy, but also from supply and demand sides of financial services.

Pre-Fintech

Generally, in 2014, approximately 36.1% of adult population in Indonesia owned bank account, both account in financial institution (35.9%) and electronic account which is accessible by mobile phone (mobile money) (0.4%). The percentage has improved compared to the number in 2011, where only 20% Indonesian citizens had bank accounts. An increase in the number of citizens owning bank accounts in 2014 indicated that financial inclusion is widening in Indonesia. However, there is still a gap in terms of owning bank accounts with large deposit in them. It is proven as among 40% of adult population with low income, only 22.2% of them have bank accounts; while the rest of them have not been reached by financial service. Moreover, a gap between male-female proportion with bank account also provides more challenges. From the total of adult female population in Indonesia, there is only 37.5% of them who have bank accounts.

According to a survey by World Bank (2014), comparing Indonesia and other countries, access to save money and obtain loans from financial institution remained at moderate level. However, in terms of bank account ownership, Indonesia belonged to low category at approximately 36%. This number was lower than the average in East Asia and Pacific which were recorded at 69% and also lower than low- and mid-income countries' average which were recorded at 42%. In Southeast Asia, Indonesia is left behind Thailand whose 78% of population have bank accounts. It signals that Indonesia is a country with low penetration level of banking sector.

According to data from Global Findex 2014, approximately 69.3% of Indonesia adult population in Indonesia obtained saving service and owned several forms of saving accounts. However, based on the data, there was only 26.6% population who owned saving account in formal financial institution. The rest of them owned saving account in informal settings, namely informal saving among saving group or entrusting the money to nuclear family. Furthermore, from 69.3% of those having formal saving accounts, 33.3% of them saved money for education fund or school tuition; and 27.1% of them admitted that they are saving for old age; and 22.6% saved money for agribusiness or other business. There are only 13% of adult population who make use of loan fund from financial institution. Moreover, 42% of citizens prefer to borrow money from family or friends to financial institutions. This fact indicates how big is the potential funding.

This number has a huge gap with the number of mobile phone's penetration. Based on Digital in 2016 Report by We Are Social, 88% of Indonesian citizens own mobile phone and 43% of them own smartphones. The number of mobile phone users are even higher than Indonesia population, which are 326.3 million users or 126% of the total population. The large number of mobile phone users can be taken advantage of reaching financial system through digital financial service. It means that tens of million people, especially smartphone users with internet access, can be reachable by financial system through smartphone's technology.

Financial inclusion in Indonesia was supported by government policy, namely SNLKI 2013. This policy is a guidance to increase knowledge, understanding, and utilization of financial products and services. When this program was launched in 2013, literacy index was recorded at 21.8% and inclusion index was at 59.7%. These numbers increased in 2016 become 29.7% for the literacy index and 67.8% for the inclusion index. However, in the press release of OJK (2017), Mrs. Soetiono, Member of the Board of Commissioners for Consumer Education and Protection, stated that based on the evaluation from 2013-2016 and information technology advancements, financial education activities still need improvement. She added that even though the literacy index and inclusion index have increased, it is necessary to accelerate the achievement of the financial literacy and inclusion index. The acceleration aims to achieve the 75% financial inclusion index target in 2019 as stated in Presidential Regulation No. 82 of 2016 concerning National Strategy for Inclusive Finance (SNKI).

Post-Fintech

In 2017, OJK launched the revision version of SNLKI 2013, which called revisit SNLKI 2017. This version has some adjustments from the previous one. One of the adjustments is digital financial services. Digital financial services include in revisit SNLKI 2017 core actions for Strategic Program 1: Competent Finance and Strategic Program 3: Financial Access. For the first strategic program, the core action is conducting financial education regarding the usage of digital financial services for financial transactions. For the third strategic program, there are two core actions related with digital financial service. The first action is encouraging financial service industry to expand service network both traditionally and digitally and the second action is encouraging financial service institutions to develop products and services with digital based.

Digital financial service will improve access to financial service and provide benefits for national economy. Based on a study by the World Bank, an increase in inclusive financial system by 1% can boost Gross Domestic Product (GDP) per capita by 0.03%. Economic growth will lead to growth in job opportunities. An increase in financial inclusion by 20% through digital service creates 1.7 million new jobs. Moreover, along with the increase of banking access, business enterprises, particularly UMKM, will also grow. New entrepreneurs shall be born as the ease to obtain financial services upgraded.

Technology advancement and progressive digital development bring about some changes in business. Two decades ago, innovation in financial technology is still centered in internal banking institution. Afterwards, digital era brings about some ease, so that customers can access financial service in their palm. Customers can easily conduct various transactions through smartphones, namely through SMS banking and internet banking. Currently innovation of technology has reached more potential consumers. This shift has made technology-based financial institutions (Fintech) flourished.

Based on some occurring facts, Fintech will mainly be attractive, because the existing financial institutions in Indonesia have not successfully solved financial problems. Fintech also offers more advantages compared to conventional bank. Contrary to the prejudice that Fintech can threaten conventional bank, both institutions can actually collaborate to find common solution. By collaborating, banking institution can take advantage of Fintech's technology to reach potential customers in secluded areas without having to establish a physical branch. Fintech can also offer affordable loan service to enhance bank activities.

Fintech serves the needs of the unbanked and those unwilling to use conventional financial industry services. The large potential market of the unbanked because of prudent lending and more strict lending standards required by banks and other financial institutions. Meanwhile, communities are unwilling to use conventional financial industry services because of the view that Fintech could change the financial industry's model into a more democratic, transparent and inexpensive industry that could serve many consumers.

Furthermore, according to OJK (2017), Fintech is expected to reduce the cost of financial inclusion programs with greater efficiency so that can reach more consumers in remote areas. Fintech also includes in OJK Strategy Map 2018. The financial inclusion performance targets will be measured based on credible consumer protection, expanding microfinance products and optimizing the use of Fintech. To optimize the role of Fintech through adequate regulation, licensing and supervision, OJK has two programs. First, strengthen the regulation and supervision of Fintech development in Indonesia; and second, establish the National Financial Technology Centre.

According to a research conducted by Phan, Narayan, Rahman, and Hutabarat (2018), the existing Fintech institutions in Indonesia have influenced the performance of conventional banks. The research stated that banks with highly valuable market value, long-standing banks, and banks owned by State-Owned Enterprises (BUMN) are the most-affected institutions. Generally, the performances of those three kinds of conventional banks are corrected as negative. Fintech's impacts are tremendously strong and swift so that the existing financial institutions are forced to create some innovations to compensate their negatively-corrected performance. In addition, a research conducted by Mahardhika and Inggis (2017) found that Fintech Peer-to-Peer Lending platform may become the solution for short-term loan for UMKM which in turn increase UMKM's capital. With the increase of UMKM's capital from the loan, the owner is willing to expand their business. The benefit for Fintech firms is that their profitability is increasing as well as their business is expanding.

CONCLUSION

Financial inclusion is one of important parts in achieving sustainable development. Indonesia financial inclusion has been recognized worldwide and it is a proof that Indonesia is committed to support financial inclusion. Fintech as a new technology in financial industry has grown and reached people who are not familiar with financial products and services. Fintech in Indonesia has expanded rapidly and has been supported by formal regulation from government. In the end, financial inclusion and fintech contribution are determined by government. The support from government not only by formal regulation but also followed by a synergy from all stakeholders so as to create an ecosystem that supports financial inclusion.

Furthermore, for the Fintech firms, Indonesia is one of the big markets to expand the business, especially with the support from the government to enhance the development of Fintech in Indonesia as stated in revisit SNLKI 2017 as well as OJK Strategy Map 2018. The target to accelerate financial literacy and financial inclusion index in the coming years through digitalization helps Fintech industry to expand.

REFERENCES

Abubakar, L., & Handayani, T. (2018). Financial technology: Legal challenges for Indonesia financial sector. In *IOP Conference Series: Earth and Environmental Science* (Vol. 175, No. 1, p. 012204). IOP Publishing. 10.1088/1755-1315/175/1/012204

Arner, D. W., Barberies, J., & Buckley, R. P. (2015). The evolution of Fintech: A new post-crisis paradigm. *Georgetown Journal of International Law*, *47*, 1271.

Business Insider Intelligence. (2016). *Fintech could be bigger than ATMs, PayPal, and Bitcoin combined.* Retrieved from https://www.businessinsider.com.au/fintech-could-be-bigger-than-atms-paypal-and-bitcoin-combined-2016-10

Citi. (2016). *How FinTech is forcing banking to a tipping point: Digital disruption*. Citibank.

Davis, K., Maddock, R., & Foo, M. (2017). Catching up with Indonesia's fintech industry. *Law and Financial Markets Review*, *11*(1), 33–40. doi:10.1080/17521440.2017.1336398

Demirguc-Kunt, A., Klapper, L., Singer, D., Ansar, S., & Hess, J. (2018). *The Global Findex Database 2017: Measuring Financial Inclusion and the Fintech Revolution*. The World Bank. doi:10.1596/978-1-4648-1259-0

Ernst & Young (2018). *ASEAN Fintech Census*. EY.

Febriana, P. (2016). Fintech: Funding Alternative for start-ups. *The Jakarta Post*. Retrieved from https://www.thejakartapost.com/news/2016/05/25/fintech-funding-alternative-start-ups.html

Haddad, C., & Hornuf, L. (2016). The emergence of the global fintech market: Economic and technological determinants. *Small Business Economics*, 1–25.

International Monetary Fund. (2018). *The Bali Fintech Agenda: A Blueprint for Successfully Harnessing Fintech's Opportunities.* Press Release, No.18/388. IMF.

Mahardhika, G. S., & Inggis, R. A. (2017). Peer-to-peer lending in Surabaya: How it drives regional economy? *Journal of Development Economics*, *2*(2), 58–78.

Minerva, R., Asaba, C. P. S., Aiba, D. P. K., & Hirano, M. (2016). *The potential of the Fintech industry to support the growth of SMEs in Indonesia* (Unpublished master thesis). Waseda University, Japan.

Nicoletti, B. (2017). *The future of FinTech*. Springer. doi:10.1007/978-3-319-51415-4

Otoritas Jasa Keuangan. (2013). *Peraturan OJK Nomor 1/POJK.07/2013 tentang Perlindungan Konsumen Sektor Jasa Keuangan.*

Otoritas Jasa Keuangan. (2016). *Peraturan OJK Nomor 76/POJK.07/2016 tentang Peningkatan Literasi dan Inklusi Keuangan di Sektor Jasa Keuangan bagi Konsumen dan/atau Masyarakat.*

Otoritas Jasa Keuangan. (2017a). *The Global Inclusion Awards 2017: Sebuah Pengakuan Internasional untuk Indonesia.*

Otoritas Jasa Keuangan. (2017b). *Annual Report.*

Otoritas Jasa Keuangan. (2017c). *Revisit strategi nasional literasi keuangan Indonesia (SNLKI) sebagai upaya akselerasi pencapaian indeks literasi dan inklusi keuangan.* Press Release, No.SP 82/DKSN/OJK/VII/2017.

Phan, D., Narayan, P. K., Rahman, R. E., & Hutabarat, A. R. (2018). *Do Financial Technology Firms Influence Bank Performance?* Paper was presented on September 4th, 2018 in Universitas Airlangga Presiden.

Republik Indonesia. (2016). *Peraturan Presiden Republik Indonesia Nomor 82 tahun 2016 tentang Strategi Nasional Keuangan Inklusif.* SNKI.

Shinozaki, S. (2012). *A New Regime of SME Finance in Emerging Asia: Empowering Growth-Oriented SMEs to Build Resilent National Economics.* Asia Development Bank. Working Paper Series on Regional Economic integration No. 104/ December 2012, Asia Development Bank.

We Are Social. (2016). *Digital in 2016: Global Overview*. Retrieved from https://wearesocial.com/special-reports/digital-in-2016

World Economic Forum. (2015). *Global Agenda Council on the future of Financing and Capital.* Author.

World Economic Forum. (2015). *The Future of Fintech: A Paradigm Shift in Small Business Finance*. Author.

KEY TERMS AND DEFINITIONS

Financial Inclusion: A condition where individuals and business have access to useful and affordable financial products and services that meet their needs.

FinTech: A new technology that aims to improve and automate the delivery and use of financial services.

OJK: Indonesian Financial Service Authority. It is an independent institution free from external interference, mandated with regulating, supervising, inspecting and investigating the financial services sector.

Peer-to-Peer Lending: The practice of lending money to individuals or businesses through online services which match lenders with borrowers.

SNKI: Indonesia national strategy as stated in a document that contains the vision, mission, goals, and policies of inclusive finance in order to support economic growth, accelerate poverty reduction in order to realize the welfare of the Indonesian people.

SNLKI: A guidelines for OJK or financial institutions in Indonesia in conducting financial education activities to improve public financial literacy.

Unbanked: Individuals who do not use banks or banking institutions in any capacity.

Chapter 9
Customer Adoption and Perception Towards Fintech in Indonesia:
A Diamond in the Rough or a Dime a Dozen?

Nofie Iman
Universitas Gadjah Mada, Indonesia

ABSTRACT

While fintech is relatively new in Indonesia, it is visibly emerging and setting for a new path. This chapter is attempting to shed a light on customer adoption and their perceptions toward fintech products and services in Indonesia. This study is descriptive and exploratory by nature. Data gathered from primary surveys as well as secondary sources. This study identifies several factors that significantly affect customer adoption and perception towards fintech products and services, namely relative advantages, trialability, and simplicity. Trust, responsiveness, and empathy are also served as important variables that should be considered as well. It is expected that this study will help researchers and academics who are interested in studying the phenomenon of fintech more broadly.

DOI: 10.4018/978-1-5225-9183-2.ch009

Copyright © 2020, IGI Global. Copying or distributing in print or electronic forms without written permission of IGI Global is prohibited.

INTRODUCTION

Fintech, a portmanteau of financial and technology, is growing rapidly in the last couple of years. More than USD 12 billion has been invested in fintech sector (Accenture, 2015). In the US, fintech transaction has amounted USD 7 trillion while in China it has passed USD 4 trillion (PwC, 2016). The rise of fintech inevitably lead to change the role of technology, the consumer behavior, the ecosystems, as well as the industry and regulation itself (Puschmann, 2017). Some recent studies even predicted that fintech provides opportunity to disrupt the market and fundamentally change the business landscape (e.g. Arner et al., 2017; Gomber et al., 2017; Iman, 2018; Lee and Shin, 2018, Ng and Kwok, 2017; among others).

Unfortunately, the study on customer perception and adoption of fintech is fairly limited, especially in the context of emerging countries such as Indonesia (Iman, 2018). In particular, a gap between user experience and convenience perspective in conventional banking industry appeared to be widening (Arslanian, 2016). This niche, in turn, encourages fintech industry to jump in and capture this opportunity. Since financial related services like fintech require high level of risk control and motivation due to its direct link to personal wealth and well-being, thus, it is important to examine the market dynamics toward this emerging technology.

Indonesia is particularly interesting in a sense that only around 36 percent of adult population there has conventional banking accounts (Global Findex, 2014). As many as 170 million Indonesian use mobile phones, where 130 millions of them use mobile phones to access the internet but 80 millions of them do not have access to conventional banking and financial services (Euromonitor, 2017). At the same time, however, the government of the Republic of Indonesia launched the vision of "Indonesia Digital Economy 2020" and "National Movement of 1000 Digital Startups" (Iman, 2018).

This study aims to map the dynamic of fintech in Indonesia by focusing on factors that encourage or inhibit customer adoption. Primarily guided by diffusion of innovations theory (Rogers, 1995) and SERVQUAL framework (Parasuraman et al., 1988), this study attempted to capture the dynamics of user adoption and perception toward fintech products and services provision. It is expected that the findings will contribute toward stimulating academic discussion on fintech, assisting policy makers and regulatory bodies, as well as promoting development of the sector in the country.

For this reason, this article is divided into 5 (five sections). The first section is the introduction and background of the study. The second section is the discussion on theoretical basis and conceptual framework to support this research. The third section briefly reviews the methodology used. The fourth section is the findings and analysis of this study, while the last section, section five, becomes conclusions and limitations.

WHAT IS FINTECH AND WHY IS IT IMPORTANT?

Unarguably, there are various concepts and diverse definitions regarding fintech. For example, Puschmann (2017) defines fintech as "[…] incremental or disruptive innovations in or in the context of the financial services industry induced by IT developments resulting in new intra- or inter-organizational business models, products and services, organizations, processes and systems" (p74). Meanwhile, Gomber et al. (2017) considered fintech as initiatives in the financial sector that are challenging established roles, business models and service offerings by introducing technology-based innovations.

Moreover, Ng and Kwok (2017) classified fintech organization into four different categories: efficient payment process, robo-advisor, peer-to-peer load and deposit platform, as well as crowdfunding. In stark contrast to their study, Iman (2018) categorized fintech according to the type of interaction and their business processes (see Table 1). Equally, if not more interesting, Lee and Shin (2018) identified fintech ecosystems into five different elements: fintech startups, technology developers, government, financial customers, and traditional financial institutions.

Table 1. Business process of fintech

Type of interaction	Business process	Some examples
Customer-to-customer (C2C)	Payment	Digital wallet, peer-to-peer (P2P) payment
	Investment	Peer-to-peer (P2P) lending, equity crowdfunding
Business-to-customer (B2C)	Lending	Crowdfunding, micro loan, credit facilities
	Insurance	Risk management
Business-to-business (B2B)	Infrastructure	Security, data management
	Multi-processes	Big data analytics, predictive modeling

Source: Iman (2018)

As this brief overview has shown, there have been quite a number of studies in the literature that do take fintech rather seriously. However, it appears that we do not have a unified definition of fintech just yet. Some are focusing on the roles and structures (e.g. Arner et al., 2017; Lee and Shin, 2018), while some others are emphasizing on the attributes and (product and service) provision (e.g. Iman, 2018; Ng and Kwok, 2017). This article distinguishes itself by focusing on the customer adoption and perceptions toward fintech product and services. If we are to minimize this gap, it is particularly important to know not only why and how fintech works in Indonesia, but also how customers adopt the technology and how they perceive the quality of fintech products and services.

Diffusion of innovation theory (Rogers, 1995) provides a useful framework to analyze the adoption process.

According to him, perceived attributes of an innovation consist of relative advantage—whether an innovation is perceived as better than the idea it supersedes, compatibility—whether an innovation is perceived as consistent with the existing values and experiences, complexity—whether an innovation is perceived as relatively easy (difficult) to use, observability—whether the results of an innovation are visible, trialability—whether an innovation may be experimented with.

Meanwhile, SERVQUAL instrument (Parasuraman et al., 1988) is perhaps the most widely-used instrument to analyze customer satisfaction, especially in service sectors such as fintech. SERVQUAL incorporates 22 statements to examine customers' general expectation and 22 matching statements to examine customers' assessment of a particular service. These instrument being categorized into five dimensions: tangibles—physical facilities, equipment, staff appearance, etc., reliability—ability to perform service independently and accurately, responsiveness—willingness to respond to customers' need, assurance—ability to inspire confidence and trust, and empathy—the extent to which caring individual service is given.

METHODOLOGY

This study aims to examine customer adoption as well as their perceptions towards fintech products and services in Indonesia. Thus, survey is probably the most suitable method for that purpose (Bryman and Bell, 2007). It included sections comprising questions about fintech product and service attributes, adoption factors, customer experiences and expectations. The overall study uses diffusion of innovation (Rogers, 1995) and SERVQUAL (Parasuraman et al., 1988) framework. Response to those questions was measured on five-point Likert-type scales. The items for this scale were derived from previous adoption and quality research.

Data were collected in the second semester of 2018. Survey respondent were chosen using convenience sampling in Jakarta and Yogyakarta who had actually using fintech products and services. This study distributed email and mobile message invitations to fill the online questionnaire. As an attempt to reach non-respondents, researcher contacted non-respondents to request that they fill in the survey. When necessary, an additional enumerator was available to help respondents in completing the survey. The premise behind this is to increase survey response rates (Dillman, 2000).

In total, 129 responses were collected, but four of them were incomplete, resulted in 125 valid responses to be analyzed further. The sample demographics of this study were illustrated in Table 2 as follows.

Table 2. Descriptive statistics

Gender	Male	60	48.0%
	Female	65	52.0%
Marital Status	Single	108	86.4%
	Married	15	12.0%
	Others	2	1.6%
Age	15 or under	-	-
	16-20 years old	22	17.6%
	21-25 years old	79	63.2%
	26-30 years old	15	12.0%
	31-35 years old	7	5.6%
	36-40 years old	1	0.8%
	41-45 years old	1	0.8%
	46-60 years old	-	-
	60 or more	-	-
Occupation	Private employee	18	14.4%
	Public sector employee	7	5.6%
	Civil servant	13	10.4%
	Entrepreneur/business owner	4	3.2%
	Student	75	60.0%
	Unemployed	8	6.4%

continued on following page

Table 2. Continued

Educational background	Elementary School	-	-
	Junior High School	-	-
	Senior High School	57	45.6%
	Diploma	14	11.2%
	University/Undergraduate	47	37.6%
	Postgraduate	7	5.6%
	Doctorate (PhD)	-	-
Annual income	IDR 50 million (USD 34,263) or less	93	74.4%
	IDR 50-100 million (USD 6,852)	17	13.6%
	IDR 100-150 million (USD 10,279)	8	6.4%
	IDR 150-200 million (USD 13,705)	3	2.4%
	IDR 200-250 million (USD 17,132)	1	0.8%
	IDR 250-300 million (USD 20,558)	-	-
	IDR 300 million or more	3	2.4%
Fintech provider being used (may choose more than one)	Amartha	3	2.4%
	Ayopop	3	2.4%
	Bareksa	10	8.0%
	Blockchain Indonesia	2	1.6%
	BluePay Wallet	2	1.6%
	Bukadompet (Bukalapak)	23	18.4%
	Cekaja.com	1	0.8%
	Cermati	1	0.8%
	Cicil	2	1.6%
	Crowde	3	2.4%
	Dimo	1	0.8%
	Doku	15	12.0%
	Finaccel (Kredivo)	2	1.6%
	Finansialku	3	2.4%
	Finpay	2	1.6%
	Flip	8	6.4%
	Gandeng Tangan	1	0.8%
	Gift Card	4	3.2%
	Go Cash	8	6.4%
	GoPay (Gojek)	115	92.0%
	Grab Pay (Grab)	40	32.0%
	Gudang Voucher	2	1.6%
	HaloMoney	1	0.8%

continued on following page

Table 2. Continued

	Igrow	3	2.4%
	Indves	1	0.8%
	Investree	2	1.6%
	Julo	1	0.8%
	Kartuku	3	2.4%
	Kitabisa	16	12.8%
	Koinworks	2	1.6%
	Kudo	3	2.4%
	Midtrans	2	1.6%
	Mol (Money Online)	2	1.6%
	NicePay	1	0.8%
	Ovo	42	33.6%
	Pefindo Biro Kredit	1	0.8%
	Pundi X	1	0.8%
	PT. Rintis Sejahtera (Jaringan Prima)	1	0.8%
	Rupiah Plus	1	0.8%
	Stockbit	1	0.8%
	Tanihub	1	0.8%
	Tokopedia	38	30.4%
	TunaiKita	1	0.8%
	Uangku	4	3.2%
	Uang Teman	1	0.8%
	Others (currently not being listed under Indonesian Fintech Association)	18	14.4%
Type of service used (may choose more than one)	Asset management	8	6.4%
	Crowdfunding	16	12.8%
	Insurance	8	6.4%
	Investment	35	28.0%
	P2P lending	10	8.0%
	Payments	115	92.0%
	Point of sales	20	16.0%
	Others	1	0.8%
How did they know about the service?	Advertisement	12	9.6%
	Friends/family	17	13.6%
	Internet	52	41.6%
	Social media	44	35.2%
	Newspaper/magazine	-	-
	Others	-	-

continued on following page

Table 2. Continued

How many times usually use the service?	Daily	17	13.6%
	Several times a week	56	44.8%
	Once a week	2	1.6%
	A couple times in a month	35	28.0%
	Once in a month	5	4.0%
	Once in a couple months	10	8.0%
Approximate value per transaction	Less than IDR 100,000 (USD 6.85)	83	66.4%
	IDR 100,000 to IDR 500,000 (USD 34.27)	30	24.0%
	IDR 500,000 to IDR 1,000,000 (USD 68.53)	9	7.2%
	IDR 1,000,000 to IDR 5,000,000 (USD 342.63)	3	2.4%
	More than IDR 5,000,000 (USD 342.63)	-	-
Satisfied with the service?	Yes	119	95.2%
	No	6	4.8%

Data showed that the majority of the respondents was female, single, aged between 21 to 25 years old, which can be classified as millennials. As predicted, most of them were student and employees with the education level of at least high school. The majority of the respondents earned IDR 50 million (or about US$ 34,000) annually. Meanwhile, the most popular fintech applications being used are GoPay (Gojek) followed by Ovo, Grab Pay (Grab), and Tokopedia. The respondents were mostly using fintech for payment services (92%). They were mostly conducted financial transactions through fintech several times a week (44.8%) with less than IDR 100,000 (or about US$ 6.85) per transaction. Interestingly, most of them (95.2%) said that they were already satisfied with the service.

TALES FROM THE FIELD: RESULTS AND DISCUSSION

Indonesia is the world's largest island country with more than 17,000 islands (The Jakarta Post, 2017). It is the 7th largest country (see Figure 1) with over 261 million people, the majority of which are under 35 years old (Seeking Alpha, 2017). As we already know, Indonesia is also the largest economy in Southeast Asia. It is also a member of G20 and becomes one of the emerging market economies. PwC (2017) predicted that Indonesia could be the 4th largest economies in the world by 2050. Even though fintech in Indonesia is growing rapidly, with growing mobile phone and Internet penetration, it still a treasure trove of untapped fintech opportunities (Fintechnews Singapore, 2018).

Indonesian fintech market has also indicated a significant amount growth of 16.3% annually with the total disclosed investment into fintech initiatives standing at USD 176.75 million in 2017 (Fintechnews Singapore, 2018). Most of fintech operating in Indonesia are engaged in the payment sector, followed by investment and lending (Iman, 2018). Those fintech companies are joined together to form an association, namely Indonesian Fintech Association (*Asosiasi Fintech Indonesia*). As of December 2018, there are 154 startup companies, 24 financial institutions, as well as 9 associate partner within the association.[1] There are also many government policies in relation to fintech. For instance, the Central Bank (*Bank Indonesia*) Regulation No. 16/8/PBI/2014 concerning Electronic Money, the Financial Services Authority (*Otoritas Jasa Keuangan*/OJK) Regulation No. 77/POJK.01/2016 concerning Information Technology-Based Lending and Borrowing Services, as well as No. 13/POJK.02/2018 on Digital Financial Innovation in Financial Services Sector.

As of October 2018, there are 73 fintech companies currently registered and licensed by OJK. Those fintech companies are Danamas, Koinworks, Amartha, Investree, Modalku, Danacepat, AwanTunai, KlikACC, CROWDO,

Figure 1. Digital infrastructure map of Indonesia
Source: APJII (2015)

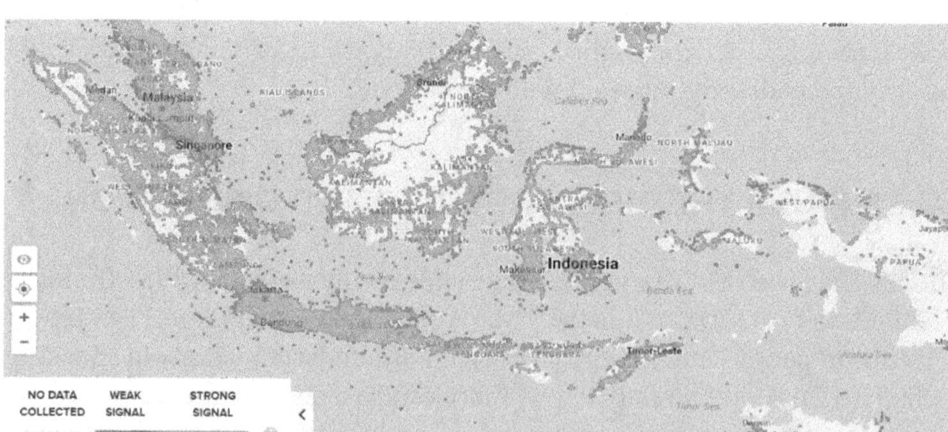

**For a more accurate representation see the electronic version.*

Akseleran, UangTeman, Dompet Kilat, Taralite, FINTAG, Involla, KIMO, TunaiKita, Igrow, Qreditt, Cicil, Dana Merdeka, Cash Wagon, Esta Kapital, Ammana, Gradana, Dana Mapan, Aktivaku, Danakini, Finmas, Rupiah Plus, Tokomodal, Indodana, Kredivo, Mekar.id, PinjamanGo, iternak.id, Kredit Pintar, Kredito, Crowde, PinjamGampang, TaniFund, Danain, Indofund. id, SGPIndonesia, KreditPro, Avantee, Do-It, RupiahCepat, Danarupiah, Danabijak, Cashcepat, Danalaut, Danasyariah, Telefin, Modalrakyat, Kawancicil, Sanders One Stop Solution, Kreditcepat, Uangme, Pinjam Duit, Pinjam Yuk, Pinjam Modal, Julo, Easy Cash, Maucash, RupiahOne, Pohon Dana, Dana Cita, DANAdidik, TrustIQ, Danai, Pinduit, and Pinjam.[2]

In analyzing customer adoption, inter-item correlations, means and standard deviations were calculated. The perceived attributes items were factor analyzed to examine whether the clustered items are align with diffusion of innovation theory (Rogers, 1995), thereby assessing factorial validity. Two types of rotations were used: varimax rotation and promax rotation to confirm the previous findings. In examining the perceived attributes, Pearson correlation coefficient is calculated to examine the association between perceptions and customer adoptions. The stronger the correlation implies that the construct validity of the scale is better.

From the correlation matrix (Table 3), all items presented were of positive values, ranging from 0.052 to 0.686. The highest correlation were found for items PB 18/17 on complexity/simplicity, while the lowest correlation were found in PB 15/9 on complexity/simplicity and relative advantage/ comparability. The highest mean appears in PB 14 (4.30), while the lowest mean score was found in PB 1 (3.42). all correlations were indeed in predicted direction and were significant at the $P < .05$ level.

Table 4 shows the rotated component matrix while Table 5 displays the correlation matrix among five different attributes. From here, it can be interpreted that the strongest relationship with adoption of fintech products and services was with relative advantage/compatibility (r=0.869), followed by trialability (r=791) and then complexity/simplicity (r=774). Again, all correlations aforementioned above were in the expected direction and were significant at the $P < .01$ level.

Moving on to the quality perceptions and expectations of fintech customers, the mean score of such attributes were shown in Table 6. Almost all attributes showed a gap except for Tangible 2 (the physical facilities at fintech companies will be visually appealing) and Tangible 3 (employees at fintech companies will be neat in their appearance) attributes. This result is not surprising since

Table 3. Correlations matrix of adoption attributes

	Relative Advantage/Compatibility										Complexity/Simplicity							Trialability				Observability			Mean	Stdev
	1	2	3	4	5	6	7	8	9	10	11	12	13	14	15	17	18	19	20	22	23	34	26	29		
PB1																									3.42	0.87
PB2	.451**																								3.67	0.96
PB3	.465**	.452**																							3.47	0.95
PB4	.401**	.455**	.535**																						3.51	0.99
PB5	.342**	.413**	.501**	.566**																					3.66	0.97
PB6	.451**	.539**	.495**	.472**	.488**																				3.64	0.93
PB7	.605**	.400**	.504**	.422**	.414**	.453**																			3.60	0.80
PB8	.337**	.505**	.390**	.363**	.520**	.419**	.351**																		3.93	0.93
PB9	.338**	.427**	.673**	.506**	.504**	.447**	.360**	.422**																	3.44	1.01
PB10	.341**	.332**	.543**	.588**	.558**	.529**	.476**	.460**	.502**																3.76	0.87
PB11	.298**	.172*	.196*	.235**	.242**	.256**	.453**	.248**	.199*	.414**															4.16	0.73
PB12	.185*	.211**	.095	.255**	.312**	.238**	.295**	.445**	.163*	.332**	.550**														4.17	0.88
PB13	.073	.166*	.168*	.130	.144	.158*	.127	.239**	.248**	.199*	.476**	.428**													4.06	0.89
PB14	.196*	.287**	.308**	.249**	.281**	.255**	.327**	.441**	.252**	.359**	.463**	.525**	.492**												4.30	0.73
PB15	.201**	.159*	.121	.166*	.347**	.215**	.244**	.306**	.052	.201**	.493**	.587**	.454**	.518**											4.21	0.78
PB17	.241**	.230**	.216**	.207**	.301**	.256**	.325**	.448**	.147	.306**	.478**	.546**	.429**	.678**	.558**										4.24	0.74
PB18	.150	.202**	.107	.190*	.267**	.225**	.207**	.383**	.100	.275**	.549**	.666**	.464**	.617**	.600**	.686**									4.21	0.79
PB19	.247**	.314**	.262**	.334**	.476**	.336**	.369**	.468**	.228**	.366**	.467**	.440**	.342**	.452**	.480**	.450**	.435**								4.11	0.81
PB20	.238**	.380**	.210**	.272**	.393**	.345**	.282**	.458**	.214**	.298**	.393**	.499**	.391**	.524**	.502**	.465**	.465**	.628**							4.06	0.81
PB22	.190*	.155*	.175*	.202**	.407**	.284**	.305**	.346**	.204**	.406**	.362**	.265**	.196*	.320**	.324**	.397**	.264**	.462**	.302**						3.75	0.89
PB23	.254**	.389**	.218**	.291**	.418**	.336**	.344**	.392**	.198*	.298**	.376**	.348**	.280**	.471**	.480**	.420**	.394**	.645**	.586**	.459**					4.04	0.79
PB24	.191*	.348**	.246**	.273**	.275**	.324**	.261**	.339**	.283**	.307**	.220**	.210**	.266**	.360**	.194*	.225**	.188*	.272**	.320**	.257**	.398**				3.70	0.87
PB26	.148	.256**	.179*	.256**	.211**	.191*	.189*	.302**	.264**	.343**	.388**	.352**	.413**	.419**	.369**	.379**	.321**	.347**	.286**	.299**	.394**	.347**			3.96	0.75
PB29	.265**	.408**	.440**	.339**	.437**	.362**	.328**	.411**	.374**	.376**	.222**	.188*	.312**	.371**	.289**	.298**	.308**	.265**	.293**	.324**	.389**	.435**	.371**		3.67	0.86

**. Correlation is significant at the 0.01 level (2-tailed). *. Correlation is significant at the 0.05 level (2-tailed).

Table 4. Rotated COMPONENT Matrix[a]

	Factor 1: Relative Advantage/ Compatibility	Factor 2: Complexity/ Simplicity	Factor 3: Trialability	Factor 4: Observability
PB1	0.698	0.153	0.137	-0.171
PB2	0.565	0.015	0.312	0.292
PB3	0.797	0.052	-0.035	0.257
PB4	0.710	0.089	0.135	0.166
PB5	0.607	0.101	0.446	0.148
PB6	0.669	0.082	0.278	0.129
PB7	0.701	0.265	0.195	-0.136
PB8	0.445	0.255	0.407	0.271
PB9	0.698	0.041	-0.066	0.409
PB10	0.680	0.241	0.138	0.193
PB11	0.264	0.732	0.125	-0.018
PB12	0.155	0.762	0.216	0.016
PB13	0.019	0.644	-0.040	0.463
PB14	0.172	0.673	0.225	0.338
PB15	0.038	0.691	0.377	0.060
PB17	0.153	0.730	0.268	0.116
PB18	0.069	0.807	0.204	0.098
PB19	0.229	0.386	0.693	0.065
PB20	0.163	0.426	0.611	0.156
PB22	0.193	0.217	0.566	0.114
PB23	0.154	0.267	0.755	0.242
PB24	0.194	0.065	0.312	0.628
PB26	0.105	0.407	0.133	0.560
PB29	0.361	0.138	0.219	0.606
Mean	3.61	4.19	3.99	3.78
Standard deviation	0.93	0.79	0.82	0.83
Cronbach alpha	0.895	0.887	0.805	0.652

[a]Extraction Method: Principal Component Analysis. Rotation Method: Varimax with Kaiser Normalization. Rotation converged in 6 iterations.

we already suspected that SERVQUAL framework is perhaps more suitable for tangible services rather than intangible services such as fintech.

As shown in the Table 7 below, all five SERVQUAL dimensions were proved to be positive. The quality gap of the fintech services was calculated and Wilcoxon test demonstrated that the difference between the expectation

Table 5. Correlations matrix of adoption attributes

	Relative Advantage/ Compatibility	Complexity/ Simplicity	Trialability	Observability	Perceived Benefits of Adopting Fintech
Relative Advantage/ Compatibility	1	.420**	.536**	.545**	.869**
Complexity/ Simplicity		1	.642**	.495**	.774**
Trialability			1	.521**	.791**
Observability				1	.719**

**. Correlation is significant at the 0.01 level (2-tailed).

Table 6. Mean score, customers' expectation and perception of quality attributes

SERVQUAL attributes	Expectation	STDev	Perception	STDev	Gap	STDev
Tangible 1	4.296	0.783	4.152	0.741	0.144	0.715
Tangible 2	3.952	0.878	4.056	0.796	-0.104	0.840
Tangible 3	3.608	0.982	3.680	0.885	-0.072	0.943
Tangible 4	4.192	0.779	4.152	0.783	0.040	0.700
Reliability 1	4.120	0.713	4.064	0.839	0.056	0.909
Reliability 2	4.160	0.892	4.016	0.842	0.144	0.981
Reliability 3	4.352	0.743	4.088	0.740	0.264	0.742
Reliability 4	4.312	0.827	4.080	0.848	0.232	0.804
Reliability 5	4.216	0.768	3.984	0.897	0.232	0.814
Responsiveness 1	4.240	0.766	3.920	0.838	0.320	0.866
Responsiveness 2	4.320	0.768	4.024	0.807	0.296	0.842
Responsiveness 3	4.408	0.708	4.056	0.765	0.352	0.775
Responsiveness 4	4.112	0.863	3.920	0.819	0.192	0.895
Assurance 1	4.312	0.723	4.008	0.767	0.304	0.753
Assurance 2	4.472	0.690	4.184	0.744	0.288	0.669
Assurance 3	4.344	0.794	4.056	0.806	0.288	0.749
Assurance 4	4.464	0.666	3.984	0.761	0.480	0.747
Empathy 1	4.176	0.833	3.824	0.871	0.352	0.882
Empathy 2	4.280	0.725	4.008	0.837	0.272	0.722
Empathy 3	4.120	0.828	3.872	0.924	0.248	0.912
Empathy 4	4.312	0.711	4.056	0.806	0.256	0.739
Empathy 5	4.192	0.829	3.984	0.803	0.208	0.785

Table 7. SERVQUAL dimensions and quality gap of Fintech services

SERVQUAL dimensions	Expectation	STDev	Perception	STDev	Gap	STDev	P value
Tangibility	4.012	0.856	4.010	0.801	0.002	0.799	<0.001
Reliability	4.232	0.789	4.046	0.834	0.186	0.850	<0.001
Responsiveness	4.270	0.776	3.980	0.808	0.290	0.845	<0.001
Assurance	4.398	0.718	4.058	0.770	0.340	0.730	<0.001
Empathy	4.216	0.786	3.949	0.848	0.267	0.808	<0.001
Total Quality	4.225	0.785	4.007	0.815	0.218	0.807	<0.001

and perception of the patients was statistically significant in all of dimensions. Among those dimensions, the highest gap score was related to assurance (0.340), followed by responsiveness (0.290) and empathy (0.267). On the other hand, the lowest gap score was associated with tangibility (0.002), followed by reliability (0.186). All items were significant at the $P < .001$ level.

This study suggest that, in general, fintech adoption had several desirable important properties: (1) the advantages of fintech products and services must be superior compared to traditional banking and financial products and services, (2) fintech products and services must be easy to try by prospected customers, and (3) fintech products and services should be as simple as possible. These properties were also supported by the SERVQUAL measurement which displayed similar theme.

On the other hand, SERVQUAL measurement indicated that fintech companies must pay attention to assurance factor. Even though there are many regulations concerning fintech in Indonesia, fintech companies should not take consumer trust and confidence for granted (Arner et al., 2017). In conjunction with this factor, responsiveness and empathy should be the priority of any fintech providers (Lee and Shin, 2018). This study also perhaps implies some of the predominant explanations, namely cultural idiosyncrasies, on the one extreme, and the universal imperatives of a latecomer notion or of technological innovation, on the other.

CONCLUSION AND FUTURE DIRECTIONS

The present study reveals the way customers adopt fintech products and services in Indonesia and analyzes their perceptions toward the quality of fintech products and services. Unlike traditional banking/financial products and services, fintech customers are expecting not only superior advantages, but also trialability and simplicity of fintech products and services. Moreover, fintech companies should also take into account trust, empathy, and responsiveness as their focus priorities.

Indonesia is also not a financial center like Hong Kong or Singapore, thus probably there will be no significant consequences on direct job losses as a result of fintech innovation. However, the government should carefully examine job shift in fintech-related industries such as law firms, accounting firms, technology vendors, among others. While the number is perhaps substantially smaller, there will be a very different skill sets and regulations required for today's bankers and financiers compared to decades ago.

Indeed, this study suffers from several limitations. First, even though this study was carefully chosen its sample, the data obtained were still considered to be small. Theoretically speaking, diffusion theory (Rogers, 1995) and SERVQUAL (1988) have been widely criticized. Thus, examining similar phenomenon using more recent framework would complement the study. Last but not least, while examining customer behavior and preferences seemed like a natural fit for anyone interested in technological innovation such as fintech, but that potential has somewhat surprisingly only been realized to a very limited extent.

REFERENCES

Accenture. (2015). *Future of FinTech and Banking*. Available at http://www.accenture.com/us-en/insight-future-fintech-banking.aspx

Arner, D. W., Zetzsche, D. A., Buckley, R. P., & Barberis, J. N. (2017). FinTech and RegTech: Enabling Innovation While Preserving Financial Stability. *Georgetown Journal of International Affairs*, *18*(3), 47–58. doi:10.1353/gia.2017.0036

Arslanian, H. (2016). How FinTech is Shaping the Future of Banking. *TEDx Talks*. Available at https://youtu.be/pPkNtN8G7q8

Bryman, A., & Bell, E. (2007). *Business Research Methods*. New York: Oxford University Press.

Dillman, D. A. (2000). *Mail and Internet Surveys: The Tailored Design Method* (2nd ed.). New York: Wiley.

Euromonitor. (2017). *Mobile Phones in Indonesia*. Retrieved from http://www.euromonitor.com/mobile-phones-in-indonesia/report

Fintechnews Singapore. (2018). Fintech Indonesia Report 2018 – The State of Play for Fintech Indonesia. *Fintechnews Singapore*. Available at http://fintechnews.sg/20712/indonesia/fintech-indonesia-report-2018/

Global Findex. (2014). *The Global Findex database: Indonesia*. Retrieved from http://datatopics.worldbank.org/financialinclusion/country/indonesia

Gomber, P., Koch, J. A., & Siering, M. (2017). Digital Finance and FinTech: Current research and future research directions. *Journal of Business Economics*, *87*(5), 537–580. doi:10.100711573-017-0852-x

Iman, N. (2018). Assessing the dynamics of fintech in Indonesia. *Investment Management and Financial Innovations*, *15*(4), 296–303. doi:10.21511/imfi.15(4).2018.24

Lee, L., & Shin, Y. J. (2018). Fintech: Ecosystem, business models, investment decisions, and challenges. *Business Horizons*, *61*(1), 35–46. doi:10.1016/j.bushor.2017.09.003

Ng, A. W., & Kwok, B. K. B. (2017). Emergence of Fintech and cybersecurity in a global financial centre: Strategic approach by a regulator. *Journal of Financial Regulation and Compliance*, *25*(4), 422–434. doi:10.1108/JFRC-01-2017-0013

Parasuraman, A., Zeithaml, V. A., & Berry, L. L. (1988). SERVQUAL: A multiple-item scale for measuring consumer perception of service quality. *Journal of Retailing*, *64*(1), 12–40.

Puschmann, T. (2017). Fintech. *Business & Information Systems Engineering*, *59*(1), 69–76. doi:10.100712599-017-0464-6

PwC. (2016). *FinTech*. Available at http://www.pwc.com/us/en/financial-services/fintech.html

PwC. (2017). *The Long View: How will the global economic order change by 2050?* Available at https://www.pwc.com/gx/en/issues/economy/the-world-in-2050.html

Rogers, E. M. (1995). *Diffusion of Innovation* (4th ed.). New York: Free Press.

Seeking Alpha. (2017). Indonesia - The Next Major Oil Importer? *Seeking Alpha*. Available at https://seekingalpha.com/article/4035779-indonesia-next-major-oil-importer

The Jakarta Post. (2017). 16,000 Indonesian islands registered at UN. *The Jakarta Post*. Available at https://www.thejakartapost.com/news/2017/08/21/16000-indonesian-islands-registered-at-un.html

ENDNOTES

1 https://fintech.id/

2 https://www.ojk.go.id/id/berita-dan-kegiatan/publikasi/Pages/Penyelenggara-Fintech-Terdaftar-di-OJK-per-Oktober-2018.aspx

Chapter 10
The Growing Opportunities of Financial Technology in Brunei

Fakhriyah Abdullah Thani
Universiti Brunei Darussalam, Brunei

ABSTRACT

This chapter aims to address the current FinTech situation in Brunei as well as the possibility of encouraging the growth opportunities and adoption of FinTech into the nation's daily life. Although the development of FinTech has been prevalent across the globe, Brunei has only begun to creep up to its Association of South East Asian Nations (ASEAN) counterparts in the race of FinTech growth. Although existing research on FinTech adoption is prevalent, there is little evidence to indicate a substantive research has been conducted on ASEAN FinTech, particularly in Brunei.

DOI: 10.4018/978-1-5225-9183-2.ch010

Copyright © 2020, IGI Global. Copying or distributing in print or electronic forms without written permission of IGI Global is prohibited.

INTRODUCTION

In 2016, the Bruneian government identified its financial sector to be a key driver in ameliorating the national economy. In an effort to diversify and develop the economy further, Brunei has moved its focus away from its dependence of oil and gas, to venturing into other areas of economic development. In an attempt to accommodate the fast changing nature of ICT in the financial sector and the potential adoption of new technologies and trends, the Autoriti Monetari Brunei Darussalam (AMBD) established its Financial Technology (FinTech) Unit in 2016. This unit acts as a regulatory board for FinTech developments and innovation in the nation. While traditional banking is still popular, there is a slow adoption of FinTech with the emergence of applications such as ProgresifPay, BruPay and Bank Islam Brunei Darussalam (BIBD) NEXGEN.

The rise of Industry 4.0 has transformed the traditional financial platform with many organizations and financial institutions rapidly adopting its digital counterpart. While FinTech is becoming an increasingly popular trend, its adoption and growth in Brunei is slower in comparison to its Association of South East Asian Nation (ASEAN) neighbors. According to the report by United Overseas Bank Group and Ernest & Young Corporation in 2016, Brunei was ranked amongst the lowest in the region with an estimated number of 2 FinTech accelerators, incubators and innovation labs in comparison to Singapore which houses approximately 50 FinTech related companies. The numbers indicate a growing opportunity for companies and startups to tap into the FinTech and accelerate the growth of such industry.

In an effort to identify the underlying opportunities of FinTech in Brunei, there is a need to understand the existing FinTech industry in Brunei and its potential. More specifically, the paper will attempt to address the following questions:

1. What are the main drivers of FinTech industry in Brunei?
2. What are the main challenges of adopting and encouraging FinTech growth in Brunei?

This paper aims to provide an insight to the potential opportunities that exists in Brunei by evaluating the financial environment in Brunei. The main objective of this study is to fill in the gap of a non-existent literature review on ASEAN FinTech, particularly in Brunei. Furthermore, the paper aims to provide evidence of the current financial movement of FinTech in Brunei. The outcome of this study will provide an overview/insight to the development of FinTech industry in Brunei.

BACKGROUND

FinTech has become one of today's popular buzzword, not only among academics but also amongst professionals and the public alike. Despite its recent popularity, the integration of technology in the area of financial services dates as early as the 1950s with the introduction of credit cards and later in 1960's, the Automated Teller Machine (ATM) (Desai, 2015; Ma & Liu, 2017). Developed with convenience in mind, the introduction of the ATM presented an easier alternative for bank customers and bankers alike in conducting financial transactions (Ogunsemor, 1991; Hone, Graham, Maguire, Baber & Johnson, 1998; Fasan, 2014; Mahmud, Islam & Naher, 2015). The rise of the Internet in the 1990's saw the development of an Internet based business model such as e-commerce and e-banking which further resulted in the introduction of a digitized trading platform (Arner, Berberis & Buckley, 2015; Desai, 2015).

The emergence of Industry 4.0 further facilitated the growth of FinTech subsequently altering the existing financial service industry. Numerous literature have attempted to define FinTech with some describing it to be the use of traditional financial activities with that of modern technology such as cloud computing, big data etc. FinTech is a technological revolution of the financial industry as it uses innovative technology to provide new products, solutions and services (Puschmann, 2012; Koffi, 2016; Wonglimpiyarat, 2017). Kim et al. (2015, pp.136-140) defines FinTech to be "an industry which uses mobile-centered IT technology to enhance the efficiency of the financial system". Gomber et al., (2017) and Vives (2017) identified FinTech as disruptive innovators of financial institutions that takes advantage of the interconnectivity of today's devices through the use of the Internet. Ozili (2018) further define FinTech as the emergence of a digital financial and banking service with the use of today's technological advancement.

The broad and complex nature of FinTech development, there is yet to be a generally accepted classification of FinTech innovation. Numerous literature (Arner et al., 2015; Zalan & Toufaily, 2017; Martínez-Climent,

Zorio-Grima & Robeiro-Soriano, 2018) defined FinTech to include a variety of financing technologies such as crowdfunding, peer-to-peer lending as well as technology based financial services. This chapter will highlight the different FinTech elements as categorized by Dorfleitner et al. (2017). In their research, Dorfleitner et al. (2017) identified four main categorizes in which FinTech innovation can be classified, namely: Financing, Asset Management, Payments and Other FinTechs.

CROWDFUNDING

Originally coined in 2006 by Michael Sullivan, the rapid development of the Internet has facilitated the advent of crowdfunding and has since become one of today's popular financing methods (Guan, 2016). Its advent has been described as the public's attempt to balance out the need for the supply and demand of capital brought about by the economic disruption in the early 2000's (Bruton et al., 2015). Numerous scholars (Kappel, 2008; Belleflame, Lambert & Schwienbacher, 2010, 2014) defined crowdfunding as an informal way of

Figure 1. Segments and elements of FinTech
Source: Dorfleitner et al, 2017.

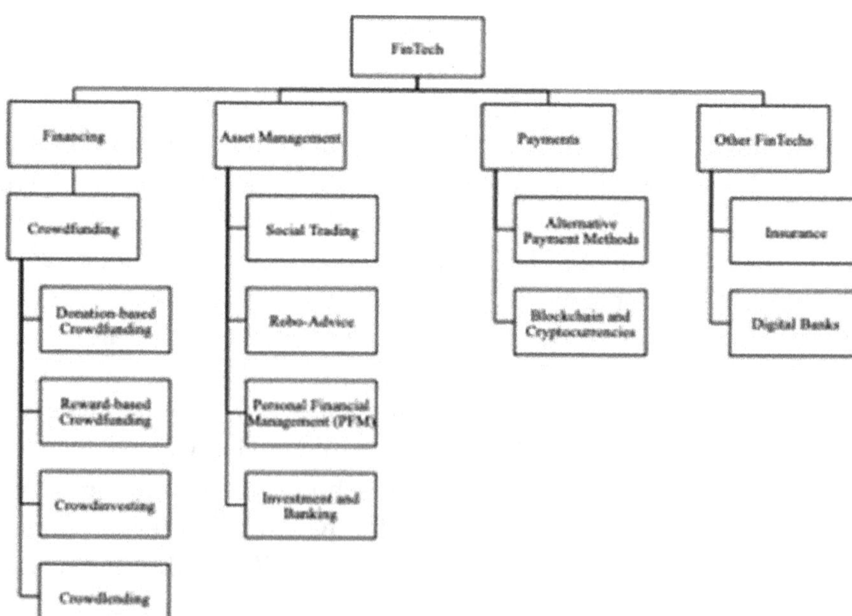

gathering finances by engaging the public (easily identified as crowd) in order to raise the required funds instead of relying on traditional sources of funds such as loans or investments. Couffinhal (2014) described crowdfunding as a lateral funding model, which enables the easy transfer of funds between two parties via an Internet based platform.

Over the years, scholars have further noted the four models of crowdfunding based on the successful outcome of the funding. Such crowdfunding models have been identified as donation-based crowdfunding, reward-based crowdfunding, crowdinvesting and crowdlending. *Donation-based crowdfunding* is one such model that relies on the public or crowd's philanthropic nature in contributing funds to the project.

Reward-based crowdfunding, on the other hand, is one of more known crowdfunding model. These models have been emulated by many online platforms such as Indiegogo and Kickstarter; and social networking sites such as Facebook and Twitter. This model remains popular as supporters are rewarded with incentives or physical rewards as a token of appreciation for their contribution to a successful project (Agrawal, Catalini & Goldfarb, 2015).

Crowdinvesting, more commonly known as equity-based crowdfunding, is similar to that of the model discussed above. However, instead of providing supporters with tangible rewards, supporters are given the avenue to invest in start-ups and business ventures with the aim of gaining a share of such ventures (Guan, 2016).

Crowdlending, also known as peer-to-peer (P2P) lending, allows supporters to provide a certain amount of money in exchange for a certain amount of financial gain such as return of interest rates (Guan, 2016). Crowdlending can also be seen as a form of loan due to the nature of its transactions that occurs between borrowers and lenders. While similar to traditional loans, crowdlending allows projects or businesses to be financed by the crowd.

Despite its perceived benefits, Guan (2016) raised his concerns in particular regards to crowdinvesting and crowdlending as he identifies them to be a "special financial tools" which in turn requires a specific regulatory framework that can help address issues relating to crowdinvesting and crowdlending.

ASSET MANAGEMENT

The development of technological innovations has since altered the financial environment. As a result, traditional financial services such as asset management has faced much disruption from the development of such innovation. Today, the introduction of such innovation has facilitated the growth of innovative asset management solutions and services such as Social Trading, Robo-Advisors, Personal Finance Management as well as Investment and Banking (Haddad & Hornuf, 2018).

SOCIAL TRADING

Social trading is a novel way of trading as it allows investors to observe and emulate trading patterns and strategies of their peers on the social platform (Pelster & Hofmann, 2018). Wohlgemuth et al., (2016) further described social trading as a type of online community that allows its investors to analyze and imitate investments that are made by trusted investors. Additionally, social trading further enables traders and investors to participate in the field of supply and demand with a low entry barrier (Pelster & Hofmann, 2018). While authors argued the disruption it can cause towards traditional trading and for investors, it does provide benefit to novice trading as it increases their likelihood for a successful trade (Pan, Altschuler & Pentland, 2012).

ROBO-ADVISORS

Also known as digital advisors, these solutions makes use of the innovative technological advancements to demonstrate a novel way of providing clients financial advice and services. With the use of models and algorithms, companies are able to provide its clients with a specialized financial advice as well as portfolio management services that caters to their clients' needs (Kaya, 2017). While its introduction has been slow, the recent technological advancements allowed robo-advisors to offer a wide range of services that takes into account the preference of individual potential investors (Phoon & Koh, 2018). Due to its simplicity and inexpensive nature, an increasing amount of investors are engaging with robo-advisors as opposed to its traditional counterparts. While robo-advisors has disrupted the existing financial advice service, Phoon & Koh (2018) indicated that traditional asset managers are still the main choice for highly sophisticated clients and investors due to the complex nature of their requests.

PAYMENTS

The development of digital technologies has tremendously disrupted the field of financial services, particularly in the payment methods. Digital payment has its roots in online or internet-based payments such as PayPal. Leveraging on existing platforms, traditional financial institutions and company began to integrate mobile-based applications to provide payment services via mobile.

ALTERNATIVE PAYMENT METHODS

The increasingly rapid development of FinTech technologies and innovation has facilitated the growth of an alternative payment method, better known as e-Wallets. Mobile applications such as Apple Pay and ProgresifPay provide users the platform to conduct in financial transactions at the tip of their fingertips via the Internet (Ryabova, 2015; Lu, 2018a, 2018b). As technological advancements progress, so has the development of alternative payments with many providers incorporating Quick Response (QR) code as part of their mobile app functionality (Lu, 2018a, 2018b).

BLOCKCHAIN AND CRYPTO-PRODUCTS

In the recent years, a new form of digital currency, Bitcoin, has been developed as an attempt to provide an alternative form of payment that is independent from a central authority (Swan, 2015). Swan (2015) describes Bitcoin as a form of digital money that can be exchanged over the Internet using 'decentralized cryptocurrency technology' (Shrier, Canale & Pentland, 2016). Though Bitcoin payments are decentralized, Bitcoin transactions are recorded in a dispersed public ledger known as Blockchain (Swan, 2015; Iansiti & Lakhani, 2017). Lee & Shin (2018) further highlighted the impact Blockchain technology has on numerous traditional financial services as such technology boasts better services with secured transactions both locally and globally. Despite its traceability, its unique ability to maintain users' security makes it a popular form of payment amongst its users (Olleros & Zhegu, 2016).

Although Bitcoin is the more notable example of Blockchain, Crosby et al. (2016) highlighted its versatility due to its successful application in both the financial and non-financial sectors. Such versatility can be attributed to its characteristics – distributed consensus and anonymity, further encouraging the use of Blockchain technology in non-financial sectors. The advent of Blockchain has given rise to the development of crypto-product or Blockchain technologies that disrupts existing financial sector.

OTHER FINTECH

The rapid innovative development of FinTech has also transformed traditional financial services such as insurance and banking institutions.

INSURTECH

Based on the prevailing growth of FinTech, there is an increasing growth to incorporate technology on existing financial products. In 2017, the World Bank reported a $2.3 billion has been spent on InsureTech funding in countries such as the US and the UK (Wrede, 2018). With an increasing startups and investments in the area, many experts are anticipating the boom of InsureTech in the financial industry. Despite receiving global investments, the power and future of InsureTech has been shrouded with doubt and uncertainty as Deda (2017) highlighted the lack of awareness of such innovation in the insurance industry.

Similar to FinTech, InsureTech is the integration of technology to alter and disrupt the existing insurance industry. Shai (2018) describes InsureTech as the incorporation of technology with companies or products to add value in the traditional insurance value chain. Braun & Schreiber (2017) further defined InsureTech as *'the application of modern technologies in the risk transfer sector'*. The emergence of such disruptive technology is expected to change consumers' perception on the current insurance industry (Passler, 2018). Despite its potential disruptive in the insurance sector, Braun & Schreiber (2017) discovered that many InsureTech startups and technologies is merely a digitization of the existing process and products.

DIGITAL BANKS

Since the emergence of the Internet, traditional financial institutions and banks have extended their offerings to provide services over the Internet. With the accessibility and availability of smartphones and Industry 4.0, banks and financial institutions began to offer the services over mobile. Digital-only banks is the complete digitization of banks, removing the need for a physical store in favor of internet-based and mobile-based applications to provide traditional banking services (Money Super Market, 2018). Leveraging on technologies of Industry 4.0, digital banks rely on consumers' data to craft a personalized offerings ranging from financing and payments to asset management (Lipton, Shrier & Pentland, 2016).

ASEAN FINTECH INDUSTRY

Despite the ASEAN region still at its developing stage, its FinTech industry shows promising signs of continuous growth. In a report published by Deloitte, FinTech growth in the ASEAN region have reached over US$5 billion worth of investment in 2017 alone and is expected to escalade up to at least US$70 billion in the near future (Cassiopeia Services, 2019). While Singapore continues to pilot the ASEAN FinTech industry, other nations are slowly making a name for themselves in various fields of FinTech.

FINTECH INDUSTRY IN BRUNEI DARUSSALAM

One of the smallest nations in the ASEAN region with a population of approximately 400,000 people, Brunei is ranked as the world's 4th country with the highest social media penetration (Rajak, 2018) and number 1 in the ASEAN region with a penetration rate of 94.6% (Internet World Stats, 2018). Despite such rankings, Brunei has been slow to adopt and encourage the growth of its FinTech industry. In an effort to encourage the development of such FinTech innovations, a regulatory sandbox was established under the direction of the nation's Autoriti Monetari Brunei Darussalam (AMBD) (Biz Brunei, 2017). The establishment of the regulatory sandbox is the nation's first step towards encouraging the development of its FinTech industry. Additionally, Hj Md Khairul Zaki Hj Mohidin – the Head of AMBD's FinTech unit, elaborated the role of the regulatory sandbox in acting as a hub of information as well as a networking platform for keen investing groups (Biz Brunei, 2017).

Although Brunei's FinTech industry is still at its infancy, FinTech startups and financial institutions are progressively developing FinTech innovations as an attempt to introduce and illustrate the potential of FinTech innovations. In 2011, Bank Islam Brunei Darussalam (BIBD) launched its BIBD Debit Card and mobile banking as their first step towards achieving a cashless society (Kon, 2018). Today, Brunei's FinTech industry has evolved from mobile banking to the development of numerous FinTech innovations such as alternative payment methods such as QR code payments and e-Wallet payment platform with the introduction of the BIBD NEXGEN. Brunei's FinTech startup such as BruPay and WasapPay attempts to provide an alternative payment solution, while Jana Model Ethis (JME) is an Islamic crowdfunding platform where as Chynge is a digital remittance service (Wong, 2018).

THE GROWING OPPORTUNITIES OF FINTECH IN BRUNEI

Despite boasting a high penetration rate of 94.3%, the research discovered a relatively low level of FinTech awareness among majority of the Bruneian public, which explains the relatively slow growth of FinTech adoption. Additionally, the reported concerns expressed by respondents could signify additional factors limiting Brunei's FinTech adoption rate. In order to overcome such slow growth, an increased level of awareness and knowledge sharing should be encouraged banks, financial institutions as well as FinTech startups.

ENVIRONMENT

The findings of the research suggest there are several factors driving Brunei's FinTech industry. Amongst the factors are the rapid technological advancements that provide online sellers with a digital platform to offer products and services to members of the public with ease. Such convenience has propelled the development of financial technology in the nation. Additionally, the fast growth of youth and its digitally ready and connected young population is conducive in encouraging FinTech growth in the nation. However, such readiness and sophistication should be supported with a level of awareness and education from stakeholders to increase the level of awareness necessary to boost FinTech adoption and development.

OPPORTUNITIES

The research revealed that while the opportunities of FinTech growth and adoption is vast, it is important for key FinTech player to emulate characteristics of its traditional counterparts, i.e., simplicity and security. Offering consumers '*peace of mind*' can alter consumers' views on FinTech services to adopt such practices. With the increasing growth of e-payments in Brunei, it is crucial for such services to be perceived as simple and secure so to gain the population's trust.

The introduction of a diverse FinTech service in Brunei can help provide the nation with more opportunities to push the boundaries of its economic diversity. By recognizing the population's level of sophistication in the digital platform, Brunei has an opportunity to become a hub for both established as well as emerging FinTech companies and startups to experiment the viability and usability of their FinTech products. Furthermore, its strong Islamic brand and identity can help build the foundation for Brunei to towards developing Islamic FinTech services and establishing themselves as an *Abode of Islamic FinTech.*

Although blockchain technologies such as crypto-currencies and crypto-products have been popular around the globe, it has yet to gain its footing in the nation with the public opting for services such as e-Trading. The introduction of currency trading application has removed the need for intermediaries, as the public is able to become traders themselves. With easy access for foreign exchange (Forex) trading, many of the nation's population have delved into Forex trading as a means of income. Acknowledging the nation's increasing Forex activity, there is potential opportunity for Brunei to adopt a fully-fledged, digitally run stock market as well as a stock market system and ancillary services to be developed.

In realizing the nation's potential to become a hub for FinTech experimentation as well as an Abode for Islamic FinTech, the government can build on such opportunity to develop FinTech based education. Such move would contribute to the nation's efforts to diversify its economy and propel them into a nation that encourages innovative development.

CHALLENGES

Although FinTech services has numerous opportunities to expand further beyond e-payments, there presents numerous challenges in adopting FinTech related services. One such challenge is the consumers' perception towards FinTech services. Although existing FinTech services has managed to successfully offer FinTech services such as e-payment platforms, concerns such as security and protection of personal data remains a challenge.

With the rise and adoption of FinTech services in the nation, it is crucial for relevant parties to look into the rise of potential threats of fraud and illicit activities. While crowdfunding is a novel concept, it is often scrutinized and adopted with caution due to the risk associated with it. As crowdfunding involves other people's money, a certain degree of trust and transparency should be practiced in order to fully adopt such services.

One particular challenge that exists in the adoption of FinTech services in Brunei is the existing business model that is adopted in the nation. While the nation's regulatory bodies and the government is proactive in encouraging the development and adoption of FinTech services, many businesses are often slow and some are reluctant to engage with FinTech adoption. The long established businesses of today are built on the mums-and-dads business model that relies heavily on cash. With their business as their main source of income, several, if not, majority of businesses are reluctant to incorporate FinTech services into their business due to concerns mentioned previously.

RECOMMENDATIONS

In order to ameliorate the nation's economy and leverage FinTech innovations as a way of economic diversification, the research provides various alternatives for Brunei and its financial institutions to venture into. In order to develop a strong economic development and generate a stronghold on FinTech, it is recommended for the stakeholders to look into the challenges relating to FinTech adoption.

Furthermore, it is necessary for the Brunei government to invest in adequate financial and network infrastructure to encourage the public toward adopting FinTech services in the nation. Similarly, it is suggested that the government invest in providing support and guidance for local businesses to fully integrate and accept FinTech services without implementing a minimum spending fee on its customers. In doing so, the government needs to take an even more proactive approach in not only encouraging the development of FinTech services but also the acceptance of FinTech services in local businesses.

Additionally, financial institutions and FinTech companies should look into the strong Islamic identity to offer more shari'ah compliant FinTech services. Doing so will enable Brunei to work towards establishing Brunei as a hub for Islamic FinTech and realizing Brunei as not only an *'Abode of Peace'* but also an *'Abode of Islamic FinTech'*. Additionally, its young and digitally abled population act as a breeding ground for testing potential FinTech developments and innovation giving AMBD a strong position to act as a strong RegTech in the region.

FUTURE RESEARCH DIRECTIONS

With the limited literature in the field, it is recommended future research to be conducted to not only extend the potential of such research but also to further investigate the feasibility of adopting FinTech towards achieving a cashless society. Furthermore, future research is encouraged to further assess the viability of FinTech services as the nation's attempt to diversify and ameliorate the national economy.

Although adopting a variety of FinTech services in the nation could diversify the economy and encourage economic growth, the full incorporation of FinTech services, as a mode of transaction should be assessed.

CONCLUSION

The rise of Industry 4.0 and rapid technological advancements in a digitally ready population, FinTech startups such as Jana Modal Ethis and financial institutions such as Bank Islam Brunei Darussalam are at the edge of providing Financial technological advancements that have the potential to alter and disrupt the existing financial industry in Brunei.

In an attempt to provide literature in the field, the research looks into existing Brunei environment to investigate circumstances behind the slow adoption rate of FinTech in the nation. The author discovered that while there are numerous opportunities that could be adopted, the potential risk that comes with such opportunities should be taken into consideration. By taking such challenges into consideration, Brunei can be a potential powerhouse in the FinTech industry, particularly in the emergence of Industry 4.0.

REFERENCES

Agrawal, A., Catalini, C., & Goldfarb, A. (2015). Crowdfunding: Geography, Social Networks and the Timing of Investment Decisions. *Journal of Economics & Management Strategy*, *24*(2), 253–274. doi:10.1111/jems.12093

Arner, D. W., Barberis, J., & Buckley, R. P. (2015). The evolution of FinTech: a new post-crisis paradigm. *Georgetown Journal of International Law,* (47), 1271.

Bauer, R. M., & Gegenhuber, T. (2015). Crowdsourcing: Global search and the twisted roles of consumers and producers. *Organization*, *22*(5), 661–681. doi:10.1177/1350508415585030 PMID:27524930

Beaulieu, T., Sarker, S., & Sarker, S. (2015). A conceptual framework for understanding crowdfunding. CAIS, 37, 1.

Belleflame, P., Lambert, T., & Schwienbacher, A. (2010). *Crowdfunding: An industrial organization perspective. In Workshop Digital Business Models: Understanding Strategies* (pp. 25–26). Paris: Citeseer.

Belleflamme, P., Lambert, T., & Schwienbacher, A. (2014). Crowdfunding: Tapping the right crowd. *Journal of Business Venturing*, *29*(5), 585–609. doi:10.1016/j.jbusvent.2013.07.003

Belleflamme, P., Omrani, N., & Peitz, M. (2015). The economics of crowdfunding platform. *Information Economics and Policy*, *33*, 11–28. doi:10.1016/j.infoecopol.2015.08.003

Biz Brunei. (2017). AMBD launches sandbox under new FinTech unit. *Biz Brunei*. Retrieved from: https://www.bizbrunei.com/2017/03/amdb-launches-sandbox-new-fintech-unit/

Bofondi, M., & Gobbi, G. (2017). The Big Promise of FinTech. *European Economy*, *2*(2), 107–120.

Braun, A., & Schreiber, F. (2017). *The Current InsurTech Landscape: Business Models and Disruptive Potential*. St Gallen: Institute of Insurance Economics I.VW-HSG, University of St. Gallen.

Bruton, G. D., Khavul, S., Siegel, D. S., & Wright, M. (2015). New Financial Alternatives in Seeding Entrepreneurship: Microfinance, Crowdfnding and Peer-to-Peer Innovations. *Entrepreneurship Theory and Practice*, *39*(1), 9–26. doi:10.1111/etap.12143

Cassiopeia Services. (2019). All eyes on Southeast Asia for FinTech growth in 2019. *Medium*. Retrieved from https://medium.com/@cassiopeiaservicesltd/all-eyes-on-southeast-asia-for-fintech-growth-in-2019-97aec593a93

Consulus. (2013). BIBD: Bruneian at Heart. *Consulus*. Retrieved from: http://consulus.com/bibd-bruneian-at-heart/

Couffinhal, B. (2014). *The use of crowdfunding as an alternative way to finance small businesses in France*. Dublin: Dublin Business School.

Crosby, M., Nachiappan, P., Verma, S., & Kalyanaraman, V. (2016). BlockChain Technology: Beyond Bitcoin. *Applied Innovation Review (AIR)*, (2), 6 - 19.

Deda, B. (2017). What is InsurTech and how can you harness its disruptive power? *Vertafore*. Retrieved from: https://www.vertafore.com/resources/blog-posts/what-insurtech-and-how-can-you-harness-its-disruptive-powers

Desai, F. (2015). The Evolution of FinTech. *Forbes*. Retrieved from: https://www.forbes.com/sites/falgunidesai/2015/12/13/the-evolution-of-fintech/#758f05787175

Dorfleitner, G., Hornuf, L., Schmitt, M., & Weber, M. (2017). FinTech in Germany. In G. Dorfleitner, L. Hornuf, M. Schmitt, & M. Weber (Eds.), The FinTech Market in Germany (pp. 34 - 36). Springer International Publishing. doi:10.1007/978-3-319-54666-7

Fasan, R. (2014). Banks, customer relation and use of ATM cards. *Business Day Newspapers*. Retrieved from: www.businessdayonline.com

Gomber, P., Koch, J.-A., & Siering, M. (2017). Digital Finance and FinTech: Current research and future research direction. *Journal of Business Economics*, *87*(5), 537–580. doi:10.100711573-017-0852-x

Guan, L. (2016). *A Short Literature Review on Reward-based Crowdfunding*. Academic Press.

Haddad, C., & Hornuf, L. (2018). The emergence of the global fintech market: Economic and technological determinants. *Small Business Economics*, 1–25.

Hone, K. S., Graham, R., Maguire, M., Baber, C., & Johnson, G. (1998). Speech technology for automatic teller machines: An investigation of user attitude and performance. *Ergonomics*, *41*(7), 962–981. doi:10.1080/001401398186531

Hyman, L., Lamb, J., & Bulmer, M. (2006). The Use of Pre-Existing Survey Questions: Implications for Data Quality. *European Conference on Quality in Survey Statistics*.

Iansiti, M., & Lakhani, K. R. (2017). The Truth about Blockchain. *Harvard Business Review*, 3–11.

Internet World Stats. (2018). Internet Usage in Asia. *Internet World Stats: Usage and Population Statistics*. Retrieved from: https://www.internetworldstats.com/stats3.htm

Kappel, T. (2008). Ex ante crowdfunding and the recording industry: A model for the US. *Loyola of Los Angeles Entertainment Law Review*, *29*, 375.

Kaya, O. (2017). Robo-advice - a true innovation in asset management. *Deutsche Bank Research: EU Monitor Global financial markets*. Retrieved from: http://www.dbresearch.com/PROD/RPS_EN-PROD/PROD0000000000449125/Robo-advice_–_a_true_innovation_in_asset_managemen.PDF

Kim, Y., Park, Y.-J., Choi, J., & Yeon, J. (2015). An Empirical Study on the Adoption of "FinTech" Service: Focused on Mobile Payment Services. *Advanced Science and Technology Letters*, *114*, 136–140. doi:10.14257/astl.2015.114.26

Kleemann, F., Voß, G., & Rieder, K. (2008). Un(der)paid innovators: The commercial utiliza-tion of consumer work through crowdsourcing. *Science, Technology & Innovation Studies*, *4*(1), 5.

Koffi, H. (2016). The Fintech Revolution: An Opportunity for the West African Financial Sector. *Open Journal of Applied Sciences*, *6*(11), 771–782. doi:10.4236/ojapps.2016.611068

Kon, J. (2018). Progresif launches Brunei's first mobile wallet. *Borneo Bulletin* Retrieved from: https://borneobulletin.com.bn/progresif-launches-bruneis-first-mobile-wallet/

Lakhani, K., Lifshitz-Assaf, H., & Tushman, M. (2013). Open Innovation and Organizational Boundaries: The Impact of Task Decomposition and Knowledge Distribution on the Locus of Innovation. In A. Grandori (Ed.), *Handbook of Economic Organization: Integrating Economic and Organization Theory* (pp. 355–382). Northampton, UK: Edward Elgar. doi:10.4337/9781782548225.00030

Lee, I., & Shin, Y. J. (2018). Fintech: Ecosystem, business models, investment decisions and challenges. *Business Horizons*, *61*(1), 35–46. doi:10.1016/j.bushor.2017.09.003

Leong, C., Tan, B., Xiao, X., Tan, F. T., & Sun, Y. (2017). Nurturing a FinTech ecosystem: The case of a youth microloan startup in China. *International Journal of Information Management*, *37*(2), 92–97. doi:10.1016/j.ijinfomgt.2016.11.006

Lipton, A., Shrier, D., & Pentland, A. (2016). *Digital banking manifesto: the end of banks?* Massachusetts Institute of Technology.

Lu, L. (2018a). *Decoding Alipay: Mobile Payments, a Cashless Society and Regulatory Challenges. Butterworths Journal of International Banking and Financial Law.*

Lu, L. (2018b). *How a Little Ant Challenges Giant Banks? The Rise of Ant Financial (Alipay)'s Fintech Empire and Relevant Regulatory Concerns. International Company and Commercial Law Review.*

Ma, Y., & Liu, D. (2017). Introduction to the special issue on Crowdfunding and FinTech. *Financial Innovation, 3*(1).

Mahmud, B., Islam, M., & Naher, K. (2015). Empirical Study of the Use of Automated Teller Machine (ATM) among Bank Customers in Dhaka City, Bangladesh. *European Journal of Business and Management*, *7*(1).

Martínez-Climent, C., Zorio-Grima, A., & Robeiro-Soriano, D. (2018). Financial return crowdfunding: Literature review and bibliometric analysis. *The International Entrepreneurship and Management Journal, 14*(3), 527–553. doi:10.100711365-018-0511-x

Money Super Market. (2018). Our guide to 'digital-only' banks. *Money Seuper Market | Digital Banking*. Retrieved from: https://www.moneysupermarket.com/current-accounts/digital-banking/digital-only-guide/

Ogunsemor, A. (1991, January). *Banking Services: The Emergence and Impact of electronic Banking. The Bangladeshi Banker.*

Olleros, F., & Zhegu, M. (Eds.). (2016). *Research Handbook on Digital Transformation*. Cheltenham, UK: Academic Press. doi:10.4337/9781784717766

Ozili, P. K. (2018). *Impact of digital finance on financial inclusion and stability*. Borsa Istanbul Review. doi:10.1016/j.bir.2017.12.003

Pan, W., Altschuler, Y., & Pentland, A. S. (2012). Decoding Social Influence and the Wisdom of the Crowd in Financial Trading Network. In *International Conference on Privacy, Security, Risk and Trust and International Conference on Social Computing* (pp. 203 - 209). Institute of Electrical and Electronics Engineers.

Passler, K. H. (2018). "Real" InsurTech Startups do it Differently! In S. Chishti & J. Barberis (Eds.), The InsurTech Book: The Insurance Technology Handbook for Investors, Entrepreneurs and FinTech Visionaries (pp. 24 - 27). FINTECH Circle Ltd. doi:10.1002/9781119444565.ch6

Pelster, M., & Hofmann, A. (2018). About the fear of reputational loss: Social trading and the disposition effect. *Journal of Banking & Finance, 94*, 75–88. doi:10.1016/j.jbankfin.2018.07.003

Phoon, K., & Koh, F. (2018). Robo-Advisors and Wealth Management. *Journal of Alternative Investments, 20*(3), 79–94. doi:10.3905/jai.2018.20.3.079

Puschmann, T. (2012). The Rise of Customer-Oriented Banking-Electronic Markets Are Paving the Way for Change in the Financial Industry. *Electronic Markets, 22*(4), 203–215. doi:10.100712525-012-0106-2

Rajak, W. (2018). Brunei is world's 4th highest in social media penetration. *The Bruneian.* Retrieved from: https://www.thebruneian.news/brunei-is-worlds-4th-highest-in-social-media-penetration

Ryabova, A. (2015). Emerging FinTech market: Types and features of new financial technologies. *Journal of Economics and Social Sciences*, *7*(4).

Shai, G. (2018). InsurTech and the Promise of "Property Value Hedging Technology". In S. Chishti & J. Barberis (Eds.), The InsurTech Book: The Insurance Technology Handbook for Investors, Entrepreneurs and FinTech Visionaries, (pp. 280-282). Academic Press.

Shrier, D., Canale, G., & Pentland, A. (2016). *Mobile money & payments: Technology trends. In Connection Science & Engineering* (pp. 2–27). Massachusetts Institute of Technology.

Swan, M. (2015). Blockchain: Blueprint for a new economy. O'Reilly.

United Overseas Bank Group, Ernest & Young Corporation. (2016). United Overseas Bank (UOB): State of FinTech in ASEAN. *UOB Group: Tech Eco System.* Retrieved from: https://www.uobgroup.com/techecosystem/pdf/UOB-State-of-FinTech-in-ASEAN.pdf

Vives, X. (2017). The Impact of Fintech on Banking. *European Economy*, *2*, 97–106.

Wang, T., & Shin, N. (2010). An empirical study of customers' perceptions of security and trust in e-payment systems. *Electronic Commerce Research and Applications*, *9*(1), 84–95. doi:10.1016/j.elerap.2009.04.014

Warner, J. (2017). Future of FinTech | Consumer Survey 2017 Presented by Telegraph. *The Telegraph.* Retrieved from: https://www.telegraph.co.uk/content/dam/business/spark/Fintech/Telegraph_Fintech_Report%202017.pdf

Wohlgemuth, V., Berger, E. S., & Wenzel, M. (2016). More than just financial performance: Trusting investors in social trading. *Journal of Business Research*, *69*(11), 4970–4974. doi:10.1016/j.jbusres.2016.04.061

Wong, A. (2018). BruPay received AMBD aproval for trial phase. *Biz Brunei.* Retrieved from: https://www.bizbrunei.com/2018/08/brupay-receives-ambd-approval-for-trial-phase-sandbox/

Wonglimpiyarat, J. (2017). FinTech Crowdfunding of Thailand 4.0. *Journal of Private Equity*, *21*(1), 55–63. doi:10.3905/jpe.2017.21.1.055

Wrede, P. (2018). InsureTech for development. *The World Bank Blog*. Retrieved from: http://blogs.worldbank.org/psd/insuretech-development

Zalan, T., & Toufaily, E. (2017). The promise of FinTech in emerging markets: not as disruptive. *Contemporary Economics, 11*(4).

Chapter 11
Advancing Towards a Cashless Society:
The Acceptance of eWallet in Brunei Darussalam

Munirah Ajeerah Arine
Universiti Brunei Darussalam, Brunei

Hidayatul Aziyah Zain
Universiti Brunei Darussalam, Brunei

Norzaidah Hidayah Rashid
Universiti Brunei Darussalam, Brunei

ABSTRACT

This exploratory research study looked into the younger population of Brunei Darussalam in terms of the feasibility of eWallets. By utilizing the unified theory of acceptance and use of technology (UTAUT) model established by Venkatesh et al., this research hoped to assess the country's technological readiness and the level of acceptance of eWallet adoption in a future of an e-Payment economy for the purpose of to improve the efficiency of financial institutions as well as for the provision of new services for the convenience of the customers. The study found that none of the main four constructs of the UTAUT model to be predictors of behavioral intention but rather, attitude towards using technology and anxiety. This may be as a result of the younger populace being in constant interaction with various types of technology, paired with the rising internet connectivity which led to the minimal impact of a new technology, in this case, eWallets.

DOI: 10.4018/978-1-5225-9183-2.ch011

Copyright © 2020, IGI Global. Copying or distributing in print or electronic forms without written permission of IGI Global is prohibited.

INTRODUCTION

In light of understanding the potential market for FinTech in Brunei, the increase in internet and smartphone usage and infrastructure poses as a pressing stimulus for the change in local consumers' buying behavior which increases online payments via smartphone, which then lead to a rise in e-commerce activities amongst the populace, especially the millennials (AITI, 2018). According to the statistics provided in the Brunei Darussalam Statistical Yearbook of 2016, the country is inhabited by a total of 422,678 individuals with a population growth rate of 1.5 percent (Economic Planning and Development Board, 2017). It was then highlighted in a news article published by Borneo Bulletin that the mobile phone penetration rate in Brunei is at 125.5 percent which is a 14.1 percent increase from 2015 (AITI, 2016). This shows that the population growth rate and the smartphone penetration is progressing parallely, resulting in a technologically savvy community. This aforementioned trends driven by the current trend advances has created FinTech opportunities for SMEs, startups, FinTech companies and individuals.

Hence, this study is done to investigate the familiarity with the service to ensure that the implementation of eWallets is feasible within the country with the implementation of local eWallets have already been done within the Sultanate. Since the idea for this technology is relatively new in the Brunei market, the key objectives of this study are to examine the population's level of familiarity and awareness towards eWallets by utilizing Unified Theory of Acceptance and Use of Technology model (UTAUT) (Venkatesh et al., 2003).

LITERATURE REVIEW

The FinTech 3.5 and Its Impact to Mobile Financial Services

In addition to continuous technological advancement and the widespread Internet usage, The Global Financial Crisis of 2008 was a climacteric for the emergence of the FinTech 3.0 era (Arner, Barberis and Buckley, 2015). However Arner et al. (2015) clarified that the unfolding of the FinTech 3.5 era was deeply motivated by the emerging countries' efforts in progressing economically. They also highlighted that the younger communities are typically equipped with smart devices earlier on and are technologically shrewd in this era (Arner et al., 2015). The Internet and mobile communications payments is noted to be a predominant focal point for FinTech 3.5 which provides opportunities to fintech companies. Furthermore, the continual and exponential rise in technological advancements may encourage merchants to provide alternatives to physical cash and cheque payments and opt for contactless payments to customers as this may help to reduce operating costs whilst simultaneously increase revenues. Hence, eWallet service is introduced as an alternative where it can store user details such as multiple credit and debit card account numbers, bank account information, passwords, loyalty cards and vouchers, whilst also allowing the user to make a transaction allowing for a more efficient payments between the customers and merchants.

Brunei Darussalam: Moving Towards a Cashless Economy

Brunei Darussalam is a small country with a high income per capita of $72,914 with a small population of less than 430 thousand individuals (Economic Planning and Development Board, 2017). It was recorded that 99% of the country's total population owned a smartphone, and 350,000 of the population were mobile internet users where mobile penetration in Brunei Darussalam was at 125.5% in 2016 (AITI, 2016) - surpassing Brunei's population undoubtedly increasing the digital activity within the country.

As a result, there was in an increase in e-commerce activities in Brunei Darussalam, mainly driven by the millennials (AITI, 2018) where there was a rise in online shopping activities occurring within the country where respondents found this mode of shopping to be most convenient. From these statistical facts alone, it has become evident that the smartphone adoption, internet usage and e-commerce activity are considerably increasing in the country. However, the adoption of e-Wallets are not yet prominent, where instead they prefer to utilize mobile banking channels (AMDB, 2017). This was apparent in a study by AITI (2018) where while many still prefer payments via online credit and debit cards and bank transfers instead.

Autoriti Monetari Brunei Darussalam (AMBD) (2017) aspires for the provision of eWallets will aid in enhancing innovation, cost reduction, as well as improve the efficiency and effectiveness of mobile payments by streamlining both conventional face-to-face payments with online transactions between the consumer and businesses. Adding to this, the revitalization of the entrepreneurism growth within the country could be made possible, boosting the economy as well as creating opportunities for private sectors i.e. SMEs and establish a greater competitive advantage as means to achieve Brunei's national vision, *Wawasan 2035* (HAB, 2018). This spurred the introduction of local eWallets: *ProgresifPay* - an eWallet introduced by a local telecommunication company Progresif Cellular Sdn Bhd (PCSB) and BIBD's *QuickPay* - an upgrade from their mobile internet payment service platform, *eTunai* that was previously introduced in 2013. Following this, the proliferation of effective implementation and adoption of e-Wallets would be a step in achieving AMBD's goal in making Brunei Darussalam a cashless society (AMBD, 2017).

Technology Adoption in the Younger Generations

It is apparent in the studies by Venkatesh & Morris (2000) and Wilkowska & Ziefle (2012) indicated that age differences influences the decision to adopt to new technology where findings of the study concluded that the younger generation find it easier to adopt a new technology compared to the older generation, hence the attitudes towards using a new technology was found to be more salient in the younger generation.

RESEARCH FRAMEWORK

The framework for this study is adapted from the Unified Theory of Acceptance and Use of Technology (UTAUT) developed by Venkatesh et al. (2003). This model is utilized for studies relating individual intentions to adopt or accept a particular information technology (IT) (Venkatesh et al. (2003). Some studies have made extensive research with regards to eWallets (Shin, 2009; Yahid & Nobakht, 2013; Tang et al., 2014) or in relation to them (Truman, Sandoe & Rifkin, 2003; Helander & Khalid, 2000; Hobololo & Malewa, 2017).

The willingness of a user to utilize a technology or continue using the said technology is noted to be behavioural intention (Venkatesh et al., 2012; Thomas et al., 2010). This, along with a user's particular beliefs set by the probabilities of the outcome if the technology is utilized as well as attitude will provide a basis of understanding on a user's perception of the said technology (Lin & Lu, 2000). This is important as to ensure that investments made to create the particular technology is not left to waste due to limited acceptance (Park, 2009; Liu, Liao & Pratt, 2009).

Figure 1. Conceptual framework of the research study

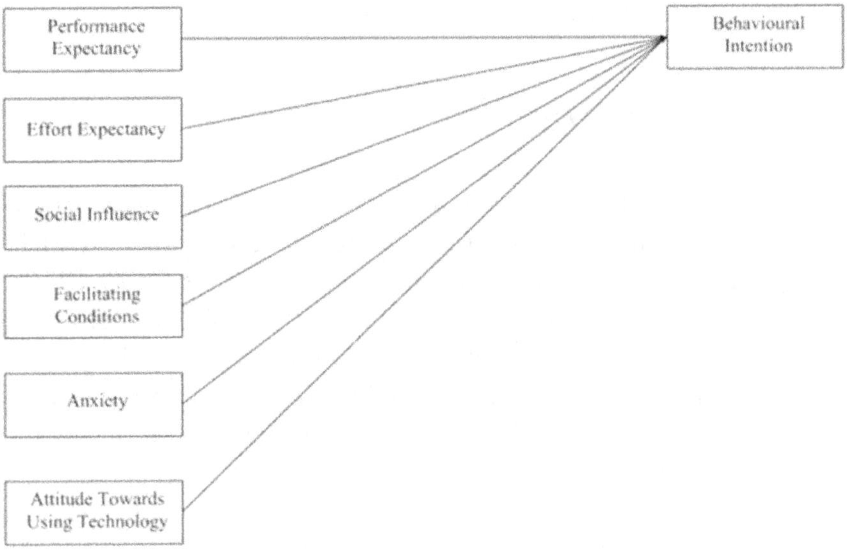

In the UTAUT framework, there are four main constructs in which these directly measure the usage intention and behaviour (Tan & Ouyang, 2004): Performance Expectancy (PE), Effort Expectancy (EE), Social Influence (SI) and Facilitating Conditions (FC). Moran et al. (2010) identified PE, EE, SI, FC and Attitude Towards Using Technology (ATT) to have significant roles in influencing an individual's behavioural intention. Therefore, in this study, attitude towards using technology (ATT) will also be used to measure Behavioural Intention (BI). In addition to attitude towards using technology (ATT), Venkatesh et al. (2003) also identified Anxiety (ANX) to also have some influence to behavioural intention which will also be assessed in this research study.

METHODOLOGY

This study was a cross-sectional study conducted in 2018 in Brunei Darussalam. The collection of data was done using a quantitative method where it was done in the form of electronic questionnaires and the link was distributed through social network platforms such as WhatsApp, Facebook and Twitter.

The target population for this study was the younger population where a sample size of 100 (n = 100) was obtained.

RESULTS AND DISCUSSION

This study examined the population's familiarity and awareness of eWallet in Brunei Darussalam as well as to investigate whether this may influence users' adoption rate and consumer acceptance by using the Unified Theory of Acceptance and Use of Technology (UTAUT). It was found that there were almost a 1:1 ratio in all three demographic information collected namely gender, age group and current level of education. As aforementioned, the participants were comprised of 49 males and 51 females. In terms of their age groups, 55 participants were Generation Y i.e. millennials and 45 were Generation Z i.e. digital natives (Chaney, Touzani & Slimane, 2017). It was also found that 44 participants are currently in their pre-university level while 56 participants are university students.

Prior to the provision of a definition, 67 of the respondents claimed to understand what an eWallet is while 21 of them said 'no' and 12 answered 'maybe'. The subsequent question then provided a definition of what eWallets are; distinguishing it from the traditional online payment methods; in which 63 of them affirmed to have used an ewallet. However, it was also found that some of the respondents are still unclear with the concept of an eWallet as 13 of them listed applications not classified as eWallets like Netteler and PointzMatter. The study then found Paypal as the most ubiquitous eWallet amongst the respondents (52). In terms of frequency of use, only 3 of the respondents professed to always using the service while a majority uses it rarely. The most common use for eWallets found (35) were for online shopping while only eight of the respondents use eWallets for making physical purchase.

The study then tried to fathom the respondent's awareness on local eWallet providers in which 63 of them knew of such service whilst 37 of them does not. It was also found that only 17 of the respondents utilize these local eWallets and 83 of them did not. Lastly, the study was able to observe that Quickpay is the most used local eWallet (6), followed by ProgresifPay (5).

Looking into the analysis for the relationship between the behavioural intention and the other constructs, it was found that attitude towards using technology and anxiety are the main predictors of behavioral intention rather than the main constructs of the UTAUT model where effort expectancy (EE), social influence (SI), facilitating conditions (FC) and attitude towards using technology (ATT) have positive relationships with behavioural intention (BI) on the adoption of eWallets while performance expectancy (PE) and anxiety (ANX) have negative relationships with behavioural intention (BI) on the adoption of eWallets. Attitude towards using technology (ATT) has the strongest impact on BI on the adoption of eWallets as per the model below:

$$Y = 6.743 - 0.148\,(PE) + 0.017\,(EE) + 0.013\,(SI) + 0.047\,(FC) + 0.523^{**}\,(ATT) - 0.118^{**}\,(ANX)$$

As per above model, it was noted that effort expectancy (EE), social influence (SI), facilitating conditions (FC) and attitude towards using technology (ATT) have positive relationships with behavioural intention (BI) on the adoption of eWallets while performance expectancy (PE) and anxiety (ANX) have negative relationships with behavioural intention (BI) on the adoption of eWallets. Attitude towards using technology (ATT) has the strongest impact on BI on the adoption of eWallets. This is not inline with previous studies where these four constructs were found to be determinants for behavioural intention: performance expectancy (PE) (Kijsanayotian et al., 2009; AlAwadhi & Morris, 2008); effort expectancy (EE) (Ha & Stoel, 2009; Liao,Tsou & Huang, 2007; Chong, 2013); social influence (SI) (Chong, 2013; Venkatesh et al., 2012); facilitating conditions (FC) (Venkatesh et al., 2012).

Technology is seen as a functional and serviceable but it does not help to improve their performance and hence, the negative relationship between performance expectancy (PE) and behavioural intention (BI) (Marchewaka & Kostiwa, 2007). Additionally, Zhou et al. (2010) constructed two conditions for adoption: (1) the task that is supposed to be completed using the said technology requires the user to be swift and quick whilst completing the task; (2) the said technology will help to improve and give the user a more convenient method for completing the task. Only when the technology fulfills both of these conditions, will a pro relationship be made. Thereby, the reason for such finding could be because the respondents of this study uses eWallets sparingly - as found in the findings where only three respondents out of 100 claim to always use eWallets - and that they do not find eWallets useful in aiding them to complete a transaction swiftly.

Youths are perceived to be aware of new innovations and may have more experience on using different technologies, thus, may already be equipped with a solid foundation on the technology know-how which will not influence their decision to use the said technology (Tsui Wei et al, 2009; Cho et al., 2007). This is also mentioned by researchers where the young generation grew up with technology which makes them pervasive to various technologies in their daily lives (Wang et al.,2014; Prensky, 2001) which could explain why effort expectancy (EE) had not significant impact on the behavioural intention (BI). Correspondingly, youths are also not influenced by social norms as they are using the said technology because of their community identification, thus, allowing them to gain a sense of belonging (Hsu & Lin, 2008; Venkatesh & Davis, 2000). To further add, SI was only found to influence BI in the later stages of technological adoption in older generations which may explain why this particular relationship was not evident in the research study (Venkatesh et al, 2012).

Facilitating conditions (FC) is noted to not be a determining factor for behavioural intention as it is an antecedent of effort expectancy, thus, capturing its effects (Venkatesh et al., 2012). Furthermore, facilitating conditions were also seen to have more effects on older generations (Venkatesh et al, 2012) especially when linked to anxiety where the learning and participating in said technology may be difficult for them (Hobololo & Mawela, 2017). In addition to this, a well established infrastructure will help to reduce anxiety towards the adoption of eWallets (Hourahine & Howard, 2004). Anxiousness could also be conjured from the lack of exposure to the technology (Achuonye & Ezekoka, 2011) where they may have concerns in security and privacy especially for tasks involving monetary transactions (Hourahine & Howard, 2004). Considering the fact that a majority of the respondents for this study constitute of the younger generation who are still studying and are not earning a monthly income, it can be inferred that they lack exposure to eWallets as they might not find a significant use for it just yet. This can be further backed by the data collected from the survey where it was found that albeit they are familiar with eWallets, a significant fraction (n=39) of them does not use it and also a fraction of those who claim to use eWallets are not able to distinguish between eWallets and traditional online payments. Nonetheless, it could be inferred that the respondents of this study well perceives eWallets as useful where, they are more inclined to use it. This could be due to the respondents' level of awareness of the advantage that the technology brings, ergo instilling a positive attitude towards it (Tan, 2013; Kim & Kankanhalli, 2009).

CONCLUSION

In this study, we found ATT and ANX to be predictors of BI rather than the four main constructs of the UTAUT model established by Venkatesh et al. (2003). This may be attributed to the small sample size of only a 100 as well as the target population being only the younger generation who was born in 1981 and onwards. Nevertheless, our findings were still aligned with other similar technology acceptance studies across various type of IT whereby younger people, in this case, millennials and the digital natives were indifferent towards the perceived beliefs (PE, EE, SI, FC) on the behavioural intention which may be due to the embeddedness of the internet paired with the advancements of technology where these two are already highly integrated into their daily lives. Millennials, and especially digital natives are in constant interaction with these two daily, which could explain that the impact for the adoption or acceptance of eWallets was less pronounce. In a sense, they have already perceived eWallet to be an existing technology that they can simply adopt in their everyday lives but with perceived risks where technologies that involve monetary transactions may be a deciding factor on whether or not they would adopt eWallets.

REFERENCES

Achuonye, K. A., & Ezekoka, G. K. (2011). Technophobia among female undergraduate students: A challenge to attainment of the MDGs in Nigeria. *British Journal of Educational Research, 1*(1), 49–57.

AITI. (2016, September). *Brunei Darussalam Household ICT Survey 2016*. Bandar Seri Begawan, Brunei Muara, Brunei Darussalam.

AlAwadhi, S., & Morris, A. (2008, January). The Use of the UTAUT Model in the Adoption of E-government Services in Kuwait. In *Hawaii International Conference on System Sciences, Proceedings of the 41st Annual* (pp. 219-219). IEEE. 10.1109/HICSS.2008.452

AMBD. (2018). *FinTech Office*. Retrieved September 22, 2018, from: http://www.ambd.gov.bn/fintech-office

Arner, D. W., Barberis, J., & Buckley, R. P. (2015). The evolution of Fintech: A new post-crisis paradigm. *Geo. J. Int'l L., 47*, 1271.

Autoriti Monetari Brunei Darussalam (AMBD). (2017, October). *Retail Payments Infrastructure for Brunei Darussalam*. Retrieved August 15, 2018 from: http://ambd.gov.bn/SiteAssets/Request%20for%20Information%20-%20PSS%20Retail%20Payment%20Infrastructure%20v1.1.pdf

Chaney, D., Touzani, M., & Ben Slimane, K. (2017). *Marketing to the (new) generations: summary and perspectives*. Academic Press.

Cho, D., Kwon, H., & Lee, H. (2007). Analysis of Trust in Internet and Mobile Commerce Adoption. *2007 40th Annual Hawaii International Conference On System Sciences (HICSS'07)*. doi: 10.1109/hicss.2007.76

Chong, A. (2013). A two-staged SEM-neural network approach for understanding and predicting the determinants of m-commerce adoption. *Expert Systems with Applications*, *40*(4), 1240–1247. doi:10.1016/j.eswa.2012.08.067

Economic Planning and Development Board. (2017). *Brunei Darussalam Statistical Yearbook 2016. Bandar Seri Begawan*. Brunei Darussalam: Brunei Muara.

Ha, S., & Stoel, L. (2009). Consumer e-shopping acceptance: Antecedents in a technology acceptance model. *Journal of Business Research*, *62*(5), 565–571. doi:10.1016/j.jbusres.2008.06.016

HAB. F. (2018, August 18). BIBD bolstering efforts to create cashless society. *Borneo Bulletin*. Retrieved September 24, 2018, from: https://borneobulletin.com.bn/bibd-bolstering-efforts-to-create-cashless-society/

Helander, M. G., & Khalid, H. M. (2000). Modeling the customer in electronic commerce. *Applied Ergonomics*, *31*(6), 609–619. doi:10.1016/S0003-6870(00)00035-1 PMID:11132045

Hobololo, T. S., & Mawela, T. (2017). Exploring the Use of Mobile Phones for Public Participation in the Buffalo City Metropolitan Municipality. *AGRIS On-Line Papers in Economics and Informatics*, *9*(1), 57–68. doi:10.7160/aol.2017.090105

Hobololo, T. S., & Mawela, T. (2017). Exploring the Use of Mobile Phones for Public Participation in the Buffalo City Metropolitan Municipality. *AGRIS On-Line Papers in Economics and Informatics*, *9*(1), 57–68. doi:10.7160/aol.2017.090105

Hourahine, B., & Howard, M. (2004). Money on the move: Opportunities for financial service providers in the 'third space'. *Journal of Financial Services Marketing*, *9*(1), 57–67. doi:10.1057/palgrave.fsm.4770141

Hsu, C., & Lin, J. (2008). Acceptance of blog usage: The roles of technology acceptance, social influence and knowledge sharing motivation. *Information & Management*, *45*(1), 65–74. doi:10.1016/j.im.2007.11.001

Kijsanayotin, B., Pannarunothai, S., & Speedie, S. M. (2009). Factors influencing health information technology adoption in Thailand's community health centers: Applying the UTAUT model. *International Journal of Medical Informatics*, *78*(6), 404–416. doi:10.1016/j.ijmedinf.2008.12.005 PMID:19196548

Kim, H. W., & Kankanhalli, A. (2009). Investigating user resistance to information systems implementation: A status quo bias perspective. *Management Information Systems Quarterly*, *33*(3), 567–582. doi:10.2307/20650309

Liao, C., Tsou, C., & Huang, M. (2007). Factors influencing the usage of 3G mobile services in Taiwan. *Online Information Review*, *31*(6), 759–774. doi:10.1108/14684520710841757

Lin, J. C. C., & Lu, H. (2000). Towards an understanding of the behavioural intention to use a web site. *International Journal of Information Management*, *20*(3), 197–208. doi:10.1016/S0268-4012(00)00005-0

Liu, S. H., Liao, H. L., & Pratt, J. A. (2009). Impact of media richness and flow on e-learning technology acceptance. *Computers & Education*, *52*(3), 599–607. doi:10.1016/j.compedu.2008.11.002

Marchewka, J. T., & Kostiwa, K. (2007). An application of the UTAUT model for understanding student perceptions using course management software. *Communications of the IIMA*, *7*(2), 10.

Moran, M., Hawkes, M., & Gayar, O. E. (2010). Tablet personal computer integration in higher education: Applying the unified theory of acceptance and use technology model to understand supporting factors. *Journal of Educational Computing Research*, *42*(1), 79–101. doi:10.2190/EC.42.1.d

Park, S. Y. (2009). An analysis of the technology acceptance model in understanding university students' behavioral intention to use e-learning. *Journal of Educational Technology & Society*, *12*(3), 150–162.

Prensky, M. (2001). Digital Natives, Digital Immigrants Part 1. *On the Horizon*, *9*(5), 1–6. doi:10.1108/10748120110424816

Shin, D. H. (2009). Towards an understanding of the consumer acceptance of mobile wallet. *Computers in Human Behavior*, *25*(6), 1343–1354. doi:10.1016/j.chb.2009.06.001

Tan, P. J. B. (2013). Students' adoptions and attitudes towards electronic placement tests: A UTAUT analysis. *American Journal of Computer Technology and Application*, *1*(1), 14–23.

Tan, Z., & Ouyang, W. (2004). Diffusion and Impacts of the Internet and E-commerce in China. *Electronic Markets*, *14*(1), 25–35. doi:10.1080/1019678042000175270

Tang, C. Y., Lai, C. C., Law, C. W., Liew, M. C., & Phua, V. V. (2014). Examining key determinants of mobile wallet adoption intention in Malaysia: An empirical study using the unified theory of acceptance and use of technology 2 model. *International Journal of Modelling in Operations Management*, *4*(3-4), 248–265. doi:10.1504/IJMOM.2014.067383

Thomas, T., Singh, L., & Gaffar, K. (2013). The utility of the UTAUT model in explaining mobile learning adoption in higher education in Guyana. *International Journal of Education and Development Using ICT*, *9*(3).

Truman, G. E., Sandoe, K., & Rifkin, T. (2003). An empirical study of smart card technology. *Information & Management*, *40*(6), 591–606. doi:10.1016/S0378-7206(02)00046-0

Tsu Wei, T., Marthandan, G., Yee-Loong Chong, A., Ooi, K., & Arumugam, S. (2009). What drives Malaysian m-commerce adoption? An empirical analysis. *Industrial Management & Data Systems*, *109*(3), 370–388. doi:10.1108/02635570910939399

Venkatesh, M., Morris, Davis, & Davis. (2003). User Acceptance of Information Technology: Toward a Unified View. *Management Information Systems Quarterly*, *27*(3), 425. doi:10.2307/30036540

Venkatesh, V., & Davis, F. D. (2000). A theoretical extension of the technology acceptance model: Four longitudinal field studies. *Management Science*, *46*(2), 186–204. doi:10.1287/mnsc.46.2.186.11926

Venkatesh, V., Morris, M. G., Davis, G. B., & Davis, F. D. (2003). User acceptance of information technology: Toward a unified view. *Management Information Systems Quarterly*, *27*(3), 425–478. doi:10.2307/30036540

Venkatesh, V., Thong, J. Y., & Xu, X. (2012). Consumer acceptance and use of information technology: Extending the unified theory of acceptance and use of technology. *Management Information Systems Quarterly*, *36*(1), 157–178. doi:10.2307/41410412

Wilkowska, W., & Ziefle, M. (2012). Privacy and data security in E-health: Requirements from the user's perspective. *Health Informatics Journal*, *18*(3), 191–201. doi:10.1177/1460458212442933 PMID:23011814

Yahid, B., Shahbahrami, A., & Nobakht, M. B. (2013, April). Providing security for e-wallet using e-cheque. In *e-Commerce in Developing Countries: With Focus on e-Security (ECDC), 2013 7th International Conference on* (pp. 1-14). IEEE. 10.1109/ECDC.2013.6556725

Zhou, T., Lu, Y., & Wang, B. (2010). Integrating TTF and UTAUT to explain mobile banking user adoption. *Computers in Human Behavior*, *26*(4), 760–767. doi:10.1016/j.chb.2010.01.013

Chapter 12
An Overview of Financial Technology in Indonesia

Muhammad Anshari
https://orcid.org/0000-0002-8160-6682
Universiti Brunei Darussalam, Brunei

Mohammad Nabil Almunawar
Universiti Brunei Darussalam, Brunei

Masairol Masri
Universiti Brunei Darussalam, Brunei

ABSTRACT

Financial technology (FinTech) has been developing at a tremendous rate all around the globe. This chapter will show how banking and financial system has evolved by financial technology which affected the way of how society is living now. There is a rapid change of FinTech for the past few years in Indonesia. These changes have made an impact to the people in Indonesia. As for the exploration to the rise of FinTech in Indonesia, it is important to understand the development and challenges of FinTech in Indonesia by looking changing Indonesian people's behavior in terms of FinTech's adoption include payment channel system, digital banking, peer-to-peer (P2P) lending, and crowdfunding.

DOI: 10.4018/978-1-5225-9183-2.ch012

Copyright © 2020, IGI Global. Copying or distributing in print or electronic forms without written permission of IGI Global is prohibited.

INTRODUCTION

The fourth industrial revolution (Industry 4.0) will definitely contribute to an extensive and profound impact on almost all business sectors. FinTech is one of the cutting edge technology in Industry 4.0 realms. The integration of key stakeholders such as customers, machines, including information and communication technologies (ICT) are kept connected through Industry 4.0 in order to achieve ever-changing management of complex business processes (Bauer et al., 2015). In relation to the flexibility it offers, Kiel et al. (2018) stated that Industry 4.0 intends to tackle the contemporary challenges by enhancing business competition globally, managing volatile markets and demands which will be needed in dealing with dynamic, challenging requirements.

FinTech is one of the emerging sectors in Industry 4.0. The scope of FinTech is very broad, it covers almost every aspect of the financial system. There are new capabilities and modes in insurance, money transaction, digital security, investment, data analysis, crowdfunding and etc. It offers various user-friendly products that provide a positive customer experience and at the same time reduce transaction costs. FinTech has existed for many years and there is an enormous gap from when our society started establishing the system. Sandel (2016) stated that the existing financial services organizations are making a considerable investment in FinTech, while also investing in and collaborating with promising strategies that can deliver additional value. Globally and Indonesia in particular has seen the growing usage in online trading and online banking that resulted in the expansion of e-commerce. It has changed many aspects of the way society is living now.

Indonesia has become one fastest growing financial system in the world. The financial landscape in Indonesia can be categorized based on funding, lending and performance trends, and drivers. FinTech has created alternative financial ecosystems available both for customers and businesses. It exists to compete with the traditional and established financial sectors in the form of services, products, and deliveries. In the next five years, it is expected that US$500 billion will be invested to develop the necessary infrastructure for FinTech in Indonesia. Since 2015, FinTech's startups in Indonesia have grown up to 78% with their increasing markets for lending, cards, and payments (Cekindo, 2018). Amartha, GoPay from Go-Jek, Finansialku, Midtrans, T-Cash, and Doku are among visible FinTech companies in Indonesia that offers financial services.

The established banking and the financial sector in Indonesia is dominated by the Big Four Banks, three are state-owned banks - Bank Mandiri, Bank Rakyat Indonesia (BRI), and Bank Negara Indonesia (BNI), and one private bank – Bank Central Asia (BCA). Indonesia Banking statistic stated that the big four take up 41% of national leading (Cekindo, 2018). Next, larger commercial banks are CIMB Niaga, Danamon, Permata, Maybank Indonesia, Bank Tabungan Negara (BTN), and Panin Bank with 16% retail and corporate lending in Indonesia. While other smaller commercial banks are 33% of national lending are 9 branches of foreign-owned banks, 12 joint-venture banks, 27 regional development banks, 13 Shariah Banks, and 44 conventional banks (Cekindo, 2018). In addition, there are 1,630 Rural Banks (BPRs) and Micro Finance Institution (MFIs) those are 2% of the national lending in Indonesia. Finally, Multi-finance Companies – 8% of their national lending are built up to more than 200 multi-finance companies in Indonesia. These companies are licensed to offer leasing, consumer financing, credit card financing and other lending services these companies are Adira Dinamika Finance, Clipan Finance, BFI Finance and Astra Sedaya Finance (Cekindo, 2018).

FinTech comes to challenge conventional financial services from crowdfunding, peer-to-peer lending and another alternative up and coming FinTech lenders are growing over the years (Anshari et.al, 2019). In the near future, most platforms are being tested and are set to achieve this stage of lending. Significant investments from foreign investors are increasing rapidly with customers. Indonesia is one of the countries that adopt unfold technology as its important opportunities. One of Indonesia large unbanked population have rapidly spiked innovation. Mobile banking and Fintech have changed the financial landscape of Indonesia.

FinTech in Indonesia

Financially under-served population, those who have no account in any financial institution and millenniums are currently adopting FinTech and start participating in e-commerce. FinTech in Indonesia have included money transfer and payments, investments, accounting, point of sale, comparison, financial planning, crowdfunding, and cryptocurrency. Currently, money transfer and digital payments are two FinTech services highly adopted by people (Riyanto, Primiana, & Azis, 2018), however, other services such as digital lending and crowdfunding are growing in their visibility. Even though

China is the leader of the emerging market of Fintech in Asia (Bloomberg, 2019), FinTech in Indonesia is growing at a faster pace and just a next place to China. This is expected to grow further in the near future. Having 17,504 islands, Indonesia is the biggest archipelago country on the planet, however, this gives Indonesia financial inclusion challenges as credit information and infrastructures are limited. With a very large young population and the growing Internet penetration, and low access to the conventional finance, and the growing adoption of e-commerce, there is ample room for FinTech to grow. Some of the growing factors of FinTech in Indonesia are customer behavior, moving into cashless society, and financial inclusion. The following are some factors that push for FinTech to grow in Indonesia.

Firstly, FinTech is driven by customer behavior. It is very convenient to customers as FinTech can be easily access anytime and anywhere and registering an account is easy. The mode of services in FinTech is very different from conventional banks such as their lower fee and less restrictions. The government encourage financial services to expand so they can reach the under-served segments and give customers lower transaction fees. Bank loans are hard to get so this can affect small and medium businesses of making use particular banking services.

Secondly, FinTech will transform society from cash-based to cashless society. Before FinTech, almost every transactions in Indonesia were by cash. Nowadays, with the emergence of FinTech startups, people favored more to cashless transactions. Payment gateway providers such as GoPay, GrabPay, DOKU, Midtrans and Xendit with other hundreds of FinTech innovation are on the rise.

Thirdly, Indonesia is said to be the highest unbanked populations in the world. Over 50 million of small and medium businesses Indonesia, only 12% have access to credit because of the deficiency of credit history, statements or collateral. Interestingly these SMEs give more than half of the percentage of the total GDP in Indonesia. Indonesia's government supported for financial inclusion and this has opens up opportunities for both the institution with traditional finance model as well as FinTech new entrants.

Finally, The Financial Services Authority (OJK) of Indonesia and relevant agencies constantly held and organise FinTech festivals to increase customers' awareness and access to new applications (Cekindo, 2018). Investors, founders, entrepreneurs, students, and startups were invited to join an event to develop Fintech and discuss the future of FinTech and this shows the purpose of sharing knowledge and ideas on financial service ecosystem.

Development

FinTech has transformed smartphones into portable ATMs, which makes it convenient for people to use their finance through the comfort of their own home. The introduction of electronic money has also patch up the issues for the "unbanked" people because online payments/finance are not necessarily tied to the money you have in your bank account or credit card. QR code payments are also common today especially in street vendors as introduction of FinTech made electronic payments possible at low costs. (Iwasaki, 2018). FinTech has also allowed financial service provider to acquire customer information quicker through the use of technology such as biometrics. FinTech pledges to give more towards profitable business models, highly efficient services with quality assurance and upgrading the conditions of certain workplace apart from being exposed to the escalating competitions in the business world as well as the challenges of change management (Kagermann et al., 2013).

In 2016, Southeast Asia's e-commerce has overtaken their number of investment by the amount of US$421M (Freischlad, 2016). Similar to its other South East Asian counterparts, like Singapore and Malaysia, payments and lending are the large part of the FinTech ecosystem in Indonesia. Indonesia have broken that record in 2017 and to be expected high results in 2018. Digital payments hit a total transactions of US $18M in 2017. The market has shown and proved us a great amount of growth. The annual growth rate is 16.3% with the total investment standing at USD 176.75 million into FinTech companies in 2017 alone (Fintechnews, 2018). Indonesia's government has called for Fintech integration for better use of payment infrastructure as a key for e-commerce. With over 260 million and growing smartphone and Internet market penetration, this has makes Indonesia to become one of the highest countries for FinTech adoption amongst ASEAN countries. With FinTech companies looking forward to expand their services in other South East Asia countries, it will be helpful for the government to give further encouragement and support FinTech development in Indonesia. For example, the financial regulator would need to carefully craft regulations to encourage innovations while protecting consumers from frauds and security issues. This will positively encourage further growth and undertake financial inclusion issues.

Bank Indonesia's decision to ban on cryptocurrency payments late last year has not discourage Coinhako, a Singapore establish startup that operates a trading platform and e-wallet services for bitcoin and other Cryptocurrencies. As the future of FinTech in Indonesia has so much potential, Coinhako started to make some changes to his platform in Jakarta back in August 2018. The Indonesian FinTech Association said that there are more than 200 FinTech companies in the country, including the 31 e-payment providers that have obtained licenses from Bank Indonesia. Also, more than 60 peer-to-peer (P2P) lending companies registered with the Financial Services Authority (Maulia, 2018).

There are many wealthy investors from outside Indonesia whom has invested in the Indonesian market, turning four of the country's startups into unicorns (Nikkei, 2018). In April 2016 it launching of mobile wallet Go-Pay and Go-Jek, Indonesia's first unicorn has raised more than $2 billion through three funding rounds. In August 2016, it raised $550 million from KKR, Warburg Pincus, Sequoia and other private equity funds. In February it closed a $1.5 billion funding round from investors including Tencent Holdings, JD.com, Google, Temasek, and local conglomerate Astra International. In April, German insurance company Allianz Group announced a $35 million investment in Go-Jek.

Chinese e-commerce giant Alibaba Group Holding led an investment of $1.1 billion in online marketplace Tokopedia, another local unicorn that has created its own e-payment service, TokoCash. In March, Alibaba launched mobile wallet Dana with local media company Elang Mahkota Teknologi. Despite still seeing FinTech companies as potential threats, Indonesia's major banks are also investing in local startups. Bank Mandiri has invested in peer-to-peer (P2p) lending startups Amartha and KoinWorks through its venture capital arm Mandiri Capital Indonesia.

Nevertheless not everything that has been planned might went smoothly due to worries on the potential systemic risks to the economy. Bank Indonesia has enacted policies that some see as restricting market access. In May, the central bank issued a regulation capping foreign ownership in e-money providers at

49% which may explain the suspension of some e-wallets like TokoCash and GrabPay, a mobile wallet originally used by Singapore based Grab.

Challenges

Some of the notified challenges for FinTech startups is on FinTech payment. In Indonesia, payment are made through both in person and online transactions of which are not widely available for customers. If they are offered to choose an option, customers have to pay an extra percentage for transactions. Thus, to develop a cashless society will definitely take up some time.

Other issue that need to be address is on the legal aspect of the Fintech companies. For example, some companies run e-wallets without business licenses. This might be due to the slow development and enactment of rules and regulations by the regulators. This will negatively affect Fintech lending startups that will face competitions with their foreign counterparts. Thus, the government needs to take positive steps to ensure the regulatory requirements bring better environment for FinTech Startups in Indonesia. This will definitely help to boost the confidence of Fintech startup founders and investors in Indonesia.

CONCLUSION

The chapter mainly focuses on the development of FinTech in Indonesia, which definitely has a high impact on the society to switch from the traditional cash-based to cashless society. It focuses on how FinTech can be further develop. Most transactions in the past use cash and some shifted to a credit card. With FinTech cashless transactions using e-wallet or simply using a smartphone can easily and cost-effectively done. The growing internet penetration in Indonesia was the main cause of the development of FinTech in the country. FinTech offers alternative solutions for many financial-related problems. It will help address the financial inclusion of the large unbanked population and help in financial literacy. The future of FinTech in Indonesia is definitely bright, and the traditional financial system to adapt accordingly. The government needs to carefully craft rules and regulations to encourage innovation but at the same time to protect the society from frauds and uncertainties.

REFERENCES

Anshari, M., Almunawar, M. N., Masri, M., & Hamdan, M. (2019). *Digital Marketplace and FinTech to Support Agriculture Sustainability. Energy Procedia, 156C*, 234–238.

Bauer, W., Hammerle, M., Schlund, S., & Vocke, C. (2015). Transforming to a Hyper-connected Society and Economy - Towards an "Industry 4.0". *Procedia Manuf., 3*, 417-424.

Bloomberg. (2019). *Why Asia is leading the fintech revolution.* Retrieved from https://www.bloomberg.com/professional/blog/asia-leading-fintech-revolution/

Cekindo. (2018). *Everything you need to know about fintech in Indonesia.* Retrieved from https://www.cekindo.com/fintech-indonesia.html

Fintechnews. (2018). *Fintech Indonesia Report 2018 – The State of Play for Fintech Indonesia.* Retrieved from http://fintechnews.sg/20712/indonesia/fintech-indonesia-report-2018/

Freischlad, N. (2016). *Many options, little awareness: fintech startups in Indonesia have a long way to go.* Retrieved from https://www.techinasia.com/indonesia-fintech-report-2016

Iwasaki, K. (2018). Emergence of fintech companies in Southeast Asia: rising hopes of a solution to financial issues. *Pacific Business and Industries, 18*(68), 1-32. Retrieved from https://www.jri.co.jp/MediaLibrary/file/english/periodical/rim/2018/68.pdf

Kagermann, H., Washlster, W., & Helbig, J. (2013). Recommendations for Implementing the Strategic Initiative Industrie 4.0 - Final Report of the Industrie 4.0 Working Group. Acatech - National Academy of Science and Engineering.

Kiel, D., Muller, J., Arnold, C., & Voigt, K. (2017). Sustainable Industrial Value Creation: Benefits and Challenges of Industry 4.0. *International Journal of Innovation Management, 21*(8), 3–10. doi:10.1142/S1363919617400151

Maulia, E. (2018). *Indonesia offers a fresh battleground for fintech.* Retrieved from https://asia.nikkei.com/Spotlight/Cover-Story/Indonesia-offers-a-fresh-battleground-for-fintech

Nikkei. (2018). *Indonesia offers a fresh battleground for fintech*. Retrieved from https://asia.nikkei.com/Spotlight/Cover-Story/Indonesia-offers-a-fresh-battleground-for-fintech

Riyanto, A., Primiana, I., & Azis, Y. (2018). Disruptive Technology: The Phenomenon of FinTech towards Conventional Banking in Indonesia. *IOP Conference Series. Materials Science and Engineering*, *407*(1), 012104. doi:10.1088/1757-899X/407/1/012104

Sandel, T. (2016, December 21). *The fintech revolution*. Retrieved from https://www.jpmorgan.com/europe/merchant-services/fin-tech-revolution

Chapter 13
Using Blockchain and Smart Contracts for Waqf Institutions

Farrukh Habib
International Shari'ah Research Academy for Islamic Finance, Malaysia

Abu Umar Faruq Ahmad
King Abdulaziz University, Saudi Arabia

ABSTRACT

The institution of Waqf always played a pivotal role of sustainable economic development in a Muslim society throughout the history of Islam. However, recently, even with the introduction of the modern Islamic finance a few decades ago, the institution has been struggling to rejuvenate its past glory. The key issues are lack of availability of data and historical records, weak transparency and public disclosure, improper audit and compliance practices. The advent of the blockchain has offered a ray of hope for the revival of the Waqf institution. The blockchain has already proved itself as a game changing breakthrough. Similarly, the Waqf institution could be invigorated with the innovative and efficient use of the blockchain. Moreover, the use of smart contracts on blockchain could further enhance the performance and efficacy of the Waqf institution. It is strongly believed that with the firm Islamic jurisprudential foundations of the Waqf, blockchain, and smart contracts will ensure that the Waqf institution could partake in the economic development of the whole Muslim world.

DOI: 10.4018/978-1-5225-9183-2.ch013

Copyright © 2020, IGI Global. Copying or distributing in print or electronic forms without written permission of IGI Global is prohibited.

INTRODUCTION

Waqf is a voluntary charitable endowment characterized by perpetuity. Giving *sadaqah* (voluntary charity) is one of the noblest acts in Islam, for which the reward is immensely huge. The Messenger of Allah (ﷺ) is reported to have said:

When a man dies, his deeds come to an end except for three things: ceaseless charity (sadaqah jariyah); a knowledge which is beneficial, or a virtuous descendant who prays for him (for the deceased). (Muslim, 2000, Book 14, Hadith 1631)

The importance of charity is emphasized strongly as it is one of the five pillars of Islam. The essentials of giving alms is advocated in many verses of the Qur'an and quoted in many traditions of the Messenger of Allah (ﷺ) (*hadith*). In fact, *sadaqah and zakah* are mentioned in Qur'an on a total of 32 occasions separately; and on 82 occasions in combination with the other pillars of Islam (Al-Qaradawi, 1999). That is why, according to the Islamic believe, if utilization of wealth is according to the manner guided by Islam, it will be a way of receiving reward in the hereafter.

Additionally, the concept of *sadqah* is designed to re-circulate surplus wealth from the rich to the poor so as to advocate social justice. According to Bremer (2004): "Islamic societies have a rich heritage to philanthropic institutions, a heritage that reflects the central place of philanthropy within Islam". Islamic approach to reduce poverty and wealth disparity is unique through using plethora of instruments (Mohieldin et al., 2012). They are intended for just and fair distribution of wealth, creation, circulation and re-circulation of resources.

That is why, Islam encourages people to get involved in charity and altruistic acts, no matter big or small. And Sharī'ah provides a complete eco-system for Islamic philanthropy to ensure that wealth does not revolve among only the rich of a society. One of the major pillars of that eco-system is *Waqf*. *Waqf* is a charitable unchangeable devotion of a share of one's wealth to Allah's sake. Once given, a *Waqf* corpus is not subject to receive as gift, inheritance, or sale, as it should always remain intact, because it belongs to Allah. In this way, *Waqf* has been institutionalized by Sharī'ah, and became very popular from the early stage.

The institution of *Waqf* always played a pivotal role of sustainable economic development in a Muslim society throughout the history of Islam. It was an integral element of the financial empowerment program of the people which actively contributed in the financial inclusion, poverty alleviation and fruitful mutual community initiatives. However, recently, this important institution has been generally neglected by the Muslim community for various reasons. There is an array of issues and challenges facing *Waqf* in the contemporary world. This chapter discusses those issue and presents their solutions based on blockchain and smart contracts.

The organization of the outline of the chapter is as follows. It is divided into 5 sections. Section 1 is the introduction to this research, followed by a section on the definition of Waqf, its types and characteristic features. Section 3 discusses the authority of *Waqf* that has been derived from the primary sources of Sharī'ah. While the origin and historical development of Waqf is highlighted in section 4 followed by the discussion on socio-economic contributions of Waqf in section 5. Section 6 concentrates on the challenges facing Waqf and the way forward in section 7 followed by the concluding section.

WAQF: DEFINITION, TYPES AND CHARACTERISTIC FEATURES

Meaning and Origins of Waqf

The Arabic term '*Waqf*' is taken from the root verb '*waqafa*", which literally means cause to halt, immobilise and 'come to a standstill' (Oxford Dictionaries). In Islamic Law, *Waqf* refers to a charitable and perpetual devotion of a person's wealth or a share of it, in cash or kind, and its distribution for Sharī'ah compliant ventures. The classical Muslim jurists defined the term *Waqf* according to their own understandings. However, all four *madhahib* (schools of Islamic law) hold the same idea in their definitions of *Waqf*; i.e., the corpus of the *Waqf* or its value must remain intact, becomes restricted on a perpetual basis, and be used for general charitable purposes in which the recipients are the public or the underprivileged.

Some contemporary scholars defined *waqf* as "holding certain property and preserving it for the confined benefit of certain philanthropy and prohibiting any use or disposition of it outside its specific objective" (Kahf, 2007). *The Wakf Act 1954* of India describes *Waqf* as, "Wakf means the permanent dedication by a person professing the Islam, of any movable or immovable property for any purpose recognized by Muslim Law as religious, pious, or charitable" (*LII of India*). The legal devices establishing a *Waqf* links three parties: a benefactor, an administrator and recipients. The benefactor passes resources to *Waqf*, and it becomes the responsibility of *Waqf* manager to look after the assets and direct the benefits of those assets to poor and needy as per the direction of the donor.

Waqf is similar to *zakah* in the sense that it is a type of *sadaqah*. However, at least four significant differences exist between these two charitable instruments of Islam. First, while *zakah* is considered as obligatory and contemporary charity, Waqf is optional and perpetual charity (Mahmood, 2006). Second, Waqf involves using one's wealth for religious purpose over and above the minimum and obligated threshold of *zakah* (Mobin & Ahmad, 2017). Third, Waqf falls under a specific form of *sadaqah* termed as *sadqah jarriyah* (unceasing charity) (Ali, 2009). Last but not the least, Waqf extends the role of *zakah*, which ensures the flow of cash fund to those in need.

Cizacka (2000) and Mahamood (2006) state: "the origin of *Waqf* remains contentious and cannot be traced to any single source". Abu Zahrah (2007), Cizacka (2000), Abdel-Mohsin (2009), and Singer (2008) claim that the notion of *Waqf* originated from ancient human civilization like Mesopotamia, Greece and Macedonia. As per their claim, similar structures had existed earlier civilizations such as Persia, Egyptian, Turkish, Byzantine and Roman Empires. Koehler (2010) claims *Waqf* to be originated in the era of Prophet Muhammad (ﷺ) rather than a later stage of the history of Islam, and provides evidence that Europeans were unprotected to *Waqf* in Jerusalem. The following narrative of events by Ibn Sa`ad provides evidence of *waqf* practised by the Messenger of Allah (ﷺ):

Umar Ibn al Khattab earned some lands in Khyber and came to the Messenger of Allah (ﷺ) and asked him what to do with it. He said, "I got land in Khyber and I did not get any property dearer to me than it. What do you command me to do with it?" The Messenger of Allah (ﷺ) advised him to make it as Waqf and said, "If you wish, you should lock to its original and use the revenue for charity." Umar gave it as charity.... the first charity given in Islam were the fruits of the charity of Umar Ibn al Khattab. (Ibn Sa'd, 2013)

The Types of Waqf

According to Abdel-Mohsin (2009), *Waqf*, according to the recipients, is classified into three key types: *Waqf Khayri* (public or philanthropic *Waqf*), *Waqf Ahli or Dhurri* (posterity or family *Waqf*) and *Waqf Mushtarak* (combination of public and family *Waqf*).

Waqf Khairi (Public Waqf)

The Messenger of Allah (ﷺ) himself practiced and encouraged his noble companions to establish public *Waqf*. This type of *Waqf* is designed to sponsor ventures that benefits the public; and has a humanitarian side to benefit the poor and needy segment of the community. Examples include masjid, water wells, and public universities.

Waqf Ahli (Family Waqf)

This type of *Waqf* is formed when it is specified that the recipients of the property made as *Waqf* are the members of *Waqif* or donor's family. The profit accrued from the family *Waqf* is divided in accordance with the proportions stated in the *Waqfiyyah* (Islamic Trust agreement). Only surplus profit is passed on to the poor and needy as charity. This type of *Waqf* is preferably administered by the relatives of donor (*Waqif*). The Messenger of Allah (ﷺ) permitted many of his companions to generate *Waqf* for their close families and relatives (Abdel-Mohsin, 2009).

Waqf Mushtarak (The Combination of Public and Family Waqf)

The joint public and family *Waqf* is formed when the *Waqif* donates a part of his own property to his kith and kin, while another share to the community.

Characteristics of Waqf

Waqf has three features, which differentiate *Waqf* from other Islamic Trust deeds. First, the *perpetuity* or *permanency* of *Waqf* averts appropriation of the *Waqf* property by the management or entities (including the *Waqif*). This safeguards continuity of the delivery of social services to *Waqf* recipients. Second, irrevocability of *Waqf* safeguards that once the *Waqif* promises to donate his property as *Waqf*, it is unalterable and as such his successors cannot make any alteration in the status of the *Waqf*. This is to avoid the *Waqif* or his successors' execution of rights to withdraw the endowed assets, once it has been avowed as a *Waqf*. Finally, Inalienability of *Waqf* guarantees that no one can own a *Waqf's* assets once they are endowed. Besides, sooner the ownership of the *Waqf* assets is transferred to Allah, its real owner, and the *Waqf* assets become frozen. By law, the *Waqf* assets, once donated, cannot be vended, transferred, pledged, gifted, inherited or subjected to any form of alienation (Abdel-Mohsin, 2009).

All these features of *Waqf* are intended to confirm the perpetuity of *Waqf* assets in order to protect the incessant stream of profits accrued from the *Waqf* assets which can be used for public or family well-being. Although Kahf (1998) and Kuran (2004) have argued that the sole features of permanency of *Waqf* has hindered the growth, Lev (2005) has stated that the perpetual nature of *Waqf* together with non-perishable feature as well as uninterrupted benefits make *Waqf* a much superior form of charity.

AUTHORITY OF WAQF IN PRIMARY SOURCES OF SHARĪ'AH

No direct reference of the word '*Waqf*' is found in the Qur'an. So, one may ask "what are the motivational factors for Muslims to give away his/her property to *Waqf*"? The motivation to contribute to *Waqf* institution is due to religious encouragement. Islamic scholars trace its conformity to the law from the Qur'an, and the *Sunnah*.

Evidence From the Qur'an

The Qur'an gives a spiritual background for acquiring wealth and practical guidelines for its circulation. Using the analogy that Allah is the owner of everything in this universe and mankind is just His trustee on this earth, it is appropriate for Muslims to spend everything they have beyond what is necessary for the sake of Allah. This is stated in the Qur'an:

They ask you how much they should spend. Say, `The surplus (what you can spare after spending on your basic requirement). (Al-Qur'an, 2:219)

The worshippers who are neither extravagant nor niggardly; when they spend they do not play the prodigal nor do they act parsimoniously, but they use a mean. (Al-Qur'an, 25:67)

Both the above verses reveal that mankind needs to maintain a balance between extravagance and miserliness. As human beings, humans possess dual desire of compassion and an inherent love of wealth. Islam's spiritual teachings urge selflessness and generosity.

Some Islamic scholars seek to argue that lending to Allah is in effect creating a *Waqf*. It is a common Muslims' belief that Allah's reward is the best to one who lends to his fellow human being:

You shall, however, observe Prayer (regularly five times a day in all events). And go on presenting Zakah and set apart a goodly portion (of your possessions to give for (the sake of) Allah. And whatever good you send on before for yourselves, you will find it with Allah as the best of things meriting the greatest reward. (Al-Qur'an, 73:20)

Muslims also believe that charity is a tool for attaining Allah's utmost satisfaction and rewards in the hereafter, through righteousness. Islam motivates its followers to perform the acts of charity for fellow human beings as it is evidenced in the following two verses of the Qur'an:

It is not benignancy that you turn your faces around in the direction of East and West; but benignancy is (in him) who believes in Allah, and the Last Day, and the Angels, and the Book, and the Messengers of Allah (ﷺ), and brings wealth in spite of his love for it (Or: offers out of love for Him) to near kinsmen, and the orphans, and the indigent, and the wayfarer, and the beggars, and (to ransom) necks, (i.e. captives "slaves") and keeps up the prayer, and bring the Zakat, (i.e. pay the poor-dues). (Al-Qur'an, 2:177)

You can never have extended virtue and righteousness unless you spend part of what you dearly love for the cause of Allah. Allah knows very well whatever you spend for His cause. (Al-Qur'an, 3:92)

Evidence From the Sunnah

The creation of *Waqf* has been encouraged by the Messenger of Allah (ﷺ) in many *ahadith*. An imperative enthusiasm for bequeathing to *Waqf* is repeated or permanent charity as stated in a *hadith* as mentioned above at the outset.

In one case, Messenger of Allah (ﷺ) arrived at Madinah where there was insufficient drinking water aside from what was available in the well of Rumah. He motivated his companions to purchase the well so as to have a continuous stream of unrestricted drinking water for the dwellers of Madinah. Uthman Ibn Affan (may Allah be pleased with him) purchased the well of Rumah from its landlord and donated it to the inhabitant of Madinah as *Waqf*. In return for his donation or charity, he was assured by the Messenger of Allah (ﷺ) of a better well in the hereafter (Raissouni, 2001).

The following *ahadith* provide crystal clear evidence on how to establish and manage a *Waqf*:

Narrated by Ibn 'Umar: During the time of Allah's Messenger (ﷺ) 'Umar Ibn Al Khattab (may Allah be pleased with him) donated as charity some of his belongings, a garden of date-palms called Thamgh. 'Umar said: "O Allah's Messenger! I have some property which I prize highly, and I want to give it in charity?" The Messenger of Allah (ﷺ) said: "Give it in charity (i.e. endowment) with its land and trees on the condition that the land and trees will neither be sold nor given as a present, nor bequeathed, but the fruits are to be spent in charity". So, 'Umar donated it as an endowment, and it was in the cause of Allah, in freeing slaves, for the poor and needy, for guests, for wayfarers and for kinsmen. The person assigned to act as its administrator was allowed to consume it sensibly and justly. His friends were also permitted to consume it without having any intention of becoming well-off by using these resources. (Bukhari, 2000, hadith # 2532)

THE ORIGIN AND HISTORICAL DEVELOPMENT OF WAQF

The Origin of Waqf

Scholars on *Waqf* have mixed versions on the first *Waqf* which was recognized in the Islamic history. Kahf (1998) claims that the first *Waqf* on which the legal *Waqf* contexts function as a base was the *Waqf* of Umar Ibn al- Khattab. Ahmed (2004) claims that the first *Waqf* was founded by the Messenger of Allah (ﷺ) was the *masjid* in Madinah whereby the land was purchased on which the *masjid* was erected. Today, that *masjid* is widely known as *al-Masjid al-Nabawi* (the *masjid* of the Messenger of Allah (ﷺ)) and is the second most sacred place for Muslims.

Cizakca (2000) proclaims that the first *Waqf* is the *masjid* in Quba, which was built personally by the Messenger of Allah (ﷺ) together with other Muslim migrants upon their arrival in Madinah in 622 AD. Gil (1998) published that the first *Waqf* is the property which was donated to the Messenger of Allah (ﷺ) by a wealthy Jewish Rabbi called Mukhayriq.

Historical Development of Waqf

The concept of *Waqf* demonstrates a remarkable tradition of Islamic philanthropy. Although, the historical basis of charity is much older than the era the Messenger of Allah (ﷺ), the Arabs before his time had knowledge regarding the legacies of charity and "it is most likely that Islam may have been influenced by earlier civilizations", as Cizakca (2000) claims. The first *Waqf* from pre-Prophetic era was the *Waqf* established by Prophet Ibrahim in the form of Kaabah (Al-Humaidan, 2007).

The *Waqf institutions* continued to develop all over the Muslim world after the demise of the Messenger of Allah (ﷺ). During the 9th century, Fatima al-Fihri, used her bequest to bequeath a *masjid* and the al-Qarawiyyin University in Fes, Morocco, which is considered as the world's oldest university. Fatima's sister, Maryam al-Fihri also followed her by using her bequest to endow the Al-Andalus *masjid* (Andalusian Mosque) in Fes.

Agricultural industry was vibrant as it provided the largest basis of revenue collection from *Waqf* assets. As White (2006) mentions "*Waqf* agricultural land constituted half of the size of land in Algeria and one-third in Tunisia; and even in the mid-20th century, one-eighth in Egypt." Moreover, a significant amount of cash (money) was donated as *Waqf* and the revenue generated from cash *Waqf* comprised 32% of all the yields generated from *Waqf* in the 18th century. It is also projected that in 1931, the percentage of human resource employed by *Waqf* institutions to those employed by Turkey was 40% to 60% (Cizakca, 2000).

The Ottoman era (1299–1453) is a remarkable illustration of *Waqf* foundations enchanting the main role of socio-economic development which set a precedent for the world. These *Waqf* foundations were the centrepiece of the Ottoman economy and were contributory to funding a sophisticated market welfare. The Ottoman economy was flexible and worthwhile enough to provide adequate economic set-up to the *Waqf* institutions (Shechter, 2005). It has been projected that three-fourth of all the arable land during the Ottoman empire was under the domain of *Waqf* institutions. The total budget for health, education and welfare used to generate from its *Waqf* foundations and government expenditures on the social services towards fulfilling the needs of community was nominal or insignificant.

Waqf also provided employment during the Ottoman era. Well-reputed people played role in the *Waqf* institutions as trustees and they had significant responsibilities such as collection of revenues, intensifying the sources of income, supervising new erections, carrying out maintenances, and distributing incomes and resources. The task of supervising all the public *Waqf* was given to the Sharī‘ah court, while the individuals used to manage the family *Waqf*. The number of *Waqf* established at that time reached its highest owing to the sound supervision and transparency of *Waqf* institutions by the relevant authorities such as trustees and Sharī‘ah court.

The *Waqf* institution during the Ottoman era witnessed a tremendous success due to the fact that its administration was de-centralized. Besides, some other factors also worked behind this success such as open-handedness, insight, autonomy, good governance of the relevant authorities towards *Waqf* institution and vow to help the humanity, without the need to restore to administration (Abdel-Mohsin, 2009). Likewise, Bremer (2004) elucidates "Islamic philanthropy has been able to play these important and diverse roles in part because it was among the most transparent, formalized and rule-based segments of Islamic society".

At the commencement of the 19th century, the *Waqf* institution started a downward descend, over a period of one and a half century, beginning from the declining of the Ottoman Empire over the ages of colonization period of the Middle East and South Asia and into the nationalization and sovereign state-governed direction (Bremer, 2004). The waning of *Waqf* institution attributed to the downfall of the Ottoman Empire, colonization and government's involvement with the administration of *Waqf* institution.

Governments took control of *Waqf* institution as *Waqf* was well-looked-after to distribute wealth and form an elite group capable of founding benevolent institutions. This put the government in danger and the governments found this as a unique opportunity to take the ownership of the *Waqf* assets and administer them. As soon as the government took over the *Waqf* assets it caused to lose transparency and people did not find it much attractive to contribute.

During the past couple of decades, there was an increasing demand and consciousness among the people and governments in *Waqf* institution and they found it as one of the significant tools for their economic developments. More importantly, during the recent years, governments in Muslim countries have witnessed the revival of *Waqf* in a significant manner. But sadly, many of them started interfering with the autonomy of *Waqf* institution and hindered the freedom of its administration. The situation became so complex that some countries nationalized *Waqf* institutions, while others vested powers to the relevant ministries to even regulate them.

Waqf institutions have also been introduced in countries where Muslims are minority. These include *inter alia* Australia, New Zealand, India and South Africa. In Muslim minority environments, *Waqf* is registered as a charitable trust.

SOCIO-ECONOMIC CONTRIBUTIONS OF WAQF

Waqf institutions were the indispensable components for economic distribution and re-distribution of excess of wealth whereby the circulation of wealth took place from the rich to the destitute and underprivileged in order to eliminate poverty. The profit accrued from *Waqf* funds were utilized to target identified areas which had constructive social effect and additional significance to the community.

Ahmed (1998) claims: "once people heard about the establishment of *Waqf* by `Umar there was not a single able (rich) companion who did not make *Waqf*'. The Messenger of Allah (ﷺ) used the profits from the endowment to help the warriors, the Muslims, for the Messenger of Allah's (ﷺ) family expenses and the *fuqara* (poor/needy) of migrants to Madinah (Gil,1998).

As highlighted in the above section, the *Waqf* of *Rumah* established by Uthman ibn Affan and the land in Khyber established as a *Waqf* by Umar Ibn al- Khattab were both created under the advice and directions of the Messenger of Allah (ﷺ). Both of these *Waqf* were designed with social purposes in mind and are examples showcasing the socio-economic contributions of *Waqf* to the public benefits and welfare of the community. Centuries have passed, but the *Waqf* of the well of *Rumah* has always been in service of mankind until today. Cultivation of date trees is extensively made dependent on the well of *Rumah*. The dates are sold in markets of Madinah and elsewhere all over the world. Fifty percent of the proceeds from the date cultivation investment are distributed to beneficiaries such as orphans. The other fifty percent of the profits are used for further investment. The returns on the date cultivation have been so profitable that the *Waqf* was able to purchase prime land near Al-Masjid al-Nabawi in Madinah on which hotels are being constructed. The investment in hotel business is estimated to generate revenue in the region of 50 million riyals per annum (AwqafSA, n.d.).

THE CHALLENGES FACING WAQF AND THE WAY FORWARD

Even with the inception of Islamic finance a few decades ago, *Waqf* has been struggling to rejuvenate its past glory. Many reasons are collectively responsible for this dilemma. For instance, there is lack of availability of comprehensive data and historical records. The key issues and challenges facing *Waqf* also include in some jurisdictions *inter alia*: (a) highly centralized *Waqf* administration, (b) inadequate manpower, (c) lack of organizational and administrative competency, (d) unregistered *Waqf* properties, (e) absence of provisions in pertinent laws and regulations, (f) lack of social awareness, (g) illegal occupation, (h) misappropriation of *Waqf* properties, (i) operational inefficiency, (j) integrity and qualification of trustees and (k) lack of Sharī'ah supervision. These challenges lead among others to weak transparency and public disclosure of *Waqf* institutions. Subsequently, there is little scope for proper audit and compliance practices. Moreover, most of the time, good governance structures and well-planned development and business strategies are ignored in such institutions. In addition to that, legal and regulatory challenges in every jurisdiction are considered to be some of the major issues with the *Waqf* institutions in the contemporary world.

What Is Blockchain?

Blockchain is a digital ledger of transactional data which is distributed on a decentralized peer-to-peer (P2P) network (PwC FinTech, 2016). In other words, it is a decentralized database which records transactions that have been performed or events that have been occurred and shares them through a digital network among participating parties (Crosby, Nachiappan, Pattanayak, Verma, & Kalyanaraman, 2015).

Though the blockchain database is maintained by many people, it is not 'controlled' by anyone (Grant Thornton, n.d.). Each transaction is entered on the blockchain based on the confirmation of certain number of people endorsing it. Furthermore, it is verified by consensus of the majority of participating parties on the blockchain network. The data of transactions once entered on blockchain cannot be deleted. Moreover, the data of even a single transaction remain verifiable by any participating party at any point in time (Crosby, Nachiappan, Pattanayak, Verma, & Kalyanaraman, 2015). Figure 01 below shows the work flow of a blockchain system.

Figure 1. Transaction work flow of blockchain system
Source: https://blockgeeks.com/guides/what-is-blockchain-technology/

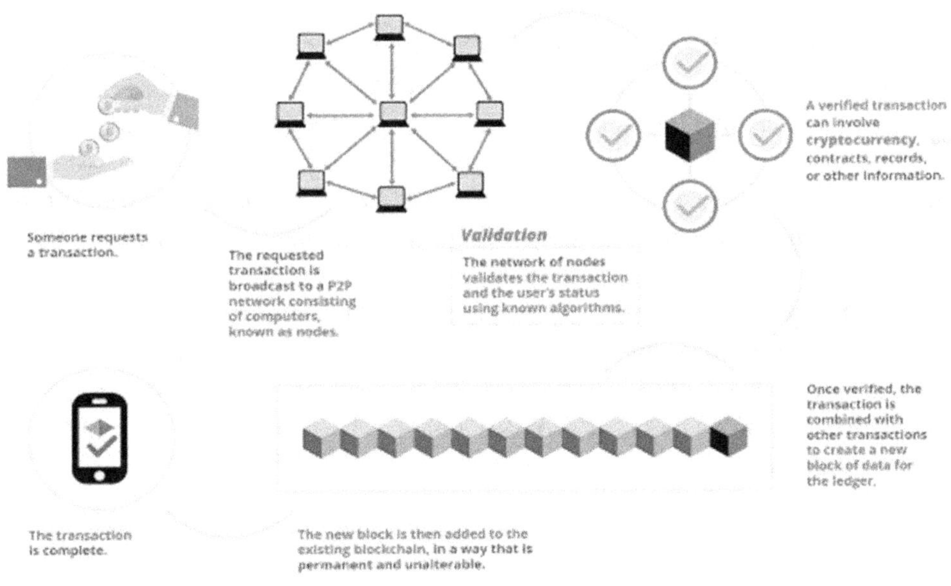

How Blockchain Can Help?

The advent of technological advancements, particularly the introduction of the blockchain, has offered a ray of hope for the revival of the waqf institutions in the modern world. Having transparency at the core of its system, it possesses various attractive features which are naturally required by waqf institutions. For example, data entry is done through a decentralized consensus system which can provide more reliability and trust among the parties involved. Once the data is entered it is immutable. Since the records at the blockchain are unalterable; it is very difficult to corrupt or manipulate those records or data entries.

The blockchain, though still at its infancy stage, has already proved itself as a game changing breakthrough for the global financial sphere. In fact, its utilization is not limited to only financial sector, but it also affords promising features and usage for non-financial sectors. Similarly, the *Waqf* institution could be invigorated with the innovative and efficient use of the blockchain. The block chain and *Waqf* is indeed naturally a perfect match, because interestingly, the blockchain addresses many, if not all, of the issues and problems currently facing the *Waqf* in the contemporary world.

Using Smart Contracts for *Waqf*

Szabo (2016) introduced the idea of 'Smart Contracts' establish contract law through electronic commerce protocols and to design business practices through computer programs on internet among strangers. He stated:

A smart contract is a set of promises, specified in digital form, including protocols within which the parties perform on these promises. (Szabo, 1996)

It is actually a computer program or algorithm that automatically executes when pre-defined conditions are met. In other words, it is a general-purpose computation or calculation typically occurs on a distributed ledger or blockchain. In this respect, it is more generic than a traditional contract, because it can be any kind of algorithm.

The idea behind them is to convert terms and conditions of a transaction into codes; if the conditions are met, the contract is immediately concluded. Previously, the challenge was to automatically ensure that conditions are met, and that this event automatically triggers the conclusion of the contract, and perhaps its execution. With blockchain, conditions - being written into lines of code – could exist across a distributed, decentralized blockchain network in which it could be verified against the pre-set conditions by anonymous parties without the need for a central authority, legal system, or external enforcement mechanism. This renders transactions traceable, transparent, and irreversible (Investopedia, n.d).

A smart contract can easily satisfy common contractual conditions and minimize exceptions both malicious and accidental. It does not need intervention; hence, it minimizes the need for trusted intermediaries. Subsequently, its usage would reduce fraud loss; and lower arbitrations, enforcement and other transactional costs. Figure 02 below shows how a smart contract works.

Figure 2. How a smart contract works?
Source: https://www.thesecuritybuddy.com/blockchain/smart-contracts-and-blockchain/

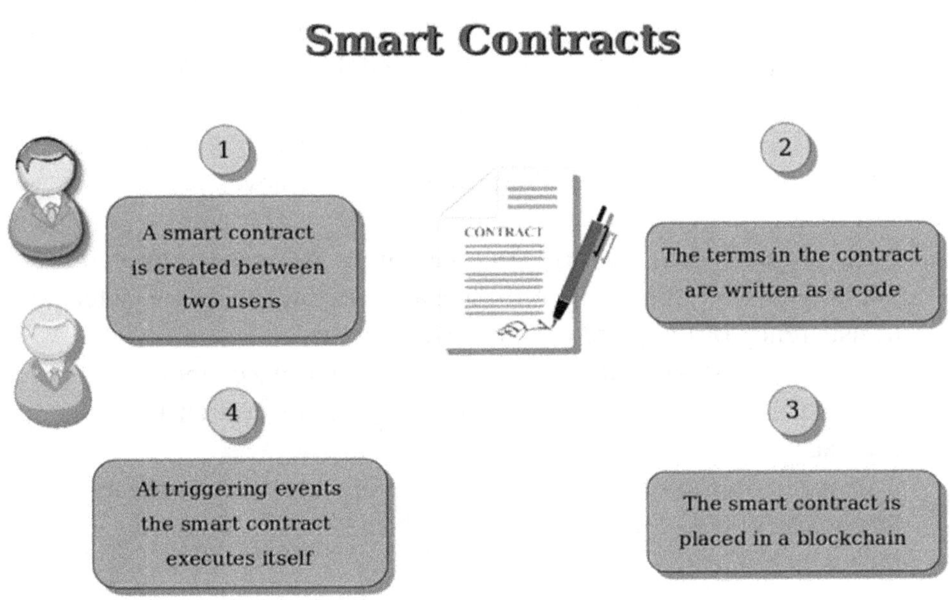

It can be effectively used in *Waqf*. For instance, a *Waqf* deed can be converted into an algorithm or code. The algorithm or code then can be inserted in the Blockchain platform in the form of a smart contract. The execution of the smart contract is automated. The smart contract can avoid the usage of *Waqf* property against the stipulations of the *Waqf* giver. In this way, the *Waqf* deed can be protected and adhered to. This is a simple example where *Waqf* can benefit from smart contract.

From macro perspective, the use of smart contracts could further enhance the performance and efficacy of the *Waqf* institution. Incorporating smart contracts could also reduce the cost, while further increase the security and adherence to the *Waqf* stipulations.

Use Case: Waqf Chain by Finterra

Finterra has developed a crowdfunding platform that uses blockchain to create smart contracts that would be tied to specific waqf projects. This can provide a more efficient way to raise money, manage and transfer ownership of waqf.

The Waqf Chain allows participants to create project proposals to develop and invigorate endowment properties. Others can fund these project proposals by contributing funds. If the project goals are met, the project proposal is accepted, and a certain number of endowment tokens are created and distributed to the participating funders. The tokens can be held to gain stakeholder rights and revenue sharing or transferred and exchanged in the wider Finterra ecosystem (and on other networks) through the Finterra Inter-Chain Protocol.

Among the key benefits that Finterra wants to achieve:

- Each project's 'real world' documentation is stored immutably and publicly for all stakeholder to see and review, ensuring safety and transparency of the project as it moves forward.
- Contribution, stakeholder voting, and special terms cannot be tampered with because they are enforced by blockchain consensus via smart contract.
- Token distribution and project revenue are handled automatically in the smart contract logic guaranteeing fairness and accounting accuracy for token holders.

- Specific project terms are encoded into (and enforced by) a smart contract in a tamper proof manner.

SUMMARY, CONCLUSION, AND POLICY RECOMMENDATIONS

The blockchain, though still in its infancy stage, has already proved itself as a game changing breakthrough for the global financial sphere. In fact, its utilisation is not limited to only the financial sector, but it also affords promising features and usage for non-financial sectors.

Similarly, the waqf institutions could be invigorated with the innovative and efficient use of the blockchain and smart contracts. The blockchain technology and such institutions can indeed have a perfect natural match because, interestingly, the blockchain addresses many, if not all, of the issues and problems currently facing such institutions in the contemporary world.

However, there is an urgent need to focus on this technology for the betterment of waqf institutions. More research with interdisciplinary collaboration should be promoted with the focus on development of proofs of concepts and their implementation related to waqf. Most importantly, shariah scholars need to be well equipped with an in-depth understanding of the technological advancements to the minimum level which is sufficient to guide and advise those efforts in a shariah compliant manner.

Comprehensive shariah governance framework should be developed in order to harness the potential of blockchain and smart contracts phenomenon for invigorating waqf institutions, and other Islamic social financing institutions in general. Shariah standards and parameters need to be prepared for regulatory sand boxes, business incubators, accelerator programs, and technology parks at universities for this purpose.

It is strongly believed that with the firm fiqhi foundations of such institutions, an innovative approach consisting of technological advancements, like blockchain and smart contracts, towards their reinforcement will ensure that they could dynamically participate in the societal and economic development of the whole Muslim world. Such remarkable initiatives will also crystallise the ethical and social dimensions of Islamic finance in a robust manner.

REFERENCES

Abdel-Mohsin, M. (2009). *Cash Waqf: A New Financial Product*. Petaling Jaya: Prentice Hall.

Abdul-Karim, S. (2010). *Contemporary Shari'ah Structuring for the Development and Management of Waqf Assets in Singapore, Durham thesis*. Durham: Durham University.

Abu-Zahrah, M. (2007). *Waqf According to Religion and Laws (Wakaf Menurut Agama dan Undang-undang)*. Selangor: Berlian Publications Sdn Bhd.

Ahmed, H. (1998). *Strategies to Develop Waqf Administration in India*. Research Paper No. 50. Islamic Research and Training Institute, Islamic Development Bank, Jeddah, Saudi Arabia.

Al-Bukhari, M. (2000). *Al-Jami' al-Musnad al-Sahih al-Mukhtasar min Umur Rasul Allah s.a.w. wa Sunanihi wa Ayyamihi in Mawsu'ah al-Hadith al-Sharif al-Kutub al Sittah*. Riyadh: Dar al-Salam.

Al-Humaidan, M. (2007). *Women and Waqf - A series of Translations of Philanthropic and Voluntary Work (12)*. Kuwait Awqaf Public Foundation. Retrieved from http://www.archive.org/stream/WomenAndWaqf/WomenAndWaqf_djvu.txt

Al-Qaradawi, Y. (1999). *Fiqh Al-Zakat: A Comparative Study: The Rules, Regulations and Philosophy of Zakat in the Light of the Quran and Sunna* (K. Monzer, Trans.). Dar Al Taqwa Ltd.

Ali, I. (2009). *WAQFA Sustainable Development Institution for Muslim Communities*. Takaaful T&T Friendly Society.

Awqaf, S. A. (n.d.). *Waqf Hotel 'Uthman ibn 'Affan'(RA)*. Available at: http://www.awqafsa.org.za/waqf-hotel-uthman-ibn-affanra/

Bremer, J. (2004). Islamic Philanthropy: Reviving Traditional Forms for Building Social Justice. *CSID Fifth Annual Conference*. Retrieved from https://www.csidonline.org/documents/pdf/5th_Annual_Conference-Bremer_paper.pdf

Cizakca, M. (2000). *A History of Philanthropic Foundations: The Islamic World from the Seventh Century to the Present*. Bogazici University Press.

Crosby, M., Nachiappan, P., Verma, S., & Kalyanaraman, V. (2015). *Blockchain Technology Beyond Bitcoin*. Sutardja Center for Entrepreneurship & Technology Technical Report.

Fawzan, S. (2005). *A Summary of Islamic Jurisprudence (Al-Mulakhkhas al-Fiqhi)*. Riyadh: Almaiman Publishing House.

Gil, M. (1998). The Earliest Waqf Foundations. *Journal of Near Eastern Studies*, *57*(2), 125-140.

Investopedia. (n.d.). *Smart Contracts*. Available at: https://www.investopedia.com/terms/s/smart-contracts.asp

Kahf, M. (1998). *Financing Development of Awqaf Properties*. International Conference on Awqaf and Economic Development, Kuala Lumpur, Malaysia.

Koehler, B. (2010). Early Islamic Charities as Catalysts of Institutional Innovation. *Economic Affairs*, *30*(3), 6–8. doi:10.1111/j.1468-0270.2010.02014.x

Kuran, T. (2004). Why the Middle East Is Economically Underdeveloped: Historical Mechanism of Institutional Stagnation. *The Journal of Economic Perspectives*, *18*(3), 71–90. doi:10.1257/0895330042162421

Lev, Y. (2005). *Charity Endowments and Charitable Institutions in Medieval Islam*. University Press of Florida.

Mahmood, M. (2006). Waqf in Malaysia: Legal and Administrative Perspective. *IIUM Law Journal, 16*(2). Retrieved from http://journals.iium.edu.my/iiumlj/index.php/iiumlj/article/view/56

Mobin, M., & Ahmad, A. (2017). Achieving Sustainable Economic Development Through Islamic Microfinance and Potential of Proposed Two Tier *Mudarabah Waqf* Business Model. In M. K. Hassan (Ed.), *Handbook of empirical research on Islam and economic life* (pp. 193–212). Edward Elgar Publishing. doi:10.4337/9781784710736.00016

Mohieldin, M., Iqbal, Z., Rostom, A., & Fu, X. (2012). The Role of Islamic Finance in Enhancing Financial Inclusion in Organization of Islamic Cooperation (OIC) Countries. *Islamic Economic Studies*, *20*(2), 55–120. Retrieved from http://elibrary.worldbank.org/docserver/download/5920.pdf?expires=1379735184&id=id&accname=guest&checksum=2AA02676694EA4827E71A356C9E4D7AC

Muslim, H. (2000). *Al-Musnad al-Sahih al-Mukhtasar min al-Sunan bi Naql al-'Adl 'an Rasul Allah Sallallahu Alaihi wa Sallam* in *Mawsu'ah al-Hadith al-Sharif al-Kutub al-Sittah*. Riyadh: Dar al-Salam. Oxford Dictionaries. Retrieved from https://en.oxforddictionaries.com/definition/waqf

PwC FinTech. (2016). *What is Blockchain?* PwC's Financial Services Institute.

Rahman, T. (1980). *A code of Muslim personal law* (Vol. 2). Oxford, UK: Oxford University Press.

Raissouni, A. (2001). *"Waqf Endowment" Scope and Implications*. Morocco: ISESCO. Retrieved from http://isesco.org.ma/english/publications/WAQF/waqf.php

Shechter, R. (2005). Market Welfare in the Early-Modern Ottoman Economy - A Historiographic Overview with Many Questions. *Journal of Economic and Social History of the Orient*, *48*(2), 253–276. doi:10.1163/1568520054127130

Singer, A. (2008). *Charity in Islamic Society*. New York: Cambridge University Press.

Szabo, N. (1996). *Smart Contracts: Building Blocks for Digital Markets*. Retrieved from http://www.fon.hum.uva.nl/rob/Courses/InformationInSpeech/CDROM/Literature/LOTwinterschool2006/szabo.best.vwh.net/smart_contracts_2.html

White, A. (2006). The Role of the Islamic Waqf in Strengthening South Asian Civil Society: Pakistan As Case Study. *International Journal of Civil Society Law*, *4*(2), 7–37. Retrieved from http://www.iccsl.org/pubs/06-04_IJCSL.pdf

Compilation of References

Abdel-Mohsin, M. (2009). *Cash Waqf: A New Financial Product*. Petaling Jaya: Prentice Hall.

Abdul-Karim, S. (2010). *Contemporary Shari'ah Structuring for the Development and Management of Waqf Assets in Singapore, Durham thesis*. Durham: Durham University.

Abubakar, L., & Handayani, T. (2018). Financial technology: Legal challenges for Indonesia financial sector. In *IOP Conference Series: Earth and Environmental Science* (Vol. 175, No. 1, p. 012204). IOP Publishing. 10.1088/1755-1315/175/1/012204

Abu-Zahrah, M. (2007). *Waqf According to Religion and Laws (Wakaf Menurut Agama dan Undang-undang)*. Selangor: Berlian Publications Sdn Bhd.

Accenture. (2015). *Future of FinTech and Banking*. Available at http://www.accenture.com/us-en/insight-future-fintech-banking.aspx

Accenture. (2016). *FinTech and the Evolving Landscape: Landing Points for the Industry*. Retrieved from https://www.finextra.com/finextra-downloads/newsdocs/accentureFinTech2016.pdf

Accenture. (2018, February 28). *Newsroom Main*. Retrieved from Accenture: https://newsroom.accenture.com/news/global-venture-capital-investment-in-fintech-industry-set-record-in-2017-driven-by-surge-in-india-us-and-uk-accenture-analysis-finds.htm

Achuonye, K. A., & Ezekoka, G. K. (2011). Technophobia among female undergraduate students: A challenge to attainment of the MDGs in Nigeria. *British Journal of Educational Research*, *1*(1), 49–57.

African Business Magazine. (2017, August 30). Fintech can cut remittance costs to a fraction. *African Business*.

Agrawal, A., Catalini, C., & Goldfarb, A. (2015). Crowdfunding: Geography, Social Networks and the Timing of Investment Decisions. *Journal of Economics & Management Strategy*, *24*(2), 253–274. doi:10.1111/jems.12093

Ahmed, H. (1998). *Strategies to Develop Waqf Administration in India*. Research Paper No. 50. Islamic Research and Training Institute, Islamic Development Bank, Jeddah, Saudi Arabia.

AITI. (2016, September). *Brunei Darussalam Household ICT Survey 2016*. Bandar Seri Begawan, Brunei Muara, Brunei Darussalam.

Akinyomi, O. J. (2012) Examination of fraud in the Nigerian banking sector and its prevention. *Asian Journal Of Management Research*, *3*(1), 184 – 192.

Al-Alawi, A. I. (2014). Cybercrimes, Computer Forensics and their Impact in Business Climate: Bahrain Status, *Research. Journal of Business and Management*, *8*, 139–156. doi:10.3923/rjbm.2014.139.156

AlAwadhi, S., & Morris, A. (2008, January). The Use of the UTAUT Model in the Adoption of E-government Services in Kuwait. In *Hawaii International Conference on System Sciences, Proceedings of the 41st Annual* (pp. 219-219). IEEE. 10.1109/HICSS.2008.452

Al-Bukhari, M. (2000). *Al-Jami' al-Musnad al-Sahih al-Mukhtasar min Umur Rasul Allah s.a.w. wa Sunanihi wa Ayyamihi in Mawsu'ah al-Hadith al-Sharif al-Kutub al Sittah*. Riyadh: Dar al-Salam.

Al-Humaidan, M. (2007). *Women and Waqf - A series of Translations of Philanthropic and Voluntary Work (12)*. Kuwait Awqaf Public Foundation. Retrieved from http://www.archive.org/stream/WomenAndWaqf/WomenAndWaqf_djvu.txt

Ali, L., Ali, F., Surendran, P., & Thomas, B. (2017). The Effects of Cyber Threats on Customer's Behaviour in e-Banking Services. *International Journal of e-Education, e-Business, e-Management and e-Learning*, *7*(1), 70 – 78. doi:10.17706/ijeeee.2017.7.1.7

Ali, I. (2009). *WAQFA Sustainable Development Institution for Muslim Communities*. Takaaful T&T Friendly Society.

Al-Qaradawi, Y. (1999). *Fiqh Al-Zakat: A Comparative Study: The Rules, Regulations and Philosophy of Zakat in the Light of the Quran and Sunna* (K. Monzer, Trans.). Dar Al Taqwa Ltd.

AMBD. (2018). *FinTech Office*. Retrieved September 22, 2018, from: http://www.ambd.gov.bn/fintech-office

Ancri, C. (2016, October 19). *FinTech Innovation: An Overview*. Washington, DC: Board of Governors of the Federal Reserve System.

Andreasson, K. (2018). FinTech in ASEAN: Unlock the opportunity. *The Economist*.

Anshari, M., Almunawar, M.N., & Masri, M. (2019b). Financial Technology and Disruptive Innovation in Business. *International Journal of Asian Business and Information Management*.

Anshari, M., Almunawar, M. N., & Masri, M. (2019a). Financial Technology and Disruptive Innovation in Business. *International Journal of Asian Business and Information Management, 12*(3).

Anshari, M., Almunawar, M. N., Masri, M., & Hamdan, M. (2019). *Digital Marketplace and FinTech to Support Agriculture Sustainability. Energy Procedia, 156C*, 234–238.

Anshari, M., Almunawar, M. N., Masri, M., & Hamdan, M. (2019)... *Digital Marketplace and FinTech to Support Agriculture Sustainability, Energy Procedia, Elsevier, 156C*, 234–238.

Anshari, M., Almunawar, M. N., Masri, M., & Hamdan, M. (2019a). *Digital Marketplace and FinTech to Support Agriculture Sustainability. In Energy Procedia*. Elsevier.

Anshari, M., Almunawar, M. N., Masri, M., & Hamdan, M. (2019b). *Digital Marketplace and FinTech to Support Agriculture Sustainability. Energy Procedia, Elsevier, 156C*, 234–238.

Antonescu, M., & Birau, R. (2014). Financial and non-financial implications of cybercrimes in emerging countries. *Procedia - Economics and Finance, 32*, 618 – 621. doi:10.1016/S2212-5671(15)01440-9

Arbor Ventures. (2018). *FinTech—Past, present and future.* Retrieved from https://medium.com/@ArborVentures1/fintech-past-present-and-future-eac0f8df2722

Arner, D. W. (2016). *FinTech: Evolution and regulation.* Retrieved from https://law.unimelb.edu.au/__data/assets/pdf_file/0011/1978256/D-Arner-FinTech-Evolution-Melbourne-June-2016.pdf

Arner, D. W., Barberis, J. N., & Buckle, R. P. (2015). *The Evolution of FinTech: A New Post-Crisis Paradigm?* Retrieved December 10, 2018 from https://papers.ssrn.com/sol3/papers.cfm?abstract_id=2676553

Arner, D. W., Barberis, J. N., & Buckle, R. P. (2015). *The Evolution of FinTech: A New Post-Crisis Paradigm?* Retrieved from https://papers.ssrn.com/sol3/papers.cfm?abstract_id=2676553

Arner, D. W., Barberis, J., & Buckley, R. P. (2015). The evolution of FinTech: a new post-crisis paradigm. *Georgetown Journal of International Law,* (47), 1271.

Arner, D. W., Barberies, J., & Buckley, R. P. (2015). The evolution of Fintech: A new post-crisis paradigm. *Georgetown Journal of International Law*, *47*, 1271.

Arner, D. W., Barberis, J., & Buckley, R. P. (2015). The evolution of Fintech: A new post-crisis paradigm. *Geo. J. Int'l L.*, *47*, 1271.

Arner, D. W., Barberis, J., & Buckley, R. P. (2015). The evolution of FinTech: A new post-crisis paradigm. *Geo. J. Int'l L.*, *47*, 1271.

Arner, D. W., Buckley, R. P., & Zetzsche, D. A. (2018). *Fintech for financial inclusion: A framework for digital financial transformation.* Alliance for Financial Inclusion.

Arner, D. W., Zetzsche, D. A., Buckley, R. P., & Barberis, J. N. (2017). FinTech and RegTech: Enabling Innovation While Preserving Financial Stability. *Georgetown Journal of International Affairs*, *18*(3), 47–58. doi:10.1353/gia.2017.0036

Arslanian, H. (2016). How FinTech is Shaping the Future of Banking. *TEDx Talks*. Available at https://youtu.be/pPkNtN8G7q8

Arumuga Perumal, S. (2008). *Impact of Cyber Crime on Virtual Banking*. Available at SSRN: https://ssrn.com/abstract=1289190

ASEANtoday. (2018). *Better late than never? Brunei and its role in the Fintech revolution*. Retrieved 30 October 2018 from https://www.aseantoday.com/2018/06/better-late-than-never-brunei-and-its-role-in-the-fintech-revolution/

Autoriti Monetari Brunei Darussalam (AMBD). (2017, October). *Retail Payments Infrastructure for Brunei Darussalam*. Retrieved August 15, 2018 from: http://ambd.gov.bn/SiteAssets/Request%20for%20Information%20-%20PSS%20Retail%20Payment%20Infrastructure%20v1.1.pdf

Awqaf, S. A. (n.d.). *Waqf Hotel 'Uthman ibn 'Affan' (RA)*. Available at: http://www.awqafsa.org.za/waqf-hotel-uthman-ibn-affanra/

Baker, R. C. (1999). An analysis of fraud on the Internet. *Internet Research, Emerald Publishing Limited*, *9*(5), 348–360. doi:10.1108/10662249910297750

Banks willing to work with fintech companies. (2016, June 6). *The Sun Daily*.

Barreiro, V. (2017). *PH has slowest average internet speed in Asia Pacific – report*. Retrieved 20 October 2018 from https://www.rappler.com/technology/news/171680-philippines-akamai-broadband-adoption-internet-speed-rankings

Barry, B., & Maya, B. (2016). *PwC Global FinTech Survey: Beyond automated advice: How FinTech is shaping asset & wealth management*. Pricewaterhouse Coopers.

Bauer, W., Hammerle, M., Schlund, S., & Vocke, C. (2015). Transforming to a Hyper-connected Society and Economy - Towards an "Industry 4.0". *Procedia Manuf.*, *3*, 417-424.

Bauer, R. M., & Gegenhuber, T. (2015). Crowdsourcing: Global search and the twisted roles of consumers and producers. *Organization*, *22*(5), 661–681. doi:10.1177/1350508415585030 PMID:27524930

BBVA. (2017). *FinTech in emerging ASEAN: Trends and prospects*. Madrid, Spain: BBVA Research.

Beaulieu, T., Sarker, S., & Sarker, S. (2015). A conceptual framework for understanding crowdfunding. CAIS, 37, 1.

Belleflame, P., Lambert, T., & Schwienbacher, A. (2010). *Crowdfunding: An industrial organization perspective. In Workshop Digital Business Models: Understanding Strategies* (pp. 25–26). Paris: Citeseer.

Belleflamme, P., Lambert, T., & Schwienbacher, A. (2014). Crowdfunding: Tapping the right crowd. *Journal of Business Venturing*, *29*(5), 585–609. doi:10.1016/j.jbusvent.2013.07.003

Belleflamme, P., Omrani, N., & Peitz, M. (2015). The economics of crowdfunding platform. *Information Economics and Policy*, *33*, 11–28. doi:10.1016/j.infoecopol.2015.08.003

Bernama. (2017, December). Malaysia's fintech industry poised for growth. *New Strait Times*. Retrieved from https://www.nst.com.my/business/2017/12/311888/malaysias-fintech-industry-poised-growth

Bhasin, M. L. (2015). Menace of Frauds in the Indian Banking Industry: An Empirical Study. *Australian Journal of Business and Management Research*, *4*(12). Available at SSRN: https://ssrn.com/abstract=2676466

BIBD. (2018). *BIBD QuickPay*. Retrieved 30 October 2018 from http://www.bibd.com.bn/personal/digital-banking/bibd-quickpay/

Birau, R. (2016a). A framework for investigating the influence of sociopathic behavior in the case of corporate management. *International Journal of Core Engineering and Management*, *3*(8), 9 – 11.

Birau, R. (2016b). Investigating the influence of psychiatric disorders and internet addiction on human behavior. *International Journal of Business Quantitative Economics and Applied Management Research, 3*(6), 48 – 52.

Birau, R. (2017). The implications of free internet access on the sociopathic and psychopathic personality based on childhood trauma. *International Journal of Core Engineering and Management*, *4*(1), 16 - 20.

Biz Brunei. (2017). AMBD launches sandbox under new FinTech unit. *Biz Brunei*. Retrieved from: https://www.bizbrunei.com/2017/03/amdb-launches-sandbox-new-fintech-unit/

BizBrunei. (2017, March 1). AMBD launches sandbox under new FinTech unit: Local start-ups can now test financial technology products and services through the regulatory sandbox. *Biz Brunei*. Retrieved from https://www.bizbrunei.com/2017/03/amdb-launches-sandbox-new-FinTech-unit/

BizBrunei. (2018). *BruPay receives AMBD approval for trial phase*. Retrieved 30 October 2018 from https://www.bizbrunei.com/2018/08/brupay-receives-ambd-approval-for-trial-phase-sandbox/

Blenkinsop, C. (2018). Why making in-app game purchases using crypto is about to get easier. *Coin Telegraph*. Retrieved from https://cointelegraph.com/news/why-making-in-app-game-purchases-using-crypto-is-about-to-get-easier

BlockchainHub. (n.d.). *Smart contracts*. Retrieved from https://blockchainhub.net/smart-contracts/

Bloomberg. (2019). *Why Asia is leading the fintech revolution*. Retrieved from https://www.bloomberg.com/professional/blog/asia-leading-fintech-revolution/

Bofondi, M., & Gobbi, G. (2017). The Big Promise of FinTech. *European Economy*, *2*(2), 107–120.

Botsman, R., & Rogers, R. (2011). *What's Mine is Yours: How Collaborative Consumption is Changing the Way We Live*. Collins.

Braun, A., & Schreiber, F. (2017). *The Current InsurTech Landscape: Business Models and Disruptive Potential*. St Gallen: Institute of Insurance Economics I.VW-HSG, University of St. Gallen.

Bregant, J., & Bregant, R. (2014). Cybercrime and Computer Crime. In The Encyclopedia of Criminology and Criminal Justice. John Wiley & Sons, Inc. Doi:10.1002/9781118517383.wbeccj244

Bremer, J. (2004). Islamic Philanthropy: Reviving Traditional Forms for Building Social Justice. *CSID Fifth Annual Conference*. Retrieved from https://www.csidonline.org/documents/pdf/5th_Annual_Conference-Bremer_paper.pdf

Broadhurst, R. (2006). Developments in the Global Law Enforcement of Cyber-Crime. *Policing: an International Journal of Police Strategies and Management*, *29*(3), 408 – 433. Available at SSRN: https://ssrn.com/abstract=2089650

Broby, D., & Karkkainen, T. (2016). *FINTECH in Scotland: building a digital future for the financial sector*. Academic Press.

Brummer, C., & Gorfine, D. (2014). FinTech: building a 21st century regulator's toolkit. Milken Institute.

Bruton, G. D., Khavul, S., Siegel, D. S., & Wright, M. (2015). New Financial Alternatives in Seeding Entrepreneurship: Microfinance, Crowdfnding and Peer-to-Peer Innovations. *Entrepreneurship Theory and Practice*, *39*(1), 9–26. doi:10.1111/etap.12143

Bryman, A., & Bell, E. (2007). *Business Research Methods*. New York: Oxford University Press.

BSP. (2015). *National Baseline Survey on Financial Inclusion*. Retrieved 20 October 2018 from http://www.bsp.gov.ph/downloads/publications/2015/NBSFIFullReport.pdf

Business Insider Intelligence. (2016). *Fintech could be bigger than ATMs, PayPal, and Bitcoin combined*. Retrieved from https://www.businessinsider.com.au/fintech-could-be-bigger-than-atms-paypal-and-bitcoin-combined-2016-10

Businesstimes. (2018). *What is the ASEAN Economic Community?* Retrieved 30 October 2018 from https://www.businesstimes.com.sg/hub-projects/deepening-asean-economic-integration/what-is-the-asean-economic-community

Cassiopeia Services. (2019). All eyes on Southeast Asia for FinTech growth in 2019. *Medium*. Retrieved from https://medium.com/@cassiopeiaservicesltd/all-eyes-on-southeast-asia-for-fintech-growth-in-2019-97aec593a93

CB Insights. (2015, November 19). *Disrupting Banking: The FinTech Startups That Are Unbundling Wells Fargo, Citi and Bank of America*. Retrieved from https://www.cbinsights.com/blog/disrupting-banking-fintech-startups/

CB Insights. (2018). *FinTech Trends to Watch in 2018*. Retrieved from / research/report/FinTech-trends-2018/

Cekindo. (2018). *Everything you need to know about fintech in Indonesia*. Retrieved from https://www.cekindo.com/fintech-indonesia.html

Cham, T. H., Low, S. C., Lim, C. S, Aye, A.K., & Ling, R. L. B. (2018). Preliminary study on consumer attitude toward fintech products and services in Malaysia. *International Journal of Engineering & Technology, 7*(2.29), 166-169.

Chaney, D., Touzani, M., & Ben Slimane, K. (2017). *Marketing to the (new) generations: summary and perspectives*. Academic Press.

Chen, M. (2018). Mobile payment firms eye city transport. *China Daily*. Retrieved from http://www.chinadaily.com.cn/a/201805/21/WS5b022003a3103f6866ee98d7.html

Chen, L. (2016). From FinTech to Finlife: The case of FinTech Development in China. *China Economic Journal, 9*(3), 225–239. doi:10.1080/17538963.2016.1215057

Chin, C. S., & Collao, J. B. (2018, April 1). *It's time for more FinTech in the Philippines*. Retrieved from https://www.rappler.com/thought-leaders/199315-time-more-FinTech-philippines

Chishti, S., Barberis, J., & Telfer, J. (2017). *The FINTECH Book: The Financial Technology Handbook for Investors, Entrepreneurs and Visionaries (Unabridged edition)*. Audible Studios on Brilliance Audio.

Chizurum, C. (2018). Cryptocurrency versus fiat money: Pros and cons. *Cryptoblockwire*. Retrieved from https://cryptoblockwire.com/cryptocurrency-vs-fiat-money/

Cho, D., Kwon, H., & Lee, H. (2007). Analysis of Trust in Internet and Mobile Commerce Adoption. *2007 40th Annual Hawaii International Conference On System Sciences (HICSS'07)*. doi: 10.1109/hicss.2007.76

Chong, A. (2013). A two-staged SEM-neural network approach for understanding and predicting the determinants of m-commerce adoption. *Expert Systems with Applications, 40*(4), 1240–1247. doi:10.1016/j.eswa.2012.08.067

Choudhury, R. R., Basak, S., & Guha, D. (2013). Cyber Crimes - Challenges & Solutions. *International Journal of Computer Science and Information Technologies, 4*(5), 729 - 732.

Chowbe, V. S. (2011). *An Introduction to Cyber Crime: General Considerations*. Available at SSRN: https://ssrn.com/abstract=1766234

Christopher, M. (2018). *FinTech Industry in Thailand holds Unlimited Prospects*. Retrieved from https://www.opengovasia.com/FinTech-industry-in-thailand-holds-unlimited-prospects/

Chuen, D. L., & Teo, E. G. (2015, September 30). *Emergence of Fintech and the Lasic Principles*. Retrieved from https://papers.ssrn.com/sol3/papers.cfm?abstract_id=2668049

Chuen, K., Lee, D., & Teo, E. G. (2015). Emergence of FinTech and the LASIC principles. *Journal of Financial Perspectives, 3*(3).

CIMB Group Holdings Berhad. (2017). *CIMB Annual Report 2017*. Retrieved from www.cimb.com

Citi. (2016). *How FinTech is forcing banking to a tipping point: Digital disruption*. Citibank.

Citigroup. (2016a). *Digital Money: Releasing The Flow Of Digital Money Hitting The Tipping Point Of Adoption*. January.

Citigroup. (2016b). *Citi GPS: Global Perspectives & Solutions*. March.

Citigroup. (2018, March). *Citi GPS: Global Perspectives & Solutions*

Cizakca, M. (2000). *A History of Philanthropic Foundations: The Islamic World from the Seventh Century to the Present*. Bogazici University Press.

Collective, T. (2018). *Why is Asia leading the Fintech race?* Retrieved 30 October 2018 from https://techcollectivesea.com/2018/01/19/why-is-asia-leading-the-fintech-race/

Consulus. (2013). BIBD: Bruneian at Heart. *Consulus*. Retrieved from: http://consulus.com/bibd-bruneian-at-heart/

Couffinhal, B. (2014). *The use of crowdfunding as an alternative way to finance small businesses in France*. Dublin: Dublin Business School.

Crosby, M., Nachiappan, P., Verma, S., & Kalyanaraman, V. (2015). *Blockchain Technology Beyond Bitcoin*. Sutardja Center for Entrepreneurship & Technology Technical Report.

Crosby, M., Nachiappan, P., Verma, S., & Kalyanaraman, V. (2016). BlockChain Technology: Beyond Bitcoin. *Applied Innovation Review (AIR),* (2), 6 - 19.

Cryptoboer. (2018). *Cryptocurrencies vs. fiat money: major differences and similarities.* Retrieved from https://www.cryptoboer.nl/2018/01/27/cryptocurrencies-vs-fiat-money-major-differences-and-similarities/

Cuthbertson, A. (2018). Bitcoin market opens to 1.6 billion Muslims as cryptocurrency declared halal under Islamic law. *The Independent.* Retrieved from https://www.independent.co.uk/life-style/gadgets-and-tech/news/bitcoin-islamic-law-muslims-cryptocurrency-market-permissible-sharia-news-price-surge-a8302761.html'

daCosta, F. (2013). *Rethinking the Internet of Things: A Scalable Approach to Connecting Everything*. New York: Apress. doi:10.1007/978-1-4302-5741-7

Danchainam, N. (2018). *10th Digital Finance Working Group in Lao PDR is a clarion call for Digital Finance.* Retrieved 28 October 2018 from http://www.uncdf.org/article/3302/10th-digital-finance-working-group-in-lao-pdr-is-a-clarion-call-for-digital-finance

Dapp, T. F. (2014). *Fintech-The digital (r)evolution in the financial sector:Algorithm-based banking with the human touch.* Frankfurt: Deutsche Bank.

Davies, H. (2015, December 11). *The US News.* Retrieved from The Guardian: https://www.theguardian.com/us-news/2015/dec/11/senator-ted-cruz-president-campaign-facebook-user-data

Davis, K., Maddock, R., & Foo, M. (2017). Catching up with Indonesia's fintech industry. *Law and Financial Markets Review*, *11*(1), 33–40. doi:10.1080/17521440.2017.1336398

Dawson, R. (2014). The New Layer of the Economy Enabled by M2M Payments in the Internet of Things. *Trends in the Living Networks.* Retrieved from http://rossdawsonblog.com/weblog/archives/2014/09/new-layer-economy-enabled-m2mpayments-internet-things.html

DBS Group Research. (2015, April 14). ASEAN Banks, Regional Industry Focus.

de Luna, I. R., Liébana-Cabanillas, F., Sánchez-Fernández, J., & Muñoz-Leiva, F. (2018). Mobile payment is not all the same: The adoption of mobile payment systems depending on the technology applied. *Technological Forecasting and Social Change*. doi:10.1016/j.techfore.2018.09.018

Deda, B. (2017). What is InsurTech and how can you harness its disruptive power? *Vertafore*. Retrieved from: https://www.vertafore.com/resources/blog-posts/what-insurtech-and-how-can-you-harness-its-disruptive-powers

Demirguc-Kunt, A., Klapper, L., Singer, D., Ansar, S., & Hess, J. (2018). *The Global Findex Database 2017: Measuring Financial Inclusion and the Fintech Revolution*. The World Bank. doi:10.1596/978-1-4648-1259-0

Desai, F. (2015). The Evolution of FinTech. *Forbes*. Retrieved from: https://www.forbes.com/sites/falgunidesai/2015/12/13/the-evolution-of-fintech/#758f05787175

Desai, F. (2015). *The Evolution of Fintech*. Retrieved from https://www.forbes.com/sites/falgunidesai/2015/12/13/the-evolution-of-fintech/2/#454f8b0e3dd0

Detwiler, D. (2018). One nation's move to increase food safety with blockchain. *IBM*. Retrieved from https://www.ibm.com/blogs/blockchain/2018/02/one-nations-move-to-increase-food-safety-with-blockchain/

Dharmesh, M. (2016). *Racing from Digital Engagement to Customer Intimacy*. Retrieved from https://www.temenos.com/en/market-insight/2016/racing-from-digital-engagement-to-customer-intimacy/

Dhar, V. (2016). When to trust robots with decisions and when not to. *Harvard Business Review*.

Dillman, D. A. (2000). *Mail and Internet Surveys: The Tailored Design Method* (2nd ed.). New York: Wiley.

Dorfleitner, G., Hornuf, L., Schmitt, M., & Weber, M. (2017). *FinTech in Germany*. Springer International Publishing. Retrieved from https://www.fintechweekly.com/fintech-definition

Dorfleitner, G., Hornuf, L., Schmitt, M., & Weber, M. (2017). *FinTech in Germany*. Springer International Publishing. doi:10.1007/978-3-319-54666-7

Duflos, E. (2015). *New Accounts in China Drive Global Financial Inclusion Figures*. Retrieved October 2, 2017, from http://blogs.worldbank.org/eastasiapacific/new-accounts-china-drive-global-financial-inclusion-figures

Economic Planning and Development Board. (2017). *Brunei Darussalam Statistical Yearbook 2016. Bandar Seri Begawan*. Brunei Darussalam: Brunei Muara.

EdgeVerve Systems. (2017). Blockchain technology: from hype to reality.

Egorova, K. (2018). Gaming company allows players to win cryptocurrency in its new first-person shooter. *Coin Telegraph*. Retrieved from https://cointelegraph.com/news/gaming-company-allows-players-to-win-cryptocurrency-in-its-new-first-person-shooter

Empirica.com. (2018, March 12). *Top Fintech companies in lending space*. Retrieved March 12, 2018, from http://empirica-software.com/fintech-companies-lending/

Ernst & Young (2018). *ASEAN Fintech Census*. EY.

Ernst and Young. (2017). *Unleashing the Potential of FinTechs*. Retrieved from http://www.ey.com/Publication/vwLUAssets/ey-unleashing-the-potential-of-fin-tech-in-banking/$File/ey-unleashing-the-potential-of-fin-tech-in-banking.pdf

Ernst and Young. (2018). *ASEAN FinTech Census 2018*. Retrieved from https://www.ey.com/Publication/vwLUAssets/EY-asean-fintech-census-2018/$FILE/EY-asean-fintech-census-2018.pdf

Euromonitor. (2017). *Mobile Phones in Indonesia*. Retrieved from http://www.euromonitor.com/mobile-phones-in-indonesia/report

EY FinTech adoption index. (2017). Retrieved from http://www.ey.com/gl/en/industries/financial-services/ey-FinTech-adoption-index#market_link

EY FinTech Global Network. (2017). EY FinTech Adoption Index 2017. *The Rapid Emergence of FinTech*. Retrieved from http://www.ey.com/GL/en/Industries/Financial-Services/ey-fintech-adoption-index

EY. (2018). *ASEAN FinTech Census 2018*. Retrieved 30 October 2018 from https://www.ey.com/Publication/vwLUAssets/EY-asean-fintech-census-2018/$FILE/EY-asean-fintech-census-2018.pdf

Fasan, R. (2014). Banks, customer relation and use of ATM cards. *Business Day Newspapers.* Retrieved from: www.businessdayonline.com

Fawzan, S. (2005). *A Summary of Islamic Jurisprudence (Al-Mulakhkhas al-Fiqhi).* Riyadh: Almaiman Publishing House.

Febriana, P. (2016). Fintech: Funding Alternative for start-ups. *The Jakarta Post.* Retrieved from https://www.thejakartapost.com/news/2016/05/25/fintech-funding-alternative-start-ups.html

Ferro, S. (2017). Regulators just demonstrated they are serious about making digital currency companies follow the rules. *Business Insider.* Retrieved from https://www.businessinsider.com/ripple-just-got-slapped-with-a-700000-fine-2015-5/?IR=T

Financial Planning Standards Board. (2016). FinTech and the Future of Financial Planning.

Finextra. (2018). *Alipay targets China's public transportation networks.* Retrieved from https://www.finextra.com/newsarticle/31977/alipay-targets-chinas-public-transportation-networks

FinTech Global. (2018). *2018 is already a record year for global FinTech investment.* Retrieved from http://fintech.global/2018-is-already-a-record-year-for-global-fintech-investment

FinTech trends to watch in 2018. (2018). Retrieved from https://www.cbinsights.com/reports/CB-Insights_FinTech-Trends-2018.pdf

Fintechnews Singapore. (2018). Fintech Indonesia Report 2018 – The State of Play for Fintech Indonesia. *Fintechnews Singapore.* Available at http://fintechnews.sg/20712/indonesia/fintech-indonesia-report-2018/

FinTechnews. (2017). *FinTech in Myanmar, an Overview.* Retrieved 28 October 2018 from http://FinTechnews.sg/8637/myanmar/FinTech-myanmar-overview/

Fintechnews. (2017a). *Fintech Singapore 2017 in Review*. Retrieved 30 October 2017 from http://fintechnews.sg/15601/fintech/fintech-singapore-2017-review/

Fintechnews. (2018). *Fintech for financial inclusion in Vietnam*. Retrieved from http://fintechnews.sg/21608/vietnam/fintech-for-financial-inclusion-in-vietnam/

Fintechnews. (2018). *Fintech Indonesia Report 2018 – The State of Play for Fintech Indonesia*. Retrieved from http://fintechnews.sg/20712/indonesia/fintech-indonesia-report-2018/

FinTechnews. (2018). *FinTech startups in Philippines*. Retrieved 28 October 2018 from http://FinTechnews.sg/FinTech-startups-philippines/

Flint, M. (2018). Cash flow % of small businesses fail. *Reason*, *82*.

Fong, V. (2016). *The emergence of FinTech: Where does Malaysia stand?* Retrieved from http://www.banktechasia.com/FinTech-in-malaysia-2016/

Fontes, T., Costa, V., Ferreira, M. C., Shengxiao, L., Zhao, P., & Dias, T. G. (2017). Mobile payments adoption in public transport. *Transportation Research Procedia*, *24*, 410–417. doi:10.1016/j.trpro.2017.05.093

Frankel, M. (2018). How many crytocurrencies are there? *Fool*. Retrieved from https://www.fool.com/investing/2018/03/16/how-many-cryptocurrencies-are-there.aspx

Freischlad, N. (2016). *Many options, little awareness: fintech startups in Indonesia have a long way to go*. Retrieved from https://www.techinasia.com/indonesia-fintech-report-2016

FTSE Country Classification. (n.d.). Retrieved from http://www.ftse.com/products/indices/country-classificatio.

Fundingsocieties. (2018). *Here are the reasons for Fintech's rapid growth in Southeast Asia*. Retrieved 30 October from http://brands.dollarsandsense.sg/fundingsocieties/tag/asean/

Gabor, D., & Brooks, S. (2017). The digital revolution in financial inclusion: International development in the fintech era. *New Political Economy*, *22*(4), 423–436. doi:10.1080/13563467.2017.1259298

Gai, K., Qiu, M., & Sun, X. (2018). A survey on FinTech. *Journal of Network and Computer Applications, 103*(January), 262–273. doi:10.1016/j.jnca.2017.10.011

Ganeshwaran, K. (2016, November 26). FinTech seen as threat to business of institutions. *The Star Online*.

Gansky, L. (2010). *The Mesh: Why the Future of Business Is Sharing*. Portfolio Penguin.

Gaumer, Q., Mortier, S., & Moutaib, A. (2016). Financial institutions and cyber crime – Between vulnerability and security. *Financial Stability Review, 20*, 45 - 52.

Gavril, M. (2017). *The Financial Revolution And The Many Benefits It Brings: Cryptocurrency & Blockchain Technology*. Academic Press.

Gem. (n.d.). *Healthcare solutions.* Retrieved from https://enterprise.gem.co/health/

Gil, M. (1998). The Earliest Waqf Foundations. *Journal of Near Eastern Studies, 57*(2), 125-140.

Global Banking & Finance Review. (2018). *The three biggest FinTech challenges facing the industry right now.* Retrieved from https://www.globalbankingandfinance.com/the-three-biggest-fintech-challenges-facing-the-industry-right-now/

Global Findex. (2014). *The Global Findex database: Indonesia.* Retrieved from http://datatopics.worldbank.org/financialinclusion/country/indonesia

Gnirck, M., & Visser, G. (2016). Singapore, the FinTech Hub for Southeast Asia. *The FinTech Book: The financial technology handbook for investors, entrepreneurs and visionaries*, 58-60.

Gnrick, M. (2017, Aug 22). *The 5 driving factors behind ASEAN's imminent FinTech boom.* Retrieved from https://www.forbes.com/sites/outofasia/2017/08/22/the-5-driving-factors-behind-aseans-imminent-FinTech-boom/#cff91055cf3b

Gomber, P., Koch, J. A., & Siering, M. (2017). Digital Finance and FinTech: Current research and future research directions. *Journal of Business Economics, 87*(5), 537–580. doi:10.100711573-017-0852-x

Google Trends. (2018). *fintech.* Retrieved from https://trends.google.com/trends/explore?date=all&q=fintech

Goyal, S. (2018). The difference between fiat money and cryptocurrencies. *Yahoo.* Retrieved from https://finance.yahoo.com/news/difference-between-fiat-money-cryptocurrencies-132027811.html

Gromex, M. (2018). *What Can FinTech Expect In The Next 24 Months In The Central And Eastern Europe.* Retrieved 30 October 2018 from https://www.forbes.com/sites/michalgromek/2018/07/27/what-can-fintech-expect-in-the-next-24-months-in-the-central-and-eastern-europe/#5694db9548e2

Guan, L. (2016). *A Short Literature Review on Reward-based Crowdfunding.* Academic Press.

Gudowicz, Z. (2018). *ASEAN Thailand ICO market.* Retrieved from https://www.cyberius.com/wp-content/uploads/2018/03/ASEAN-Insights-Thailand.pdf

Gulamhuseinwala, I., Bull, T., & Lewis, S. (2015). *FinTech is gaining traction and young, high-income users are the early adopters.* Academic Press.

Gupta, A., & Xia, C. (2018). A Paradigm Shift in Banking: Unfolding Asia's FinTech Adventures. In Banking and Finance Issues in Emerging Markets (pp. 215-254). Emerald Publishing Limited.

HAB. F. (2018, August 18). BIBD bolstering efforts to create cashless society. *Borneo Bulletin.* Retrieved September 24, 2018, from: https://borneobulletin.com.bn/bibd-bolstering-efforts-to-create-cashless-society/

Haddad, C., & Hornuf, L. (2016). The emergence of the global fintech market: Economic and technological determinants. *Small Business Economics*, 1–25.

Hamin, Z., Othman, R., & Selamat, H. S. (2016). Funding terror in cyberspace: Challenges in the financial investigation of cyber terrorist financing. *Information Journal Elsevier B.*, *19*(10), 4725–4730.

Hannig, A. (2017, December 20). FinTech: What's in it for financial inclusion? Alliance for Financial Inclusion.

Härle, P, Havas, A, Kremer, A, Rona, D, Samandari, H (2015). The future of bank risk management.

Ha, S., & Stoel, L. (2009). Consumer e-shopping acceptance: Antecedents in a technology acceptance model. *Journal of Business Research, 62*(5), 565–571. doi:10.1016/j.jbusres.2008.06.016

Hayen, R. (2016). *FinTech: The Impact and Influence of Financial Technology on Banking and the Finance Industry*. Createspace Independent Publishing Platform.

Helander, M. G., & Khalid, H. M. (2000). Modeling the customer in electronic commerce. *Applied Ergonomics, 31*(6), 609–619. doi:10.1016/S0003-6870(00)00035-1 PMID:11132045

Hitcher, W. (2006). *The Innovation Paradigm*. Retrieved from https://www.icd-ps.org/en/common/viewfile?FilePath=~/Uploads/publication/doc/20171205113348810IFDIReport2017.pdf

Hobololo, T. S., & Mawela, T. (2017). Exploring the Use of Mobile Phones for Public Participation in the Buffalo City Metropolitan Municipality. *AGRIS On-Line Papers in Economics and Informatics, 9*(1), 57–68. doi:10.7160/aol.2017.090105

Hoesin, S. (2018). *Unrealized Potential in Indonesia's Growing FinTech industry*. Retrieved 30 October 2018 from https://ifcextapps.ifc.org/IFCExt/Pressroom/IFCPressRoom.nsf/0/E26207B6540F40A9852582DB001098C9

Hone, K. S., Graham, R., Maguire, M., Baber, C., & Johnson, G. (1998). Speech technology for automatic teller machines: An investigation of user attitude and performance. *Ergonomics, 41*(7), 962–981. doi:10.1080/001401398186531

Hong Leong Bank Berhad. (2017). *Sustainability Report 2017*.

Hong Leong Bank Berhad. (2018). *Annual Report 2018*.

Hoontrakul, P. (2018). Asia's Digital Economy. In *Economic Transformation and Business Opportunities in Asia* (pp. 269–312). Cham: Palgrave Macmillan. doi:10.1007/978-3-319-58928-2_8

Hourahine, B., & Howard, M. (2004). Money on the move: Opportunities for financial service providers in the 'third space'. *Journal of Financial Services Marketing, 9*(1), 57–67. doi:10.1057/palgrave.fsm.4770141

Hsu, C., & Lin, J. (2008). Acceptance of blog usage: The roles of technology acceptance, social influence and knowledge sharing motivation. *Information & Management, 45*(1), 65–74. doi:10.1016/j.im.2007.11.001

Huei, C. T., Cheng, L. S., Seong, L. C., Khin, A. A., & Bin, R. L. L. (2018). Preliminary Study on consumer attitude towards FinTech products and services in Malaysia. *International Journal of Engineering & Technology, 7*(2.29), 166-169.

Hyman, L., Lamb, J., & Bulmer, M. (2006). The Use of Pre-Existing Survey Questions: Implications for Data Quality. *European Conference on Quality in Survey Statistics.*

Iansiti, M., & Lakhani, K. R. (2017). The Truth about Blockchain. *Harvard Business Review*, 3–11.

Ibrahim, M. (2016, April 4). Accelerating the migration to electronic payments in Malaysia [Speech of the Deputy Governor of the Central Bank of Malaysia]. In Inaugural Malaysian E-Payments Excellence Awards, Kuala Lumpur.

Iman, N. (2018). Assessing the dynamics of fintech in Indonesia. *Investment Management and Financial Innovations, 15*(4), 296–303. doi:10.21511/imfi.15(4).2018.24

Iman, N. (2018). Is mobile payment still relevant in the fintech era? *Electronic Commerce Research and Applications, 30*, 72–82.

International Monetary Fund. (2018). *The Bali Fintech Agenda: A Blueprint for Successfully Harnessing Fintech's Opportunities.* Press Release, No.18/388. IMF.

International Monetary Fund. (2018). The Core Principles for Islamic Finance Regulations and Assessment Methodology. *Staff Report, 18/193*(May), 35.

Internet World Stats. (2018). Internet Usage in Asia. *Internet World Stats: Usage and Population Statistics.* Retrieved from: https://www.internetworldstats.com/stats3.htm

Internet World Stats. (n.d.). Retrieved from https://www.internetworldstats.com/stats.htm

Investment, I. (2018). *Rapid Development of Fintech Industry in Indonesia.* Retrieved 30 October 2018 from https://www.indonesia-investments.com/id/finance/financial-columns/rapid-development-of-fintech-industry-in-indonesia/item8949

Investopedia. (2015). *Is fiat money more prone to inflation than commodity money?* Retrieved from https://www.investopedia.com/ask/answers/041515/fiat-money-more-prone-inflation-commodity-money.asp

Investopedia. (n.d.). *Smart Contracts.* Available at: https://www.investopedia.com/terms/s/smart-contracts.asp

ITA. (2016). *FinTech Top Markets Report.* Retrieved from https://www.trade.gov/topmarkets/pdf/Financial_Technology_Executive_Summary.pdf

Iwamoto, K., & Lee, J. (2018). *Banks, regulators lack skills to cope with pace of fintech innovation.* Retrieved from https://asia.nikkei.com/Spotlight/Asia300-Summit-2018/Banks-regulators-lack-skills-to-cope-with-pace-of-fintech-innovation

Iwasaki, K. (2018). Emergence of FinTech companies in Southeast Asia: rising hopes of a solution to financial issues. *Journal of Pacific Business and Industries, 18*. Retrieved from https://www.jri.co.jp/MediaLibrary/file/english/periodical/rim/2018/68.pdf

Iwasaki, K. (2018). Emergence of fintech companies in Southeast Asia: rising hopes of a solution to financial issues. *Pacific Business and Industries, 18*(68), 1-32. Retrieved from https://www.jri.co.jp/MediaLibrary/file/english/periodical/rim/2018/68.pdf

Iwasaki, K. (2018). Emergence of FinTech companies in Southeast Asia: Rising hopes of a solution to financial issues. *Pacific Business and Industries, 18*(68), 1–32.

Jagtiani, J., & Lemieux, C. (2017). *FinTech Lending: Financial Inclusion, Risk Pricing, and Alternative Information (SSRN Scholarly Paper No. ID 3005260).* Rochester, NY: Social Science Research Network. Retrieved from https://papers.ssrn.com/abstract=3005260

Jamieson, S. (2017). *Wonga data breach could affect nearly 250,000 customers' bank details.* Retrieved from https://www.fintech.finance/01-news/wonga-data-breach-could-affect-nearly-250000-customers-bank-details

Jomo, K. S. (1997). *Southeast Asia's misunderstood miracle: Industrial policy and economic development in Thailand, Malaysia and Indonesia.* Boulder, CO: Westview Press.

Jones, B. (2016). *Mobile Money at The Report.* Myanmar: Oxford Business Group.

Juniper Research. (2016). *FinTech AI Revenue to Grow 960% by 2021, Driven by Big Data, Distributed Computing & Connectivity.* Retrieved from https://www.juniperresearch.com/press/press-releases/FinTech-ai-revenue-to-grow-960-by-2021-driven-by

Kagermann, H., Washlster, W., & Helbig, J. (2013). Recommendations for Implementing the Strategic Initiative Industrie 4.0 - Final Report of the Industrie 4.0 Working Group. Acatech - National Academy of Science and Engineering.

Kahf, M. (1998). *Financing Development of Awqaf Properties.* International Conference on Awqaf and Economic Development, Kuala Lumpur, Malaysia.

Kamruzzaman, J., & Sarker, R. A. (2006). Artificial neural networks: Applications in finance and manufacturing. In *Artificial Neural Networks in Finance and Manufacturing* (pp. 1–27). IGI Global. doi:10.4018/978-1-59140-670-9.ch001

Kappel, T. (2008). Ex ante crowdfunding and the recording industry: A model for the US. *Loyola of Los Angeles Entertainment Law Review*, *29*, 375.

Karim, S. S. (2016). Cyber-crime Scenario in Banking Sector of Bangladesh: An Overview. *The Cost and Management*, *44*(2), 13 – 19.

Kartawijaya, R., & Hamsal, I. (2018). FINTECH: FinTech Entrepreneurs versus Banks in Indonesia. *Advanced Science Letters*, *24*(1), 264–266. doi:10.1166/asl.2018.11978

Kaya, O. (2017). Robo-advice - a true innovation in asset management. *Deutsche Bank Research: EU Monitor Global financial markets*. Retrieved from: http://www.dbresearch.com/PROD/RPS_EN-PROD/PROD0000000000449125/Robo-advice_–_a_true_innovation_in_asset_managemen.PDF

Khan, F. (2018). Evolution of fintech—A timeline. *Datadriveninvestor*. Retrieved from https://www.datadriveninvestor.com/2018/06/15/evolution-of-fintech%E2%80%8A-%E2%80%8Aa-timeline/

Kharpal, A. (2017). Singapore aims to finish its own cryptocurrency trial next year. *CNBC*. Retrieved from https://www.cnbc.com/2017/10/26/singapore-cryptocurrency-blockchain-trial.html

Kharpal, A. (2018). Bitcoin market share is at the level it was just after it hit its near-$20,000 record high. *CNBC*. Retrieved from https://www.cnbc.com/2018/08/07/bitcoin-market-share-near-level-when-price-hit-record-high.html

Kiel, D., Muller, J., Arnold, C., & Voigt, K. (2017). Sustainable Industrial Value Creation: Benefits and Challenges of Industry 4.0. *International Journal of Innovation Management*, *21*(8), 3–10. doi:10.1142/S1363919617400151

Kijsanayotin, B., Pannarunothai, S., & Speedie, S. M. (2009). Factors influencing health information technology adoption in Thailand's community health centers: Applying the UTAUT model. *International Journal of Medical Informatics*, *78*(6), 404–416. doi:10.1016/j.ijmedinf.2008.12.005 PMID:19196548

Kim Do, H. T., Nguyen, N. T. M., & Le, T. H. (2017). Effects of the Credit Boom on the Soundness of Vietnamese Commercial Banks. *International Journal of Financial Research*, *8*(3). Doi:10.5430/ijfr.v8n3p57

Kim, H. T., Chu, L. K., & Nguyen, P. M. (2017). Vietnamese Banking System in the Context of ASEAN Financial Integration. *International Journal of Financial Research*, *8*(1). Doi:10.5430/ijfr.v8n1p155

Kim, H. W., & Kankanhalli, A. (2009). Investigating user resistance to information systems implementation: A status quo bias perspective. *Management Information Systems Quarterly*, *33*(3), 567–582. doi:10.2307/20650309

Kim, Y., Park, Y.-J., Choi, J., & Yeon, J. (2015). An Empirical Study on the Adoption of "FinTech" Service: Focused on Mobile Payment Services. *Advanced Science and Technology Letters*, *114*, 136–140. doi:10.14257/astl.2015.114.26

King, B. (2014). *Breaking Banks: The Innovators, Rogues, and Strategists Rebooting Banking* (1st ed.). Wiley. doi:10.1002/9781118958247

Kleemann, F., Voß, G., & Rieder, K. (2008). Un(der)paid innovators: The commercial utiliza-tion of consumer work through crowdsourcing. *Science, Technology & Innovation Studies, 4*(1), 5.

Kocherlakota, N. (1998). The technological role of fiat money. *Federal Reserve Bank of Minnianapolis Quarterly Review*, *22*(3), 2–10.

Koehler, B. (2010). Early Islamic Charities as Catalysts of Institutional Innovation. *Economic Affairs*, *30*(3), 6–8. doi:10.1111/j.1468-0270.2010.02014.x

Koffi, H. (2016). The Fintech Revolution: An Opportunity for the West African Financial Sector. *Open Journal of Applied Sciences*, *6*(11), 771–782. doi:10.4236/ojapps.2016.611068

Kon, J. (2018). Progresif launches Brunei's first mobile wallet. *Borneo Bulletin* Retrieved from: https://borneobulletin.com.bn/progresif-launches-bruneis-first-mobile-wallet/

Kong, A. (2016). *The State of FinTech In Laos*. Retrieved 28 October 2018 from https://yostartups.com/the-state-of-FinTech-in-laos/

Kong, A. (2016). *The state of FinTech in Thailand*. Retrieved from https://yostartups.com/the-state-of-FinTech-in-thailand/

Kumar, S. (2018). Financial inclusion can leapfrog with blockchain technology. *Yourstory*. Retrieved from https://yourstory.com/2018/01/financial-inclusion-leapfrog-blockchain-technology/

Kuran, T. (2004). Why the Middle East Is Economically Underdeveloped: Historical Mechanism of Institutional Stagnation. *The Journal of Economic Perspectives*, *18*(3), 71–90. doi:10.1257/0895330042162421

Kursh, S. R., & Gold, N. A. (2016). Adding FinTech and blockchain to your curriculum. *Business Education Innovation Journal, 8*.

Lagarde, C. (2018). *IMF and World Bank unveil Fintech Agenda*. Retrieved 30 October 2018 from https://www.finextra.com/pressarticle/75832/imf-and-world-bank-unveil-fintech-agenda

Lagazio, M., Sherif, N., & Cushman, M. (2014). A multi-level approach to understanding the impact of cyber crime on the financial sector. *Computers & Security, Elsevier, 45*, 58–74. doi:10.1016/j.cose.2014.05.006

Lago, C. (2018). How Singapore is using blockchain outside of cryptocurrencies. *CIO-Asia*. Retrieved from https://www.cio-asia.com/article/3291758/blockchain/how-singapore-is-using-blockchain-outside-of-crypto-currencies.html

Lakhani, K., Lifshitz-Assaf, H., & Tushman, M. (2013). Open Innovation and Organizational Boundaries: The Impact of Task Decomposition and Knowledge Distribution on the Locus of Innovation. In A. Grandori (Ed.), *Handbook of Economic Organization: Integrating Economic and Organization Theory* (pp. 355–382). Northampton, UK: Edward Elgar. doi:10.4337/9781782548225.00030

Larios-Hernández, G. J. (2017). Blockchain entrepreneurship opportunity in the practices of the unbanked. *Business Horizons*, *60*(6), 865–874. doi:10.1016/j.bushor.2017.07.012

Laven, M., & Bruggink, D. (2016). How FinTech is transforming the way money moves around the world: An interview with Mike Laven. *Journal of Payments Strategy & Systems*, *10*(1), 6–12.

Lee, J. (2017). OCBC chatbot 'Emma' helps customers sign $70m in home loans. *StraitsTimes*. Retrieved from https://www.straitstimes.com/business/banking/ocbc-chatbot-emma-helps-customers-sign-70m-in-home-loans

Lee, S. H., & Lee, D. W. (2016). *Review on FinTech Industry in Oversea*. Academic Press.

Lee, D. K., & Teo, E. G. (2015). Emergence of FinTech and the LASIC principles. *The Journal of Financial Perspective*, *3*(3), 24–37.

Lee, I., & Shin, Y. J. (2018). FinTech: Ecosystem, business models, investment decisions, and challenges. *Business Horizons*, *61*(1), 35–46. doi:10.1016/j.bushor.2017.09.003

Lee, T., & Kim, H. (2015). An exploratory study on FinTech industry in Korea: Crowdfunding case. *International conference on Innovative Engineering Technologies*, 58-64.

Leong, C., Tan, B., Xiao, X., Tan, F. T., & Sun, Y. (2017). Nurturing a FinTech ecosystem: The case of a youth microloan startup in China. *International Journal of Information Management*, *37*(2), 92–97. doi:10.1016/j.ijinfomgt.2016.11.006

Leukfeldt, E. R., Lavorgna, A. & Kleemans, E. R. (2017). Organised Cybercrime or Cybercrime that is Organised? An Assessment of the Conceptualisation of Financial Cybercrime as Organised Crime. *European Journal on Criminal Policy and Research, 23*(3), 287 – 300. doi:10.100710610-016-9332-z

Lev, Y. (2005). *Charity Endowments and Charitable Institutions in Medieval Islam*. University Press of Florida.

Liao, C., Tsou, C., & Huang, M. (2007). Factors influencing the usage of 3G mobile services in Taiwan. *Online Information Review*, *31*(6), 759–774. doi:10.1108/14684520710841757

Lin, J. C. C., & Lu, H. (2000). Towards an understanding of the behavioural intention to use a web site. *International Journal of Information Management*, *20*(3), 197–208. doi:10.1016/S0268-4012(00)00005-0

Lipton, A., Shrier, D., & Pentland, A. (2016). *Digital banking manifesto: the end of banks?* Massachusetts Institute of Technology.

Lisk Academy. (n.d.). *Blockchain transparency explained.* Retrieved from https://lisk.io/academy/blockchain-basics/benefits-of-blockchain/blockchain-transparency-explained

Liu, S. H., Liao, H. L., & Pratt, J. A. (2009). Impact of media richness and flow on e-learning technology acceptance. *Computers & Education*, *52*(3), 599–607. doi:10.1016/j.compedu.2008.11.002

Lokman, A. M., Ilyas, S. S. M., & Tsuchiyac, T. (2017). A Qualitative Exploration of Phishing and its Affect to Trust in Online Banking. *International Journal of Control Theory and Applications*, *10*(30), 63-70.

Lopez-de-Silanes, F., Phalippou, L., & Gottschalg, O. (2015). Giants at the gate: Investment returns and diseconomies of scale in private equity. *Journal of Financial and Quantitative Analysis*, *50*(3), 377–411. doi:10.1017/S0022109015000113

Lu, L. (2018a). *Decoding Alipay: Mobile Payments, a Cashless Society and Regulatory Challenges. Butterworths Journal of International Banking and Financial Law.*

Lu, L. (2018b). *How a Little Ant Challenges Giant Banks? The Rise of Ant Financial (Alipay)'s Fintech Empire and Relevant Regulatory Concerns. International Company and Commercial Law Review.*

Ma, Y., & Liu, D. (2017). Introduction to the special issue on Crowdfunding and FinTech. *Financial Innovation, 3*(1).

Mahardhika, G. S., & Inggis, R. A. (2017). Peer-to-peer lending in Surabaya: How it drives regional economy? *Journal of Development Economics*, *2*(2), 58–78.

Mahmood, M. (2006). Waqf in Malaysia: Legal and Administrative Perspective. *IIUM Law Journal, 16*(2). Retrieved from http://journals.iium.edu.my/iiumlj/index.php/iiumlj/article/view/56

Mahmud, B., Islam, M., & Naher, K. (2015). Empirical Study of the Use of Automated Teller Machine (ATM) among Bank Customers in Dhaka City, Bangladesh. *European Journal of Business and Management*, *7*(1).

Mansfield-Devine, S. (2017). Beyond Bitcoin: Using blockchain technology to provide assurance in the commercial world. *Computer Fraud & Security*, *2017*(5), 14–18. doi:10.1016/S1361-3723(17)30042-8

Marchewka, J. T., & Kostiwa, K. (2007). An application of the UTAUT model for understanding student perceptions using course management software. *Communications of the IIMA*, *7*(2), 10.

Martínez-Climent, C., Zorio-Grima, A., & Robeiro-Soriano, D. (2018). Financial return crowdfunding: Literature review and bibliometric analysis. *The International Entrepreneurship and Management Journal*, *14*(3), 527–553. doi:10.100711365-018-0511-x

Maulia, E. (2018). *Indonesia offers a fresh battleground for fintech*. Retrieved from https://asia.nikkei.com/Spotlight/Cover-Story/Indonesia-offers-a-fresh-battleground-for-fintech

Maybank. (2017). Annual Report 2017.

Micu, I., & Micu, A. (2016). Financial Technology (FinTech) And Its Implementation on The Romanian Non-Banking Capital Market. *SEA-Practical Application of Science*, *11*, 379–384.

Middleton, C. (2018). FinTech: Intelligent automation could add $512 billion to finance sector. *Internet of Business*. Retrieved from https://internetofbusiness.com/fintech-intelligent-automation-could-add-512-billion-to-finance-sector/

Milne, A. (2015, November 16). *Achieving European policy objectives through Financial Technology*. Brussels, Belgium: ECRI.

Milne, A. (2015). *Achieving European Policy Objectives through Financial Technology*. European Credit Research Institute.

Minerva, R., Asaba, C. P. S., Aiba, D. P. K., & Hirano, M. (2016). *The potential of the Fintech industry to support the growth of SMEs in Indonesia* (Unpublished master thesis). Waseda University, Japan.

Mobin, M., & Ahmad, A. (2017). Achieving Sustainable Economic Development Through Islamic Microfinance and Potential of Proposed Two Tier *Mudarabah Waqf* Business Model. In M. K. Hassan (Ed.), *Handbook of empirical research on Islam and economic life* (pp. 193–212). Edward Elgar Publishing. doi:10.4337/9781784710736.00016

Mohamed, H., & Ali, H. (2019). Blockchain, Fintech and Islamic Finance — Building the Future of the New Islamic Digital Economy. DeIG Press.

Mohieldin, M., Iqbal, Z., Rostom, A., & Fu, X. (2012). The Role of Islamic Finance in Enhancing Financial Inclusion in Organization of Islamic Cooperation (OIC) Countries. *Islamic Economic Studies*, *20*(2), 55–120. Retrieved from http://elibrary.worldbank.org/docserver/download/5920.pdf?expires=1379735184&id=id&accname=guest&checksum=2AA02676694EA4827E71A356C9E4D7AC

Money Super Market. (2018). Our guide to 'digital-only' banks. *Money Seuper Market | Digital Banking*. Retrieved from: https://www.moneysupermarket.com/current-accounts/digital-banking/digital-only-guide/

Mongid, A. (2015). Cost Efficiency of the ASEAN Banking Market. *International Business Management*, *9*(7), 1580–1586. doi:10.3923/ibm.2015.1580.1586

Moran, M., Hawkes, M., & Gayar, O. E. (2010). Tablet personal computer integration in higher education: Applying the unified theory of acceptance and use technology model to understand supporting factors. *Journal of Educational Computing Research*, *42*(1), 79–101. doi:10.2190/EC.42.1.d

More, M. M., Jadhav, M. P., & Nalawade, K. M. (2015). Online Banking and Cyber Attacks: The Current Scenario. *International Journal of Advanced Research in Computer Science and Software Engineering*, *5*(12), 743 - 749.

Morgan, R. (2017, September 5). The top fintech trends driving the next decade. *ABA Banking Journal*.

Muslim, H. (2000). *Al-Musnad al-Sahih al-Mukhtasar min al-Sunan bi Naql al-'Adl 'an Rasul Allah Sallallahu Alaihi wa Sallam* in *Mawsu'ah al-Hadith al-Sharif al-Kutub al-Sittah*. Riyadh: Dar al-Salam. Oxford Dictionaries. Retrieved from https://en.oxforddictionaries.com/definition/waqf

Nakamoto, S. (2008). Bitcoin: a peer-to-peer electronic cash system.

Nakashima, T. (2018). Creating credit by making use of mobility with FinTech and IoT. *IATSS Research*, *42*(2), 61–66. doi:10.1016/j.iatssr.2018.06.001

Nanayakkara, N., Smith, C., Nassir, Z., Hatch, M., Crespigny, A. C., & Hinkis, R. (2017). *Blockchain innovation in wealth and asset management: Benefits and key challenges to adopting this technology*. Ernst & Young LLP.

Nasdaq. (2018). Nasdaq blockchain strategy. Retrieved from https://business.nasdaq.com/media/Blockchain Mutual Fund Strategy SEB and Nasdaq 2018_tcm5044-61791.pdf

Nazri, M and Hoolash, R. (2017). Are Malaysian banks doing okay with the FinTech wave? *Malaysian Business*.

Ng, A. W., & Kwok, B. K. B. (2017). Emergence of Fintech and cybersecurity in a global financial centre: Strategic approach by a regulator. *Journal of Financial Regulation and Compliance*, *25*(4), 422–434. doi:10.1108/JFRC-01-2017-0013

Nguyen, T. L. A. (2018). Diversification and bank efficiency in six ASEAN countries. *Global Finance Journal*, *37*, 57 - 78. . doi:10.1016/j.gfj.2018.04.004

Nicoletti, B. (2017). The Future of FinTech: Integrating Finance and Technology in Financial Services. Cham: Palgrave Macmillan.

Nicoletti, B. (2017). *The future of FinTech*. Springer. doi:10.1007/978-3-319-51415-4

Nikkei. (2018). *Indonesia offers a fresh battleground for fintech*. Retrieved from https://asia.nikkei.com/Spotlight/Cover-Story/Indonesia-offers-a-fresh-battleground-for-fintech

Nimtrakoon, S. (2015). The relationship between intellectual capital, firms' market value and financial performance: Empirical evidence from the ASEAN. *Journal of Intellectual Capital*, *16*(3), 587–618. doi:10.1108/JIC-09-2014-0104

Noman, A. H. M., Gee, C. S., & Isa, C. R. (2017). Does competition improve financial stability of the banking sector in ASEAN countries? An empirical analysis. *PLoS ONE. Europe PMC*, *12*(5), e0176546. doi:10.1371/journal.pone.0176546 PMID:28486548

Noordin, KA. (2017, July 5). Disrupting Islamic finance. The Edge Malaysia.

O'Dwyer, M. (2017). Reducing security breaches in FinTech is a business priority. *IPSwitch*. Retrieved from https://blog.ipswitch.com/reducing-security-breaches-in-fintech-is-a-business-priority

Ogunsemor, A. (1991, January). *Banking Services: The Emergence and Impact of electronic Banking. The Bangladeshi Banker*.

Olleros, F., & Zhegu, M. (Eds.). (2016). *Research Handbook on Digital Transformation*. Cheltenham, UK: Academic Press. doi:10.4337/9781784717766

Olsen, T., Judah, M., Fielding, J., Nielsen, N. P., & Phillips, S. (2017). *New Bank Strategies Require New Operating Models*. Singapore: Bain & Company's Financial Services.

Otoritas Jasa Keuangan. (2013). *Peraturan OJK Nomor 1/POJK.07/2013 tentang Perlindungan Konsumen Sektor Jasa Keuangan.*

Otoritas Jasa Keuangan. (2016). *Peraturan OJK Nomor 76/POJK.07/2016 tentang Peningkatan Literasi dan Inklusi Keuangan di Sektor Jasa Keuangan bagi Konsumen dan/atau Masyarakat.*

Otoritas Jasa Keuangan. (2017a). *The Global Inclusion Awards 2017: Sebuah Pengakuan Internasional untuk Indonesia.*

Otoritas Jasa Keuangan. (2017b). *Annual Report.*

Otoritas Jasa Keuangan. (2017c). *Revisit strategi nasional literasi keuangan Indonesia (SNLKI) sebagai upaya akselerasi pencapaian indeks literasi dan inklusi keuangan.* Press Release, No.SP 82/DKSN/OJK/VII/2017.

Ozili, P. K. (2018). *Impact of digital finance on financial inclusion and stability. Borsa Istanbul Review*. doi:10.1016/j.bir.2017.12.003

Pan, W., Altschuler, Y., & Pentland, A. S. (2012). Decoding Social Influence and the Wisdom of the Crowd in Financial Trading Network. In *International Conference on Privacy, Security, Risk and Trust and International Conference on Social Computing* (pp. 203 - 209). Institute of Electrical and Electronics Engineers.

Parasuraman, A., Zeithaml, V. A., & Berry, L. L. (1988). SERVQUAL: A multiple-item scale for measuring consumer perception of service quality. *Journal of Retailing*, *64*(1), 12–40.

Park, S. Y. (2009). An analysis of the technology acceptance model in understanding university students' behavioral intention to use e-learning. *Journal of Educational Technology & Society*, *12*(3), 150–162.

Passler, K. H. (2018). "Real" InsurTech Startups do it Differently! In S. Chishti & J. Barberis (Eds.), The InsurTech Book: The Insurance Technology Handbook for Investors, Entrepreneurs and FinTech Visionaries (pp. 24 - 27). FINTECH Circle Ltd. doi:10.1002/9781119444565.ch6

Paulsen, D. (2012). Why fiat money is a safe asset. *Economics Letters*, *116*(2), 193–198. doi:10.1016/j.econlet.2012.02.016

Pelster, M., & Hofmann, A. (2018). About the fear of reputational loss: Social trading and the disposition effect. *Journal of Banking & Finance*, *94*, 75–88. doi:10.1016/j.jbankfin.2018.07.003

Pesin, I. (2017, May 10). *FinTech in Cambodia 2017*. Retrieved 28 October 2018 from https://medium.com/@igorpesin/FinTech-in-cambodia-2017-d74f82f46b7d

Phan, D., Narayan, P. K., Rahman, R. E., & Hutabarat, A. R. (2018). *Do Financial Technology Firms Influence Bank Performance?* Paper was presented on September 4th, 2018 in Universitas Airlangga Presiden.

Philippon, T. (2016). *The fintech opportunity (No. w22476). National Bureau of Economic Research*. doi:10.3386/w22476

Philstar. (2017). *Phl leads in internet speed increase*. Retrieved 20 October 2018 from https://www.philstar.com/business/2017/06/04/1706696/phl-leads-internet-speed-increase

Phong, K., Srou, L., & Solá, J. (2016). *Mobile Phones and Internet Use in Cambodia 2016*. Academic Press.

Phoon, K., & Koh, F. (2018). Robo-Advisors and Wealth Management. *Journal of Alternative Investments*, *20*(3), 79–94. doi:10.3905/jai.2018.20.3.079

Pisani, B. (2010). *Man vs machine: how stock trading got so complex*. Retrieved December 10, 2018 from https://www.cnbc.com/id/38978686

Pollari, I., & Raisbeck, M. (2018). *The pulse of fintech*. KPMG.

Powell, R. J., & McMillan, D. (2017). New perspectives on bank risk in Malaysia. *Cogent Economics & Finance, Taylor & Francis*, *5*(1). doi:10.1080/23322039.2017.1326217

Pradhan, R. P., Arvin, M. B., Hall, J. H., & Norman, N. R. (2017). ASEAN economic growth, trade openness and banking-sector depth: The nexus. *EconomiA. Elsevier B.*, *18*, 359–379. doi:10.1016/j.econ.2017.05.002

Preetha, N. (2015) Digital Disruption: Game Changer for the Capital Market Industry. engage@SIDC, 1(2), 4-6.

Prensky, M. (2001). Digital Natives, Digital Immigrants Part 1. *On the Horizon*, *9*(5), 1–6. doi:10.1108/10748120110424816

Puschmann, T. (2012). The Rise of Customer-Oriented Banking-Electronic Markets Are Paving the Way for Change in the Financial Industry. *Electronic Markets*, *22*(4), 203–215. doi:10.100712525-012-0106-2

Puschmann, T. (2017). FinTech. *Business & Information Systems Engineering*, *59*(1), 69–76. doi:10.100712599-017-0464-6

PwC FinTech. (2016). *What is Blockchain?* PwC's Financial Services Institute.

PwC. (2016). *Customers in the spotlight: How FinTech is reshaping banking*. Retrieved from https://www.pwc.com/gx/en/industries/financial-services/publications/fintech-is-reshaping-banking.html

PwC. (2016). *FinTech*. Available at http://www.pwc.com/us/en/financial-services/fintech.html

PwC. (2017). *The Long View: How will the global economic order change by 2050?* Available at https://www.pwc.com/gx/en/issues/economy/the-world-in-2050.html

Quickonomics. (2016). *The four different types of money*. Retrieved from https://quickonomics.com/different-types-of-money/

Rahman, A. R. (2017). We need responsible disruption. Accountants Today, (Mar/Apr), 18–20.

Rahman, A. J. (2018). Deflationary policy under digital and fiat currency competition. *Research in Economics*, *72*(2), 171–180. doi:10.1016/j.rie.2018.04.004

Rahman, T. (1980). *A code of Muslim personal law* (Vol. 2). Oxford, UK: Oxford University Press.

Raikwar, M., Mazumdar, S., Ruj, S., Gupta, S. S., Chattopadhyay, A., & Lam, K. Y. (2018, February). A blockchain framework for insurance processes. In *2018 9th IFIP International Conference on New Technologies, Mobility and Security (NTMS)* (pp. 1-4). IEEE. 10.1109/NTMS.2018.8328731

Raissouni, A. (2001). *"Waqf Endowment" Scope and Implications*. Morocco: ISESCO. Retrieved from http://isesco.org.ma/english/publications/WAQF/waqf.php

Rajak, W. (2018). Brunei is world's 4th highest in social media penetration. *The Bruneian.* Retrieved from: https://www.thebruneian.news/brunei-is-worlds-4th-highest-in-social-media-penetration

Rampton, J. (2017). Move fast, but be careful: The challenges of FinTech. *Due*. Retrieved from https://due.com/blog/move-fast-careful-challenges-fintech/

Raza, S. (2018). FinTech – the evolution of modern financial technology in the 21st century. *Value Walk*. Retrieved from https://www.valuewalk.com/2018/03/fintech-evolution-financial-technology/

Republik Indonesia. (2016). *Peraturan Presiden Republik Indonesia Nomor 82 tahun 2016 tentang Strategi Nasional Keuangan Inklusif*. SNKI.

Riyanto, A., Primiana, I., & Azis, Y. (2018, August). Disruptive Technology: The Phenomenon of FinTech towards Conventional Banking in Indonesia. *IOP Conference Series. Materials Science and Engineering*, *407*(1), 012104. doi:10.1088/1757-899X/407/1/012104

Rob, M. (2017, September 5). The top fintech trends during the next decade. *ABA Banking Journal*.

Rogers, E. M. (1995). *Diffusion of Innovation* (4th ed.). New York: Free Press.

Rooney, K. (2018). After the crisis, a new generation puts its trust in tech over traditional banks. *CNBC*. Retrieved from https://www.cnbc.com/2018/09/14/a-new-generation-puts-its-trust-in-tech-over-traditional-banks.html

Rotman, S. (2014). Bitcoin Versus Electronic Money. *Cgap*, (January), 4. Retrieved from https://openknowledge.worldbank.org/bitstream/handle/10986/18418/881640BRI0Box30WLEDGENOTES0Jan02014.pdf?sequence=1&isAllowed=y

Ryabova, A. (2015). Emerging FinTech market: Types and features of new financial technologies. *Journal of Economics and Social Sciences*, *7*(4).

Sandel, T. (2016, December 21). *The fintech revolution.* Retrieved from https://www.jpmorgan.com/europe/merchant-services/fin-tech-revolution

Santander InnoVentures & Oliver Wyman. (2015). Rebooting Financial Services.

Sanusi, Z. M., Rameli, M. N. F., & Isa, Y. M. (2015). Fraud Schemes in the Banking Institutions: Prevention Measures to Avoid Severe Financial Loss, 7th International Conference on Financial Criminology 2015, 13-14 April 2015, Wadham College, Oxford, United Kingdom. *Procedia Economics and Finance*, *28*, 107–113. doi:10.1016/S2212-5671(15)01088-6

Schindele, A., & Szczesny, A. (2016). The impact of Basel II on the debt costs of German SMEs. *Journal of Business Economics*, *86*(3), 197–227. doi:10.100711573-015-0775-3

Schindler, J. (2017). *FinTech and Financial Innovation: Drivers and Depth.* Finance and Economics Discussion Series 2017-081. Washington, DC: Board of Governors of the Federal Reserve System.

Schwab, K. (2016, January 14). *The Fourth Industrial Revolution: What it means and how to respond.* Retrieved from World Economic Forum: https://www.weforum.org/agenda/2016/01/the-fourth-industrial-revolution-what-it-means-and-how-to-respond/

Scott-Briggs, A. (2017, May 30). *Fintech News: Tech Bullion.* Retrieved March 15, 2018, from https://www.techbullion.com/fintech-money-transfer-sector-improving-remittance-industry/

Secretariat A. S. E. A. N. World Bank. (2013). *ASEAN Integration Monitoring Report.* Jakarta: ASEAN Secretariat and the World Bank. Retrieved from https://openknowledge. worldbank.org/handle/10986/16695

Seeking Alpha. (2017). Indonesia - The Next Major Oil Importer? *Seeking Alpha.* Available at https://seekingalpha.com/article/4035779-indonesia-next-major-oil-importer

Serey, C. (2017). *FinTech could be 'game changer'.* Retrieved 28 October 2018 from https://m.phnompenhpost.com/business/FinTech-could-be-game-changer

Serrels, M. (2018). Someone just bought a cryptocurrency cat for $172,000. *CNET*. Retrieved from https://www.cnet.com/news/cryptokitties-bought-a-digital-cat-for-172000/

Shai, G. (2018). InsurTech and the Promise of "Property Value Hedging Technology". In S. Chishti & J. Barberis (Eds.), The InsurTech Book: The Insurance Technology Handbook for Investors, Entrepreneurs and FinTech Visionaries, (pp. 280-282). Academic Press.

Sharf, S. (2016, November 7). The FinTech 50: The Complete List 2016. *Forbes*.

Shechter, R. (2005). Market Welfare in the Early-Modern Ottoman Economy - A Historiographic Overview with Many Questions. *Journal of Economic and Social History of the Orient*, *48*(2), 253–276. doi:10.1163/1568520054127130

Shekokar, N. M., Shah, C., Mahajan, M., & Rachh, S. (2015). An Ideal Approach for Detection and Prevention of Phishing Attacks, ICAC3′15. *Procedia Computer Science*, *49*, 82–91. doi:10.1016/j.procs.2015.04.230

Shim, Y., & Shin, D.-H. (2016). Analyzing China's FinTech Industry from the Perspective of Actor – Network Theory, *40*, 2015–2017.

Shim, Y., & Shin, D. H. (2016). Analyzing China's FinTech industry from the perspective of actor–network theory. *Telecommunications Policy*, *40*(2-3), 168–181. doi:10.1016/j.telpol.2015.11.005

Shin, D. H. (2009). Towards an understanding of the consumer acceptance of mobile wallet. *Computers in Human Behavior*, *25*(6), 1343–1354. doi:10.1016/j.chb.2009.06.001

Shinozaki, S. (2012). *A New Regime of SME Finance in Emerging Asia: Empowering Growth-Oriented SMEs to Build Resilent National Economics*. Asia Development Bank. Working Paper Series on Regional Economic integration No. 104/ December 2012, Asia Development Bank.

Shiva. (2016). *Fintech Outlook for 2017: Report discussing trends, opportunities and challenges.* Schaumburg: Opus Consulting.

Shrier, D., Canale, G., & Pentland, A. (2016). *Mobile money & payments: Technology trends. In Connection Science & Engineering* (pp. 2–27). Massachusetts Institute of Technology.

Singer, A. (2008). *Charity in Islamic Society.* New York: Cambridge University Press.

Sironi, P. (2016). *FinTech Innovation: From Robo-Advisors to Goal Based Investing and Gamification* (1st ed.). Wiley. doi:10.1002/9781119227205

Skinner, C. (2016). *ValueWeb: How FinTech firms are using bitcoin blockchain and mobile technologies to create the Internet of value.* Marshall Cavendish International Asia Pte Ltd.

Spulbar, C., & Niţoi, M. (2012). *Comparative analysis of banking systems.* SITECH Publishing House Craiova.

Spulbar, C., & Nitoi, M. (2015). An Examination of Banks' Cost Efficiency in Central and Eastern Europe. *Procedia Economics and Finance, 22*, 544–551. doi:10.1016/S2212-5671(15)00256-7

Spulbar, C., & Nitoi, M. (2016). The relationship between bank efficiency and risk and productivity patterns in Romanian banking system. *Romanian Journal of Economic Forecasting, 19*(1), 39–53.

State of FinTech in ASEAN. (2017). *EY report.* Retrieved on 04-02-2019 from https://www.ey.com/Publication/vwLUAssets/ey-state-of-FinTech-in-asean/%24File/ey-state-of-FinTech-in-asean.pdf

Stefik, M., & Stefik, B. (2006). *Breakthrough: Stories and Strategies of Radical Innovation* (illustrated edition). The MIT Press. Retrieved from http://gen.lib.rus.ec/book/index.php?md5=B1A5F9B3FFE65BF5C53490B52C7B78D6

Straitstimes. (2016). *New fintech innovation hub to take shape in the heart of Singapore's CBD.* Retrieved 30 October 2018 from https://www.straitstimes.com/business/banking/new-fintech-innovation-hub-to-take-shape-in-the-heart-of-singapores-cbd

Suchit, L. N. (2017). *Thailand lags in FinTech development in Asia*. Retrieved from https://www.bangkokpost.com/tech/local-news/1373711/thailand-lags-in-FinTech-development-in-asia

Sundarajan, S. (2017, November 28). *Top 10 fintech trends that could infuence the banking industry in 2018*. Retrieved March 10, 2018, from https://yourstory.com/2017/11/top-10-fintech-trends-influence-banking-industry-2018/

Sustainable Development knowledge Platform, Division For Sustainable Development, UN-DESA, the United Nations, Department of Economic and Social Affairs. (n.d.). Retrieved from https://sustainabledevelopment.un.org/

Swan, M. (2015). Blockchain: Blueprint for a new economy. O'Reilly.

Sy.ngo. (2018). *How Financial Technologies (FinTech) Market Evolves in Vietnam?* Retrieved 28 October, 208 from http://www.antconsult.vn/news/how-financial-technologies-FinTech-market-evolves-in-vietnam.html#ixzz5OuiQSLzE

Syadullah, M. (2018) ASEAN Banking Efficiency Review Facing Financial Services Liberalization: The Indonesian Perspective. *Asian Development Policy Review*, *6*(2), 88-99. Doi:10.18488/journal.107.2018.62.88.99

Szabo, N. (1996). *Smart Contracts: Building Blocks for Digital Markets*. Retrieved from http://www.fon.hum.uva.nl/rob/Courses/InformationInSpeech/CDROM/Literature/LOTwinterschool2006/szabo.best.vwh.net/smart_contracts_2.html

Tahir, I. M., & Mongid, A. (2013). The Interrelationship between Bank Cost Efficiency, Capital and Risk-Taking in ASEAN Banking. *International Journal of Economics and Management Sciences*, *2*(12), 1 - 15. Available at SSRN: https://ssrn.com/abstract=2766904

Tang, C. Y., Lai, C. C., Law, C. W., Liew, M. C., & Phua, V. V. (2014). Examining key determinants of mobile wallet adoption intention in Malaysia: An empirical study using the unified theory of acceptance and use of technology 2 model. *International Journal of Modelling in Operations Management*, *4*(3-4), 248–265. doi:10.1504/IJMOM.2014.067383

Tan, P. J. B. (2013). Students' adoptions and attitudes towards electronic placement tests: A UTAUT analysis. *American Journal of Computer Technology and Application*, *1*(1), 14–23.

Tan, Z., & Ouyang, W. (2004). Diffusion and Impacts of the Internet and E-commerce in China. *Electronic Markets*, *14*(1), 25–35. doi:10.1080/1019678042000175270

Tapscott, D., & Tapscott, A. (2016). *Blockchain Revolution: How the Technology Behind Bitcoin Is Changing Money, Business, and the World.* Penguin.

Tay, V. (2018). OCBC Bank's Emma: How a chatbot aided in generating leads and conversions. *Marketing Interactive*. Retrieved from https://www.marketing-interactive.com/ocbc-banks-emma-how-a-chatbot-aided-in-generating-leads-and-conversions/

Thaivisa. (2018). *Thai people spend NINE hours per day online, new study finds*. Retrieved 30 October 2018 from https://tech.thaivisa.com/thai-people-spend-nine-hours-per-day-online-new-study-finds/27033/

The Jakarta Post. (2017). 16,000 Indonesian islands registered at UN. *The Jakarta Post*. Available at https://www.thejakartapost.com/news/2017/08/21/16000-indonesian-islands-registered-at-un.html

The New Arab. (2018). *Is Bitcoin halal? Islamic scholars wade into cryptocurrency debate.* Retrieved from https://www.alaraby.co.uk/english/news/2018/4/9/is-bitcoin-halal-islamic-scholars-wade-into-cryptocurrency-debate

The official website of the Association of Southeast Asian Nations. (n.d.). Retrieved from https://asean.org/

The official website of the European Commission – Eurostat. (n.d.). Retrieved from http://ec.europa.eu/eurostat/

The official website of the UNESCO. (n.d.). Retrieved from www.unesco.org

The official website of the United Nations. (n.d.). Retrieved from http://www.un.org/

The official website of the World Bank. (n.d.). Retrieved from http://data.worldbank.org/-

TheCityUK. (2017). *Transformation and innovation: a guide to partnerships between financial services institutions and FinTechs*. Retrieved from https://www.thecityuk.com/assets/research-report/Transformation-and-innovation-A-guide-to-partnerships-between-financial-services-institutions-and-FinTechs.pdf

Thienes, C. (2016, June 16). *What's the difference between mobile and digital wallets?* Retrieved March 20, 2018, from http://www.tmgfinancialservices.com/the-future-of-credit/future-of-credit-blog/whats-the-difference-between-mobile-and-digital-wallets

Thomas, T., Singh, L., & Gaffar, K. (2013). The utility of the UTAUT model in explaining mobile learning adoption in higher education in Guyana. *International Journal of Education and Development Using ICT*, *9*(3).

Thompson, B. S. (2017). Can Financial Technology Innovate Benefit Distribution in Payments for Ecosystem Services and REDD+? *Ecological Economics*, *139*, 150–157. doi:10.1016/j.ecolecon.2017.04.008

Totka, M. (2018). 7 Secrets for using fintech to manage small business cash flow revealed. *SmallBiztrends*. Retrieved from https://smallbiztrends.com/2018/11/managing-cash-flow-with-fintech.html

Trade. (2016). *2016 Top Markets Report Financial Technology Country Case Study*. Retrieved 30 October 2018 from https://www.trade.gov/topmarkets/pdf/Financial_Technology_Singapore.pdf

TradingEconomics. (2018). *Thailand GDP Growth Rate*. Retrieved 27 October 2018 from https://tradingeconomics.com/thailand/gdp-growth)

Treleaven, P. (2015). Financial regulation of FinTech Financial regulation. EY Global Financial Services Institute, 3(3).

Truman, G. E., Sandoe, K., & Rifkin, T. (2003). An empirical study of smart card technology. *Information & Management*, *40*(6), 591–606. doi:10.1016/S0378-7206(02)00046-0

Truong, O. (2016). *How FinTech industry is changing the world.* Retrieved December 10, 2018 from https://www.theseus.fi/bitstream/handle/10024/123633/TRUONG_OANH.pdf?sequence=1

Tsai, C., & Peng, K.-J. (2017). *The FinTech Revolution and Financial Regulation: The Case of Online Supply Chain Financing (SSRN Scholarly Paper No. ID 3035386).* Rochester, NY: Social Science Research Network. Retrieved from https://papers.ssrn.com/abstract=3035386

Tsu Wei, T., Marthandan, G., Yee-Loong Chong, A., Ooi, K., & Arumugam, S. (2009). What drives Malaysian m-commerce adoption? An empirical analysis. *Industrial Management & Data Systems, 109*(3), 370–388. doi:10.1108/02635570910939399

Tung, C. (2015). *Cambodia and Laos: the challenge of altering attitudes towards startups.* Retrieved from https://e27.co/cambodia-laos-challenge-altering-attitudes-towards-startups-20151118/

Uche, C. U. (2001). Nigeria: Bank Fraud. *Journal of Financial Crime, Emerald Publishing Limited, 8*(3), 265–275. doi:10.1108/eb025992

United Overseas Bank Group, Ernest & Young Corporation. (2016). United Overseas Bank (UOB): State of FinTech in ASEAN. *UOB Group: Tech Eco System.* Retrieved from: https://www.uobgroup.com/techecosystem/pdf/UOB-State-of-FinTech-in-ASEAN.pdf

UOBgroup. (2017). *State of FinTech in ASEAN.* Retrieved 27 October 2018 from https://www.uobgroup.com/techecosystem/pdf/UOB-State-of-FinTech-in-ASEAN.pdf

Venkatesh, M., Morris, Davis, & Davis. (2003). User Acceptance of Information Technology: Toward a Unified View. *Management Information Systems Quarterly, 27*(3), 425. doi:10.2307/30036540

Venkatesh, V., & Davis, F. D. (2000). A theoretical extension of the technology acceptance model: Four longitudinal field studies. *Management Science, 46*(2), 186–204. doi:10.1287/mnsc.46.2.186.11926

Venkatesh, V., Thong, J. Y., & Xu, X. (2012). Consumer acceptance and use of information technology: Extending the unified theory of acceptance and use of technology. *Management Information Systems Quarterly*, *36*(1), 157–178. doi:10.2307/41410412

Viknesh, V., & Abdulwahab, A. S. (2017). The Impact of Digitalization of Retail Banks in Malaysia on Customer Experience. *International Journal of Accounting & Business Management*, *5*(2), 197–213.

Villasenor, J. (2016). *Ensuring Cybersecurity in FinTech: Key Trends and Solutions*. Retrieved May 11, 2018, from https://www.forbes.com/sites/johnvillasenor/2016/08/25/ensuring-cybersecurity-in-FinTech-key-trends-and-solutions/

Viray, G. (2018). *4 things fintech startups can learn from the mobile payments boom in Cambodia*. Retrieved 12 November 2018 from https://e27.co/4-things-fintech-startups-can-learn-mobile-payments-boom-cambodia-20180326/

Vives, X. (2017). The Impact of Fintech on Banking. *European Economy*, *2*, 97–106.

Wang, T., & Shin, N. (2010). An empirical study of customers' perceptions of security and trust in e-payment systems. *Electronic Commerce Research and Applications*, *9*(1), 84–95. doi:10.1016/j.elerap.2009.04.014

Warner, J. (2017). Future of FinTech | Consumer Survey 2017 Presented by Telegraph. *The Telegraph.* Retrieved from: https://www.telegraph.co.uk/content/dam/business/spark/Fintech/Telegraph_Fintech_Report%202017.pdf

We Are Social. (2016). *Digital in 2016: Global Overview*. Retrieved from https://wearesocial.com/special-reports/digital-in-2016

White, A. (2006). The Role of the Islamic Waqf in Strengthening South Asian Civil Society: Pakistan As Case Study. *International Journal of Civil Society Law*, *4*(2), 7–37. Retrieved from http://www.iccsl.org/pubs/06-04_IJCSL.pdf

Wigglesworth, R. (2016, January 20). *FinTech: Search for super-logo*, Retrieved from http://mypages.iit.edu/~mdixon7/FinancialTimesArticle_SearchForASuperAlgo_Jan_20_2016.pdf

Wilkowska, W., & Ziefle, M. (2012). Privacy and data security in E-health: Requirements from the user's perspective. *Health Informatics Journal, 18*(3), 191–201. doi:10.1177/1460458212442933 PMID:23011814

Woetzel, J., Seong, J., Wang, K. W., Manyika, J., Chui, M., & Wong, W. (2017). Digital China: Powering the Economy to Global Competitiveness.

Wohlgemuth, V., Berger, E. S., & Wenzel, M. (2016). More than just financial performance: Trusting investors in social trading. *Journal of Business Research, 69*(11), 4970–4974. doi:10.1016/j.jbusres.2016.04.061

Wong, A. (2018). BruPay received AMBD aproval for trial phase. *Biz Brunei.* Retrieved from: https://www.bizbrunei.com/2018/08/brupay-receives-ambd-approval-for-trial-phase-sandbox/

Wong, A. (2018). BruPay receives AMBD approval for trial phase. *Biz Brunei.* Retrieved from https://www.bizbrunei.com

Wonglimpiyarat, J. (2017). FinTech Crowdfunding of Thailand 4.0 Policy. *Journal of Private Equity, 21*(1), 55–63. doi:10.3905/jpe.2017.21.1.055

Wonglimpiyarat, J. (2018). Challenges and dynamics of FinTech crowd funding: An innovation system approach. *The Journal of High Technology Management Research, 29*(1), 98–108. doi:10.1016/j.hitech.2018.04.009

Wong, W. P., & Deng, Q. (2016). Efficiency analysis of banks in ASEAN countries, *Benchmarking. An International Journal, Emerald Publishing Limited, 23*(7), 1798–1817. doi:10.1108/BIJ-11-2013-0102

World Bank. (2018). *Financial inclusion on the rise, but gaps remain, global findex database shows.* Retrieved from https://www.worldbank.org/en/news/press-release/2018/04/19/financial-inclusion-on-the-rise-but-gaps-remain-global-findex-database-shows

World Economic Forum. (2015). *Global Agenda Council on the future of Financing and Capital.* Author.

World Economic Forum. (2015). *The Future of Fintech: A Paradigm Shift in Small Business Finance.* Author.

Wrede, P. (2018). InsureTech for development. *The World Bank Blog.* Retrieved from: http://blogs.worldbank.org/psd/insuretech-development

Yahid, B., Shahbahrami, A., & Nobakht, M. B. (2013, April). Providing security for e-wallet using e-cheque. In *e-Commerce in Developing Countries: With Focus on e-Security (ECDC), 2013 7th International Conference on* (pp. 1-14). IEEE. 10.1109/ECDC.2013.6556725

Yang, S. (2015). Why Wall Street is pouring money into companies that want to eat its lunch. *Business Insider*. Retrieved from https://www.businessinsider.com.au/wall-street-invests-in-fintech-startups-2015-3

Yu, E. (2017). *More Singapore consumers choose e-payments over cash.* Retrieved 30 October 2017 from https://www.zdnet.com/article/more-singapore-consumers-choose-e-payments-over-cash/

Zainuddin, A. (n.d.). Guide to centralized cryptocurrencies: what makes a coin centralized? *Master the Crypto*. Retrieved from https://masterthecrypto.com/centralized-cryptocurrencies-coin-centralized/

Zalan, T., & Toufaily, E. (2017). The promise of FinTech in emerging markets: not as disruptive. *Contemporary Economics, 11*(4).

Zavolokina, L., Dolata, M., & Schwabe, G. (2016). *The FinTech phenomenon: antecedents of financial innovation perceived by the popular press*. Financial Innovation.

Zhou, T., Lu, Y., & Wang, B. (2010). Integrating TTF and UTAUT to explain mobile banking user adoption. *Computers in Human Behavior, 26*(4), 760–767. doi:10.1016/j.chb.2010.01.013

Related References

To continue our tradition of advancing information science and technology research, we have compiled a list of recommended IGI Global readings. These references will provide additional information and guidance to further enrich your knowledge and assist you with your own research and future publications.

Abtahi, M. S., Behboudi, L., & Hasanabad, H. M. (2017). Factors Affecting Internet Advertising Adoption in Ad Agencies. *International Journal of Innovation in the Digital Economy*, *8*(4), 18–29. doi:10.4018/IJIDE.2017100102

Agrawal, S. (2017). The Impact of Emerging Technologies and Social Media on Different Business(es): Marketing and Management. In O. Rishi & A. Sharma (Eds.), *Maximizing Business Performance and Efficiency Through Intelligent Systems* (pp. 37–49). Hershey, PA: IGI Global. doi:10.4018/978-1-5225-2234-8.ch002

Alnoukari, M., Razouk, R., & Hanano, A. (2016). BSC-SI: A Framework for Integrating Strategic Intelligence in Corporate Strategic Management. *International Journal of Social and Organizational Dynamics in IT*, *5*(2), 1–14. doi:10.4018/IJSODIT.2016070101

Alnoukari, M., Razouk, R., & Hanano, A. (2016). BSC-SI, A Framework for Integrating Strategic Intelligence in Corporate Strategic Management. *International Journal of Strategic Information Technology and Applications*, *7*(1), 32–44. doi:10.4018/IJSITA.2016010103

Altındağ, E. (2016). Current Approaches in Change Management. In A. Goksoy (Ed.), *Organizational Change Management Strategies in Modern Business* (pp. 24–51). Hershey, PA: IGI Global. doi:10.4018/978-1-4666-9533-7.ch002

Alvarez-Dionisi, L. E., Turner, R., & Mittra, M. (2016). Global Project Management Trends. *International Journal of Information Technology Project Management, 7*(3), 54–73. doi:10.4018/IJITPM.2016070104

Anantharaman, R. N., Rajeswari, K. S., Angusamy, A., & Kuppusamy, J. (2017). Role of Self-Efficacy and Collective Efficacy as Moderators of Occupational Stress Among Software Development Professionals. *International Journal of Human Capital and Information Technology Professionals, 8*(2), 45–58. doi:10.4018/IJHCITP.2017040103

Aninze, F., El-Gohary, H., & Hussain, J. (2018). The Role of Microfinance to Empower Women: The Case of Developing Countries. *International Journal of Customer Relationship Marketing and Management, 9*(1), 54–78. doi:10.4018/IJCRMM.2018010104

Arsenijević, O. M., Orčić, D., & Kastratović, E. (2017). Development of an Optimization Tool for Intangibles in SMEs: A Case Study from Serbia with a Pilot Research in the Prestige by Milka Company. In M. Vemić (Ed.), *Optimal Management Strategies in Small and Medium Enterprises* (pp. 320–347). Hershey, PA: IGI Global. doi:10.4018/978-1-5225-1949-2.ch015

Aryanto, V. D., Wismantoro, Y., & Widyatmoko, K. (2018). Implementing Eco-Innovation by Utilizing the Internet to Enhance Firm's Marketing Performance: Study of Green Batik Small and Medium Enterprises in Indonesia. *International Journal of E-Business Research, 14*(1), 21–36. doi:10.4018/IJEBR.2018010102

Atiku, S. O., & Fields, Z. (2017). Multicultural Orientations for 21st Century Global Leadership. In N. Baporikar (Ed.), *Management Education for Global Leadership* (pp. 28–51). Hershey, PA: IGI Global. doi:10.4018/978-1-5225-1013-0.ch002

Atiku, S. O., & Fields, Z. (2018). Organisational Learning Dimensions and Talent Retention Strategies for the Service Industries. In N. Baporikar (Ed.), *Global Practices in Knowledge Management for Societal and Organizational Development* (pp. 358–381). Hershey, PA: IGI Global. doi:10.4018/978-1-5225-3009-1.ch017

Ávila, L., & Teixeira, L. (2018). The Main Concepts Behind the Dematerialization of Business Processes. In M. Khosrow-Pour, D.B.A. (Ed.), Encyclopedia of Information Science and Technology, Fourth Edition (pp. 888-898). Hershey, PA: IGI Global. doi:10.4018/978-1-5225-2255-3.ch076

Bartens, Y., Chunpir, H. I., Schulte, F., & Voß, S. (2017). Business/IT Alignment in Two-Sided Markets: A COBIT 5 Analysis for Media Streaming Business Models. In S. De Haes & W. Van Grembergen (Eds.), *Strategic IT Governance and Alignment in Business Settings* (pp. 82–111). Hershey, PA: IGI Global. doi:10.4018/978-1-5225-0861-8.ch004

Bashayreh, A. M. (2018). Organizational Culture and Organizational Performance. In W. Lee & F. Sabetzadeh (Eds.), *Contemporary Knowledge and Systems Science* (pp. 50–69). Hershey, PA: IGI Global. doi:10.4018/978-1-5225-5655-8.ch003

Bedford, D. A. (2018). Sustainable Knowledge Management Strategies: Aligning Business Capabilities and Knowledge Management Goals. In N. Baporikar (Ed.), *Global Practices in Knowledge Management for Societal and Organizational Development* (pp. 46–73). Hershey, PA: IGI Global. doi:10.4018/978-1-5225-3009-1.ch003

Benmoussa, F., Nakara, W. A., & Jaouen, A. (2016). The Use of Social Media by SMEs in the Tourism Industry. In I. Lee (Ed.), *Encyclopedia of E-Commerce Development, Implementation, and Management* (pp. 2159–2170). Hershey, PA: IGI Global. doi:10.4018/978-1-4666-9787-4.ch155

Berger, R. (2016). Indigenous Management and Bottom of Pyramid Countries: The Role of National Institutions. In U. Aung & P. Ordoñez de Pablos (Eds.), *Managerial Strategies and Practice in the Asian Business Sector* (pp. 107–123). Hershey, PA: IGI Global. doi:10.4018/978-1-4666-9758-4.ch007

Bharwani, S., & Musunuri, D. (2018). Reflection as a Process From Theory to Practice. In M. Khosrow-Pour, D.B.A. (Ed.), Encyclopedia of Information Science and Technology, Fourth Edition (pp. 1529-1539). Hershey, PA: IGI Global. doi:10.4018/978-1-5225-2255-3.ch132

Bhatt, G. D., Wang, Z., & Rodger, J. A. (2017). Information Systems Capabilities and Their Effects on Competitive Advantages: A Study of Chinese Companies. *Information Resources Management Journal*, *30*(3), 41–57. doi:10.4018/IRMJ.2017070103

Bhushan, M., & Yadav, A. (2017). Concept of Cloud Computing in ESB. In R. Bhadoria, N. Chaudhari, G. Tomar, & S. Singh (Eds.), *Exploring Enterprise Service Bus in the Service-Oriented Architecture Paradigm* (pp. 116–127). Hershey, PA: IGI Global. doi:10.4018/978-1-5225-2157-0.ch008

Bhushan, S. (2017). System Dynamics Base-Model of Humanitarian Supply Chain (HSCM) in Disaster Prone Eco-Communities of India: A Discussion on Simulation and Scenario Results. *International Journal of System Dynamics Applications*, *6*(3), 20–37. doi:10.4018/IJSDA.2017070102

Biswas, A., & De, A. K. (2017). On Development of a Fuzzy Stochastic Programming Model with Its Application to Business Management. In S. Trivedi, S. Dey, A. Kumar, & T. Panda (Eds.), *Handbook of Research on Advanced Data Mining Techniques and Applications for Business Intelligence* (pp. 353–378). Hershey, PA: IGI Global. doi:10.4018/978-1-5225-2031-3.ch021

Bücker, J., & Ernste, K. (2018). Use of Brand Heroes in Strategic Reputation Management: The Case of Bacardi, Adidas, and Daimler. In A. Erdemir (Ed.), *Reputation Management Techniques in Public Relations* (pp. 126–150). Hershey, PA: IGI Global. doi:10.4018/978-1-5225-3619-2.ch007

Bureš, V. (2018). Industry 4.0 From the Systems Engineering Perspective: Alternative Holistic Framework Development. In R. Brunet-Thornton & F. Martinez (Eds.), *Analyzing the Impacts of Industry 4.0 in Modern Business Environments* (pp. 199–223). Hershey, PA: IGI Global. doi:10.4018/978-1-5225-3468-6.ch011

Buzady, Z. (2017). Resolving the Magic Cube of Effective Case Teaching: Benchmarking Case Teaching Practices in Emerging Markets – Insights from the Central European University Business School, Hungary. In D. Latusek (Ed.), *Case Studies as a Teaching Tool in Management Education* (pp. 79–103). Hershey, PA: IGI Global. doi:10.4018/978-1-5225-0770-3.ch005

Campatelli, G., Richter, A., & Stocker, A. (2016). Participative Knowledge Management to Empower Manufacturing Workers. *International Journal of Knowledge Management, 12*(4), 37–50. doi:10.4018/IJKM.2016100103

Căpusneanu, S., & Topor, D. I. (2018). Business Ethics and Cost Management in SMEs: Theories of Business Ethics and Cost Management Ethos. In I. Oncioiu (Ed.), *Ethics and Decision-Making for Sustainable Business Practices* (pp. 109–127). Hershey, PA: IGI Global. doi:10.4018/978-1-5225-3773-1.ch007

Carneiro, A. (2016). Maturity in Health Organization Information Systems: Metrics and Privacy Perspectives. *International Journal of Privacy and Health Information Management, 4*(2), 1–18. doi:10.4018/IJPHIM.2016070101

Chan, R. L., Mo, P. L., & Moon, K. K. (2018). Strategic and Tactical Measures in Managing Enterprise Risks: A Study of the Textile and Apparel Industry. In K. Strang, M. Korstanje, & N. Vajjhala (Eds.), *Research, Practices, and Innovations in Global Risk and Contingency Management* (pp. 1–19). Hershey, PA: IGI Global. doi:10.4018/978-1-5225-4754-9.ch001

Chandan, H. C. (2016). Motivations and Challenges of Female Entrepreneurship in Developed and Developing Economies. In N. Baporikar (Ed.), *Handbook of Research on Entrepreneurship in the Contemporary Knowledge-Based Global Economy* (pp. 260–286). Hershey, PA: IGI Global. doi:10.4018/978-1-4666-8798-1.ch012

Charlier, S. D., Burke-Smalley, L. A., & Fisher, S. L. (2018). Undergraduate Programs in the U.S: A Contextual and Content-Based Analysis. In J. Mendy (Ed.), *Teaching Human Resources and Organizational Behavior at the College Level* (pp. 26–57). Hershey, PA: IGI Global. doi:10.4018/978-1-5225-2820-3.ch002

Chaudhuri, S. (2016). Application of Web-Based Geographical Information System (GIS) in E-Business. In U. Panwar, R. Kumar, & N. Ray (Eds.), *Handbook of Research on Promotional Strategies and Consumer Influence in the Service Sector* (pp. 389–405). Hershey, PA: IGI Global. doi:10.4018/978-1-5225-0143-5.ch023

Choudhuri, P. S. (2016). An Empirical Study on the Quality of Services Offered by the Private Life Insurers in Burdwan. In U. Panwar, R. Kumar, & N. Ray (Eds.), *Handbook of Research on Promotional Strategies and Consumer Influence in the Service Sector* (pp. 31–55). Hershey, PA: IGI Global. doi:10.4018/978-1-5225-0143-5.ch002

Dahlberg, T., Kivijärvi, H., & Saarinen, T. (2017). IT Investment Consistency and Other Factors Influencing the Success of IT Performance. In S. De Haes & W. Van Grembergen (Eds.), *Strategic IT Governance and Alignment in Business Settings* (pp. 176–208). Hershey, PA: IGI Global. doi:10.4018/978-1-5225-0861-8.ch007

Damnjanović, A. M. (2017). Knowledge Management Optimization through IT and E-Business Utilization: A Qualitative Study on Serbian SMEs. In M. Vemić (Ed.), *Optimal Management Strategies in Small and Medium Enterprises* (pp. 249–267). Hershey, PA: IGI Global. doi:10.4018/978-1-5225-1949-2.ch012

Daneshpour, H. (2017). Integrating Sustainable Development into Project Portfolio Management through Application of Open Innovation. In M. Vemić (Ed.), *Optimal Management Strategies in Small and Medium Enterprises* (pp. 370–387). Hershey, PA: IGI Global. doi:10.4018/978-1-5225-1949-2.ch017

Daniel, A. D., & Reis de Castro, V. (2018). Entrepreneurship Education: How to Measure the Impact on Nascent Entrepreneurs. In A. Carrizo Moreira, J. Guilherme Leitão Dantas, & F. Manuel Valente (Eds.), *Nascent Entrepreneurship and Successful New Venture Creation* (pp. 85–110). Hershey, PA: IGI Global. doi:10.4018/978-1-5225-2936-1.ch004

David, F., van der Sijde, P., & van den Besselaar, P. (2016). Enterpreneurial Incentives, Obstacles, and Management in University-Business Co-Operation: The Case of Indonesia. In J. Saiz-Álvarez (Ed.), *Handbook of Research on Social Entrepreneurship and Solidarity Economics* (pp. 499–518). Hershey, PA: IGI Global. doi:10.4018/978-1-5225-0097-1.ch024

David, R., Swami, B. N., & Tangirala, S. (2018). Ethics Impact on Knowledge Management in Organizational Development: A Case Study. In N. Baporikar (Ed.), *Global Practices in Knowledge Management for Societal and Organizational Development* (pp. 19–45). Hershey, PA: IGI Global. doi:10.4018/978-1-5225-3009-1.ch002

Delias, P., & Lakiotaki, K. (2018). Discovering Process Horizontal Boundaries to Facilitate Process Comprehension. *International Journal of Operations Research and Information Systems*, *9*(2), 1–31. doi:10.4018/IJORIS.2018040101

Denholm, J., & Lee-Davies, L. (2018). Success Factors for Games in Business and Project Management. In *Enhancing Education and Training Initiatives Through Serious Games* (pp. 34–68). Hershey, PA: IGI Global. doi:10.4018/978-1-5225-3689-5.ch002

Deshpande, M. (2017). Best Practices in Management Institutions for Global Leadership: Policy Aspects. In N. Baporikar (Ed.), *Management Education for Global Leadership* (pp. 1–27). Hershey, PA: IGI Global. doi:10.4018/978-1-5225-1013-0.ch001

Deshpande, M. (2018). Policy Perspectives for SMEs Knowledge Management. In N. Baporikar (Ed.), *Knowledge Integration Strategies for Entrepreneurship and Sustainability* (pp. 23–46). Hershey, PA: IGI Global. doi:10.4018/978-1-5225-5115-7.ch002

Dezdar, S. (2017). ERP Implementation Projects in Asian Countries: A Comparative Study on Iran and China. *International Journal of Information Technology Project Management*, *8*(3), 52–68. doi:10.4018/IJITPM.2017070104

Domingos, D., Martinho, R., & Varajão, J. (2016). Controlled Flexibility in Healthcare Processes: A BPMN-Extension Approach. In M. Cruz-Cunha, I. Miranda, R. Martinho, & R. Rijo (Eds.), *Encyclopedia of E-Health and Telemedicine* (pp. 521–535). Hershey, PA: IGI Global. doi:10.4018/978-1-4666-9978-6.ch040

Domingos, D., Respício, A., & Martinho, R. (2017). Reliability of IoT-Aware BPMN Healthcare Processes. In C. Reis & M. Maximiano (Eds.), *Internet of Things and Advanced Application in Healthcare* (pp. 214–248). Hershey, PA: IGI Global. doi:10.4018/978-1-5225-1820-4.ch008

Dosumu, O., Hussain, J., & El-Gohary, H. (2017). An Exploratory Study of the Impact of Government Policies on the Development of Small and Medium Enterprises in Developing Countries: The Case of Nigeria. *International Journal of Customer Relationship Marketing and Management*, *8*(4), 51–62. doi:10.4018/IJCRMM.2017100104

Durst, S., Bruns, G., & Edvardsson, I. R. (2017). Retaining Knowledge in Smaller Building and Construction Firms. *International Journal of Knowledge and Systems Science*, *8*(3), 1–12. doi:10.4018/IJKSS.2017070101

Edvardsson, I. R., & Durst, S. (2017). Outsourcing, Knowledge, and Learning: A Critical Review. *International Journal of Knowledge-Based Organizations*, *7*(2), 13–26. doi:10.4018/IJKBO.2017040102

Edwards, J. S. (2018). Integrating Knowledge Management and Business Processes. In M. Khosrow-Pour, D.B.A. (Ed.), Encyclopedia of Information Science and Technology, Fourth Edition (pp. 5046-5055). Hershey, PA: IGI Global. doi:10.4018/978-1-5225-2255-3.ch437

Ejiogu, A. O. (2018). Economics of Farm Management. In *Agricultural Finance and Opportunities for Investment and Expansion* (pp. 56–72). Hershey, PA: IGI Global. doi:10.4018/978-1-5225-3059-6.ch003

Ekanem, I., & Abiade, G. E. (2018). Factors Influencing the Use of E-Commerce by Small Enterprises in Nigeria. *International Journal of ICT Research in Africa and the Middle East*, *7*(1), 37–53. doi:10.4018/IJICTRAME.2018010103

Ekanem, I., & Alrossais, L. A. (2017). Succession Challenges Facing Family Businesses in Saudi Arabia. In P. Zgheib (Ed.), *Entrepreneurship and Business Innovation in the Middle East* (pp. 122–146). Hershey, PA: IGI Global. doi:10.4018/978-1-5225-2066-5.ch007

El Faquih, L., & Fredj, M. (2017). Ontology-Based Framework for Quality in Configurable Process Models. *Journal of Electronic Commerce in Organizations*, *15*(2), 48–60. doi:10.4018/JECO.2017040104

El-Gohary, H., & El-Gohary, Z. (2016). An Attempt to Explore Electronic Marketing Adoption and Implementation Aspects in Developing Countries: The Case of Egypt. *International Journal of Customer Relationship Marketing and Management*, *7*(4), 1–26. doi:10.4018/IJCRMM.2016100101

Entico, G. J. (2016). Knowledge Management and the Medical Health Librarians: A Perception Study. In J. Yap, M. Perez, M. Ayson, & G. Entico (Eds.), *Special Library Administration, Standardization and Technological Integration* (pp. 52–77). Hershey, PA: IGI Global. doi:10.4018/978-1-4666-9542-9.ch003

Faisal, M. N., & Talib, F. (2017). Building Ambidextrous Supply Chains in SMEs: How to Tackle the Barriers? *International Journal of Information Systems and Supply Chain Management*, *10*(4), 80–100. doi:10.4018/IJISSCM.2017100105

Fernandes, T. M., Gomes, J., & Romão, M. (2017). Investments in E-Government: A Benefit Management Case Study. *International Journal of Electronic Government Research*, *13*(3), 1–17. doi:10.4018/IJEGR.2017070101

Fouda, F. A. (2016). A Suggested Curriculum in Career Education to Develop Business Secondary Schools Students' Career Knowledge Management Domains and Professional Thinking. *International Journal of Technology Diffusion*, *7*(2), 42–62. doi:10.4018/IJTD.2016040103

Gallardo-Vázquez, D., & Pajuelo-Moreno, M. L. (2016). How Spanish Universities are Promoting Entrepreneurship through Your Own Lines of Teaching and Research? In L. Carvalho (Ed.), *Handbook of Research on Entrepreneurial Success and its Impact on Regional Development* (pp. 431–454). Hershey, PA: IGI Global. doi:10.4018/978-1-4666-9567-2.ch019

Gao, S. S., Oreal, S., & Zhang, J. (2018). Contemporary Financial Risk Management Perceptions and Practices of Small-Sized Chinese Businesses. In I. Management Association (Ed.), Global Business Expansion: Concepts, Methodologies, Tools, and Applications (pp. 917-931). Hershey, PA: IGI Global. doi:10.4018/978-1-5225-5481-3.ch041

Garg, R., & Berning, S. C. (2017). Indigenous Chinese Management Philosophies: Key Concepts and Relevance for Modern Chinese Firms. In B. Christiansen & G. Koc (Eds.), *Transcontinental Strategies for Industrial Development and Economic Growth* (pp. 43–57). Hershey, PA: IGI Global. doi:10.4018/978-1-5225-2160-0.ch003

Gencer, Y. G. (2017). Supply Chain Management in Retailing Business. In U. Akkucuk (Ed.), *Ethics and Sustainability in Global Supply Chain Management* (pp. 197–210). Hershey, PA: IGI Global. doi:10.4018/978-1-5225-2036-8.ch011

Giacosa, E. (2016). Innovation in Luxury Fashion Businesses as a Means for the Regional Development. In L. Carvalho (Ed.), *Handbook of Research on Entrepreneurial Success and its Impact on Regional Development* (pp. 206–222). Hershey, PA: IGI Global. doi:10.4018/978-1-4666-9567-2.ch010

Giacosa, E. (2018). The Increasing of the Regional Development Thanks to the Luxury Business Innovation. In L. Carvalho (Ed.), *Handbook of Research on Entrepreneurial Ecosystems and Social Dynamics in a Globalized World* (pp. 260–273). Hershey, PA: IGI Global. doi:10.4018/978-1-5225-3525-6.ch011

Gianni, M., & Gotzamani, K. (2016). Integrated Management Systems and Information Management Systems: Common Threads. In P. Papajorgji, F. Pinet, A. Guimarães, & J. Papathanasiou (Eds.), *Automated Enterprise Systems for Maximizing Business Performance* (pp. 195–214). Hershey, PA: IGI Global. doi:10.4018/978-1-4666-8841-4.ch011

Gianni, M., Gotzamani, K., & Linden, I. (2016). How a BI-wise Responsible Integrated Management System May Support Food Traceability. *International Journal of Decision Support System Technology*, *8*(2), 1–17. doi:10.4018/IJDSST.2016040101

Glykas, M., & George, J. (2017). Quality and Process Management Systems in the UAE Maritime Industry. *International Journal of Productivity Management and Assessment Technologies*, *5*(1), 20–39. doi:10.4018/IJPMAT.2017010102

Glykas, M., Valiris, G., Kokkinaki, A., & Koutsoukou, Z. (2018). Banking Business Process Management Implementation. *International Journal of Productivity Management and Assessment Technologies*, *6*(1), 50–69. doi:10.4018/IJPMAT.2018010104

Gomes, J., & Romão, M. (2017). The Balanced Scorecard: Keeping Updated and Aligned with Today's Business Trends. *International Journal of Productivity Management and Assessment Technologies, 5*(2), 1–15. doi:10.4018/IJPMAT.2017070101

Gomes, J., & Romão, M. (2017). Aligning Information Systems and Technology with Benefit Management and Balanced Scorecard. In S. De Haes & W. Van Grembergen (Eds.), *Strategic IT Governance and Alignment in Business Settings* (pp. 112–131). Hershey, PA: IGI Global. doi:10.4018/978-1-5225-0861-8.ch005

Grefen, P., & Turetken, O. (2017). Advanced Business Process Management in Networked E-Business Scenarios. *International Journal of E-Business Research, 13*(4), 70–104. doi:10.4018/IJEBR.2017100105

Haider, A., & Saetang, S. (2017). Strategic IT Alignment in Service Sector. In S. Rozenes & Y. Cohen (Eds.), *Handbook of Research on Strategic Alliances and Value Co-Creation in the Service Industry* (pp. 231–258). Hershey, PA: IGI Global. doi:10.4018/978-1-5225-2084-9.ch012

Haider, A., & Tang, S. S. (2016). Maximising Value Through IT and Business Alignment: A Case of IT Governance Institutionalisation at a Thai Bank. *International Journal of Technology Diffusion, 7*(3), 33–58. doi:10.4018/IJTD.2016070104

Hajilari, A. B., Ghadaksaz, M., & Fasghandis, G. S. (2017). Assessing Organizational Readiness for Implementing ERP System Using Fuzzy Expert System Approach. *International Journal of Enterprise Information Systems, 13*(1), 67–85. doi:10.4018/IJEIS.2017010105

Haldorai, A., Ramu, A., & Murugan, S. (2018). Social Aware Cognitive Radio Networks: Effectiveness of Social Networks as a Strategic Tool for Organizational Business Management. In H. Bansal, G. Shrivastava, G. Nguyen, & L. Stanciu (Eds.), *Social Network Analytics for Contemporary Business Organizations* (pp. 188–202). Hershey, PA: IGI Global. doi:10.4018/978-1-5225-5097-6.ch010

Hall, O. P. Jr. (2017). Social Media Driven Management Education. *International Journal of Knowledge-Based Organizations, 7*(2), 43–59. doi:10.4018/IJKBO.2017040104

Hanifah, H., Halim, H. A., Ahmad, N. H., & Vafaei-Zadeh, A. (2017). Innovation Culture as a Mediator Between Specific Human Capital and Innovation Performance Among Bumiputera SMEs in Malaysia. In N. Ahmad, T. Ramayah, H. Halim, & S. Rahman (Eds.), *Handbook of Research on Small and Medium Enterprises in Developing Countries* (pp. 261–279). Hershey, PA: IGI Global. doi:10.4018/978-1-5225-2165-5.ch012

Hartlieb, S., & Silvius, G. (2017). Handling Uncertainty in Project Management and Business Development: Similarities and Differences. In Y. Raydugin (Ed.), *Handbook of Research on Leveraging Risk and Uncertainties for Effective Project Management* (pp. 337–362). Hershey, PA: IGI Global. doi:10.4018/978-1-5225-1790-0.ch016

Hass, K. B. (2017). Living on the Edge: Managing Project Complexity. In Y. Raydugin (Ed.), *Handbook of Research on Leveraging Risk and Uncertainties for Effective Project Management* (pp. 177–201). Hershey, PA: IGI Global. doi:10.4018/978-1-5225-1790-0.ch009

Hassan, A., & Privitera, D. S. (2016). Google AdSense as a Mobile Technology in Education. In J. Holland (Ed.), *Wearable Technology and Mobile Innovations for Next-Generation Education* (pp. 200–223). Hershey, PA: IGI Global. doi:10.4018/978-1-5225-0069-8.ch011

Hassan, A., & Rahimi, R. (2016). Consuming "Innovation" in Tourism: Augmented Reality as an Innovation Tool in Digital Tourism Marketing. In N. Pappas & I. Bregoli (Eds.), *Global Dynamics in Travel, Tourism, and Hospitality* (pp. 130–147). Hershey, PA: IGI Global. doi:10.4018/978-1-5225-0201-2.ch008

Hawking, P., & Carmine Sellitto, C. (2017). Developing an Effective Strategy for Organizational Business Intelligence. In M. Tavana (Ed.), *Enterprise Information Systems and the Digitalization of Business Functions* (pp. 222–237). Hershey, PA: IGI Global. doi:10.4018/978-1-5225-2382-6.ch010

Hawking, P., & Sellitto, C. (2017). A Fast-Moving Consumer Goods Company and Business Intelligence Strategy Development. *International Journal of Enterprise Information Systems, 13*(2), 22–33. doi:10.4018/IJEIS.2017040102

Hawking, P., & Sellitto, C. (2017). Business Intelligence Strategy: Two Case Studies. *International Journal of Business Intelligence Research, 8*(2), 17–30. doi:10.4018/IJBIR.2017070102

Haynes, J. D., Arockiasamy, S., Al Rashdi, M., & Al Rashdi, S. (2016). Business and E Business Strategies for Coopetition and Thematic Management as a Sustained Basis for Ethics and Social Responsibility in Emerging Markets. In M. Al-Shammari & H. Masri (Eds.), *Ethical and Social Perspectives on Global Business Interaction in Emerging Markets* (pp. 25–39). Hershey, PA: IGI Global. doi:10.4018/978-1-4666-9864-2.ch002

Hee, W. J., Jalleh, G., Lai, H., & Lin, C. (2017). E-Commerce and IT Projects: Evaluation and Management Issues in Australian and Taiwanese Hospitals. *International Journal of Public Health Management and Ethics, 2*(1), 69–90. doi:10.4018/IJPHME.2017010104

Hernandez, A. A. (2018). Exploring the Factors to Green IT Adoption of SMEs in the Philippines. *Journal of Cases on Information Technology, 20*(2), 49–66. doi:10.4018/JCIT.2018040104

Hernandez, A. A., & Ona, S. E. (2016). Green IT Adoption: Lessons from the Philippines Business Process Outsourcing Industry. *International Journal of Social Ecology and Sustainable Development, 7*(1), 1–34. doi:10.4018/IJSESD.2016010101

Hollman, A., Bickford, S., & Hollman, T. (2017). Cyber InSecurity: A Post-Mortem Attempt to Assess Cyber Problems from IT and Business Management Perspectives. *Journal of Cases on Information Technology, 19*(3), 42–70. doi:10.4018/JCIT.2017070104

Igbinakhase, I. (2017). Responsible and Sustainable Management Practices in Developing and Developed Business Environments. In Z. Fields (Ed.), *Collective Creativity for Responsible and Sustainable Business Practice* (pp. 180–207). Hershey, PA: IGI Global. doi:10.4018/978-1-5225-1823-5.ch010

Ilahi, L., Ghannouchi, S. A., & Martinho, R. (2016). A Business Process Management Approach to Home Healthcare Processes: On the Gap between Intention and Reality. In M. Cruz-Cunha, I. Miranda, R. Martinho, & R. Rijo (Eds.), *Encyclopedia of E-Health and Telemedicine* (pp. 439–457). Hershey, PA: IGI Global. doi:10.4018/978-1-4666-9978-6.ch035

Iwata, J. J., & Hoskins, R. G. (2017). Managing Indigenous Knowledge in Tanzania: A Business Perspective. In P. Jain & N. Mnjama (Eds.), *Managing Knowledge Resources and Records in Modern Organizations* (pp. 198–214). Hershey, PA: IGI Global. doi:10.4018/978-1-5225-1965-2.ch012

Jabeen, F., Ahmad, S. Z., & Alkaabi, S. (2016). The Internationalization Decision-Making of United Arab Emirates Family Businesses. In N. Zakaria, A. Abdul-Talib, & N. Osman (Eds.), *Handbook of Research on Impacts of International Business and Political Affairs on the Global Economy* (pp. 1–22). Hershey, PA: IGI Global. doi:10.4018/978-1-4666-9806-2.ch001

Jain, P. (2017). Ethical and Legal Issues in Knowledge Management Life-Cycle in Business. In P. Jain & N. Mnjama (Eds.), *Managing Knowledge Resources and Records in Modern Organizations* (pp. 82–101). Hershey, PA: IGI Global. doi:10.4018/978-1-5225-1965-2.ch006

Jamali, D., Abdallah, H., & Matar, F. (2016). Opportunities and Challenges for CSR Mainstreaming in Business Schools. *International Journal of Technology and Educational Marketing*, *6*(2), 1–29. doi:10.4018/IJTEM.2016070101

James, S., & Hauli, E. (2017). Holistic Management Education at Tanzanian Rural Development Planning Institute. In N. Baporikar (Ed.), *Management Education for Global Leadership* (pp. 112–136). Hershey, PA: IGI Global. doi:10.4018/978-1-5225-1013-0.ch006

Janošková, M., Csikósová, A., & Čulková, K. (2018). Measurement of Company Performance as Part of Its Strategic Management. In R. Leon (Ed.), *Managerial Strategies for Business Sustainability During Turbulent Times* (pp. 309–335). Hershey, PA: IGI Global. doi:10.4018/978-1-5225-2716-9.ch017

Jean-Vasile, A., & Alecu, A. (2017). Theoretical and Practical Approaches in Understanding the Influences of Cost-Productivity-Profit Trinomial in Contemporary Enterprises. In A. Jean Vasile & D. Nicolò (Eds.), *Sustainable Entrepreneurship and Investments in the Green Economy* (pp. 28–62). Hershey, PA: IGI Global. doi:10.4018/978-1-5225-2075-7.ch002

Jha, D. G. (2016). Preparing for Information Technology Driven Changes. In S. Tiwari & L. Nafees (Eds.), *Innovative Management Education Pedagogies for Preparing Next-Generation Leaders* (pp. 258–274). Hershey, PA: IGI Global. doi:10.4018/978-1-4666-9691-4.ch015

Joia, L. A., & Correia, J. C. (2018). CIO Competencies From the IT Professional Perspective: Insights From Brazil. *Journal of Global Information Management, 26*(2), 74–103. doi:10.4018/JGIM.2018040104

Juma, A., & Mzera, N. (2017). Knowledge Management and Records Management and Competitive Advantage in Business. In P. Jain & N. Mnjama (Eds.), *Managing Knowledge Resources and Records in Modern Organizations* (pp. 15–28). Hershey, PA: IGI Global. doi:10.4018/978-1-5225-1965-2.ch002

K., I., & A, V. (2018). Monitoring and Auditing in the Cloud. In K. Munir (Ed.), *Cloud Computing Technologies for Green Enterprises* (pp. 318-350). Hershey, PA: IGI Global. doi:10.4018/978-1-5225-3038-1.ch013

Kabra, G., Ghosh, V., & Ramesh, A. (2018). Enterprise Integrated Business Process Management and Business Intelligence Framework for Business Process Sustainability. In A. Paul, D. Bhattacharyya, & S. Anand (Eds.), *Green Initiatives for Business Sustainability and Value Creation* (pp. 228–238). Hershey, PA: IGI Global. doi:10.4018/978-1-5225-2662-9.ch010

Kaoud, M. (2017). Investigation of Customer Knowledge Management: A Case Study Research. *International Journal of Service Science, Management, Engineering, and Technology, 8*(2), 12–22. doi:10.4018/IJSSMET.2017040102

Kara, M. E., & Fırat, S. Ü. (2016). Sustainability, Risk, and Business Intelligence in Supply Chains. In M. Erdoğdu, T. Arun, & I. Ahmad (Eds.), *Handbook of Research on Green Economic Development Initiatives and Strategies* (pp. 501–538). Hershey, PA: IGI Global. doi:10.4018/978-1-5225-0440-5.ch022

Katuu, S. (2018). A Comparative Assessment of Enterprise Content Management Maturity Models. In N. Gwangwava & M. Mutingi (Eds.), *E-Manufacturing and E-Service Strategies in Contemporary Organizations* (pp. 93–118). Hershey, PA: IGI Global. doi:10.4018/978-1-5225-3628-4.ch005

Khan, M. A. (2016). MNEs Management Strategies in Developing Countries: Establishing the Context. In M. Khan (Ed.), *Multinational Enterprise Management Strategies in Developing Countries* (pp. 1–33). Hershey, PA: IGI Global. doi:10.4018/978-1-5225-0276-0.ch001

Khan, M. A. (2016). Operational Approaches in Organizational Structure: A Case for MNEs in Developing Countries. In M. Khan (Ed.), *Multinational Enterprise Management Strategies in Developing Countries* (pp. 129–151). Hershey, PA: IGI Global. doi:10.4018/978-1-5225-0276-0.ch007

Kinnunen, S., Ylä-Kujala, A., Marttonen-Arola, S., Kärri, T., & Baglee, D. (2018). Internet of Things in Asset Management: Insights from Industrial Professionals and Academia. *International Journal of Service Science, Management, Engineering, and Technology*, *9*(2), 104–119. doi:10.4018/IJSSMET.2018040105

Klein, A. Z., Sabino de Freitas, A., Machado, L., Freitas, J. C. Jr, Graziola, P. G. Jr, & Schlemmer, E. (2017). Virtual Worlds Applications for Management Education. In L. Tomei (Ed.), *Exploring the New Era of Technology-Infused Education* (pp. 279–299). Hershey, PA: IGI Global. doi:10.4018/978-1-5225-1709-2.ch017

Kożuch, B., & Jabłoński, A. (2017). Adopting the Concept of Business Models in Public Management. In M. Lewandowski & B. Kożuch (Eds.), *Public Sector Entrepreneurship and the Integration of Innovative Business Models* (pp. 10–46). Hershey, PA: IGI Global. doi:10.4018/978-1-5225-2215-7.ch002

Kumar, J., Adhikary, A., & Jha, A. (2017). Small Active Investors' Perceptions and Preferences Towards Tax Saving Mutual Fund Schemes in Eastern India: An Empirical Note. *International Journal of Asian Business and Information Management*, *8*(2), 35–45. doi:10.4018/IJABIM.2017040103

Lassoued, Y., Bouzguenda, L., & Mahmoud, T. (2016). Context-Aware Business Process Versions Management. *International Journal of e-Collaboration*, *12*(3), 7–33. doi:10.4018/IJeC.2016070102

Lavassani, K. M., & Movahedi, B. (2017). Applications Driven Information Systems: Beyond Networks toward Business Ecosystems. *International Journal of Innovation in the Digital Economy*, *8*(1), 61–75. doi:10.4018/IJIDE.2017010104

Lazzareschi, V. H., & Brito, M. S. (2017). Strategic Information Management: Proposal of Business Project Model. In G. Jamil, A. Soares, & C. Pessoa (Eds.), *Handbook of Research on Information Management for Effective Logistics and Supply Chains* (pp. 59–88). Hershey, PA: IGI Global. doi:10.4018/978-1-5225-0973-8.ch004

Lederer, M., Kurz, M., & Lazarov, P. (2017). Usage and Suitability of Methods for Strategic Business Process Initiatives: A Multi Case Study Research. *International Journal of Productivity Management and Assessment Technologies*, *5*(1), 40–51. doi:10.4018/IJPMAT.2017010103

Lee, I. (2017). A Social Enterprise Business Model and a Case Study of Pacific Community Ventures (PCV). In V. Potocan, M. Üngan, & Z. Nedelko (Eds.), *Handbook of Research on Managerial Solutions in Non-Profit Organizations* (pp. 182–204). Hershey, PA: IGI Global. doi:10.4018/978-1-5225-0731-4.ch009

Lee, L. J., & Leu, J. (2016). Exploring the Effectiveness of IT Application and Value Method in the Innovation Performance of Enterprise. *International Journal of Enterprise Information Systems*, *12*(2), 47–65. doi:10.4018/IJEIS.2016040104

Lee, Y. (2016). Alignment Effect of Entrepreneurial Orientation and Marketing Orientation on Firm Performance. *International Journal of Customer Relationship Marketing and Management*, *7*(4), 58–69. doi:10.4018/IJCRMM.2016100104

Leon, L. A., Seal, K. C., Przasnyski, Z. H., & Wiedenman, I. (2017). Skills and Competencies Required for Jobs in Business Analytics: A Content Analysis of Job Advertisements Using Text Mining. *International Journal of Business Intelligence Research*, *8*(1), 1–25. doi:10.4018/IJBIR.2017010101

Leu, J., Lee, L. J., & Krischke, A. (2016). Value Engineering-Based Method for Implementing the ISO14001 System in the Green Supply Chains. *International Journal of Strategic Decision Sciences*, *7*(4), 1–20. doi:10.4018/IJSDS.2016100101

Levy, C. L., & Elias, N. I. (2017). SOHO Users' Perceptions of Reliability and Continuity of Cloud-Based Services. In M. Moore (Ed.), *Cybersecurity Breaches and Issues Surrounding Online Threat Protection* (pp. 248–287). Hershey, PA: IGI Global. doi:10.4018/978-1-5225-1941-6.ch011

Levy, M. (2018). Change Management Serving Knowledge Management and Organizational Development: Reflections and Review. In N. Baporikar (Ed.), *Global Practices in Knowledge Management for Societal and Organizational Development* (pp. 256–270). Hershey, PA: IGI Global. doi:10.4018/978-1-5225-3009-1.ch012

Lewandowski, M. (2017). Public Organizations and Business Model Innovation: The Role of Public Service Design. In M. Lewandowski & B. Kożuch (Eds.), *Public Sector Entrepreneurship and the Integration of Innovative Business Models* (pp. 47–72). Hershey, PA: IGI Global. doi:10.4018/978-1-5225-2215-7.ch003

Lhannaoui, H., Kabbaj, M. I., & Bakkoury, Z. (2017). A Survey of Risk-Aware Business Process Modelling. *International Journal of Risk and Contingency Management, 6*(3), 14–26. doi:10.4018/IJRCM.2017070102

Li, J., Sun, W., Jiang, W., Yang, H., & Zhang, L. (2017). How the Nature of Exogenous Shocks and Crises Impact Company Performance?: The Effects of Industry Characteristics. *International Journal of Risk and Contingency Management, 6*(4), 40–55. doi:10.4018/IJRCM.2017100103

Lu, C., & Liu, S. (2016). Cultural Tourism O2O Business Model Innovation-A Case Study of CTrip. *Journal of Electronic Commerce in Organizations, 14*(2), 16–31. doi:10.4018/JECO.2016040102

Machen, B., Hosseini, M. R., Wood, A., & Bakhshi, J. (2016). An Investigation into using SAP-PS as a Multidimensional Project Control System (MPCS). *International Journal of Enterprise Information Systems, 12*(2), 66–81. doi:10.4018/IJEIS.2016040105

Malega, P. (2017). Small and Medium Enterprises in the Slovak Republic: Status and Competitiveness of SMEs in the Global Markets and Possibilities of Optimization. In M. Vemić (Ed.), *Optimal Management Strategies in Small and Medium Enterprises* (pp. 102–124). Hershey, PA: IGI Global. doi:10.4018/978-1-5225-1949-2.ch006

Malewska, K. M. (2017). Intuition in Decision-Making on the Example of a Non-Profit Organization. In V. Potocan, M. Üngan, & Z. Nedelko (Eds.), *Handbook of Research on Managerial Solutions in Non-Profit Organizations* (pp. 378–399). Hershey, PA: IGI Global. doi:10.4018/978-1-5225-0731-4.ch018

Maroofi, F. (2017). Entrepreneurial Orientation and Organizational Learning Ability Analysis for Innovation and Firm Performance. In N. Baporikar (Ed.), *Innovation and Shifting Perspectives in Management Education* (pp. 144–165). Hershey, PA: IGI Global. doi:10.4018/978-1-5225-1019-2.ch007

Martins, P. V., & Zacarias, M. (2017). A Web-based Tool for Business Process Improvement. *International Journal of Web Portals*, *9*(2), 68–84. doi:10.4018/IJWP.2017070104

Matthies, B., & Coners, A. (2017). Exploring the Conceptual Nature of e-Business Projects. *Journal of Electronic Commerce in Organizations*, *15*(3), 33–63. doi:10.4018/JECO.2017070103

McKee, J. (2018). Architecture as a Tool to Solve Business Planning Problems. In M. Khosrow-Pour, D.B.A. (Ed.), Encyclopedia of Information Science and Technology, Fourth Edition (pp. 573-586). Hershey, PA: IGI Global. doi:10.4018/978-1-5225-2255-3.ch050

McMurray, A. J., Cross, J., & Caponecchia, C. (2018). The Risk Management Profession in Australia: Business Continuity Plan Practices. In N. Bajgoric (Ed.), *Always-On Enterprise Information Systems for Modern Organizations* (pp. 112–129). Hershey, PA: IGI Global. doi:10.4018/978-1-5225-3704-5.ch006

Meddah, I. H., & Belkadi, K. (2018). Mining Patterns Using Business Process Management. In R. Hamou (Ed.), *Handbook of Research on Biomimicry in Information Retrieval and Knowledge Management* (pp. 78–89). Hershey, PA: IGI Global. doi:10.4018/978-1-5225-3004-6.ch005

Mendes, L. (2017). TQM and Knowledge Management: An Integrated Approach Towards Tacit Knowledge Management. In D. Jaziri-Bouagina & G. Jamil (Eds.), *Handbook of Research on Tacit Knowledge Management for Organizational Success* (pp. 236–263). Hershey, PA: IGI Global. doi:10.4018/978-1-5225-2394-9.ch009

Mnjama, N. M. (2017). Preservation of Recorded Information in Public and Private Sector Organizations. In P. Jain & N. Mnjama (Eds.), *Managing Knowledge Resources and Records in Modern Organizations* (pp. 149–167). Hershey, PA: IGI Global. doi:10.4018/978-1-5225-1965-2.ch009

Mokoqama, M., & Fields, Z. (2017). Principles of Responsible Management Education (PRME): Call for Responsible Management Education. In Z. Fields (Ed.), *Collective Creativity for Responsible and Sustainable Business Practice* (pp. 229–241). Hershey, PA: IGI Global. doi:10.4018/978-1-5225-1823-5.ch012

Muniapan, B. (2017). Philosophy and Management: The Relevance of Vedanta in Management. In P. Ordóñez de Pablos (Ed.), *Managerial Strategies and Solutions for Business Success in Asia* (pp. 124–139). Hershey, PA: IGI Global. doi:10.4018/978-1-5225-1886-0.ch007

Muniapan, B., Gregory, M. L., & Ling, L. A. (2016). Marketing Education in Sarawak: Looking at It from the Employers' Viewpoint. In B. Smith & A. Porath (Eds.), *Global Perspectives on Contemporary Marketing Education* (pp. 112–130). Hershey, PA: IGI Global. doi:10.4018/978-1-4666-9784-3.ch008

Murad, S. E., & Dowaji, S. (2017). Using Value-Based Approach for Managing Cloud-Based Services. In A. Turuk, B. Sahoo, & S. Addya (Eds.), *Resource Management and Efficiency in Cloud Computing Environments* (pp. 33–60). Hershey, PA: IGI Global. doi:10.4018/978-1-5225-1721-4.ch002

Mutahar, A. M., Daud, N. M., Thurasamy, R., Isaac, O., & Abdulsalam, R. (2018). The Mediating of Perceived Usefulness and Perceived Ease of Use: The Case of Mobile Banking in Yemen. *International Journal of Technology Diffusion*, *9*(2), 21–40. doi:10.4018/IJTD.2018040102

Naidoo, V. (2017). E-Learning and Management Education at African Universities. In N. Baporikar (Ed.), *Management Education for Global Leadership* (pp. 181–201). Hershey, PA: IGI Global. doi:10.4018/978-1-5225-1013-0.ch009

Naidoo, V., & Igbinakhase, I. (2018). Opportunities and Challenges of Knowledge Retention in SMEs. In N. Baporikar (Ed.), *Knowledge Integration Strategies for Entrepreneurship and Sustainability* (pp. 70–94). Hershey, PA: IGI Global. doi:10.4018/978-1-5225-5115-7.ch004

Nayak, S., & Prabhu, N. (2017). Paradigm Shift in Management Education: Need for a Cross Functional Perspective. In N. Baporikar (Ed.), *Management Education for Global Leadership* (pp. 241–255). Hershey, PA: IGI Global. doi:10.4018/978-1-5225-1013-0.ch012

Ndede-Amadi, A. A. (2016). Student Interest in the IS Specialization as Predictor of the Success Potential of New Information Systems Programmes within the Schools of Business in Kenyan Public Universities. *International Journal of Information Systems and Social Change*, *7*(2), 63–79. doi:10.4018/IJISSC.2016040104

Nedelko, Z., & Potocan, V. (2016). Management Practices for Processes Optimization: Case of Slovenia. In G. Alor-Hernández, C. Sánchez-Ramírez, & J. García-Alcaraz (Eds.), *Handbook of Research on Managerial Strategies for Achieving Optimal Performance in Industrial Processes* (pp. 545–561). Hershey, PA: IGI Global. doi:10.4018/978-1-5225-0130-5.ch025

Nedelko, Z., & Potocan, V. (2017). Management Solutions in Non-Profit Organizations: Case of Slovenia. In V. Potocan, M. Üngan, & Z. Nedelko (Eds.), *Handbook of Research on Managerial Solutions in Non-Profit Organizations* (pp. 1–22). Hershey, PA: IGI Global. doi:10.4018/978-1-5225-0731-4.ch001

Nedelko, Z., & Potocan, V. (2017). Priority of Management Tools Utilization among Managers: International Comparison. In V. Wang (Ed.), *Encyclopedia of Strategic Leadership and Management* (pp. 1083–1094). Hershey, PA: IGI Global. doi:10.4018/978-1-5225-1049-9.ch075

Nedelko, Z., Raudeliūnienė, J., & Črešnar, R. (2018). Knowledge Dynamics in Supply Chain Management. In N. Baporikar (Ed.), *Knowledge Integration Strategies for Entrepreneurship and Sustainability* (pp. 150–166). Hershey, PA: IGI Global. doi:10.4018/978-1-5225-5115-7.ch008

Nguyen, H. T., & Hipsher, S. A. (2018). Innovation and Creativity Used by Private Sector Firms in a Resources-Constrained Environment. In S. Hipsher (Ed.), *Examining the Private Sector's Role in Wealth Creation and Poverty Reduction* (pp. 219–238). Hershey, PA: IGI Global. doi:10.4018/978-1-5225-3117-3.ch010

Nycz, M., & Pólkowski, Z. (2016). Business Intelligence as a Modern IT Supporting Management of Local Government Units in Poland. *International Journal of Knowledge and Systems Science, 7*(4), 1–18. doi:10.4018/IJKSS.2016100101

Obaji, N. O., Senin, A. A., & Olugu, M. U. (2016). Supportive Government Policy as a Mechanism for Business Incubation Performance in Nigeria. *International Journal of Information Systems and Social Change, 7*(4), 52–66. doi:10.4018/IJISSC.2016100103

Obicci, P. A. (2017). Risk Sharing in a Partnership. In *Risk Management Strategies in Public-Private Partnerships* (pp. 115–152). Hershey, PA: IGI Global. doi:10.4018/978-1-5225-2503-5.ch004

Obidallah, W. J., & Raahemi, B. (2017). Managing Changes in Service Oriented Virtual Organizations: A Structural and Procedural Framework to Facilitate the Process of Change. *Journal of Electronic Commerce in Organizations*, *15*(1), 59–83. doi:10.4018/JECO.2017010104

Ojasalo, J., & Ojasalo, K. (2016). Service Logic Business Model Canvas for Lean Development of SMEs and Start-Ups. In N. Baporikar (Ed.), *Handbook of Research on Entrepreneurship in the Contemporary Knowledge-Based Global Economy* (pp. 217–243). Hershey, PA: IGI Global. doi:10.4018/978-1-4666-8798-1.ch010

Ojo, O. (2017). Impact of Innovation on the Entrepreneurial Success in Selected Business Enterprises in South-West Nigeria. *International Journal of Innovation in the Digital Economy*, *8*(2), 29–38. doi:10.4018/IJIDE.2017040103

Okdinawati, L., Simatupang, T. M., & Sunitiyoso, Y. (2017). Multi-Agent Reinforcement Learning for Value Co-Creation of Collaborative Transportation Management (CTM). *International Journal of Information Systems and Supply Chain Management*, *10*(3), 84–95. doi:10.4018/IJISSCM.2017070105

Ortner, E., Mevius, M., Wiedmann, P., & Kurz, F. (2016). Design of Interactional Decision Support Applications for E-Participation in Smart Cities. *International Journal of Electronic Government Research*, *12*(2), 18–38. doi:10.4018/IJEGR.2016040102

Pal, K. (2018). Building High Quality Big Data-Based Applications in Supply Chains. In A. Kumar & S. Saurav (Eds.), *Supply Chain Management Strategies and Risk Assessment in Retail Environments* (pp. 1–24). Hershey, PA: IGI Global. doi:10.4018/978-1-5225-3056-5.ch001

Palos-Sanchez, P. R., & Correia, M. B. (2018). Perspectives of the Adoption of Cloud Computing in the Tourism Sector. In J. Rodrigues, C. Ramos, P. Cardoso, & C. Henriques (Eds.), *Handbook of Research on Technological Developments for Cultural Heritage and eTourism Applications* (pp. 377–400). Hershey, PA: IGI Global. doi:10.4018/978-1-5225-2927-9.ch018

Parry, V. K., & Lind, M. L. (2016). Alignment of Business Strategy and Information Technology Considering Information Technology Governance, Project Portfolio Control, and Risk Management. *International Journal of Information Technology Project Management, 7*(4), 21–37. doi:10.4018/IJITPM.2016100102

Pashkova, N., Trujillo-Barrera, A., Apostolakis, G., Van Dijk, G., Drakos, P. D., & Baourakis, G. (2016). Business Management Models of Microfinance Institutions (MFIs) in Africa: A Study into Their Enabling Environments. *International Journal of Food and Beverage Manufacturing and Business Models, 1*(2), 63–82. doi:10.4018/IJFBMBM.2016070105

Patiño, B. E. (2017). New Generation Management by Convergence and Individual Identity: A Systemic and Human-Oriented Approach. In N. Baporikar (Ed.), *Innovation and Shifting Perspectives in Management Education* (pp. 119–143). Hershey, PA: IGI Global. doi:10.4018/978-1-5225-1019-2.ch006

Pawliczek, A., & Rössler, M. (2017). Knowledge of Management Tools and Systems in SMEs: Knowledge Transfer in Management. In A. Bencsik (Ed.), *Knowledge Management Initiatives and Strategies in Small and Medium Enterprises* (pp. 180–203). Hershey, PA: IGI Global. doi:10.4018/978-1-5225-1642-2.ch009

Pejic-Bach, M., Omazic, M. A., Aleksic, A., & Zoroja, J. (2018). Knowledge-Based Decision Making: A Multi-Case Analysis. In R. Leon (Ed.), *Managerial Strategies for Business Sustainability During Turbulent Times* (pp. 160–184). Hershey, PA: IGI Global. doi:10.4018/978-1-5225-2716-9.ch009

Perano, M., Hysa, X., & Calabrese, M. (2018). Strategic Planning, Cultural Context, and Business Continuity Management: Business Cases in the City of Shkoder. In A. Presenza & L. Sheehan (Eds.), *Geopolitics and Strategic Management in the Global Economy* (pp. 57–77). Hershey, PA: IGI Global. doi:10.4018/978-1-5225-2673-5.ch004

Pereira, R., Mira da Silva, M., & Lapão, L. V. (2017). IT Governance Maturity Patterns in Portuguese Healthcare. In S. De Haes & W. Van Grembergen (Eds.), *Strategic IT Governance and Alignment in Business Settings* (pp. 24–52). Hershey, PA: IGI Global. doi:10.4018/978-1-5225-0861-8.ch002

Perez-Uribe, R., & Ocampo-Guzman, D. (2016). Conflict within Colombian Family Owned SMEs: An Explosive Blend between Feelings and Business. In J. Saiz-Álvarez (Ed.), *Handbook of Research on Social Entrepreneurship and Solidarity Economics* (pp. 329–354). Hershey, PA: IGI Global. doi:10.4018/978-1-5225-0097-1.ch017

Pérez-Uribe, R. I., Torres, D. A., Jurado, S. P., & Prada, D. M. (2018). Cloud Tools for the Development of Project Management in SMEs. In R. Perez-Uribe, C. Salcedo-Perez, & D. Ocampo-Guzman (Eds.), *Handbook of Research on Intrapreneurship and Organizational Sustainability in SMEs* (pp. 95–120). Hershey, PA: IGI Global. doi:10.4018/978-1-5225-3543-0.ch005

Petrisor, I., & Cozmiuc, D. (2017). Global Supply Chain Management Organization at Siemens in the Advent of Industry 4.0. In L. Saglietto & C. Cezanne (Eds.), *Global Intermediation and Logistics Service Providers* (pp. 123–142). Hershey, PA: IGI Global. doi:10.4018/978-1-5225-2133-4.ch007

Pierce, J. M., Velliaris, D. M., & Edwards, J. (2017). A Living Case Study: A Journey Not a Destination. In N. Silton (Ed.), *Exploring the Benefits of Creativity in Education, Media, and the Arts* (pp. 158–178). Hershey, PA: IGI Global. doi:10.4018/978-1-5225-0504-4.ch008

Radosavljevic, M., & Andjelkovic, A. (2017). Multi-Criteria Decision Making Approach for Choosing Business Process for the Improvement: Upgrading of the Six Sigma Methodology. In J. Stanković, P. Delias, S. Marinković, & S. Rochhia (Eds.), *Tools and Techniques for Economic Decision Analysis* (pp. 225–247). Hershey, PA: IGI Global. doi:10.4018/978-1-5225-0959-2.ch011

Radovic, V. M. (2017). Corporate Sustainability and Responsibility and Disaster Risk Reduction: A Serbian Overview. In M. Camilleri (Ed.), *CSR 2.0 and the New Era of Corporate Citizenship* (pp. 147–164). Hershey, PA: IGI Global. doi:10.4018/978-1-5225-1842-6.ch008

Raghunath, K. M., Devi, S. L., & Patro, C. S. (2018). Impact of Risk Assessment Models on Risk Factors: A Holistic Outlook. In K. Strang, M. Korstanje, & N. Vajjhala (Eds.), *Research, Practices, and Innovations in Global Risk and Contingency Management* (pp. 134–153). Hershey, PA: IGI Global. doi:10.4018/978-1-5225-4754-9.ch008

Raman, A., & Goyal, D. P. (2017). Extending IMPLEMENT Framework for Enterprise Information Systems Implementation to Information System Innovation. In M. Tavana (Ed.), *Enterprise Information Systems and the Digitalization of Business Functions* (pp. 137–177). Hershey, PA: IGI Global. doi:10.4018/978-1-5225-2382-6.ch007

Rao, Y., & Zhang, Y. (2017). The Construction and Development of Academic Library Digital Special Subject Databases. In L. Ruan, Q. Zhu, & Y. Ye (Eds.), *Academic Library Development and Administration in China* (pp. 163–183). Hershey, PA: IGI Global. doi:10.4018/978-1-5225-0550-1.ch010

Ravasan, A. Z., Mohammadi, M. M., & Hamidi, H. (2018). An Investigation Into the Critical Success Factors of Implementing Information Technology Service Management Frameworks. In K. Jakobs (Ed.), *Corporate and Global Standardization Initiatives in Contemporary Society* (pp. 200–218). Hershey, PA: IGI Global. doi:10.4018/978-1-5225-5320-5.ch009

Renna, P., Izzo, C., & Romaniello, T. (2016). The Business Process Management Systems to Support Continuous Improvements. In W. Nuninger & J. Châtelet (Eds.), *Handbook of Research on Quality Assurance and Value Management in Higher Education* (pp. 237–256). Hershey, PA: IGI Global. doi:10.4018/978-1-5225-0024-7.ch009

Rezaie, S., Mirabedini, S. J., & Abtahi, A. (2018). Designing a Model for Implementation of Business Intelligence in the Banking Industry. *International Journal of Enterprise Information Systems, 14*(1), 77–103. doi:10.4018/IJEIS.2018010105

Riccò, R. (2016). Diversity Management: Bringing Equality, Equity, and Inclusion in the Workplace. In J. Prescott (Ed.), *Handbook of Research on Race, Gender, and the Fight for Equality* (pp. 335–359). Hershey, PA: IGI Global. doi:10.4018/978-1-5225-0047-6.ch015

Romano, L., Grimaldi, R., & Colasuonno, F. S. (2017). Demand Management as a Success Factor in Project Portfolio Management. In L. Romano (Ed.), *Project Portfolio Management Strategies for Effective Organizational Operations* (pp. 202–219). Hershey, PA: IGI Global. doi:10.4018/978-1-5225-2151-8.ch008

Rostek, K. B. (2016). Risk Management: Role and Importance in Business Organization. In D. Jakóbczak (Ed.), *Analyzing Risk through Probabilistic Modeling in Operations Research* (pp. 149–178). Hershey, PA: IGI Global. doi:10.4018/978-1-4666-9458-3.ch007

Rouhani, S., & Savoji, S. R. (2016). A Success Assessment Model for BI Tools Implementation: An Empirical Study of Banking Industry. *International Journal of Business Intelligence Research*, *7*(1), 25–44. doi:10.4018/IJBIR.2016010103

Ruan, Z. (2016). A Corpus-Based Functional Analysis of Complex Nominal Groups in Written Business Discourse: The Case of "Business". *International Journal of Computer-Assisted Language Learning and Teaching*, *6*(2), 74–90. doi:10.4018/IJCALLT.2016040105

Ruhi, U. (2018). Towards an Interdisciplinary Socio-Technical Definition of Virtual Communities. In M. Khosrow-Pour, D.B.A. (Ed.), Encyclopedia of Information Science and Technology, Fourth Edition (pp. 4278-4295). Hershey, PA: IGI Global. doi:10.4018/978-1-5225-2255-3.ch371

Ryan, J., Doster, B., Daily, S., & Lewis, C. (2016). A Case Study Perspective for Balanced Perioperative Workflow Achievement through Data-Driven Process Improvement. *International Journal of Healthcare Information Systems and Informatics*, *11*(3), 19–41. doi:10.4018/IJHISI.2016070102

Safari, M. R., & Jiang, Q. (2018). The Theory and Practice of IT Governance Maturity and Strategies Alignment: Evidence From Banking Industry. *Journal of Global Information Management*, *26*(2), 127–146. doi:10.4018/JGIM.2018040106

Sahoo, J., Pati, B., & Mohanty, B. (2017). Knowledge Management as an Academic Discipline: An Assessment. In B. Gunjal (Ed.), *Managing Knowledge and Scholarly Assets in Academic Libraries* (pp. 99–126). Hershey, PA: IGI Global. doi:10.4018/978-1-5225-1741-2.ch005

Saini, D. (2017). Relevance of Teaching Values and Ethics in Management Education. In N. Baporikar (Ed.), *Management Education for Global Leadership* (pp. 90–111). Hershey, PA: IGI Global. doi:10.4018/978-1-5225-1013-0.ch005

Sambhanthan, A. (2017). Assessing and Benchmarking Sustainability in Organisations: An Integrated Conceptual Model. *International Journal of Systems and Service-Oriented Engineering*, *7*(4), 22–43. doi:10.4018/IJSSOE.2017100102

Sambhanthan, A., & Potdar, V. (2017). A Study of the Parameters Impacting Sustainability in Information Technology Organizations. *International Journal of Knowledge-Based Organizations*, *7*(3), 27–39. doi:10.4018/IJKBO.2017070103

Sánchez-Fernández, M. D., & Manríquez, M. R. (2018). The Entrepreneurial Spirit Based on Social Values: The Digital Generation. In P. Isaias & L. Carvalho (Eds.), *User Innovation and the Entrepreneurship Phenomenon in the Digital Economy* (pp. 173–193). Hershey, PA: IGI Global. doi:10.4018/978-1-5225-2826-5.ch009

Sanchez-Ruiz, L., & Blanco, B. (2017). Process Management for SMEs: Barriers, Enablers, and Benefits. In M. Vemić (Ed.), *Optimal Management Strategies in Small and Medium Enterprises* (pp. 293–319). Hershey, PA: IGI Global. doi:10.4018/978-1-5225-1949-2.ch014

Sanz, L. F., Gómez-Pérez, J., & Castillo-Martinez, A. (2018). Analysis of the European ICT Competence Frameworks. In V. Ahuja & S. Rathore (Eds.), *Multidisciplinary Perspectives on Human Capital and Information Technology Professionals* (pp. 225–245). Hershey, PA: IGI Global. doi:10.4018/978-1-5225-5297-0.ch012

Sarvepalli, A., & Godin, J. (2017). Business Process Management in the Classroom. *Journal of Cases on Information Technology*, *19*(2), 17–28. doi:10.4018/JCIT.2017040102

Satpathy, B., & Muniapan, B. (2016). Ancient Wisdom for Transformational Leadership and Its Insights from the Bhagavad-Gita. In U. Aung & P. Ordoñez de Pablos (Eds.), *Managerial Strategies and Practice in the Asian Business Sector* (pp. 1–10). Hershey, PA: IGI Global. doi:10.4018/978-1-4666-9758-4.ch001

Saygili, E. E., Ozturkoglu, Y., & Kocakulah, M. C. (2017). End Users' Perceptions of Critical Success Factors in ERP Applications. *International Journal of Enterprise Information Systems, 13*(4), 58–75. doi:10.4018/IJEIS.2017100104

Saygili, E. E., & Saygili, A. T. (2017). Contemporary Issues in Enterprise Information Systems: A Critical Review of CSFs in ERP Implementations. In M. Tavana (Ed.), *Enterprise Information Systems and the Digitalization of Business Functions* (pp. 120–136). Hershey, PA: IGI Global. doi:10.4018/978-1-5225-2382-6.ch006

Seidenstricker, S., & Antonino, A. (2018). Business Model Innovation-Oriented Technology Management for Emergent Technologies. In M. Khosrow-Pour, D.B.A. (Ed.), Encyclopedia of Information Science and Technology, Fourth Edition (pp. 4560-4569). Hershey, PA: IGI Global. doi:10.4018/978-1-5225-2255-3.ch396

Senaratne, S., & Gunarathne, A. D. (2017). Excellence Perspective for Management Education from a Global Accountants' Hub in Asia. In N. Baporikar (Ed.), *Management Education for Global Leadership* (pp. 158–180). Hershey, PA: IGI Global. doi:10.4018/978-1-5225-1013-0.ch008

Sensuse, D. I., & Cahyaningsih, E. (2018). Knowledge Management Models: A Summative Review. *International Journal of Information Systems in the Service Sector, 10*(1), 71–100. doi:10.4018/IJISSS.2018010105

Sensuse, D. I., Wibowo, W. C., & Cahyaningsih, E. (2016). Indonesian Government Knowledge Management Model: A Theoretical Model. *Information Resources Management Journal, 29*(1), 91–108. doi:10.4018/irmj.2016010106

Seth, M., Goyal, D., & Kiran, R. (2017). Diminution of Impediments in Implementation of Supply Chain Management Information System for Enhancing its Effectiveness in Indian Automobile Industry. *Journal of Global Information Management, 25*(3), 1–20. doi:10.4018/JGIM.2017070101

Seyal, A. H., & Rahman, M. N. (2017). Investigating Impact of Inter-Organizational Factors in Measuring ERP Systems Success: Bruneian Perspectives. In M. Tavana (Ed.), *Enterprise Information Systems and the Digitalization of Business Functions* (pp. 178–204). Hershey, PA: IGI Global. doi:10.4018/978-1-5225-2382-6.ch008

Shaikh, A. A., & Karjaluoto, H. (2016). On Some Misconceptions Concerning Digital Banking and Alternative Delivery Channels. *International Journal of E-Business Research, 12*(3), 1–16. doi:10.4018/IJEBR.2016070101

Shams, S. M. (2016). Stakeholder Relationship Management in Online Business and Competitive Value Propositions: Evidence from the Sports Industry. *International Journal of Online Marketing, 6*(2), 1–17. doi:10.4018/IJOM.2016040101

Shamsuzzoha, A. (2016). Management of Risk and Resilience within Collaborative Business Network. In R. Addo-Tenkorang, J. Kantola, P. Helo, & A. Shamsuzzoha (Eds.), *Supply Chain Strategies and the Engineer-to-Order Approach* (pp. 143–159). Hershey, PA: IGI Global. doi:10.4018/978-1-5225-0021-6.ch008

Shaqrah, A. A. (2018). Analyzing Business Intelligence Systems Based on 7s Model of McKinsey. *International Journal of Business Intelligence Research, 9*(1), 53–63. doi:10.4018/IJBIR.2018010104

Sharma, A. J. (2017). Enhancing Sustainability through Experiential Learning in Management Education. In N. Baporikar (Ed.), *Management Education for Global Leadership* (pp. 256–274). Hershey, PA: IGI Global. doi:10.4018/978-1-5225-1013-0.ch013

Shetty, K. P. (2017). Responsible Global Leadership: Ethical Challenges in Management Education. In N. Baporikar (Ed.), *Innovation and Shifting Perspectives in Management Education* (pp. 194–223). Hershey, PA: IGI Global. doi:10.4018/978-1-5225-1019-2.ch009

Sinthupundaja, J., & Kohda, Y. (2017). Effects of Corporate Social Responsibility and Creating Shared Value on Sustainability. *International Journal of Sustainable Entrepreneurship and Corporate Social Responsibility, 2*(1), 27–38. doi:10.4018/IJSECSR.2017010103

Škarica, I., & Hrgović, A. V. (2018). Implementation of Total Quality Management Principles in Public Health Institutes in the Republic of Croatia. *International Journal of Productivity Management and Assessment Technologies, 6*(1), 1–16. doi:10.4018/IJPMAT.2018010101

Smuts, H., Kotzé, P., Van der Merwe, A., & Loock, M. (2017). Framework for Managing Shared Knowledge in an Information Systems Outsourcing Context. *International Journal of Knowledge Management, 13*(4), 1–30. doi:10.4018/IJKM.2017100101

Soares, E. R., & Zaidan, F. H. (2016). Information Architecture and Business Modeling in Modern Organizations of Information Technology: Professional Career Plan in Organizations IT. In G. Jamil, J. Poças Rascão, F. Ribeiro, & A. Malheiro da Silva (Eds.), *Handbook of Research on Information Architecture and Management in Modern Organizations* (pp. 439–457). Hershey, PA: IGI Global. doi:10.4018/978-1-4666-8637-3.ch020

Sousa, M. J., Cruz, R., Dias, I., & Caracol, C. (2017). Information Management Systems in the Supply Chain. In G. Jamil, A. Soares, & C. Pessoa (Eds.), *Handbook of Research on Information Management for Effective Logistics and Supply Chains* (pp. 469–485). Hershey, PA: IGI Global. doi:10.4018/978-1-5225-0973-8.ch025

Spremic, M., Turulja, L., & Bajgoric, N. (2018). Two Approaches in Assessing Business Continuity Management Attitudes in the Organizational Context. In N. Bajgoric (Ed.), *Always-On Enterprise Information Systems for Modern Organizations* (pp. 159–183). Hershey, PA: IGI Global. doi:10.4018/978-1-5225-3704-5.ch008

Steenkamp, A. L. (2018). Some Insights in Computer Science and Information Technology. In *Examining the Changing Role of Supervision in Doctoral Research Projects: Emerging Research and Opportunities* (pp. 113–133). Hershey, PA: IGI Global. doi:10.4018/978-1-5225-2610-0.ch005

Studdard, N., Dawson, M., Burton, S. L., Jackson, N., Leonard, B., Quisenberry, W., & Rahim, E. (2016). Nurturing Social Entrepreneurship and Building Social Entrepreneurial Self-Efficacy: Focusing on Primary and Secondary Schooling to Develop Future Social Entrepreneurs. In Z. Fields (Ed.), *Incorporating Business Models and Strategies into Social Entrepreneurship* (pp. 154–175). Hershey, PA: IGI Global. doi:10.4018/978-1-4666-8748-6.ch010

Sun, Z. (2016). A Framework for Developing Management Intelligent Systems. *International Journal of Systems and Service-Oriented Engineering, 6*(1), 37–53. doi:10.4018/IJSSOE.2016010103

Swami, B., & Mphele, G. T. (2016). Problems Preventing Growth of Small Entrepreneurs: A Case Study of a Few Small Entrepreneurs in Botswana Sub-Urban Areas. In N. Baporikar (Ed.), *Handbook of Research on Entrepreneurship in the Contemporary Knowledge-Based Global Economy* (pp. 479–508). Hershey, PA: IGI Global. doi:10.4018/978-1-4666-8798-1.ch020

Tabach, A., & Croteau, A. (2017). Configurations of Information Technology Governance Practices and Business Unit Performance. *International Journal of IT/Business Alignment and Governance*, *8*(2), 1–27. doi:10.4018/IJITBAG.2017070101

Talaue, G. M., & Iqbal, T. (2017). Assessment of e-Business Mode of Selected Private Universities in the Philippines and Pakistan. *International Journal of Online Marketing*, *7*(4), 63–77. doi:10.4018/IJOM.2017100105

Tam, G. C. (2017). Project Manager Sustainability Competence. In *Managerial Strategies and Green Solutions for Project Sustainability* (pp. 178–207). Hershey, PA: IGI Global. doi:10.4018/978-1-5225-2371-0.ch008

Tambo, T. (2018). Fashion Retail Innovation: About Context, Antecedents, and Outcome in Technological Change Projects. In I. Management Association (Ed.), Fashion and Textiles: Breakthroughs in Research and Practice (pp. 233-260). Hershey, PA: IGI Global. doi:10.4018/978-1-5225-3432-7.ch010

Tambo, T., & Mikkelsen, O. E. (2016). Fashion Supply Chain Optimization: Linking Make-to-Order Purchasing and B2B E-Commerce. In S. Joshi & R. Joshi (Eds.), *Designing and Implementing Global Supply Chain Management* (pp. 1–21). Hershey, PA: IGI Global. doi:10.4018/978-1-4666-9720-1.ch001

Tandon, K. (2016). Innovative Andragogy: The Paradigm Shift to Heutagogy. In S. Tiwari & L. Nafees (Eds.), *Innovative Management Education Pedagogies for Preparing Next-Generation Leaders* (pp. 238–257). Hershey, PA: IGI Global. doi:10.4018/978-1-4666-9691-4.ch014

Tantau, A. D., & Frăţilă, L. C. (2018). Information and Management System for Renewable Energy Business. In *Entrepreneurship and Business Development in the Renewable Energy Sector* (pp. 200–244). Hershey, PA: IGI Global. doi:10.4018/978-1-5225-3625-3.ch006

Teixeira, N., Pardal, P. N., & Rafael, B. G. (2018). Internationalization, Financial Performance, and Organizational Challenges: A Success Case in Portugal. In L. Carvalho (Ed.), *Handbook of Research on Entrepreneurial Ecosystems and Social Dynamics in a Globalized World* (pp. 379–423). Hershey, PA: IGI Global. doi:10.4018/978-1-5225-3525-6.ch017

Trad, A., & Kalpić, D. (2016). The E-Business Transformation Framework for E-Commerce Architecture-Modeling Projects. In I. Lee (Ed.), *Encyclopedia of E-Commerce Development, Implementation, and Management* (pp. 733–753). Hershey, PA: IGI Global. doi:10.4018/978-1-4666-9787-4.ch052

Trad, A., & Kalpić, D. (2016). The E-Business Transformation Framework for E-Commerce Control and Monitoring Pattern. In I. Lee (Ed.), *Encyclopedia of E-Commerce Development, Implementation, and Management* (pp. 754–777). Hershey, PA: IGI Global. doi:10.4018/978-1-4666-9787-4.ch053

Trad, A., & Kalpić, D. (2018). The Business Transformation Framework, Agile Project and Change Management. In M. Khosrow-Pour, D.B.A. (Ed.), Encyclopedia of Information Science and Technology, Fourth Edition (pp. 620-635). Hershey, PA: IGI Global. doi:10.4018/978-1-5225-2255-3.ch054

Trad, A., & Kalpić, D. (2018). The Business Transformation and Enterprise Architecture Framework: The Financial Engineering E-Risk Management and E-Law Integration. In B. Sergi, F. Fidanoski, M. Ziolo, & V. Naumovski (Eds.), *Regaining Global Stability After the Financial Crisis* (pp. 46–65). Hershey, PA: IGI Global. doi:10.4018/978-1-5225-4026-7.ch003

Turulja, L., & Bajgoric, N. (2018). Business Continuity and Information Systems: A Systematic Literature Review. In N. Bajgoric (Ed.), *Always-On Enterprise Information Systems for Modern Organizations* (pp. 60–87). Hershey, PA: IGI Global. doi:10.4018/978-1-5225-3704-5.ch004

van Wessel, R. M., de Vries, H. J., & Ribbers, P. M. (2016). Business Benefits through Company IT Standardization. In K. Jakobs (Ed.), *Effective Standardization Management in Corporate Settings* (pp. 34–53). Hershey, PA: IGI Global. doi:10.4018/978-1-4666-9737-9.ch003

Vargas-Hernández, J. G. (2017). Professional Integrity in Business Management Education. In N. Baporikar (Ed.), *Management Education for Global Leadership* (pp. 70–89). Hershey, PA: IGI Global. doi:10.4018/978-1-5225-1013-0.ch004

Vasista, T. G., & AlAbdullatif, A. M. (2017). Role of Electronic Customer Relationship Management in Demand Chain Management: A Predictive Analytic Approach. *International Journal of Information Systems and Supply Chain Management, 10*(1), 53–67. doi:10.4018/IJISSCM.2017010104

Vergidis, K. (2016). Rediscovering Business Processes: Definitions, Patterns, and Modelling Approaches. In P. Papajorgji, F. Pinet, A. Guimarães, & J. Papathanasiou (Eds.), *Automated Enterprise Systems for Maximizing Business Performance* (pp. 97–122). Hershey, PA: IGI Global. doi:10.4018/978-1-4666-8841-4.ch007

Vieru, D., & Bourdeau, S. (2017). Survival in the Digital Era: A Digital Competence-Based Multi-Case Study in the Canadian SME Clothing Industry. *International Journal of Social and Organizational Dynamics in IT*, *6*(1), 17–34. doi:10.4018/IJSODIT.2017010102

Vijayan, G., & Kamarulzaman, N. H. (2017). An Introduction to Sustainable Supply Chain Management and Business Implications. In M. Khan, M. Hussain, & M. Ajmal (Eds.), *Green Supply Chain Management for Sustainable Business Practice* (pp. 27–50). Hershey, PA: IGI Global. doi:10.4018/978-1-5225-0635-5.ch002

Vlachvei, A., & Notta, O. (2017). Firm Competitiveness: Theories, Evidence, and Measurement. In A. Vlachvei, O. Notta, K. Karantininis, & N. Tsounis (Eds.), *Factors Affecting Firm Competitiveness and Performance in the Modern Business World* (pp. 1–42). Hershey, PA: IGI Global. doi:10.4018/978-1-5225-0843-4.ch001

von Rosing, M., Fullington, N., & Walker, J. (2016). Using the Business Ontology and Enterprise Standards to Transform Three Leading Organizations. *International Journal of Conceptual Structures and Smart Applications*, *4*(1), 71–99. doi:10.4018/IJCSSA.2016010104 von Rosing, M., & von Scheel, H. (2016). Using the Business Ontology to Develop Enterprise Standards. *International Journal of Conceptual Structures and Smart Applications*, *4*(1), 48–70. doi:10.4018/IJCSSA.2016010103

Walczak, S. (2016). Artificial Neural Networks and other AI Applications for Business Management Decision Support. *International Journal of Sociotechnology and Knowledge Development*, *8*(4), 1–20. doi:10.4018/IJSKD.2016100101

Wamba, S. F., Akter, S., Kang, H., Bhattacharya, M., & Upal, M. (2016). The Primer of Social Media Analytics. *Journal of Organizational and End User Computing*, *28*(2), 1–12. doi:10.4018/JOEUC.2016040101

Wang, C., Schofield, M., Li, X., & Ou, X. (2017). Do Chinese Students in Public and Private Higher Education Institutes Perform at Different Level in One of the Leadership Skills: Critical Thinking?: An Exploratory Comparison. In V. Wang (Ed.), *Encyclopedia of Strategic Leadership and Management* (pp. 160–181). Hershey, PA: IGI Global. doi:10.4018/978-1-5225-1049-9.ch013

Wang, F., Raisinghani, M. S., Mora, M., & Wang, X. (2016). Strategic E-Business Management through a Balanced Scored Card Approach. In I. Lee (Ed.), *Encyclopedia of E-Commerce Development, Implementation, and Management* (pp. 361–386). Hershey, PA: IGI Global. doi:10.4018/978-1-4666-9787-4.ch027

Wang, J. (2017). Multi-Agent based Production Management Decision System Modelling for the Textile Enterprise. *Journal of Global Information Management*, *25*(4), 1–15. doi:10.4018/JGIM.2017100101

Wiedemann, A., & Gewald, H. (2017). Examining Cross-Domain Alignment: The Correlation of Business Strategy, IT Management, and IT Business Value. *International Journal of IT/Business Alignment and Governance*, *8*(1), 17–31. doi:10.4018/IJITBAG.2017010102

Wolf, R., & Thiel, M. (2018). Advancing Global Business Ethics in China: Reducing Poverty Through Human and Social Welfare. In S. Hipsher (Ed.), *Examining the Private Sector's Role in Wealth Creation and Poverty Reduction* (pp. 67–84). Hershey, PA: IGI Global. doi:10.4018/978-1-5225-3117-3.ch004

Wu, J., Ding, F., Xu, M., Mo, Z., & Jin, A. (2016). Investigating the Determinants of Decision-Making on Adoption of Public Cloud Computing in E-government. *Journal of Global Information Management, 24*(3), 71–89. doi:10.4018/JGIM.2016070104

Xu, L., & de Vrieze, P. (2016). Building Situational Applications for Virtual Enterprises. In I. Lee (Ed.), *Encyclopedia of E-Commerce Development, Implementation, and Management* (pp. 715–724). Hershey, PA: IGI Global. doi:10.4018/978-1-4666-9787-4.ch050

Yablonsky, S. (2018). Innovation Platforms: Data and Analytics Platforms. In *Multi-Sided Platforms (MSPs) and Sharing Strategies in the Digital Economy: Emerging Research and Opportunities* (pp. 72–95). Hershey, PA: IGI Global. doi:10.4018/978-1-5225-5457-8.ch003

Yusoff, A., Ahmad, N. H., & Halim, H. A. (2017). Agropreneurship among Gen Y in Malaysia: The Role of Academic Institutions. In N. Ahmad, T. Ramayah, H. Halim, & S. Rahman (Eds.), *Handbook of Research on Small and Medium Enterprises in Developing Countries* (pp. 23–47). Hershey, PA: IGI Global. doi:10.4018/978-1-5225-2165-5.ch002

Zanin, F., Comuzzi, E., & Costantini, A. (2018). The Effect of Business Strategy and Stock Market Listing on the Use of Risk Assessment Tools. In *Management Control Systems in Complex Settings: Emerging Research and Opportunities* (pp. 145–168). Hershey, PA: IGI Global. doi:10.4018/978-1-5225-3987-2.ch007

Zgheib, P. W. (2017). Corporate Innovation and Intrapreneurship in the Middle East. In P. Zgheib (Ed.), *Entrepreneurship and Business Innovation in the Middle East* (pp. 37–56). Hershey, PA: IGI Global. doi:10.4018/978-1-5225-2066-5.ch003

About the Contributors

Muhammad Anshari bin Ali is an Assistant Professor at School of Business and Economics, Universiti Brunei Darussalam (UBDSBE) and currently he is also a Deputy Director, Institute of Policy Studies, Universiti Brunei Darussalam. He received his Bachelor Management Information Systems (Honours) from International Islamic University Malaysia (IIUM), his Master of IT (E-Business) from James Cook University Australia, and his PhD programme from Universiti Brunei Darussalam. His professional experience started when he was IT Business Analyst at Astra International and Lecturer at Universitas Islam Negeri Sunan Kalijaga Yogyakarta, Indonesia. Dr Anshari was research fellow at National Taiwan University (Jan-Dec, 2014) funded by The Government Republic of China (Taiwan). He was also research fellow at King Saud University - the Kingdom of Saudi Arabia 2009. His research profile is internationally competitive and he has collaborated actively with researchers in several other disciplines of MIS, particularly E-Health & Mobile Health, Digital Marketplace, FinTech, Big data in business, ICT & Area Studies, and ICT in Education.

Mohammad Nabil Almunawar is currently a senior assistant professor at School of Business and Economics, Universiti Brunei Darussalam (UBDSBE), Brunei Darussalam. He was the former dean of UBDSBE. He received his bachelor degree in 1983 from Bogor Agricultural University, Indonesia, master Degree (MSc Computer Science) from the Department of Computer Science, University of Western Ontario, London, Canada in 1991 and Ph.D. from the University of New South Wales (School of Computer Science and Engineering, UNSW) in 1998. Dr Almunawar has published more than 100 papers in refereed journals, books, book chapters, and international conferences. He has more than 30 years of teaching experience in the area of computer and information systems. His overall research interests include applications of IT in Management, Electronic Business/Commerce, Digital

Platforms, Health Informatics, information security, cloud computing, Big Data and Internet of Things. He is also interested in object-oriented technology, databases, and multimedia retrieval.

Masairol Haji Masri earned his Ph.D. in Business Administration from Manchester Business School, University of Manchester, UK. He joined Universiti Brunei Darussalam in 2001 as a Tutor before pursuing his Master in Business Administration in 2002 at International Islamic University, Malaysia. Prior to that, he worked as an Audit Assistant at Deloitte & Touche, Brunei Darussalam from 1999. His research interests are in the performance measurement, financial reporting, Islamic accounting and finance with particular reference to small and medium enterprises. While in Universiti Brunei Darussalam, he has held various administrative position such as the Deputy Director for Office of Studies, the Deputy Dean of Academic and Administration at the School of Business and Economics and the Accounting Programme Coordinator. He was also a member of the Brunei Darussalam Accounting Standard (BDASC) working committee for Non-Public Interest Entities. He is currently a member of the Brunei Darussalam Public Accountant Oversight committee (PAOC) under Ministry of Finance and Economics.

* * *

Dian Agustia is a Professor of Accounting in Universitas Airlangga, Indonesia. She received her Doctoral Degree in 2005 with Accounting Major. Her research interests are management accounting, sustainable accounting, and corporate governance. She has published and presented many papers in those fields.

Abu Umar Faruq Ahmad is currently an Associate Professor at Islamic Economics Institute (IEI), King Abdulaziz University, Jeddah, Saudi Arabia. He has a significant number of published peer-reviewed refereed journal articles, books, chapters in edited books, conference proceedings, and other intellectual contributions to his credit on Shari`ah compliance of Islamic banks' products and structures, the opportunities and challenges of Islamic finance, case studies of Islamic banks and financial institutions, Islamic insurance and reinsurance, Islamic microfinance, Sukuk, and dispute resolution in Islamic banking and finance, among others. He has presented over 50 scholarly research papers at international conferences held in the USA, Ireland, Australia, UAE, Saudi Arabia, Turkey, Brunei, Qatar, Sudan, Nigeria,

Malaysia, Indonesia, Bangladesh and Pakistan. His current editorial roles include serving as founding editor, senior editor, editorial advisory board member of a plethora of internationally reputed refereed journals including some of those published by Emerald Group Publishing, UK.

Nadia Anridho received her MBA from the Chinese Culture University in 2013. She is a lecturer at Accountancy Department, Universitas Airlangga, Indonesia. She writes and presents widely on issues of digital accounting, accounting information system, strategic management, and service industry.

H. N. Au Yong received her Master in Economics from University of Tsukuba, Japan, and PhD in Technology Management from University of Science, Malaysia. She is an Assistant Professor and the Dean of the Faculty of Business and Finance, University Tunku Abdul Rahman, Malaysia. She had a professional career in a Fortune 500 company, a Forbes 2000 company and a state-own enterprise. She was the founding manager of data analysis system and information security management system of the technology companies. She has received research grants to the amount of about MYR 330,000 (USD 80,000) between 2015 and 2019, and also consulting projects from the Federation of Malaysia Chinese Guilds Association and the Overseas Vocational Training Association, Japan. She has published in international peer-reviewed journals include Web of Science and Scopus journals / Conference Proceedings, such as International Journal of Business and Society, International Journal of Operations and Quantitative Management, Journal of the Malaysian Institute of Planners, Work: A Journal of Prevention, Assessment and Rehabilitation, and PERTANIKA Journal of Social Sciences and Humanities. She serves as a reviewer for five international journals. Her work was covered by the national media, magazines, TV and digital media. She is a member of Malaysian Institute of Management and Management Science/ Operations Research Society of Malaysia. She is a recipient of Best Paper Awards from the East Coast Economic Region Regional Conference 2008, World Conference on Business and Management 2018 and the 6th International Conference on Business, Accounting, Finance and Economics 2018.

Ramona Birau is a Lecturer on the Faculty of Education Science, Law and Public Administration at the Constantin Brancusi University of Targu Jiu, Romania. Dr. Birau has more than 10 years experience as Superior Financial Inspector at the Regional Public Finances General Directorate of Craiova, Romania. In addition, she is the Editor in Chief of both the International Journal of Business Quantitative Economics and Applied Management Research (IJBEMR) and the International Journal of Core Engineering and Management (iJCEM), India. Dr. Ramona Birau was appointed as Registrar of the British American University (BAU), Florida, USA starting February 2019. In 2018 she joined the Academic Council of Adarsh Institute of Management and Information Technology, Bangalore, India and the International Advisory Board (IAB) of CT University, India. Dr. Ramona Birau has published more than 100 research papers in journals and conference proceedings and has authored/co-authored 6 books. She became a Doctor of Cybernetics and Statistics in 2013 at the University of Craiova, Faculty of Economics and Business Administration with a Ph.D. thesis titled, "Modeling and prediction of emerging capital markets." Currently, she is following her second doctorate (PhD) in the field of Sociology at the University of Craiova, Faculty of Social Sciences. Her current research interests include financial markets, economics, cybernetics and statistics, quantitative finance, financial econometrics, behavioral psychology, economic sociology, management. Dr. Birau has also served as a teaching assistant during 2010-2012 and 2014-2015 at the University of Craiova, Faculty of Economics and Business Administration. Apart from that she is also a member of the Romanian Body of Chartered and Certified Accountants since 2012. She has a Master's degree in Finance, specialization Analysis and Financial Evaluation of Organizations and another one in the field of Administrative Sciences, specialization European Public Administration.

Debra Chern is currently enrolled in University Tunku Abdul Rahman, where she majors in Business Information Systems. She began writing in secondary school for her school magazine as well as a young writer for her local newspaper, The Star. As a lifelong-learner, Debra continues to build on her knowledge of financial technology and hopes to share this through not only literary means, but also through her daily life.

Farrukh Habib is a renowned expert in Shariah, Finance and FinTech with a diverse experience and strong educational background. He is Researcher at ISRA; co-editor of ISRA Journal of Islamic Finance (indexed by ESCI and SCOPUS); and Senior Advisor of HalalChain (HLC). He also advises various Islamic FinTech projects, with the main focus on Blockchain and tokenized economy. He is also actively involved in training, consultancy, public speaking at international events and writing for journals, books, business magazines and reports.

Mahani Hamdan is an Assistant Professor at the UBD School of Business and Economics, specialising in accounting education and development. She is currently a member of the Brunei Darussalam Accounting Standards Council for the Ministry of Finance and Economics. Dr Hamdan is also a Director at the Institute of Policy Studies, overseeing both academic and administrative matters.

Manzoor Hashmani received his B.E. (Computer Systems Engineering) from Mehran University of Engineering & Technology, Jamshoro (Pakistan) in 1991, M.E in 1997 and Ph.D. in 1999 from Nara Institute of Science & Technology, Nara (Japan). He has authored and co-authored more than 100 research papers published in various journals and conferences of international repute. He has also worked as lead research and development person in a reputable Japanese company for five years. He is currently working in the University Technology Petronas (in top 300 universities in the world as per QS World Ranking). He is a Senior Member of IEEE, member of IEEE Computational Intelligence Society's executive committee, and member of Pakistan Engineering Council. His research areas of interest include: - Artificial Intelligence and Machine Learning - Soft Computing for Optimization - Image Processing, and - High Speed Communication Networks.

Nofie Iman is currently working at Faculty of Economics and Business, Universitas Gadjah Mada. He earned his PhD in Management from the London School of Economics and Political Science and an MSc in Management of Science, Technology and Innovation from the University of Manchester. His research interests are in the area of management of innovation and dynamic corporate strategy. He has worked in numerous research and consulting projects. He also regularly wrote for newspapers and magazines, and also has published several books in the areas of investment and personal finance. He is an avid mid-handicap golfer and a weekend cyclist.

Suprabha K. R. is an Assistant Professor at the School of Management, National Institute of Karnataka. She has over ten years of teaching experience. Areas of research interests include Management of Banks and Financial Institutions, Corporate Finance and Asset Pricing, Microfinance and Micro Enterprises. She has undertaken numerous research and consultancy projects while winning best paper awards and also guided doctoral scholars.

Hazik Mohamed is a business strategist with substantial market research, operational management and start-up experience. He consults for MSMEs and MNCs on various business-related issues including market penetration, operational process trouble-shooting, investment management, and strategic execution. Specialized PhD research in behavioral research and analysis using game theory in view of conventional and Islamic economics perspectives. Its applications include understanding consumer/user behavior and viral marketing strategies as well as policy formulation and regulatory implementation through effective low-cost behavioral interventions. Other interests include region-wide strategic planning as well as implementation of innovative, disruptive and scalable technologies.

Arjun R. is a doctoral candidate in School of Management, National Institute of Technology Karnataka. He is pursuing research in the field of Information Systems and Predictive Modeling. His areas of interest are Technology and Management Sciences. He has published few Scopus and Web of Science indexed research articles. He is a reviewer in international conferences.

Mobashar Rehman is currently working as Assistant Professor in Faculty of Information and Communication Technology, Universiti Tunku Abdul Rahman, Perak, Malaysia. He has more than six years of teaching and research experience. His research expertise includes Software Engineering, human factors in Software Engineering especially personality and organizational factors in the field of Software Engineering and Knowledge Management.

Cristi Spulbar is the Executive Director of the Banking and Financial Research Center (CEBAFI) at the University of Craiova, Romania, and Professor Ph.D, Habilitated Doctor at the Faculty of Economics and Business Administration, University of Craiova. Moreover, Dr. Cristi Spulbar is a Doctoral Advisor in the field of Finance at the Doctoral School of Economic Sciences, University of Craiova, Romania and was appointed Regional Director for Romania by Eurasian Doctoral Summer Academy (EDSA), Bulgaria (Varna). His habilitation thesis, "Research on Efficiency of Banking Systems and Monetary Policy," was publicly defended in 2016, and after that he became a member of the University of Craiova's Doctoral School of Economic Sciences, where he has supervised the awarding of Ph.D. degrees in the financial field. In 2018, he received the Doctor Honoris Causa award, field Economics and Finance, from British American University, Florida, USA. Dr. Spulbar has published more than 200 research papers in journals and conference proceedings and has authored/co-authored more than 20 books. He became a Doctor of Economics in 1999 at the University of Craiova, with a Ph.D. thesis titled, "Optimization of Banking Management in Terms of Market Economy." His current research interests include banking management, quantitative finance, financial markets, economics, international monetary economy, money and credit, and corporate finance. . In addition, he is the Scientific Director of both the International Journal of Business Quantitative Economics and Applied Management Research (IJBEMR) and the International Journal of Core Engineering and Management (iJCEM), India. Building his academic profile since 1995, he has also gained broad experience as a practical practitioner in the financial field. Through continuous training and study, he has achieved a benchmark level of additional professional qualifications, enabling him to serve as an investment consultant, economic and financial evaluator, securities agent, and commercial agent (including being a broker and dealer).

Sumarsono is researcher and academic staff at Faculty of Science and Technology, State Islamic University of Sunan Kalijaga. His professional experience started when he was research management training from the Government Republic of Indonesia at National Technology University Singapore (Nov, 2006).

Fakhriyah Abdullah Thani is a graduate student at University Brunei Darussalam having undergone Masters of Management. Graduated with a Bachelor's degree in Mathematics from UBD. With experience as an intern conducting research and development (R&D), her interest include statistics, research and areas of management.

Hidayatul Aziyah Zain is a Bachelor of Business graduate with a degree in Economics. She later took on a Masters in Management so as to diversify her know-how and capabilities. Residing in the country known as the Abode of Peace, Aziyah enjoys walking around the city and taking photos. For leisure, she also enjoys solving 3D puzzles, doing art and volunteering. She aspires to leave a positive impact wherever she goes.

Index

Purchase Print, E-Book, or Print + E-Book

IGI Global books can now be purchased from three unique pricing formats: Print Only, E-Book Only, or Print + E-Book. Shipping fees apply.

www.igi-global.com

Recommended Reference Books

ISBN: 978-1-5225-2016-0
© 2017; 375 pp.
List Price: $200

ISBN: 978-1-5225-0886-1
© 2017; 251 pp.
List Price: $160

ISBN: 978-1-5225-2075-7
© 2017; 2,266 pp.
List Price: $185

ISBN: 978-1-5225-1865-5
© 2017; 443 pp.
List Price: $200

ISBN: 978-1-5225-19614-4
© 2017; 365 pp.
List Price: $210

ISBN: 978-1-5225-1005-5
© 2015; 370 pp.
List Price: $205

Looking for free content, product updates, news, and special offers?
Join IGI Global's mailing list today and start enjoying exclusive perks sent only to IGI Global members.
Add your name to the list at **www.igi-global.com/newsletters.**

Publisher of Peer-Reviewed, Timely, and Innovative Academic Research

IGI Global
DISSEMINATOR OF KNOWLEDGE

www.igi-global.com Sign up at www.igi-global.com/newsletters facebook.com/igiglobal twitter.com/igiglobal

Ensure Quality Research is Introduced to the Academic Community

Become an IGI Global Reviewer for Authored Book Projects

The overall success of an authored book project is dependent on quality and timely reviews.

In this competitive age of scholarly publishing, constructive and timely feedback significantly expedites the turnaround time of manuscripts from submission to acceptance, allowing the publication and discovery of forward-thinking research at a much more expeditious rate. Several IGI Global authored book projects are currently seeking highly qualified experts in the field to fill vacancies on their respective editorial review boards:

Applications may be sent to:
development@igi-global.com

Applicants must have a doctorate (or an equivalent degree) as well as publishing and reviewing experience. Reviewers are asked to write reviews in a timely, collegial, and constructive manner. All reviewers will begin their role on an ad-hoc basis for a period of one year, and upon successful completion of this term can be considered for full editorial review board status, with the potential for a subsequent promotion to Associate Editor.

If you have a colleague that may be interested in this opportunity, we encourage you to share this information with them.

IGI Global
DISSEMINATOR OF KNOWLEDGE
www.igi-global.com

Celebrating 30 Years of Scholarly Knowledge Creation & Dissemination

InfoSci®-Books

A Collection of 4,000+ Reference Books Containing Over 87,000 Full-Text Chapters Focusing on Emerging Research

This database is a collection of over 4,000+ IGI Global single and multi-volume reference books, handbooks of research, and encyclopedias, encompassing groundbreaking research from prominent experts worldwide. These books are highly cited and currently recognized in prestigious indices such as: Web of Science™ and Scopus®.

Librarian Features:

- No Set-Up or Maintenance Fees
- Guarantee of No More Than A 5% Annual Price Increase
- COUNTER 4 Usage Reports
- Complimentary Archival Access
- Free MARC Records

Researcher Features:

- Unlimited Simultaneous Users
- No Embargo of Content
- Full Book Download
- Full-Text Search Engine
- No DRM

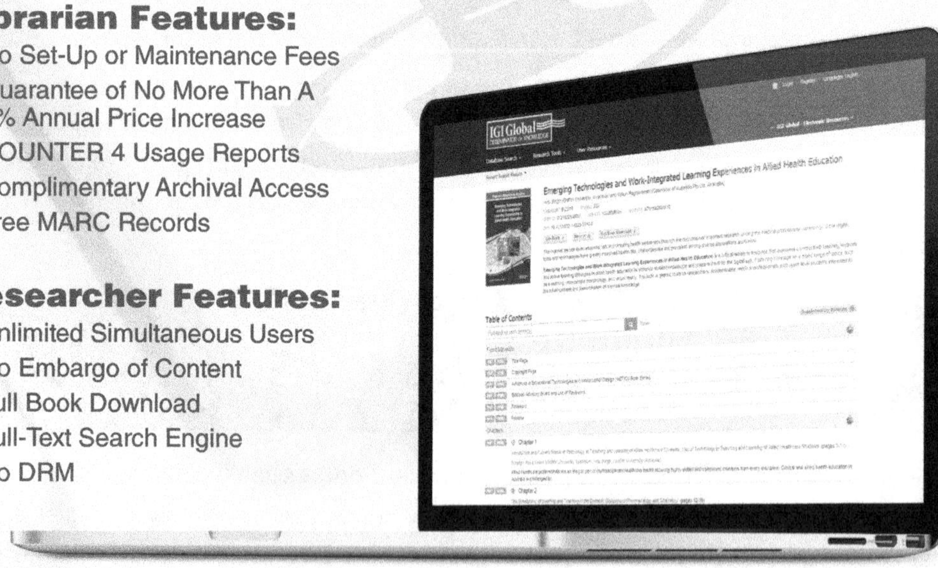

To Find Out More or To Purchase This Database:
www.igi-global.com/infosci-books
eresources@igi-global.com • Toll Free: 1-866-342-6657 ext. 100 • Phone: 717-533-8845 x100

IGI Global
DISSEMINATOR OF KNOWLEDGE
www.igi-global.com

IGI Global Proudly Partners with

eContent Pro International

Expert Copy Editing

eContent Pro International copy editors, with over 70 years of combined experience, will provide complete and comprehensive care for your document by resolving all issues with spelling, punctuation, grammar, terminology, jargon, semantics, syntax, consistency, flow, and more. In addition, they will format your document to the style you specify (APA, Chicago, etc.). All edits will be performed using Microsoft Word's Track Changes feature, which allows for fast and simple review and management of edits.

Additional Services

eContent Pro International also offers fast and affordable proofreading to enhance the readability of your document, professional translation in over 100 languages, and market localization services to help businesses and organizations localize their content and grow into new markets around the globe.

IGI Global Authors Save 25% on eContent Pro International's Services!

Scan the QR Code to Receive Your 25% Discount

The 25% discount is applied directly to your eContent Pro International shopping cart when placing an order through IGI Global's referral link. Use the QR code to access this referral link. eContent Pro International has the right to end or modify any promotion at any time.

Email: customerservice@econtentpro.com

econtentpro.com

www.ingramcontent.com/pod-product-compliance
Lightning Source LLC
LaVergne TN
LVHW080558300926
849162LV00005B/986